After
the
Disaster

After

the

Disaster

Re-Creating Community and Well-Being at Buffalo Creek
Since the Notorious Coal Mining Disaster in 1972

T. P. SCHWARTZ-BARCOTT

CAMBRIA
PRESS

AMHERST, NEW YORK

ISBN: 978-1-60497-550-5

Library of Congress Cataloging-in-Publication Data

Schwartz-Barcott, T. P. (Timothy Philip)
   After the disaster : re-creating community and well-being at Buffalo Creek since the notorious coal-mining disaster in 1972 / by T.P. Schwartz-Barcott.
       p. cm.
   Includes bibliographical references and index.
   ISBN 978-1-60497-550-5 (alk. paper)
   1. Buffalo Creek Region (Logan County, W. Va.)—Social conditions. 2. Community life—West Virginia—Buffalo Creek Region (Logan County) 3. Well-being—West Virginia—Buffalo Creek Region (Logan County) 4. Social integration—West Virginia—Buffalo Creek Region (Logan County) 5. Disasters—Social aspects—West Virginia—Buffalo Creek Region (Logan County). 6. Disasters—West Virginia—Buffalo Creek Region (Logan County)—Psychological aspects. 7. Disaster relief—West Virginia—Buffalo Creek Region (Logan County) 8. Floods—West Virginia—Buffalo Creek (Logan County)—History—20th century. 9. Coal mine accidents—West Virginia—Buffalo Creek (Logan County)—History—20th century. 10. Buffalo Creek Region (Logan County, W. Va.)—History—20th century. I. Title.

   HN79.W42B847 2008
   307.1'41660975444—dc22

2008025528

Permissions and authorization to excerpt:

Every effort has been made by the author to secure the appropriate permissions for material reproduced in this book. If there has been any oversight, efforts will be made to rectify the situation if written requests are made to the author in a timely manner.

Excerpts from *Death at Buffalo Creek: The 1972 West Virginia Flood Disaster*, by Tom Nugent, copyright © 1973, used by permission of W. W. Norton & Company, Inc.

Excerpts from *The Buffalo Creek Disaster* by Gerald M. Stern, copyright © 1976 and copyright © renewed 2004 by Gerald M. Stern. Epilogue copyright © 2008 by Gerald M. Stern. Used by permission of Random House, Inc.

Excerpts from *Everything in Its Path: Destruction of Community in the Buffalo Creek Flood*, by Kai T. Erikson, copyright © 1976, used by permission of Simon & Schuster.

Excerpts from *Against All Odds: Rural Community in the Information Age*, by John C. Allen and Don A. Dillman, copyright © 1994, used by permission of Westview Press, Inc.

Excerpts from "The Human Meaning of Total Disaster. The Buffalo Creek Experience," by Robert Jay Lifton and Eric Olson, used by permission of *Psychiatry*.

Poem "My Neighbors" by Esta Cochran, given to the author in 2005, and used with her permission.

Two black and white photos of Buffalo Creek, 1972, on the front cover, and the black and white drawing of the flash flood in 1972, used with the permission of Carlene Mowery, who drew the drawing of the flood.

Two color photographs of Buffalo Creek, 2007, on the front cover, and the map of Buffalo Creek, 2007, are the copyrighted property of the author and may not be used without written permission of the author.

Black and white icon of a scene representing contemporary Buffalo Creek was designed by the author, was rendered by Alan Greco of Alan Greco Design, Inc., and is the copyrighted property of the author.

To all good people, everywhere, who,
through no fault of their own,
suffered disasters so overwhelming
they felt totally lost;

and yet, somehow,
they kept trying
to re-create
lives worth living.

Wherefore putting away lying,
speak every man truth with his neighbor:
for we are members one of another.

—Ephesians 4:25

*   *   *

Now, more than six months later, desolation and despair are nearly all that is left in Buffalo Creek Valley…The horror of Buffalo Creek has done much to awaken the state to an awareness of its plight and to start it moving into modern times. Accountability is coming at last to the hills and hollows.

—Appalachian author Harry M. Caudill,
"Buffalo Creek Aftermath"

*   *   *

In all of these ways, Buffalo Creek epitomizes the tenuousness of so much of contemporary existence—our combination of survival of old and anticipation of new holocausts, and our struggles, equally inadequate, to confront that death-dominated precariousness as a source of new vitality and of transformation.

—Psychiatrist Robert Jay Lifton and Eric Olson,
"The Human Meaning of Total Disaster:
The Buffalo Creek Experience"

*   *   *

My neighbors are the most precious people in the world.
They may be men, women, boys or girls,
But they will stand out
like a bright flag unfurled.

They are always there in time of need,
Always ready to do a good deed,
Always help you in life
to succeed.

And when you think no one will care
Your neighbors will let you know they are there.
They are with you in the darkest night
They'll pray & guide you through the tunnel to the light.

I could search the world and never could find,
No better neighbors than mine.

—Unsolicited poem by Esta Cochran,
flood survivor and lifelong resident
of Buffalo Creek

*   *   *

Map of Buffalo Creek, 2007.

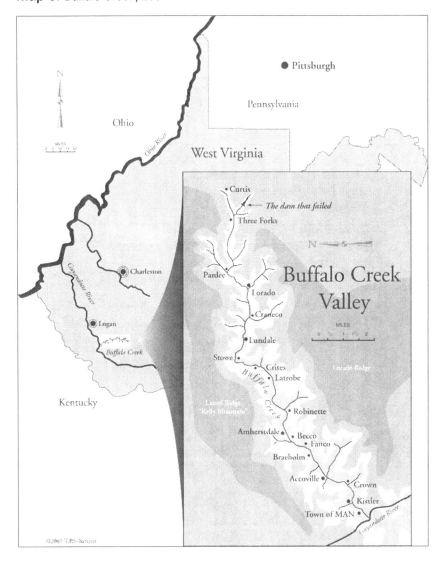

Drawing of the flash flood in 1972.

TABLE OF CONTENTS

LIST OF TABLES

FOREWORD

T. P. Schwartz-Barcott has done a great service to those of us who study, work, and live in rural communities. In this book, he provides detailed discussions with local residents, survey data, and a gift for integration that allows the reader to gain an understanding of how disasters impact communities in the short term and in the long term. The latter may be one of the most important contributions of this book.

Those of us who have studied rural people and places often have focused on a snapshot in time as we attempt to understand how human beings are impacted by change at the local community level. Community once was declared dead as a unit of analysis for social science scholars, yet the citizens who live in these places find that their attachments to place and to other people in these places are crucial to their lives. Too often, we who study such phenomena fail to examine the long-term impacts of shocks to place and people. This methodological failing often leads to exaggerated estimations of the impacts of disasters on communities and their residents. Human beings and the social structures they create are resilient. Schwartz-Barcott fills some of the gaps in our knowledge when he returns repeatedly to Buffalo Creek for several years long after the flash flood departed in 1972.

It is not often that a scholar with empathy for rural citizens returns to a place for many years in order to understand the longer-term implications of disasters for individual well-being. This monograph provides a view of place long after the tragedy took place. It illustrates how community residents struggle to re-create community and well-being after a serious ecological shock. The resilience of the human character and the adaptability of community structures are the core of this book.

Taking us through the days before the flash flood at Buffalo Creek, the author paints a portrait of human failings and of growing environmental danger. He draws on the voices that were there on the scene. He also gives us a detailed review of newspaper accounts, government documents, and research studies, including Kai Erikson's classic disaster study, *Everything in Its Path*. From these many sources, we get a multifaceted account of how the disaster occurred and how dozens of local, state, and federal agencies responded to it.

But this book is much more than an account of a return to examine a community some thirty years after a disaster. It is a human look at the pain, suffering, and survival of many individuals and the communities they inhabit. At a first cut, this book provides a clear indication of the strength of human beings and their willingness to rebuild and re-create community. Yet there is more to it than this. By drawing on sociological and psychological theories, the author empirically evaluates neighboring, social integration, social well-being, and community well-being. On all of these dimensions, residents of Buffalo Creek score higher than one would expect—given what has been published about Buffalo Creek until now by other authors.

To gain a better sense of whether Buffalo Creek lags behind other rural communities in the United States, the author then takes us to two other communities that have not been subjected to a dramatic environmental crisis. They are Elk Creek, West Virginia, and St. John, Washington (a community where I lived, worked, and neighbored for many years in the 1980s—as reported in a book that I coauthored with Don A. Dillman,

Against All Odds: Rural Community in the Information Age). These two communities are quite different from each other. Where Elk Creek is in a steep hollow only about ten miles from Buffalo Creek, St. John is surrounded by miles of soft white wheat fields and rolling hills thousands of miles away. In all three of these places, the author uses the voices and observations of a variety of their residents to illustrate how their neighboring activities influence their sense of well-being in their daily lives. This technique provides us with the language, context, and description of the locales that are essential for us to appreciate the dynamics of community life. By bringing in these other communities, the author enables us to examine issues related to community integration, well-being, and neighboring. Through this, we are able to see that all three communities have some surprising similarities in the social behaviors and attitudes of their residents.

After spending over twenty years studying how rural communities organize themselves to meet their short- and long-term needs, I am continually amazed at how resilient human beings are when it comes to finding ways to create meaningful social communities, despite very long odds against them. Fortunately, this is what has happened at Buffalo Creek for more than a few of the surviving victims of the flash flood of 1972, and for some of their successors, as well. Without this book, we would know considerably less than we do now about Buffalo Creek, about some other rural communities in the United States, about neighboring, about disasters and their consequences, and about human resilience.

John C. Allen, PhD
Professor of Sociology and
Director of the Western Rural Development Center
Utah State University

PREFACE

GUNNER McGRUFF AND GROUND ZERO, BUFFALO CREEK, WEST VIRGINIA, MARCH 1, 2000

Is this "ground zero"? Is this where it all began? Is this the origin of what has been called one of the worst "man-made" disasters in the United States in the past one hundred years, at least prior to the terrorist attacks of 2001 on the World Trade Center and the collapse of the levees that were supposed to protect New Orleans from Hurricane Katrina in 2005?

This disaster occurred when an impoundment near a coal mine collapsed after days of heavy rain at approximately 8:00 a.m. on Saturday morning, February 26, 1972. Thousands of tons of oily, black mine waste water, sludge, and suspended debris flushed down through sixteen coal camps. At least 125 people were killed (seven of the bodies never were recovered), as many as 1,000 other people were injured, more than 500 homes were destroyed, and an estimated 4,000 people were left temporarily homeless. In contrast to most disasters that involve coal mines, many of the dead and injured in this case were the wives and children of coal miners, rather than the miners themselves. And, in contrast to so many other disasters in U.S. history that involved coal mining, this disaster quickly captured national and international attention in the news media. Fortunately, it also attracted massive relief efforts and provoked a flurry of investigations by Congress, several federal agencies, and the state of West Virginia. It also led to some very famous research studies on the psychological and sociological consequences of disasters. And so it is not surprising that "the Buffalo Creek disaster" has become a common phrase and reference point whenever and wherever disasters are discussed in the United States, Canada, England, and many other societies.

*   *   *

I scan the landscape as the snow falls, slow and silent. Three steep ravines converge here. Each one bears a stream of fast-running, muddy water that seems angry and intent on getting away from this place. The middle stream is the most turbulent and troubling. It tumbles down from a jumble of railroad ties, broken branches, and truck tires. Then it rushes down along the ice-covered gravel road on which I am standing. Abandoned along the road are rusted-out metal tanks as large as barn silos, clots of broken railroad ties and twisted rails, and a three-story tipple for grading coal and loading it into dump trucks and railroad cars. There is no sign of human life here. There are no memorials or other indications that this place is more hallowed, or cursed, than any other place. And yet, somehow, it just *feels* different from the others. It almost feels…*despised*.

I notice a small square of plywood nailed ten feet up a telephone pole near the road.

BUFFALO MINING CO.
#5 PREP PLANT
PERMIT #0-98-83

Beneath it is a smaller sign, more recent, in neon orange with black letters:

CAUTION MEN
WORKING

Just then I hear a vehicle engine laboring its way up the road. Large snowflakes float lazily in the still air. Moments later, a faded blue pickup truck emerges out of the snowfall, rocking from side to side as if shivering to stay warm. The insides of the windows are fogged up, but I recognize a familiar decal inside the front windshield. It is the famous gold-ringed globe-and-anchor insignia of the United States Marine Corps. I flag the driver to stop. The window rolls down slowly and releases a cloud of stale cigar smoke. Behind it is a little old man, wizened and hunched down like a troll. He stares at me without expression; a stub of a masticated cigar droops from beneath his tobacco-stained moustache. I introduce myself and tell him what I am looking for. He just stares at me. Then I mention his Marine Corps decal and say something about Iwo Jima and Okinawa. When he finally speaks, it takes concerted effort for me to understand much of what he is saying in his mountaineer dialect made worse by labored wheezing and fits of coughing:

> Yup. This here is the place, awright. Ry cheer. It come down that holler. Ry char. Tha's Middle Fork. Coal camp houses was all along in thar. Where those tracks is. Wiped out, mostly. Was a house left. Up over on the rise thar. Couple over thar, too. Wasn't washed-out. The paper says they was all gone. But they wasn't. I hiked up over that mountain thar', two days after. Was still some people livin' over thar. Had a big fire going. Baileys. I was livin' down in Lorado camp when that water come down. I was with the wife and kids. Jes' finish ma breakfast. We got out the back when that water come down. Hit the house and wash it away. Pain in the ass. That's what it was—just another pain in the ass.

> Then, with a sly half smirk, the little old fellow adds, "Only had my shorts on. Get in if you want. I'll show you around some."

* * *

That was the beginning of several hours of conversations that I had with Elmer "Gunner" McGruff (a pseudonym). He was the first of dozens of flood survivors whom I visited with along Buffalo Creek during the next seven years. Gunner McGruff was one of the most memorable ones.

Certainly he was the most cantankerous one. We rode his truck up and down the hollows. Gunner was "scroungin'" for scrap sheet metal for his junkyard that morning. He would wave at some men, ignore others completely, and mutter disparaging remarks about others. Along the way, he commented on how things had and had not changed around Buffalo Creek over the years.

What I gathered from Gunner was that he drifted back to Buffalo Creek with his wife and kids after he somehow managed to finish twenty years with the Marine Corps, in the mid-1960s. He spent another nineteen years as a coal miner ("UMWA #17 back then, when it was still around"), had plenty of misadventures (including the flood), and more grandchildren and great-grandchildren than he could recall. He presented himself as an ornery, old cuss who did what he wanted, when he wanted, throughout his life, regardless of the consequences.

Often I had to ask Gunner the same questions several times, in various ways. I just could not get the hang of his mountaineer dialect, his way of running words together, and his mumbling while he was sucking on a stub of a Phillies Titan cigar or smoking it stuck vertically into the bowl of a grimy pipe. Gunner did not object to talking about the flood, but he did not dwell on it either. As he told his story, the flood was "mainly just another pain in the ass," just like a lot of other events in his life that he was not too fond of. Among those events were "some lousy k.p. (kitchen patrol) duty" in Tarawa, the Philippines, Korea, and Vietnam; run-ins with officers; getting busted for fights and other derelictions; and bouncing from one job to another after he mustered out of the Marines and returned to Buffalo Creek. For Gunner, life in the trailer camps that the government provided after the flood seemed only a little more chaotic and annoying than daily life in the coal camps along Buffalo Creek and at the liberty ports of the Pacific in WWII. "Kinda like living in them Quonset huts at Camp Lejeune, only with wives and babies all over the place. Was kinda noisy. Chaos at times. That's what it was." Gunner was no more enthusiastic about his current home in a crowded village about ten miles away from Buffalo Creek.

> It's good 'nuff fer me. Family's thar' most of the time. People comin'
> in and out. The neighbors ain't that much of a problem, 'cept maybe
> for raisin' hell on the weekends and pay days. And some's a little
> nosey. Gossip, too. Ain't that bad, though. I can jes' get in my truck
> here and drive on up here when I want.

Family and neighbors seemed to be less relevant to Gunner than his old
buddies, "Hacksaw" and "Bucko," whom he mentions often, and keeps
looking for, as we bounce along the back roads in his truck.

Days later, I spent two hours in Gunner's five-room home in a trailer
camp along a different creek about ten miles away. I met his wife and
some of his many in-laws. I looked at his family photos and listened to
the often salty stories that he cared to disclose about his colorful and
rather erratic life. Gunner ignored the near constant stream of kinfolk
who traipsed into his home as he reclined in a heavily padded and well-
worn rocking chair inside his front door, fumbling with his pipe and
cigars and smoking himself stuperous at midmorning in what little sunlight entered through the smoked-over front windows of his little bungalow. Introductions occurred only when I initiated them. Gunner seemed
hazy about the names of some of his in-laws and grandchildren who
walked by on their way to the kitchen. He seemed to regard his family,
kin, and neighbors matter-of-factly, without enthusiasm and with a hint
of indifference—if not annoyance.

Gunner and I posed for some photos in front of his house as I was saying good-bye. He found enough energy to feign a surprisingly energetic
punch to my belly, and mumbled, "Always wanted to do that to an officer." Looking back on it now, I am glad that I was able to oblige him.[1]

OTHER VIEWS OF BUFFALO CREEK

One of the most famous books on the subject of the disaster at Buffalo
Creek in 1972 is Kai Erikson's *Everything in Its Path: Destruction of
Community in the Buffalo Creek Flood*, published in 1976, four years
after the flood. A beautifully and compassionately written book, it

contends that the flood swept away much more than the material objects in the sixteen coal camps along the seventeen miles of the creek. The flood also damaged severely the mental health of its residents and the crucial social relationships they had with family, kin, neighbors, and friends. This damage was so extensive and profound that Buffalo Creek no longer existed as a viable social community. So complete was the destruction that Buffalo Creek might never recover—at least not on its own, and not back to where it was before February 26, 1972. It could not recover on its own because the survivors no longer could take care of their own daily needs, let alone those of others. Many people could not even care anymore about themselves, let alone about others. Anxiety disorders, depression, insomnia, and other psychological problems became commonplace. All of the social cohesion and social controls that had existed and that were essential for social order were hopelessly and perhaps permanently lost. Survivors came to believe that immorality was rampant in the forms of alcohol abuse, marital infidelity, child neglect, theft, and other forms of social conflict among their former neighbors. Virtually everything was deteriorating—that is, everything that had not died, been destroyed, or been grievously damaged by the flood and its aftereffects.

In addition to Kai Erikson's book, and dozens of research articles in scholarly journals, three other authors published books and articles about Buffalo Creek that became well known, many years ago. One of those books is by a journalist, Tom Nugent, *Death at Buffalo Creek: The Story Behind the West Virginia Flood Disaster of 1972*. The other book, *The Buffalo Creek Disaster*, is by an attorney, Gerald Stern, who led a lawsuit on behalf of some of the flood's survivors against Pittston Company and its subsidiary, Buffalo Mining Company. Both of those books generally concur with Erikson's assessment of the flood's damages to Buffalo Creek and its people. In many ways, Buffalo Creek no longer existed as a functional social community. The prospects were bleak for stable and fulfilling human social relations at Buffalo Creek in the future. These authors also concluded that the disaster occurred because of gross negligence on the part of senior officials of the coal companies and because

Buffalo Creek's residents were totally unaware of the danger posed by the coal-mine sludge ponds.

Research articles and the book, *Prolonged Psychological Effects of Disaster: A Study of Buffalo Creek*—by a team of psychologists and psychiatrists, including Bonnie L. Green and Goldine C. Gleser—were more circumspect about the permanence of the psychological damages that were suffered by many of the survivors. This is in keeping with many research studies of disasters that often have found considerable psychological recovery by many survivors within a few years of natural disasters. This book was written several years after the other three books, so Green and Gleser had more time to determine whether psychological recovery was occurring, and the survivors had more time to recover before they were studied and "written about."

NEW QUESTIONS, MOTIVATIONS, AND EFFORTS

It has been more than thirty-five years since the flood. What has been recovered or re-created since then? What damages, if any, remain in the social lives of its people? Does the flood of 1972 hang over the spirit and culture of Buffalo Creek like a curse? Do some people somehow believe it to have been a warning, a lesson to be learned, a revelation? If adversity can build character, can it also build community? Have new forms of social relationships and a new sense of community emerged? If so, how? Is Buffalo Creek once again a community with qualities similar to other small, settled places in rural America?

Since the year 2000, I have been meeting former and current residents of Buffalo Creek and other small villages and towns in the United States in order to answer these questions. What I found might surprise you, reassure you, and encourage you to think more deeply about how human beings, their families, and their communities adjust, in the long run, not only to disastrous events like floods, but also to an onslaught of modern economic, social, and technological changes. It is often claimed that automobiles, telephones, TVs, "the pill," recreational drugs, credit cards, the Internet, and globalization, among other innovations, have diminished social community and neighboring across the United States—especially in small towns in rural America that were once so vibrant, essential, and symbolic of social life in the United States. As ungrammatical as it sounds, have neighboring, communality, and well-being been re-created at Buffalo Creek despite the disaster of 1972, its unanticipated aftereffects, and all of these other changes?

*   *   *

My interest in these matters is more than sociological. It is more than professional. It is very personal—perhaps even hereditary. For, in some ways, it can be said that coal and coal mining were in my blood before I was born. They were part of my daily environment for many years after that. It might even be said that coal and coal mining still influence every breath I take; for I have had respiratory problems, on and off, ever since I was born. More directly and obviously, coal and coal mining have been in my thinking, my research, and my writing for at least the past seven years.

My mother was born in a coal camp. She was so sick with respiratory ailments that she barely survived her first year. Her father, my grandfather, was a coal miner. For his first ten years in America, he mined coal by hand (I still have his last coal pick in my basement). Each day, he descended into the depths of a small but very productive coal mine in an obscure little place misnamed Large, Pennsylvania, about ten miles south of Pittsburgh. I remember Large because I still go back there to drive the alleyways that are nearly deserted now, past the vacant lots and the few wood-frame miners' houses that remain from its heyday. I drive past the towering heap of mine waste that is now overgrown with scraggly brush; past the now irrelevant mine mouth that is stuffed with a few derelict, rusted-out trucks of WWII vintage, forty feet up a trashed hillside.

My first home was in a walk-up apartment in Monessen, Pennsylvania, across the street from blast furnaces fired by coal. The coal trains rumbled in and out all night long. My paternal grandfather worked those furnaces as a stoker and batch maker. My father worked in the mill's stockrooms and the electric motor shop. It was there that asthma caught me in my first year and plagued me for decades. Fortunately, my parents decided to move us farther away from the towering smokestacks that fouled Monessen and the Monongahela River Valley.

Somewhat safer was the town, Latrobe, Pennsylvania, where I grew up. Though not as smoke choked as Monessen, it was surrounded by smoldering coke ovens and cramped little coal camps when I first arrived there: Dorothy, St. Vincent's Shaft, Lloydsville, Whitney, Hostetter, Lycippus, and so many others. Even now, decades later, coal trains rumble through Latrobe late at night on their way to electric power plants downriver near Pittsburgh. But Latrobe is now known more for its golf legend (Arnold Palmer) and its beer (Rolling Rock) than for its coal and steel, which are still produced there, albeit on much smaller scales than in the 1950s.

When I was growing up in Latrobe, we heard shocking reports of collapses of local coal mines that injured miners and sometimes buried them forever. Often we heard of sudden and rather mysterious explosions in the mills, and of other industrial accidents. I remember how the Loyalhanna Creek drained Latrobe like an open sewer—sulfurous and toxic with vomit-colored effluence from the coal mines, steel mills, and tool and die works. Filthy brown floodwaters from heavy rains in late winter flushed under the town's bridges—sometimes even over them—with flotsam of derelict farm wagons, miner's sheds, railroad ties, carcasses of chickens, hogs, and cows, and masses of strangely buoyant metal debris from the strip mines and mills. Low-lying coal camps—Dorothy and St. Vincent's Shaft among them—flooded out and had to be evacuated until the floodwaters receded. Coal miners' families were crammed into wood rowboats and pulled to higher ground by the miners and local firemen. At times like these, our teachers and our newspapers would remind us that flash floods were part of our cultural legacy in coal mining and steelmaking country. They told us yet again of an infamous flash flood in 1889 that killed more than 2,000 residents in and around Johnstown, Pennsylvania, when an earthen dam collapsed and released millions of tons of coal-mine wastewater onto low-lying coal camps. This incident had special relevance for us because Johnstown is only thirty miles "upriver" from Latrobe, and our hard-nosed high-school football teams occasionally battled theirs.[2]

And so, with childhood experiences like these, I was appalled, but not particularly surprised, in 1972, when I read of the massive devastation that occurred down along Buffalo Creek, West Virginia. I read that sixteen coal camps—including one named Latrobe, just like my hometown—had been swept away when slurry ponds suddenly collapsed above them. I read that nothing was left of them. I read that there had been no warning. I read that all the victims had been caught totally by surprise, sleeping in their beds like helpless infants and totally unaware of the danger. Even then I had some doubts about the sweeping absolutism of these claims. Few, if any, of the many coal miners I had known were likely to be helpless infants totally unaware of the dangers around them, their families, and their coal camps. The same was true of many of their children—kids I had known growing up.

What did surprise me, and please me, was that the disaster at Buffalo Creek got so much attention—so quickly—from so many powerful newspapers, relief and charitable organizations, political leaders, and Congress. In the years since then, I have been glad to see that a considerable amount of stimulating and sympathetic research has been published about the disaster. However, I have long lamented the fact that so little has been written about the many concerted efforts to rebuild the communities along Buffalo Creek and to repair the lives of its many victims who survived the flood. It seems to me that the published literature has not gone far enough to tell us what has been sustained and accomplished by the good people of Buffalo Creek and by the people and organizations from outside Buffalo Creek who have cared about it. But then again, this is a common pattern. There are many more books about disasters—particularly about the more sensational and destructive features of disasters—than about the arduous, frustrating, and decades-long efforts to recover from disasters. Apparently, the general public tires of hearing about a particular disaster after a week or two. Other disasters "seem to come along" and push earlier disasters into the dark recesses of the public's memory, except for occasional reminders in the form of best-selling "disaster books." Undoubtedly, the next few years will bring us a barrage of informative books about the ravages of recent disasters including Hurricane Katrina's damage to the Gulf Coast of the United States in 2005 and the destructive tsunami in Indonesia in 2004. I hope that *this* book—about the recovery and re-creating of well-being and neighboring after disasters—will help us appreciate and anticipate some of the most difficult and often overlooked challenges that lie ahead for many decades.

This book can also encourage us to be guardedly optimistic. While the scale of the disaster at Buffalo Creek hardly matches that of Hurricane Katrina or the Indonesian tsunami, its intensity and shock effects were extraordinary, by almost any standard. Yet, looking back over the decades, the case of Buffalo Creek leads me to believe that, given the resources, the willpower, and the intelligence, social well-being and social communities often can be re-created, if not recovered, even when so much has been lost. Buffalo Creek might not be thriving as it once was—but it, and its people, are still very much alive. I hope that this book will convince you that Buffalo Creek must never be forgotten. Nor should it be remembered only for the disaster that occurred there in 1972 and only in the ways that it has been depicted in published accounts to this date. Buffalo Creek also should be remembered and known for the lives and the communities that have been re-created there, and the ways that they differ from the past.[3]

LOOKING AHEAD

My primary purpose is to provide an objective analysis of efforts to re-create Buffalo Creek since the disaster in 1972, with particular attention to social well-being and neighboring. I do this mainly by reporting on the interviews and field research that I have been doing there since 2000.

Chapter 1 describes key events that altered Buffalo Creek's sixteen coal camps before, during, and immediately after the flood of February 26, 1972. Chapter 2 reviews the accounts of the flood and its immediate aftereffects by a number of respected experts whose books and research articles constitute the core of the published literature on these topics. Chapter 3 describes efforts to rebuild the physical and economic infrastructure and the social services of Buffalo Creek since 1972, as well as changes in its population and social institutions. Have these rebuilding efforts been sufficient to produce a renewed sense of well-being in Buffalo Creek's residents? Does the infrastructure allow the residents to participate in neighboring and to create a resilient and satisfying social community? (Key concepts, including "well-being," "neighboring," and "community," are defined in the glossary).

Chapters 4 and 5 are the heart and soul of this book. Chapter 4 features my encounters, conversations, and interviews with more than twenty of Buffalo Creek's current and recent residents: young and not so young, male and female, coal miners, former coal miners, schoolteachers, students, and others. Some were seriously injured in the flood. Some lost their homes and almost all of their material possessions. Others lost no material possessions at all. Some were born after the flood. Collectively, all of these people can help us to understand the legacy of the flood and its impacts on well-being, neighboring, and sense of community, especially when we compare Buffalo Creek to other small communities in the United States. These comparisons are provided in chapter 5. It presents quantitative data on sets of residents of Buffalo Creek and Elk Creek, West Virginia, and another fascinating community more than 2,000 miles away from them: St. John, Washington. Doing this helps us determine whether Buffalo Creek and its current residents have less well-being, neighboring, and sense of community than do places that did not suffer disasters like the flood of 1972. You are likely to find some surprising similarities, as well as differences, among the residents of these three locations. Chances are that you will become fond of some of these residents—and perhaps more than a little concerned about others.

Chapter 6 summarizes my major findings and then reappraises them in the light of what "the experts" have told us about Buffalo Creek. It also considers how differences in our accounts might be attributed to differences in the research methods that we used, to the intricacies of human memory, or to other factors. It probes questions of fundamental importance whose "answers" are elusive and controversial, such as: As the years go by, do survivors of disasters tend to underestimate or overestimate the psychological and social impairments that they suffered in the days and weeks immediately after the disasters?

Chapter 7 is more speculative and suggestive than meditative and philosophical. It estimates the prospects for Buffalo Creek and other small communities in rural America over the next few decades in terms of social well-being, neighboring, and sense of community. Reluctantly, it considers the very discomforting question that so many people inevitably ask me: Could it happen again? It also considers a more pleasant prospect: Could Buffalo Creek's best days still be ahead of it? I posed these questions, and others, to a number of informed people in the Buffalo Creek Valley, Logan County, and Charleston (the state capital). I hope that their responses will encourage the good people of Buffalo Creek to take an active and constructive part in shaping the future of their beloved home. Their responses also encouraged me to propose a number of very specific suggestions to help small communities prevent, prepare for, and respond to disasters. Obviously, we want to learn as much as we can from "history"—rather than repeat so many of its mistakes.

In other words, this book is *not* just about Buffalo Creek, and it is *not* just for the people of Buffalo Creek, of West Virginia, or of Appalachia. It provides a fair amount of useful information for anyone, anywhere, who is interested in how human beings suffer in nearly cataclysmic disasters and then somehow courageously re-create social life and well-being for many years after that. I hope that this interest is shared by many people throughout this supposedly "globalized" world who care about the suffering that the tsunami inflicted upon Indonesia and that hurricanes Katrina and Wilma wreaked upon the Gulf Coast of the United States only a few years ago. Surely we have learned by now that many of us, if not all of us, are far more vulnerable to a bewildering array of natural and human-made disasters than we thought possible only a few years ago.

ENDNOTES

1. Gunner McGruff died about six months after I last talked with him. I attended his wake.
2. Of course, the Johnstown Flood of 1889 is notorious for other reasons besides the staggering number of fatalities. Before the earthen dam collapsed, it restrained a huge reservoir of hundreds of acres of surface water and wildlife habitat that isolated the coal camps from the favorite fishing and hunting club of some of the wealthiest coal, steel, and industrial barons of the age: Andrew Carnegie, Henry Frick, Henry Phipps, Jr., and Andrew Mellon, among them.

   It is also worth knowing that disastrous floods continue to plague Johnstown and the Conemaugh River Valley. For example, in July 1977, the "Laurel Run Dam of the Greater Johnstown Water Authority broke and sent a wall of water crashing through Tanneryville in West Taylor Township" that killed at least fifty-five people and idled "more than 20,000 wage earners…as a result of the flood" (from John McHugh and William Black, "Death Toll Stands at 55; At Least 100 Missing," *The Tribune-Democrat* [Johnstown, PA], July 22, 1977, 1). This disaster occurred little more than five years after the flash flood at Buffalo Creek, West Virginia, the focus of this book.
3. In order to enhance the likelihood that Buffalo Creek, the flood of 1972, and its victims will not be forgotten, I intend to donate a portion of the royalties from the sale of this book to the Buffalo Creek Memorial Committee for the purpose of creating a new, permanent, and safe memorial center for visitors and students near the source of the flash flood at Three Folks.

ACKNOWLEDGMENTS

I am particularly indebted to the residents of Buffalo Creek who allowed me to visit with them in their homes, meet their families, and converse with them many times for more than six years. First among them is Mrs. Gertie Moore. She welcomed me into her home, introduced me to dozens of informed and helpful residents, and served as a sounding board and critic when few others could or would do so. Her faith, compassion, and neighborliness makes Buffalo Creek a better place for many people. Glenna Wiley, Jo and Claude Curry, Joe and Pat Doczi, and Fonzo Jude are among the other good people to whom I am indebted for their friend-liness, insights, and trust.

Some of the other residents of Logan County who enhanced my under-standing of the people of Buffalo Creek include Reverend and Mrs. Linzel Walls, Reverend Mike Pollard, F. Raamie Barker, Dave Crawford, Dar-lene Stratton, Arthur Kirkendoll, S. Gillman Burgess, Elizabeth Tackett, and Sheila Miller. Carlene Mowery and the late Dennis Deitz encouraged my work and allowed me to borrow from their own good book about Buffalo Creek.

At St. John, Washington, Stephanie Swannack, Muriel Jordan, and Becky Dickerson were especially cordial and valuable sources of insight. At Johnstown, Pennsylvania, Linda Dinan provided me with many documents that revealed similarities between the disaster at Buffalo Creek and the many floods that have continued to damage communities in and around Johnstown for more than one hundred years.

My lady, Donna Schwartz-Barcott, helped me greatly in doing many days of research at Buffalo Creek and St. John. Others who collected data at these locations are Mark Steven Duty, Marlynda Adkins, Doug Barrett, and Stephanie Swannack.

Scholars who commented on one or more chapters of this book while it was in manuscript form include Professors Donna Schwartz-Barcott of the University of Rhode Island, John Allen of Utah State University, Virginia Aldige of North Carolina State University, Dwight Billings of the University of Kentucky, Bonnie L. Green of Georgetown University, and Emeritus Professors John Shelton Reed of the University of North Carolina, Russell R. Dynes and Enrico L. Quarantelli of the University of Delaware, and Kai Erikson of Yale University. For more than thirty years now, Erikson's book about the disaster at Buffalo Creek has stimulated my thinking about the nature of human communities and how people remember them. Besides this, Erikson also was very gracious and helpful to me in the early stages of my research. It was a pleasure to be able to show him around the re-created Buffalo Creek Valley for two days in 2002, comparing observations and attending a thirtieth-anniversary service in memory of the victims of the disaster.

George Roberts Coulter, a friend of many years, exercised his sharp eye and red pencil on an early draft of the manuscript and influenced the current subtitle of this book. Another longtime friend, Steve Applegate, provided useful recollections of the coal camps of Logan County in the 1970s. And yet another friend through the ages, George Levendis, Esq., of Levendis Law Group, PLLC, Washington, DC, helped me understand some of the complexities of the lawsuits against the coal companies following the disaster.

Highly skilled and friendly technical support was provided by Pat Chaney of One on One PC and by Alan Greco of Alan Greco Design, Inc., both of East Greenwich, RI. At Cambria Press, Toni Tan, Sharon Berger, Paul Richardson, and their colleagues have been very competent, courteous, innovative, quick, reliable, and more than a little daring. Elsewhere, Scot Danforth made helpful suggestions about the composition and content of an early version of the manuscript.

Of course, none of these people bear any responsibility for the final content of this book. Alas, that responsibility is mine alone, and I apologize if I inadvertently have misrepresented anyone or anything.

Far above all others, my lady, Donna Schwartz-Barcott, has been the most valuable and charming supporter of my efforts to tell what needs to be told, despite considerable indifference—even opposition, at times—from some quarters. For her I am most grateful.

After
the
Disaster

PART I

THEN

CHAPTER 1

BUFFALO CREEK BEFORE, DURING, AND SOON AFTER THE FLOOD

So the residents of Buffalo Creek were fairly well off in the early days of 1972. Most of the men were employed and earning good wages, and if the hollow did not quite reach the national mean on the conventional indices of wealth, the people nonetheless owned their own houses, paid modest taxes, enjoyed a certain measure of security, and were generally satisfied with their lot. They had survived the crisis of automation (of the coal mines in the early 1950s) and were even beginning to profit from it, and to that extent, at least, they were one of the most affluent groups in an otherwise impoverished region.

—Sociologist Kai Erikson, *Everything in Its Path*

Well, the day of the flood we just milled around to see what we could find. Just drifted around. Nobody knowed what to do or what they was looking for.

—A seventy-year-old survivor of the flood,
as reported by Kai Erikson

The Lord spared us, that's for sure. When we come down off that hillside our house here wasn't washed-out. So Buddy went out and told folks who was washed-out to come stay with us. We had families in every room. Everybody tried to help out as best they could. I recall one family from up the hollow come in that night all wet and cold. One of their little boys looked around at all the people in here. His eyes git real wide and he says to me real loud, "Lady, your floor here sure is muddy. You need to mop-up!"

Everybody bust-out laughin' at that.

—Goldie Cummins, lifelong resident of Lundale[1]

THE FLOOD:
FACTS, PRECURSORS, AND IMMEDIATE CONSEQUENCES

Some Precursors, Premonitions, and Precautions

Just before the flood on February 26, 1972, "Buffalo Creek" was the name many folks in Logan County, West Virginia, used to refer to sixteen unincorporated coal camps that were situated along seventeen miles of what was usually a nondescript, muddy creek, knee-deep in places, and five to ten yards wide. Both the creek and the string of camps were considered to originate at the juncture of three small streams at a place conveniently called "Three Forks" by some folks, or "Saunders" by some others (the map in the front of the book portrays the current topography of Buffalo Creek and the names and locations of the coal camps). From there, it rushed and flowed, twisted and turned, down through countless ravines and hollows (simply called "the hollow" or "the holler," in local parlance), eventually passing through Kistler, the last of the coal camps, and the incorporated town of Man, on the banks of the Guyandotte River.[2] Railroad tracks and a two-lane, secondary road, Route 16 (the "creek road"), ran along and often crisscrossed the creek on numerous bridges from Three Forks to Man. Buffalo Mining Company (BMC) and a number of smaller coal companies used these tracks to transport coal in gondola cars from the half dozen mines in the ridges above the Buffalo Creek Valley down through the town of Man, then down along the Guyandotte River to the city of Logan (the county seat, fifteen miles downstream), and eventually to shipping ports on the Kanawha River near Charleston, the state capital.

The coal camps of Buffalo Creek varied in size, composition, and services. Some of them, such as Kistler, Amherstdale, Lundale, and Lorado, had hundreds of households, as well as schools, churches, repair shops, theaters, and company stores. Others, such as Stowe and Three Forks, consisted of little more than a few dozen dwellings and a church or two. Altogether, about 4,950 people lived in Buffalo Creek's sixteen camps. Most of them depended on coal mining in some way or another, with perhaps 600 of them working regularly in the local mines. Hundreds more were retired or disabled. Housewives and children made up the bulk of the population. In contrast to many coal camps and other areas of Appalachia, Buffalo Creek's coal mines had been operating at full production, or nearly so, for the better part of a decade before 1972. The standard of living of many of Buffalo Creek's households had improved significantly during that time. Many families had achieved stable, working-class status. They had been able to purchase old, wood-frame, four-room houses without modern conveniences (often referred to as "four rooms and a path to the woods") that the coal companies had built for their miners decades before that. The new homeowners then spent years upgrading those houses with modern plumbing and heating, adding on rooms, porches, and garages, and outfitting them with an abundance of appliances and consumer goods. They were "house-proud" people who felt they belonged in neighborhoods with other house-proud people who had achieved a fair share of the American dream of economic and social well-being, if not affluence. Writing in 1976, sociologist Kai Erikson described the status of Buffalo Creek's people this way (as mentioned in the epigraph at the beginning of this chapter):

> So the residents of Buffalo Creek were fairly well off in the early days of 1972. Most of the men were employed and earning good

wages, and if the hollow did not quite reach the national mean on the conventional indices of wealth, the people nonetheless owned their own houses, paid modest taxes, enjoyed a certain measure of security, and were generally satisfied with their lot. They had survived the crisis of automation (of the coal mines in the early 1950s) and were even beginning to profit from it, and to that extent, at least, they were one of the most affluent groups in an otherwise impoverished region.[3]

Many of Buffalo Creek's people had worked their way out of the hardships their parents had known in the old coal camps, and the poverty their grandparents had known in the remote mountains of Appalachia. One of them said, "Looking back, the men and women of Buffalo Creek remember it as a secure, honest, comfortable life." The expansion of federal social welfare programs also had helped Appalachia and Buffalo Creek in the 1960s. In fact, President John F. Kennedy had visited Buffalo Creek during his campaign for the presidency. So Buffalo Creek already had some name recognition in the national press and some of its people were proud of the fact.[4]

If there was a sense of security, however, it was not held by all of Buffalo Creek's people. And, if there was a sense of security, it was about to be sorely tested as a consequence of a series of decisions and events that began at least as far back as 1947. (A brief chronology of some of these events is presented in table 1.1.)[5] It was in that year that Lorado Coal Company opened mine #5 on a steep hillside about one mile above Three Forks. It created a gob *pile* for the mine waste on the hillside adjacent to one of the tributaries of Buffalo Creek. Additional gob piles were created as needed. In the 1960s, the pace and scope of coal mining operations above Three Forks grew rapidly. In 1964 Buffalo Mining Company (BMC) purchased the mines and equipment of Lorado Coal Company and expanded mining operations all along Buffalo Creek, especially at Three Forks. It built a dam (#1) across Middle Fork and created a gob *pond* behind the dam.[6] As coal production accelerated at the mine, another dam (#2) and a second gob pond were built in 1966. Only one year later, in 1967, part of dam #2 collapsed and released hundreds of

TABLE 1.1. A chronology of some noteworthy events related to the flood.[7]

1947	Lorado Coal Company opens mine #5 in the hills above Three Forks and starts a gob pile on the hillside.
1964	Buffalo Mining Company (BMC) purchases the mines and operations of now defunct Lorado Coal Company and builds the first dam and gob pond across Middle Fork.
1966	BMC builds dam #2 and a second gob pond farther up Middle Fork.
1967	Dam #2 suffers a partial break. It floods some yards, porches, and basements in Three Forks, rips up sections of Route 16 and some railroad tracks, and frightens residents. Pearl Woodrum writes a letter to Governor Hulett Smith asking for the removal of the gob ponds.
1967	A gob pile at Proctor Bottom collapses, fills basements with mud and gob, and sweeps away several automobiles.
1969	BMC builds dam #3 and another gob pond farther up Middle Fork.
1970	The Pittston Company (Pittston), a New York-based conglomerate, purchases BMC and continues operating the eight mines along Buffalo Creek as BMC.

1972	**FEBRUARY 25 (Friday)**
2100H	The U.S. Weather Bureau in Huntington, West Virginia, announces flash flood warnings for the Buffalo Creek area after two days of heavy rains.
2300H	BMC official Jack Kent inspects dam #3 and warns employee Dennis Gibson and other residents at Three Forks of danger. He encourages them to evacuate to Lorado School.
	Several families evacuate Three Forks to Lorado School.
	Off-duty miners from Three Forks start checking on the status of dam #3 every few hours.
	Kent phones his boss, Steve Dasovich, and reports his concerns about dam #3.

1972	**FEBRUARY 26 (Saturday)**
0300H	Three Forks resident Maxine Adkins places an emergency phone call to the Logan County Sheriff's Office, explains that local miners have been checking on dam #3, and warns that it is about to collapse. She asks Deputy Sheriff Spriggs to call out the National Guard.
	Sheriff Grimmett phones BMC officials at their homes about the reports of danger. He is assured that there is no cause for alarm.
0500H	Sheriff Grimmett orders his deputies to start a full-scale alert of the sixteen settlements along Buffalo Creek and to advise residents to evacuate to safety. He instructs Deputy Spriggs to notify the National Guard and to request immediate assistance. Spriggs executes the orders.

(continued on next page)

TABLE **1.1.** (*continued*)

	Deputies Mutters and Doty drive along Buffalo Creek warning some residents about danger.
0600H	Steve Dasovich inspects dam #3 with Jack Kent and orders him to have a ditch and pipe installed at dam #3 to divert rising water and relieve pressure on the dam.
0630H	Dasovich returns to Lorado, encounters deputies Doty and Mutters, and reassures them that the dam has been secured.
	Dasovich then phones his boss in Dante, Virginia, I. C. Spotte, the president of BMC, and reports on the situation. Spotte approves Dasovich's decisions. Dasovich then reassures some concerned residents of Lorado that the situation is secure and that the mines will operate during the day.
0750H	Heavy-equipment operator Dennis Gibson arrives at dam #3 and is alarmed to find that it has "gone soft." He speeds through Three Forks and other coal camps honking his horn and warning residents to evacuate the area.
****** 0800H ******	Dam #3 collapses, releasing thousands of tons of sludge water and debris that explode through dam #2 and dam #1, smash into the settlement at Three Forks, and surge down Buffalo Creek towards the other fifteen settlements. "THE BUFFALO CREEK DISASTER" has begun.
0830H	Garland Scaggs, a miner for Amherst Coal Co. in Lundale, phones radio station WVOW in Logan and reports that the dam has broken at Buffalo Creek. Radio newsman Bill Becker confirms the news by talking with Scaggs, then reports it to the outside world (with the location of the dam mistakenly at Lorado rather than at Three Forks), just as phone service is knocked out when the flood wave hits Lorado. "The dam at Lorado has broken. Get out of low-lying areas immediately. This is Bill Becker."[8]
1100H to 1200H	The flood wave and most of the floodwater rushes into the Guyandotte River, without major downstream flooding.
1200H	Local rescue units and West Virginia State Police arrive in town of Man and start organizing rescue and relief efforts.
1500H	Logan Sheriff's Office and West Virginia State Police establish temporary morgue in Man High School in south Man.
	Governor Moore's office issues a statement that calls the flood a "major disaster" and requests emergency assistance from the White House.
	National Guard and U.S. Army Corps of Engineer units arrive in town of Man with bulldozers, trucks, and other heavy equipment and start searching for survivors and bodies and clearing piles of debris from roads and bridges.

(continued on next page)

TABLE 1.1. (*continued*)

Coal companies provide radio-equipped trucks and other machinery for search, rescue, and clearing operations.

Civil Defense helicopters arrive and aid in rescue efforts at the coal camps isolated at the upper end of Buffalo Creek Valley.

1972   FEBRUARY 27 (Sunday)
The White House (President Nixon is traveling in the Far East) announces that $20 million will be made available immediately in disaster relief funds to the relief effort at Buffalo Creek.

The Salvation Army, Red Cross, and other nongovernmental relief agencies arrive and start providing meals and many services to flood victims at Man High School and other locations.

Many homeless survivors take up temporary residence in the hallways and classrooms at Man High School.

1972   FEBRUARY 28–MARCH 12
Regional staff members of the U.S. Office of Emergency Preparedness arrive in Man and set up offices and services.

The U.S. Department of Housing and Urban Development (HUD) establishes a relief office to start planning and building thirteen temporary trailer parks with more than 700 trailers for more than 2,500 survivors.

Units from the West Virginia State Department of Highways, West Virginia Employment Office, and Southern West Virginia Regional Health Council establish offices in Man and begin delivering services.

On March 2, Governor Arch A. Moore forms an "Ad Hoc Commission" of nine members to study the Buffalo Creek flood. Composition of this commission is immediately criticized by some Buffalo Creek survivors and some interest groups for having a pro–coal-company bias.

News media in Logan, Charleston, and other West Virginia cities publish reports of emerging issues, controversies, and conflicts related to the Buffalo Creek flood and reactions to it, including:

  a. A controversy develops between the office of Governor Moore and officials at BMC as to whether the state's antipollution laws were to blame for the collapse of the dams because they prohibited BMC from draining off excess water from the gob ponds and discharging it into the creeks.
  b. Governor Moore's office charges that there is an antigovernment bias in news media reporting on the disaster at Buffalo Creek. It declares that Buffalo Creek Hollow is off-limits to news-media personnel (this order is lifted within a few days because of reactions to it).
  c. A Pittston spokesman is quoted in the *Charleston Gazette* as saying that the flood was "an act of God" (Nugent, *Death at Buffalo Creek*, 156) and that the gob pond at Three Forks has been safe. This report ignites

(*continued on next page*)

TABLE **1.1.** (*continued*)

---

angry and enduring protests and outrage from many survivors and interest groups.

d. Controversies erupt regarding some appointments to various government investigations into the disaster.

The U.S. Department of Interior Assistant Secretary for Mineral Resources Hollis M. Dole orders the U.S. Geological Survey and the U.S. Bureau of Mines to establish a task force to "study and analyze hazards associated with the disposal and storage of coal mine waste materials" and to include the Three Forks dam failure. (Nugent, *Death at Buffalo Creek*, 159)

The U.S. Department of Interior commissions a study of the Three Forks dam failure by its Bureau of Reclamation.

The U.S. Senate Labor Subcommittee starts an investigation of the Buffalo Creek disaster. It requests an in-depth analysis of the Buffalo Creek flood by the U.S. Army Corps of Engineers.

1972   MARCH 28
Pittston approves BMC setting up a disaster claims office in Man to process survivors' claims for property damages. BMC begins settling claims with survivors for property damages for up to $10,000, the West Virginia statutory limit for each case of wrongful death.

1972   APRIL
Governor Moore's Ad Hoc Commission holds public hearings in Charleston about the Buffalo Creek disaster. Controversial statements are made by many witnesses, including BMC president I. C. Spotte, BMC vice president Steve Dasovich, Pittston engineer Richard Yates, and flood survivor Wayne Brady Hatfield, among others.

1972   MAY
The U.S. Senate Labor Subcommittee holds two days of hearings on the dam collapse at Three Forks focusing on the Department of Interior's Bureau of Mines actions and investigations. A Bureau of Mines official claims that the 1969 Federal Coal Mining Health and Safety Act only gives the Bureau of Mines authority to protect miners working in coal mines— not the miners or their families in their homes.

The Citizens' Committee to Investigate the Buffalo Creek Disaster charges that Governor Moore's Ad Hoc Commission was "mainly a whitewash packed with people who had a personal interest in the findings."[9] The committee forms a twenty-member panel to independently investigate the disaster.

The state of West Virginia announces plans to build a modern, concrete, two-lane highway up through Buffalo Creek Hollow to replace the damaged Route 16. It also announces plans to build new water and sewer systems and a number of subsidized housing developments.

(*continued on next page*)

TABLE **1.1.** (*continued*)

1972	JUNE
	The Senate Labor Subcommittee and the Department of Interior call for new legislation to eliminate future disasters like the one at Buffalo Creek. They recommend passage of the pending "Mined Area Protection Bill."
1972	SEPTEMBER
	Governor Moore's Ad Hoc Commission publishes its report on its investigation into the Buffalo Creek flood. Some of the report is highly critical of Pittston and BMC. It recommends a grand jury investigation with subpoena power in order to examine more thoroughly the conflicting testimony of some witnesses and to consider whether criminal charges should be issued.
	A Logan County circuit judge follows the recommendation of the Ad Hoc Commission and orders a grand jury probe of the disaster to determine whether criminal charges should be brought against Pittston and BMC.
	The Citizens' Committee to Investigate the Buffalo Creek Disaster concludes that BMC was solely responsible for the flood and that it failed to protect the people of Buffalo Creek.
	Some survivors decide to seek additional compensatory and exemplary damages from Pittston. They hire the Washington DC law firm, Arnold & Porter, to prepare a lawsuit on their behalf.

tons of wastewater and debris—which tore up sections of Route 16 and railroad tracks at Three Forks and flooded the yards, porches, and basements of some of the dwellings. This flood frightened some of the residents enough that they petitioned Governor Hulett Smith to have the gob ponds closed down—but to no avail. Other incidents that involved other gob ponds along Buffalo Creek occurred during the next five years. In 1967 another gob pond collapsed. This one was at Proctor Bottom, about midway down Buffalo Creek. Tons of wastewater and debris swept away some vehicles and filled some basements with mud and gob. Concerns about the safety of the gob ponds became more widespread among Buffalo Creek's people, particularly when BMC built yet another dam (#3) and gob pond on Middle Fork in 1969. It was located about a half mile upstream and more than one hundred feet higher in elevation than the two gob ponds that were already blocking Middle Fork.

Production and profitability grew at most of the mines along Buffalo Creek in the late 1960s and early 1970s. In 1970 The Pittston Company, a powerful conglomerate based in New York City, purchased BMC and invested heavily in expanding operations at eight of the mines along Buffalo Creek—including the mine at Three Forks—under the name of Buffalo Mining Company. During the next two years, federal and state agencies conducted a number of routine inspections of the dams and gob ponds above Three Forks. Inspectors raised questions about the structural integrity of dam #3, but they did not require major renovations. Concern about the safety of the gob ponds increased nonetheless, especially among miners and their families who lived at or near Three Forks, and particularly during periods of sustained, heavy rains.

This is exactly what happened in the days immediately before February 26, 1972. Heavy rains had been falling for two days. Some of the miners who lived at Three Forks arranged among themselves to check on the gob ponds every few hours because they were close to overflowing. Gob pond #3 worried them the most. It covered about twenty acres on the surface and was forty feet deep at the edge of an earthen dam (#3) that was holding back hundreds of tons of wastewater, oily sludge, and mine debris. The miners feared that, if dam #3 collapsed, the fluid mass of its gob pond would race downhill, gain momentum, and wash away the other gob ponds and dams. The cumulative mass would pour into Three Forks and then race down the valley through the other coal camps.

At about 9:00 p.m. on Friday, February 25, the U.S. Weather Bureau in Huntington, West Virginia, announced flash flood warnings for the Buffalo Creek area. Two hours later, Jack Kent, a BMC supervisor at the Three Forks mine, inspected dam #3 and noticed that the gob pond was almost full. He drove down to Three Forks and warned BMC employee Dennis Gibson and some of the residents at Three Forks that the dam was of concern to him. He encouraged the residents to relocate for the night to the grade school at Lorado, a few miles downstream. Several of the families did so. Off-duty miners at Three Forks began checking on dam #3 every few hours. Jack Kent then phoned his boss, Steve Dasovich, who was in charge of all mining operations along Buffalo Creek, and reported his concerns about dam #3.

Later, at about 3:00 a.m., Maxine Adkins, a resident of Three Forks, called the Logan County Sheriff's Office and reported that some miners had just returned from checking dam #3. They were warning people that it was about to collapse. She asked Deputy Sheriff Spriggs to call out the National Guard. Shortly after that, Deputy Spriggs phoned Sheriff Grimmett at his home and reported his phone conversation with Mrs. Adkins. Sheriff Grimmett then phoned several BMC officials at their homes along Buffalo Creek and down in Man. He inquired about the safety of the dams up at Three Forks. The officials assured him that there was no cause for a general alarm. Sheriff Grimmett was not reassured. At about 5:00 a.m., after a few more hours of heavy rain and phone calls from other residents of Buffalo Creek who were concerned about the dams, Sheriff Grimmett ordered his deputies to start a full-scale alert of the coal camps and to advise people to evacuate their homes to higher ground. He instructed Deputy Spriggs to notify the National Guard and to request immediate assistance with the evacuation. Deputy Spriggs phoned National Guard Headquarters in Charleston, as instructed. He ordered Deputies Mutters and Doty to drive along Buffalo Creek, warn residents of the danger, and encourage them to evacuate their homes.

Meanwhile, at about 6:00 a.m., BMC's Steve Dasovich inspected dam #3 with Jack Kent. Dasovich instructed Kent to assemble a work crew and have a ditch dug and a drainage pipe installed to divert the rainwater that was nearing the crest of the dam. Dasovich then drove back down along Buffalo Creek to Lorado. There he encountered deputies Doty and Mutters as they drove around alerting people to the possibility of a flood and encouraging them to evacuate the area. Dasovich told the deputies that the dam had been secured and that there was no need to evacuate the people. He then went into his office in Lorado and phoned his boss, I. C. Spotte, the president of BMC, at his home in Dante, Virginia. Spotte listened to Dasovich's description of the situation at Three Forks, and he voiced his approval of Dasovich's decisions. Dasovich then went into the streets to talk with residents who were out in the rain, watching the rising waters of the creek, and worrying about the prospects of a flood.

He assured them that the dams at Three Forks had been secured and that the mines would operate normal shifts that day.

Dawn brought little light to Buffalo Creek that Saturday morning. It was still midwinter. The weather was overcast and raw. Rain alternated with wet snow. In the coal camps, small numbers of men, mainly retired and off-duty miners, milled about along the creek, nervously watching the water rise. Most of the other residents of Buffalo Creek were sleeping in, except for the miners who were ending their shifts in the local mines and those who had risen to have breakfast and prepare for their work on the day shift in the mines.

At 7:50 a.m., Dennis Gibson, who was a heavy-equipment operator for BMC, arrived at dam #3 in order to install the drainage pipe that Dasovich had ordered. Gibson was shocked to see that the dam had "gone soft." Alarmed, he then jumped into his truck and drove as fast as he could down Route 16, honking his horn to warn residents of the coal camps that the dam was about to collapse. And this is exactly what it did about ten minutes later.

At 8:00 a.m., by most accounts, dam #3 suddenly collapsed.

"The Disaster at Buffalo Creek" had begun.

PORTRAYALS OF THE COURSE OF THE FLOOD

Apparently, there were no aerial observers of the flood as it swept its way down through the convoluted ravines of Buffalo Creek Valley. Nor, to the best of my knowledge, is there any film footage to show us exactly how it surged into and through the sixteen coal camps and how it disgorged its ghastly spoils into the Guyandotte River hours later. All that we have as *primary* testimony are eyewitness descriptions by some survivors of how the flood appeared to them at certain small places along the hollow. Most of these descriptions were not recorded until days, months, and years after the flood had passed them by. These descriptions often refer to the flood as a "big, black wave," "a huge falling wall of mud and junk" that "churned," "swept," "drowned," "rolled," and "washed" through the coal camps like a violent flush, or several quick flushes, rather than a flood. The main body of water rushed through each of the coal camps in a matter of minutes, and then was gone—out of sight.

For *secondary* sources, we have many portrayals of the flood by journalists, engineers, scientists, and researchers (including yours truly, of course), some of whom spoke with eyewitnesses and acquaintances of eyewitnesses, often long after the flood had passed by. Some of these eyewitnesses had been immersed in its waters, barely escaping with their lives. Some had watched from a distance. Some arrived soon after the flood passed.

Reportedly, when the flood poured out of Middle Fork Ravine and slammed into the buildings at Three Forks, it destroyed the electric transformers at the power station there, knocked out electricity for most of Buffalo Creek, and created an explosion that resounded down the valley to the town of Man, seventeen miles away. Electric lights and appliances stopped running. An unnerving silence is said to have fallen upon the other coal camps after that first explosion. The dogs stopped barking. Everything seemed still and strange, possibly so still that some people noticed it immediately and reacted to it in time to awaken others and alert them that something had gone wrong.

Back at Three Forks, the floodwaters turned and cascaded down Buffalo Creek Valley with growing fury. Kai Erikson portrayed the flood's impact on Three Forks (Saunders) this way:

> The wave demolished Saunders entirely. It did not crush the village into mounds of rubble, but carried everything away with it—houses, cars, trailer, a church whose white spire had pointed to the slag pile for years—and scraped the ground as cleanly as if a thousand bulldozers had been at work.[10]

The height of the flood's front wave changed considerably from one coal camp to another according to the curvature, steepness, and width of the valley from one point to another. The front wave might bypass a row of houses on one side of the valley only to demolish every house on the other side. Estimated to have been at least thirty feet high when it hit Three Forks, the front wave gained momentum as it raced down mile-long straightaways and slammed into the relatively long, sprawling, and developed coal camps of Lorado and Lundale. They suffered the highest losses of lives, the most injuries, and the greatest amount of damage to private and public property. Three of the former residents described it like this to Erikson:

> I could see all the houses in Lorado just being kicked around like so many toys. I looked down at Lundale and it was completely gone, wiped out.
>
> I jumped out of bed and I looked out the door and I couldn't believe it. It was a wall of water and debris. It looked like it was about twenty-five or thirty foot high coming running at us. And it was just black-looking. It was just rumbling and roaring and the houses was popping and snapping and they was breaking up.
>
> One mass of ugliness was all it was to me, the water and houses and the gas exploding and the electricity lines buzzing and things like that. Crashing sounds. Everything was completely out of control, and the sound of it, you know, was just a roar, a heavy roar.[11]

By the time the front wave reached Kistler, the last coal camp before the town of Man, it only overflowed the banks of the creek by three to five feet in many places. To some residents, it almost seemed to be like other seasonal floods that were so common there and at many other coal camps in Logan County.[12]

By 11:00 a.m., most of the floodwater had poured into the Guyandotte River just below the town of Man. Pooled water drained into Buffalo Creek sufficiently that survivors could start assessing the damages and search through the debris that was left behind. It took more than a few days for all of the direct damages to be estimated. The indirect and long-term damages are still being estimated to this day (this book is a case in point). Eventually, the state of West Virginia officially decreed that 125 people had died in the flood. Seven of the bodies have never been recovered. Three bodies that were recovered were so severely damaged that they were unidentifiable. Seventy-one were females. Fifty-four were males. All were listed as being "White" regarding race.[13] Of the identifiable dead, all but two of them had surnames that were ostensibly "northern European." Seven of the dead had names that often are associated with feuds between clans in that part of Appalachia: four were Hatfields, three were McCoys. Most all of the dead (at least 73 percent of them) had lived in the coal camps at the upper end of the valley. Of the victims whose bodies were recovered and were identifiable, Lundale and Lorado had forty-nine and forty-two of the deceased, respectively. Latrobe had five. Amherstdale had four. Stowe had two. Crites had two. Robinette had four. Accoville had three dead. Kistler had one.

In addition to the dead, hundreds of people had almost drowned. Hundreds more were injured in collisions with broken rails and railroad ties, buildings, vehicles, and other floating debris, and when they were washed into bridge abutments, trees, and boulders. Hundreds of people had open wounds, concussions, ruptured internal organs, broken bones, and severe sprains. Physical shock was commonplace. The oily, polluted wastewater from the gob ponds caused respiratory and digestive problems. People died days later because they had ingested or inhaled too much "gob." By some accounts, even people who escaped physical injury were so stunned by what they had witnessed that they could do little more than lie down and cry, sit and stare, or stumble and slosh around aimlessly in dazed silence, feeling cold, wet, and disoriented. Many of them did not know where to go or what to do next. Kai Erikson interviewed an uninjured, seventy-year-old man who said:

> Well, the day of the flood we just milled around to see what we could find. Just drifted around. Nobody knowed what to do or what they was looking for.

A fifteen-year-old girl confided in Erikson:

> Everybody was wandering around and asking if you had seen so-and-so, and I never saw a time like it. People would just stop to go to the bathroom right beside the railroad because there wasn't anywhere to go, and dogs that had been washed down and weren't dead were running up to you and they were wet. We walked up to the bridge at Proctor [above Amherstdale] and a bulldozer picked

a little girl up, and when he saw he had her on, he dropped her off because it cut her back and her back was still pink. Her face was tore up so bad they couldn't tell who it was. Then we saw a hand under her, sticking up through the debris.[14]

Other survivors started frantic efforts to determine whether their neighbors and their relatives and friends in other coal camps had survived the flood. This was all the more difficult because most telephone and power lines were down, most roads and alleys were clogged with debris, and many vehicles were destroyed or flooded. Rumors started spreading about the extent of damages elsewhere along Buffalo Creek and about the causes and reasons for the flood. Most alarming were rumors that more dams were bursting somewhere upstream and that more flash floods were on the way. These problems were particularly severe in the coal camps in the upper half of Buffalo Creek and among neighbors who lived on the fringes of the camps.

By midday, help from outside agencies started to arrive at Man and Kistler in the form of the West Virginia State Police, firemen, ambulance crews, and volunteers from other coal camps along the Guyandotte River. The movement of these external relief forces up Buffalo Creek was impeded by derelict and broken buildings, vehicles, and railcars that clogged Route 16 (the only road that ran up the valley) and the bridges that remained standing over the creek. Because of this congestion, the coal camps at the upper end of the hollow—Stowe, Lundale, Lorado, Pardee, and Three Forks—received very little aid from external agencies until the next day, Sunday, and very few supplies for many days to come.

By some accounts, the vast majority of the survivors were without shelter that first night. By other accounts, many survivors whose dwellings still were inhabitable provided shelter, food, and succor to neighbors in need—even to complete strangers. Goldie and Buddy Cummins were among the "Good Samaritans" on that first night. In Goldie's own words:

> The Lord spared us, that's for sure. When we come down off that hillside our house here wasn't washed-out. So Buddy went out and told folks who was washed-out to come stay with us. We had

families in every room. Everybody tried to help out as best they could. I recall one family from up the hollow come in that night all wet and cold. One of their little boys looked around at all the people in here. His eyes git real wide and he says to me real loud, "Lady, your floor here sure is muddy. You need to mop-up!"

Everybody bust-out laughin' at that.[15]

SUNDAY, FEBRUARY 27

On Sunday the pace of external relief efforts picked up appreciably on the lower reaches of Buffalo Creek as news of the destructiveness of the flood spread throughout the United States.

> Details of the disaster were now being broadcast to the rest of the nation, and the roadblock at Man was crowded with survivors who wanted to get out, newsmen and relatives who wanted to get in, and a constant traffic of rescue teams passing back and forth.[16]

President Nixon sent condolences to the survivors while he was traveling in Asia. The White House announced that $20 million would be made available in disaster relief funds. The U.S. Army Corps of Engineers arrived in Man with dozens of bulldozers, trucks, and other heavy equipment to clear debris and start erecting temporary roads, bridges, water supply points, and sanitary facilities. Public health agencies started immunizing survivors against typhoid fever. The Salvation Army and the Red Cross started providing meals and clothing to flood victims at Man High School, where hundreds of homeless survivors took up temporary residence in the halls and classrooms. According to Erikson, most survivors had to wait for and rely upon aid from external agencies because they were still too shocked to help themselves. They were frantically seeking news about the status of their relatives and friends in Buffalo Creek's other coal camps.

> Most of the people of Buffalo Creek were still numbed by the savagery of the disaster, still trying to make sense of their shattered world. The first visitors to the hollow, aside from relief workers

called to the scene, were relatives who, made frantic by the early news broadcasts, hurried home to see for themselves.[17]

THE WEEK AFTER

Relief and cleanup efforts hit full stride during the next week. The Army Corps of Engineers cleared one lane of Route 16 all the way up the valley to Lorado. The corps also started clearing lots for thirteen temporary trailer camps along Buffalo Creek and the Guyandotte River. Officials from the U.S. Department of Housing and Urban Development (HUD) established an office in Man and arranged to bring in nearly 700 mobile homes for about 2,500 of Buffalo Creek's 4,950 residents at the time of the flood. Hundreds of the other survivors had already relocated outside of Buffalo Creek to live with relatives and friends, temporarily or permanently. By midweek, many of Buffalo Creek's school-aged children were attending classes again, either at their original schools or at schools outside of Buffalo Creek. Most of the mines along Buffalo Creek operated three shifts, just as they did before the flood, even though the rail lines had not been rebuilt. Most miners returned to work if they had not been injured in the flood, or if they had recovered sufficiently from their injuries.

To an outsider who read newspaper accounts of Buffalo Creek just five days after the flood, it might seem that Buffalo Creek was on its way to recovery. It might seem that the flood's damages were more or less obvious and that they were being responded to in a timely manner. Despite extensive damages to miners' houses and other buildings, more than 4,500 of Buffalo Creek's 4,950 people had not been killed or severely injured. More than 1,000 of them were still residing in their homes. Plenty of resources were pouring into the area. County, state, and federal political leaders and agencies were actively involved in the relief efforts. Relief supplies and work crews were packed into the town of Man, trying their best to contribute to the relief efforts up and down Buffalo Creek Valley. It might seem as though the flood certainly had been dramatic and destructive, but that it was like many other "natural" disasters—cyclones, tornadoes, and earthquakes that hit communities across the United States from time to time. As in so many of these other disasters, within a few years, the communities would be rebuilt and most of the survivors would recover a considerable amount of their economic, social, and emotional well-being.[18] In language that is fashionable among some contemporary social scientists, it might have been assumed that the Buffalo Creek Valley still had enough "social capital" to be "resilient" enough to bounce back into its former structure and functions as a community.[19]

However, to "insiders"—the people who were working up and down Buffalo Creek in recovery and relief efforts—it became shockingly apparent during the first week that this disaster was going to prove to be much more enduring, destructive, and controversial than so many other calamities, crises, catastrophes, and disasters they had faced or had heard about. The flash flood was long gone, but the disaster was lingering, and, in many ways, it was deepening and expanding by way of disruptive secondary effects. Badly decomposed bodies had to be buried quickly in graveyards that were not destroyed in the flood. There was little opportunity for the traditional ceremonies and rituals that were to be bestowed upon the dead. Many survivors of the flood watched as their damaged and derelict dwellings were bulldozed into rubble, burned, or trucked away because they were clogging bridges, roadways, and public property. Homeless survivors who were given temporary quarters at Man High School suddenly realized that the few prized possessions that they had brought with them were stolen while they were away from their beds. Relief workers from outside agencies, survivors of the flood, reporters, and leaders of government agencies were frustrated by lack of access to the most damaged coal camps. For days, only one lane of the only road up through the valley was open, and only at some points. Heated disagreements erupted as to which agencies had priority in access to that road and to each of the coal camps, in part because none of the coal camps were incorporated and Buffalo Creek itself never had any local government of its own.

News media in the cities of Logan, Charleston, Huntington, and other parts of southern Appalachia sent teams of their top investigative reporters to Buffalo Creek to describe the damages and to probe allegations of malfeasance. Wire services and other national news media quickly picked up on the articles that were published locally. Many of them sent their own reporters to Buffalo Creek by the end of the first week. A heated argument erupted between Governor Arch Moore and officials at BMC as to whether the state's antipollution laws were to blame for the collapse of the dams because they prohibited mining companies from draining off excess water from gob ponds and discharging it directly into creeks and rivers. BMC charged that newspaper accounts of the argument were biased against coal companies. Governor Moore charged that there was an antigovernment bias in news stories about the argument and about the flood in general. He declared that Buffalo Creek Hollow was off-limits to reporters. News media and public opposition to this declaration was so immediate and vehement that the declaration was rescinded a few days later.[20]

Shortly after that, a spokesman for Pittston Company was quoted in local newspapers as saying that the flood was an "act of God"—a "natural" disaster that was caused by three days of an extraordinary amount of rain rather than by negligence and mismanagement of the gob ponds at Three Forks. Many survivors of the flood and members of local grassroots interest groups reacted with scorn and outrage to this assertion, considering it as being tantamount to blasphemy: blaming God rather than Buffalo Mining Company. Some survivors of the flood formed a "Citizens' Committee to Investigate the Buffalo Creek Disaster" to monitor news reports about the disaster and to increase pressure on the coal companies and government agencies for compensatory payments for the damages they suffered because of the flood. Governor Arch Moore appointed nine members to his own "Ad Hoc Commission" to study the causes of the flood. Flood survivors and interest groups quickly charged that the commission was stacked in favor of the coal companies and that its findings would be deceitful and irrelevant.

WEEKS LATER

Given the furor of controversies like these at the local and state levels, it is no wonder that a number of offices of the federal government initiated formal inquiries into the causes of the flood within one month of the event. The U.S. Senate Labor Subcommittee began an investigation of the disaster and asked the Army Corps of Engineers to conduct an in-depth analysis of the sources of the flood. The U.S. Department of the Interior commissioned its Bureau of Reclamation to conduct a study of the dams and related structures at Three Forks. It also ordered its Bureau of Mines and Geological Survey divisions to establish a task force to include the Three Forks dam failure in a comprehensive study of hazards associated with the disposal and storage of coal-mine waste materials throughout the United States. Clearly, then, the disaster at Buffalo Creek quickly resonated through many agencies of the federal government. Three investigations of this magnitude might not seem very impressive by contemporary standards and in light of the numerous investigations that are held after disasters such as Hurricane Katrina on the Gulf Coast in 2005. However, back then, in the early 1970s, this was an unusual amount of timely responsiveness and scrutiny by agencies of the federal government to an event as localized, remote, and brief as the flood at Buffalo Creek.[21]

On March 28, Pittston Company approved a proposal by BMC to establish a claims office in the town of Man to process survivors' claims for property damages. Shortly after that, BMC began settling claims for up to $10,000, which was the maximum payment required by law in West Virginia for each case of wrongful death. At about that time, the state of West Virginia announced that it would build a modern, two-lane highway up through Buffalo Creek Valley to replace the significantly damaged and obsolete Route 16. This would be a much straighter and wider highway than its predecessor. As such, the state would claim by eminent domain the house lots and lands of dozens of the flood's survivors in order to clear a new course for the highway. Owners of these lots and lands would have to relocate permanently to other places along Buffalo Creek, or move elsewhere.

In May, the Citizens' Committee charged that Governor Moore's Ad Hoc Commission was "mainly a whitewash packed with people who have a personal interest in the findings."[22] Disgusted, the committee then formed a panel with twenty members to independently investigate the disaster. In so doing, the disaster now was being investigated by at least five different organizations at the local, state, and federal levels.

During the summer of 1972, agencies of the federal government started issuing some of their findings from their investigations into the causes of the flood. The Senate Labor Subcommittee and the Department of the Interior called for new legislation to eliminate future disasters like the one at Buffalo Creek. They recommended passage of the pending "Mined Area Protection Bill" and increased enforcement of existing regulations regarding residential housing near mining operations.

Then, in September 1972, hardly seven months after the flood, five major events took place that revealed how controversial the disaster had become and how dissatisfied many people were with efforts by external organizations to help them recover from the flood:

1. The governor's office announced that the state of West Virginia would join forces with the Federal Regional Council III in producing a comprehensive Buffalo Valley Redevelopment Plan so that "Buffalo Valley will be rebuilt more beautiful than before with a better life for everyone."[23] This plan ultimately called for more than $44 million in government funding, and it became the single most important blueprint for the coordinated rebuilding of Buffalo Creek by a welter of county, state, and federal agencies.

2. Governor Moore's Ad Hoc Commission published its report on its investigation into the causes of the flood. Some elements of the report were highly candid and critical of the Pittston Company and Buffalo Mining Company's actions before and after the flood. The commission recommended a grand jury investigation, with subpoena power, in order to sort through contradictory testimony by various witnesses and experts and to consider whether criminal charges should be issued.

3. In response to this recommendation, a judge in the Logan County Circuit Court ordered a grand jury probe of the disaster

to determine whether criminal charges should be brought against Pittston Company and Buffalo Mining Company.

4. The Citizens' Committee announced that it had concluded that Buffalo Mining Company was solely responsible for the flood and for failing to protect the people of Buffalo Creek.

5. A group of survivors, which eventually included more than four hundred plaintiffs, decided to seek additional compensatory and exemplary damages from Pittston Company. The group hired Arnold & Porter, a large, prestigious law firm in Washington DC, to prepare a lawsuit on the behalf of the litigants.

*   *   *

These, then, were some of the major public events and controversies that occurred during the first seven months after the flood. While they were occurring, many other events and controversies were taking place in the private lives and the social lives of the flood's survivors as they tried to come to terms with the damages that they had suffered, with the violent images that remained with them from the day of the flood, and with the disappointments that they experienced in trying to recover and rebuild their lives and their communities. These are the subjects of the next chapter and, to a considerable extent, the rest of this book.

Testimonies of many of the flood's witnesses have been recorded and published in local media in the decades since the flood. They provide us with troubling insights about just how difficult it was for some of the survivors to reestablish a sense of well-being (and of how difficult it is for researchers to understand the people they study—a subject that is addressed in chapter 6). One "anonymous female" put it this way:

> We thought everybody in Lundale was dying. It looked like they were from what we had seen. We had no idea how many had escaped. I didn't keep track of all who had died. When you see so many of your friends die like that, you try to keep your mind off of it as much as possible and not dwell on it…My doctors asked why

> I reacted the way I did, and asked if I was feeling guilty because I had lived while so many others had died. I said, "No." They put on my chart that I was emotionally disturbed. Anyone would have been emotionally disturbed a week after seeing all that.[24]

I heard a somewhat different account of how another woman reacted to barely escaping the floodwaters with her family as their house was nearly swept away. She had been a schoolgirl at the time. And although she moved away from Lorado for a number of years when she became an adult, she gladly moved back in the 1990s and has stayed ever since.

> My survival instinct must be strong. I never had survivor's guilt like they claimed people had after the flood. I figured I was spared, along with helping my family out of the house. I don't ask why. You don't question fate. And, not being a believer, I never once thought about God––not once.

And so, it seems fair to say that, several months after the flood, the prospects for rebuilding Buffalo Creek and for the recovery of its survivors were mixed, at best, and not really very promising. On the positive side, perhaps 1,000 of the valley's 4,950 residents had not been dislocated from their homes. The vast majority of the valley's people (4,825) had not been killed immediately in the flood. Many of them remained in Logan County. More than 2,000 of them were living in thirteen HUD trailer camps in the area. Many of them were inclined to move back into the valley as soon as they could. Quite a few of the families that had been dislocated had received or would receive up to $10,000 in compensation from the state of West Virginia or $8,000 from the Mine Workers Safety Fund. Massive efforts to help survivors had been made by county, state, and federal agencies and by national emergency relief organizations. The mines were operating again and most of the survivors who were uninjured miners were working again. The governor and state agencies gave many indications that the infrastructure of Buffalo Creek would be rebuilt and modernized. Investigations of the disaster by federal and state agencies were ongoing, or they had produced testimony that was critical of mining practices that contributed to the disaster. Agencies promised to make necessary reforms in their regulations and practices so that similar disasters would not occur anywhere in the United States.

On the negative side, 125 people had died, hundreds had been injured severely, and about 80 percent of the valley's residents were dislocated from their homes. Many families were disrupted, and many of the survivors were suffering from repeated disappointments and a variety of stresses from the flood and by some of the reactions to it by external agencies and the coal companies. Damages to private and public property were astounding—far more than the $20 million that the White House had allocated for disaster relief. Compensation to survivors' families for losses of real estate and personal property did not come close to covering replacement costs. The HUD trailer camps were increasingly congested, uncomfortable, constraining, and disturbing to many of the survivors who lived there. Survivors also were aggravated by controversies about culpability for the flood and plans for rebuilding the infrastructure of the valley in ways that would prolong uncertainty about whether survivors could ever move back to the sites of their former homes. And these are just a few of the reasons why many of the survivors were uncertain as to whether they—and Buffalo Creek—had a future.

ENDNOTES

1. Goldie Cummins (a pseudonym) told me this while I interviewed her and her husband, Buddy, in their home in Lundale on May 18, 2002. Much more of my interview with Goldie and Buddy is presented in chapter 4.

2. Contrary to most other published accounts, there was (and still is) at least one other former coal camp in Buffalo Creek Valley that was not directly damaged by the flood in 1972. This is the camp of Curtis, located about two miles upstream from Three Forks along one of Buffalo Creek's tributaries. From my visits there, I estimate that it has about one hundred residents in approximately thirty tiny, wood-frame cabins. A sizeable coal tipple and load-out was located close to it until 2002, when it was dismantled.

3. Kai T. Erikson, *Everything in Its Path: Destruction of Community in the Buffalo Creek Flood*, hardcover ed. (New York: Simon & Schuster, 1976), 24.

4. Three of the residents of Buffalo Creek whom I interviewed in 2001 proudly mentioned President Kennedy's visit as evidence that Buffalo Creek was a "famous place." On the expansion of federal welfare programs and their consequences for Appalachia, see Philip J. Obermiller and Michael E. Maloney, eds., *Appalachia: Social Context Past and Present* (Dubuque: Kendall-Hunt Publishing Company, 2006); and Ronald D. Eller, "Modernization, 1940–2000," in *High Mountains Rising: Appalachia in Time and Place*, ed. Richard A. Straw and H. Tyler Blethen (Champaign, IL: University of Illinois Press, 2004), 197–219.

5. The account of the major events leading up to the flood, and following it, relies heavily on Tom Nugent's book, *Death at Buffalo Creek: The 1972 West Virginia Flood Disaster* (New York: Norton, 1973), 19–76, and on government documents that report on the investigations of the flood, principally, the Senate Committee on Labor and Public Welfare, *Buffalo Creek (W.Va.) Disaster, 1972*, 99th Cong., May 30–31, 1972 (Washington, DC: U.S. Government Printing Office); and *The Buffalo Creek Flood and Disaster: Official Report from the Governor's Ad Hoc Commission of Inquiry*, 1972, http://www.marshall.edu/library/speccoll/virtual_museum/buffalo_creek/html/GAHCI-Report.pdf (accessed August 11, 2008).

6. By the mid-1960s, environmental laws were enacted by the federal government that prohibited mine operators from discharging wastewater directly into streams and rivers without decontaminating the effluent according to new standards of purity. Mine operators built gob *ponds* as a way to avoid discharging wastewater directly into the streams and rivers.

7. This chronology relies heavily on Nugent, *Death at Buffalo Creek*; and Gerald M. Stern, *The Buffalo Creek Disaster. How the Survivors of One of the Worst Disasters in Coal-Mining History Brought Suit Against the Coal Company—and Won* (New York: Vintage Books, 1976).

8. Nugent, *Death at Buffalo Creek*, 81.

9. Ibid., 181.

10. Erikson, *Everything in Its Path*, hardcover ed., 29. The assertion that Three Forks (Saunders) was totally destroyed by the flood is contradicted by the accounts of a number of eyewitnesses whom I interviewed during my visits to Buffalo Creek. These accounts are presented in the preface and in chapter 4 of this book.

11. Ibid., 32–33. Readers might note that the unnamed speaker of the first quotation claims that s/he actually saw all of the houses of Lorado being "kicked around" and that s/he was able to look down and see that all of Lundale was destroyed. In later chapters, I introduce evidence that both of these claims were probably well-meaning and honest—but that they probably were erroneous in at least two ways. Neither in Lorado nor in Lundale were all houses damaged, let alone destroyed. Also, it is highly unlikely that anyone could see all of Lorado and all of Lundale from the same vantage point unless that person was airborne at least 200 yards above the midpoint between Lorado and Lundale. I make this observation primarily to encourage readers to regard all assertions about the flood, including mine, with compassionate intelligence and a healthy dose of skepticism.

12. Several eyewitnesses to the flood at Kistler described it this way in face-to-face conversations with me in July 2001. One of them, an owner of a grocery store that is only thirty yards from the creek, gestured to the lower sill of his plateglass windows at the front of the store. "The water come up to that bottom sill there. Had maybe two feet of it in here on the floor and the low shelves. Made a mess, alright."

13. Erikson, *Everything in Its Path*, hardcover ed., 118–119. Erikson estimated that about 10 percent of Buffalo Creek's residents at the time of the flood were Black, that 10 percent of the plaintiffs in the Arnold & Porter lawsuit were Black, and that Blacks had been in the labor force along Buffalo Creek since the early 1900s, although they were often discriminated against by the coal companies. One often hears the claim along Buffalo Creek that housing discrimination actually helped Buffalo Creek's Black population avoid severe damages during the flood because most Blacks could only afford housing down at the lower end of the valley, far from the coal camps that were hit first and most furiously by the floodwaters. Interestingly, one

of the leaders of the citizen's group that hired Arnold & Porter was Charlie Cowan, a Black man who was a former professional football player and was widely respected for his integrity and leadership ability. Formal segregation of Blacks and Whites apparently ended in the early 1960s when the small high school for Blacks at Kistler was closed (it is still standing, but is vacant). Currently at Fanco, churches for Blacks and Whites sit side by side, but the congregations are not formally segregated. In my seven years of fieldwork along Buffalo Creek, I never witnessed any direct or indirect evidence of racial or ethnic discrimination or prejudice.

14. Erikson, *Everything in Its Path*, hardcover ed., 41. Readers might note that this eyewitness mentions that a bulldozer was clearing debris only hours after the flood passed. In doing so, this passage indicates that not everyone was so shocked or traumatized as to be ineffective.

15. See endnote 1.

16. Erikson, *Everything in Its Path*, hardcover ed., 43.

17. Ibid. As reported in chapter 4, some of the flood's survivors whom I interviewed along Buffalo Creek between 2000 and 2007 portray this situation quite differently than Erikson. They contend that they, and many other survivors, were *not* so numbed that they could not and did not help themselves and their neighbors for at least several days before relief workers from outside agencies such as the Red Cross arrived in their neighborhoods to help them. Chapter 6 considers some of the issues about the nature of human memory and forgetting, as well as the limitations of social research methods as they relate to this matter.

18. Chapter 2 discusses social science research on disasters and the ongoing controversy about what constitutes "natural" versus "human-made" or "technological" disasters. In chapter 6, I explain why I believe that the disaster at Buffalo Creek includes elements of both types of disasters. At this point, please consider that most or all of the rain that fell on Buffalo Creek, and many but not all of the terrain features of the Buffalo Creek Valley, were *not* human-made and were *not* primarily the consequence of applications of human technology. Yet it is also true that some of the key elements in the disaster *were* human-made (e.g., the gob ponds, the gob piles, the dams, and the locations and features of the buildings, roads, bridges, and rail lines) and *were* the consequences of applications of human technology.

19. The concepts of "social capital" and "resilience" applied to the analysis of small, rural communities are very much in vogue at this time. For examples, see Ann Dale and Jenny Onyx, *A Dynamic Balance: Social Capital and Sustainable Community Development* (Vancouver: UBC Press,

2005); and Rodriguez et al., eds., *Handbook of Disaster Research*, 1st ed. (New York: Springer, 2007). Skepticism about the utility of the concept of social capital as it might apply to small, rural communities is apparent in many venues, including Falk et al., eds., *Communities of Work: Rural Restructuring in Local and Global Contexts* (Athens, OH: Ohio University Press, 2003), 423–426. These concepts are considered again in chapters 3 and 6 of this book as they might apply to the Buffalo Creek experience.

20. In all likelihood, the Buffalo Creek disaster became so controversial at the national level—and eventually a *cause célèbre*—not just because it was so destructive to so many families and homes of miners, rather than to miners working in mines. Probably a greater reason for the controversy was that the events occurred when they did—in the early 1970s. The assassinations of President Kennedy, Senator Robert Kennedy, and the Reverend Martin Luther King, Jr., race riots, widespread arson in U.S. cities, and the excesses of the war in Vietnam led many Americans to distrust and question established institutions in the United States. Agencies of the federal government, political parties, labor unions, and huge multinational corporations such as Dow Chemical, Dupont, General Dynamics, Gulf Oil, and Standard Oil of New Jersey came under attack in the national news media. Political activism was obvious in the War on Poverty, the civil rights movement, women's liberation, the environmental protection movement, and the antiwar movement, to name but a few of its many manifestations. As a result of these forces, many political-interest groups, voluntary associations, and mass-media organizations were predisposed to portray almost any incident like the flash flood at Buffalo Creek as yet another example of the failure of governments and big businesses to protect working-class Americans in their own homes and in the poorest areas of the country.

21. For an overview of the findings of these investigations, see Gerald M. Stern's *The Buffalo Creek Disaster* and relevant references in the bibliography. Note that the subtitle of the 1976 paperback edition is slightly different: *The Buffalo Creek Disaster: How the Survivors of One of the Worst Disasters in Coal-Mining History Brought Suit Against the Coal Company—and Won*. All quotations that follow are from the paperback edition, unless noted otherwise.

22. Nugent, *Death at Buffalo Creek*, 181.

23. *Buffalo Valley Redevelopment Plan*, prepared by the Office of the Governor [of West Virginia], Federal/State Relations in Conjunction with Federal Regional Council (III), Charleston, WV: July 1973, 2. Chapter 3 of this

book describes this plan in some detail and evaluates how the plan contributed to the rebuilding of Buffalo Creek's communities.

24. "Anonymous female" as quoted in Dennis Deitz and Carlene Mowery, *Buffalo Creek: Valley of Death* (South Charleston, WV: Mountain Memory Books, 1992), 28, 33.

CHAPTER 2

EXPERTS' ACCOUNTS
OF DISASTERS
AND THE DISASTER
AT BUFFALO CREEK

[T]he traditional stereotypes have obscured the fact that disasters produce not only disruptive and disorganizing effects but also reconstructive and regenerative human responses. Both of these perspectives must be kept in mind in any balanced treatment of the social aspects of disasters.

—Charles E. Fritz, "Disasters,"
International Encyclopedia of the Social Sciences, 1968[1]

The ensuing days and weeks after the flood constituted what Kai Erikson called a second trauma, the deepening awareness that the fabric of community life had been irreparably destroyed.

The psychological impact of the disaster has been so extensive that no one in Buffalo Creek has been unaffected. The overwhelming evidence is that everyone exposed to the Buffalo Creek disaster has experienced some or all of the following manifestations of the general constellation of the survivor (syndrome).

—Robert Jay Lifton and Eric Olson, "The Human Meaning of Total Disaster: The Buffalo Creek Experience"[2]

We are a long way from having a good sense of the range of social and economic impacts that disasters may bring and how these may vary from case to case.

—Thomas E. Drabek[3]

*　　　　*　　　　*

A NOTE ON THE PSYCHOLOGY AND SOCIOLOGY OF DISASTERS

Before focusing on the accounts of experts about one disaster—the disaster at Buffalo Creek—let us briefly consider what social and behavioral scientists have discovered in their studies of hundreds of disasters since the early 1950s, when "disaster studies" emerged as a major field of study.[4]

In general, their research acknowledges that, in keeping with widely held public beliefs about disasters, many disasters create extensive damages to the physical environment and to the physical infrastructure and economies of neighborhoods, villages, towns, cities, counties, provinces, and wider regions of societies. Obviously, this was the case with the Indonesian tsunami in 2004 and Hurricane Katrina along the Gulf Coast of the United States in 2005.[5] Their work confirms that disasters often kill and injure many people, often in startling and gruesome ways, and cause widespread worry, uncertainty, misery, and rumors. However, their research also shows that initial reports of deaths and injuries often are overestimated. They also find recurring and systemic errors in many claims in the mass media, and in many beliefs of the general public, about psychological and social aspects of disasters, and about the losses being inevitably and permanently overwhelming to the impacted communities and to all of its people. Many—but certainly not all—of these researchers have found that many communities struck by disasters have been far more resilient than depicted in mass media accounts of the disasters.

Skilled, objective scientists often find that—contrary to allegations of widespread despair, looting, and other problematic behaviors—many survivors are very able and willing to cooperate with one another as families, friends, neighbors, and even as strangers. Researchers have coined phrases including "altruistic community" and "therapeutic community response" to describe some of these patterns. However, cooperation and goodwill among survivors often dissipates if the recovery process drags on for months and if it is perceived to be badly managed and inadequate. A "blaming and bitching phase" might emerge among some survivors. Researchers have found that, in addition to the informal support networks of the survivors (what some scholars refer to as an element of "social capital"), one of the keys to long-term recovery has been the effectiveness of governments, as well as other external support of agencies, in providing relief supplies and services and other resources for many months—even for years—after a disaster. Often, especially in advanced industrial societies, and contrary to popular belief, many communities struck by disasters, and many of the survivors of the disasters, are able to "return to normalcy," or to near normalcy, within a number of years, or in even less time.

One example of this research was done by one of the founding fathers of the sociology of disasters, Charles E. Fritz. He analyzed 114 studies of 103 different disaster events that had been assembled under the auspices of the National Research Council. From this investigation and his survey of dozens of other studies, Fritz reported in 1968 that

> the traditional stereotypes have obscured the fact that disasters produce not only disruptive and disorganizing effects but also reconstructive and regenerative human responses. Both of these perspectives must be kept in mind in any balanced treatment of the social aspects of disasters.[6]

Fritz goes so far as to contend that

> [t]hese integrative effects of disaster apparently provide a major stimulus for rapid restoration and social reconstruction. Virtually all modern disaster-struck communities and nations have not only been quickly restored, but in many cases they have experienced

an "amplified rebound" in which the society is carried far beyond its pre-disaster levels of solidarity, productivity, and capacity for growth.[7]

Thomas E. Drabek provides a more recent, comprehensive, and nuanced assessment of the research literature on disasters. After analyzing hundreds of studies of disasters, he reported in 1986 that there is considerable variability in impacts of disasters on the ability of individuals, families, and communities to recover, rebuild, reconstruct, and advance after them.[8] For example, Drabek reports that there are many studies which found short-term increases in social solidarity within disaster-struck communities.

> As a specialized aspect of the overall community response pattern, heightened levels of solidarity have been reported repeatedly... . One important manifestation of this process is the reduction of social distance, especially across class lines, albeit only temporary.[9]

However, Drabek also reports important exceptions to almost every general finding.

> In short, the matter of community solidarity has many side streets. Collectively all point to one central conclusion—there is a temporary focus on the event which precipitates a pulling together, albeit short-lived. Variations often emerge quickly after that.[10]

Interestingly—and very relevant to this book—Drabek repeatedly reports that sociological studies of the disaster at Buffalo Creek are the most salient *exception* to the general finding of continuity and positive impacts of disasters on human communities:

> [T]he single natural disaster that has produced the most evidence of negative impacts occurred in Buffalo Creek, West Virginia in 1972. This flash flood had many atypical qualities. It was a horrifying event that struck a population already stressed, and there was evidence of culpability. These qualities were developed brilliantly by several scholars, most especially Lifton and Olson

(1976), Erikson (1976), Titchener and Kapp (1976), and Gleser, Green, and Winget (1981, 1978).[11]

Of course, much of the chapter ahead focuses on the most famous studies of Buffalo Creek that Drabek regards so highly. Before moving on, however, it is also worth noting that Drabek reports that there is considerable variation among research studies about the long-term effects of disasters; on how quickly and thoroughly communities can rebuild, reconstruct, and "return to normalcy"; and on whether they become stronger, more cohesive, and resilient in the process.[12] He highlights famous (but controversial) studies that found that some disasters produced no discernible long-term effects, as well as studies that found mainly long-term positive effects. Drabek also reports research studies that found that the amount of external support that disaster-struck communities receive is crucial to whether they recover, rebuild, and thrive. "That is, most disaster-stricken communities within the U.S.A. receive sufficient levels of relief and are so tightly interdependent with regional economics that losses may be mitigated completely."[13]

Even more recently, in 2001, Gary Kreps summarized the state of research in the sociology of disasters in his essay "Sociology of Disasters" in the *International Encyclopedia of the Social and Behavioral Sciences*. In it, he notes a growing interest in "long-term recovery." This, of course, is the primary subject of this book—long-term recovery, and how it occurred.

> More recent research on peacetime disasters (has) highlighted the remarkable absorptive capacities of social systems, contradicting conventional notions that during a disaster victims will panic, that those expected to respond will abandon occupational roles, that community structure will break down, and that antisocial behavior will be rampant. Having systematically debunked such myths and disaster behavior, the more interesting questions to sociologists have related to describing and explaining structural continuity and change before, during and after an event…Where the majority of studies prior to the 1970s focused on collective action during the immediate emergency period, contemporary research

gives more balanced attention to disaster prevention, mitigation, preparedness, and *long-term recovery*.[14] (emphasis added)

The Distinction Between "Natural" and "Technological/Human-Caused" Disasters

Regarding long-term recovery of survivors and rebuilding of communities from disasters—the topic of primary interest in this book—a number of sociologists contend that disasters can be categorized as "natural" or as "technological/human-caused." They posit that this distinction is fundamental and crucial for understanding how disasters are changing and how governments, interests groups, and the public react to them. They assert that technological/human-caused disasters have become much more frequent and destructive since the 1960s, that their long-term impacts are especially severe and complex, and that long-term recovery is much less certain than in the cases of "natural" disasters. On the other hand, some disaster researchers now question the validity of this distinction.

> With the emergence of large-scale, human-caused disasters in the late 1960s and 1970s, however, the social and psychological significance of this typology became a source of discussion and debate in the literature. Different response patterns by victims have led researchers to investigate two distinct types of disasters—natural and technological...The empirical validity of this distinction, according to technological disaster researchers, is supported by evidence documenting that "technological disasters create a far more severe and long lasting pattern of social, economic, cultural and psychological impacts than do natural disasters" (Freudenberg 1997: 26). However, a number of natural disaster researchers have argued that such a distinction is theoretically and practically specious (Alexander 1993; Quarantelli 1992, 1998). This discourse continues to pervade much of the literature on disasters.[15]

TWO ALTERNATIVE PERSPECTIVES TO KEEP IN MIND

Rather than take sides in controversies like these at this time, let us simply keep in mind two alternative perspectives about disasters in general as we review the experts' accounts that follow about what has happened to Buffalo Creek. For convenience, we will call these the "social destruction" and the "social re-creation" perspectives.[16] Both perspectives apply to disastrous events that involve relatively large numbers (i.e., hundreds or thousands) of people who live together in residential communities such as hamlets, villages, towns, and cities. Both perspectives try to estimate the extent and duration of damage that disastrous events—such as the eruptions of volcanoes, cyclones, hurricanes, tsunamis, floods, blizzards, and other relatively sudden and violent events in the physical environment—impose on the social relations and the well-being of the people who resided in the area at the time of the event and on the residential communities that they had created. However, as suggested by their names, each perspective has a different view of the psychological and social consequences of these events.

One perspective contends that, psychologically and socially, more is destroyed by disasters than is regained by efforts to rebuild and recover from them by the survivors of disasters and by residential communities that suffered disasters. In other words, most disasters are so destructive that the psychological and social damages are never undone. The costs exceed the benefits and the losses exceed the gains, no matter how long the time frame.

The other perspective contends that—except in the most extreme disasters—most residential communities and survivors are able to rebuild, recover, or re-create considerable levels of social well-being and meaningful social relationships, even if these are never exactly the same as they were before the disaster. Most survivors and communities "bounce back" and even "bounce beyond" the levels of social well-being and viability that they had before the disaster. Given enough time, the benefits of reconstruction exceed the costs. The gains exceed the losses that were suffered in the disasters.

THE SOCIAL DESTRUCTION PERSPECTIVE

The social destruction perspective essentially contends that disasters generally overwhelm and permanently damage or destroy residential communities and the social well-being of the people who inhabit them. In the worst disasters, destruction and adversity become so overwhelming and long lasting to the (relatively few) survivors who remain in the area that they can no longer relate to one another in meaningful ways. Relations with family, friends, and neighbors are destroyed, as are social well-being, social integration, and communality—the essential features of any human social community. Of course, the most extreme form of social destruction would be a case where a sudden event quickly and thoroughly destroyed everyone and everything in a social community in such a way that nothing could ever be rebuilt there. This might be the case if, let us say, an asteroid or a tsunami smashed into a small island and annihilated all of the people, plants, and animals who lived there, the social communities that they had created, and the entire island itself. The island no longer exists. Everything is gone—washed away or submerged. It is no longer recoverable, let alone inhabitable. Surely, many people would agree that this would constitute what we might call a "total disaster." If so, then lesser amounts of destruction to the residential communities on the island would *not* constitute a "*total* disaster," however destructive they might be.

The destruction of the ancient city of Pompeii near Naples in AD 79 might constitute one of the few historical cases of "total disaster." Supposedly, the eruption of nearby Mount Vesuvius was so sudden, violent, and overwhelming that it thoroughly destroyed Pompeii and the neighboring cities of Herculaneum and Stabiae. All or most of Pompeii's inhabitants died in place or while they tried to escape from the area. Even would-be rescuers from Naples died from toxic fumes, including the famous scholar and naval commander Pliny the Elder. "Pompeii remained buried under a layer of lapilli and ash twelve feet or more deep" until the late sixteenth century, when some of the ruins were uncovered by workers who were trying to install water pipes across the area. There is no evidence that the land which Pompeii occupied was ever reoccupied by a social community.[17] It ceased to exist as a city, as a residential community, and, to some extent, as a society. Even today, the land remains barren—"populated only by vermin and stray dogs and cats," as reported to me by one recent visitor there, even though suburban Naples has expanded far beyond it.[18]

Fortunately, there have been few events in recorded history as totally disastrous as the destruction of Pompeii. Less total examples of social destruction would include cases where a disaster destroyed so much of the population, property, and infrastructure—and so many of the social relationships—that residential communities of comparable size and complexity were never rebuilt or re-created there, on that land. The place remained more destroyed than rebuilt. Even if some of the original inhabitants survive and remain in the area, and if outsiders migrate into the area after the disaster, recollections and rumors about the disaster become what can be called a "negative cultural legacy." References to the disaster provoke anxieties, suspicions, animosities, disagreements, and social conflict among residents and between residents and outsiders. Many inhabitants come to believe that the place of the disaster is degraded, unsafe, cursed, or haunted. They have difficulty forming helpful and reassuring social relationships. Their social and psychological well-being is chronically impaired. They are unable to perceive accurately the behaviors of other people. They are unable to interpret accurately the motives of other people. They are unable to influence the behavior of one another in positive ways. Power and moral authority diminish in social control agencies such as governments, police, courts, churches, and hospitals. Increases occur in deviant behaviors such as substance abuse, theft, interpersonal neglect, abandonment, abuse, and violence.

The social destruction perspective also posits that social well-being and social relations are severely damaged even in disasters that kill few, if any, inhabitants. Some inhabitants are so shocked by what they have witnessed in terms of the natural elements and property damages that they are more or less permanently damaged psychologically. Often, even when physical destruction of dwellings and public infrastructure is limited, longstanding resentments and animosities among different social classes, ethnic groups, and occupational groups ignite into social conflicts. Even if the village, town, or city is "rebuilt" physically, many of the inhabitants never regain the economic, social, and psychological well-being that they had prior to the disaster. Often this is because resources are so scarce that competition, exploitation, inequality, crime, and other social problems increase dramatically. Sometimes additional disastrous events occur within a few months or years. Social problems are exacerbated even further. Survivors with the means to do so often try to emigrate. Other survivors remain because they feel psychologically bound to the place or they believe that they have no viable alternatives.

"Corrosive Communities" and "Risk Societies"

A popular, contemporary form of the social destruction perspective is found in writing about the "corrosive communities" and the "risk society" that result from some disasters.[19] This writing generally focuses on disasters such as the Exxon Valdez oil spill in Alaska; the "accident" at the Chernobyl nuclear power plant near Kiev, Ukraine; the nuclear power plant failure at Three Mile Island, Pennsylvania; and the discharge of toxic gases at Bhopal, India, that killed (and allegedly continues to kill) thousands of inhabitants in the surrounding area. This writing generally contends that modern technological/human-caused disasters have unusually complex, delayed, long-term, pernicious effects that render communities "corrosive" and permanently "at risk." There are at least three major reasons why damages continue to occur to the physical environment and to the human population that remains in the disaster area. The toxicity of the contaminants endures for many years, perhaps indefinitely. "Recreancy" occurs in the form of institutional malfeasance—where experts and specialized organizations fail to carry out responsibilities that are expected of them in reacting to the disaster. Protracted litigation takes place among many different governments, corporations, public-interest groups, and ad hoc groups of victims, survivors, and their advocates. For these reasons, "the mental and physical health of victims is much more difficult to restore. Members of the impacted communities have heightened perceptions of risk."[20] As a consequence, according to these writings, communities struck by massive, modern "technological" disasters are more or less permanently damaged, if not destroyed. Recovery is much less likely to occur than in the cases of more traditional "natural" disasters.

THE SOCIAL RE-CREATION PERSPECTIVE

In contrast to the social destruction perspective, the social re-creation perspective purports that—despite a considerable amount of damage that disasters inflict upon property, infrastructure, population, and social relations of villages, towns, cities, and larger areas—most disasters also create common adversities, needs, and challenges for those people who survive. Many of the survivors come to understand and appreciate these commonalities, as do the leaders of agencies, voluntary associations, and interest groups inside and outside of the impacted area—at least so long as the larger society is relatively wealthy, powerful, and egalitarian. Eventually, many cooperative responses occur that mobilize resources and lead to the physical rebuilding of the place, often with consider-able improvements in the physical infrastructure (roads and bridges, water and energy delivery, and sanitation systems) of the area. Inhabit-ants and institutions create a positive cultural legacy about the disaster that emphasizes the cooperation and rebuilding that has occurred rather than the damages that the disastrous event inflicted on the place and the disruptions that immediately followed it. In time, the survivors, their progeny, and newcomers to the area re-create a considerable amount of neighboring, social integration, and social well-being.

These re-creative processes often take many months or years—even decades—to become apparent to objective, outside observers. Rarely is a residential community rebuilt exactly as it was. Perhaps only a fraction of the survivors completely recover the same kinds of social and psycho-logical well-being they had before the disastrous event, although some survivors might thrive because of the confidence and respect they have gained for their efforts in rebuilding the place and in helping others. And yet, some survivors might become less trusting of the physical environ-ment for the rest of their lives. Many of them might lament the disap-pearance of some features of the physical environment that they had enjoyed or depended upon prior to the disaster. However, given enough time and access to enough material and social resources (what is now called "social capital" by some academicians), many survivors and post-disaster newcomers are able to *re-create* satisfying lives for themselves and for others whom they care about in the area.

As discussed later in this chapter, fortunately, there are quite a few historical examples that illustrate the social re-creation perspective rather well. Two of the disasters that struck the San Francisco Bay area of California, more than one hundred years apart, are cases in point. Surely, it is readily apparent to anyone who has visited San Francisco that many impressive residential communities have been re-created since the "San Andreas Fault Earthquake" of 1997. Apparently, another impressive re-creation occurred there more than one hundred years earlier, after the "Great Fire" in 1895. I hope that we will be able to say the same thing about the thousands of villages that were destroyed in the Indonesian tsunami in 2004 and about the hundreds of towns and cities—including Gulfport, Mississippi, and New Orleans, Louisiana—that were severely damaged because of Hurricane Katrina in 2005.[21]

*　　　　*　　　　*

Now let us consider the most influential accounts that have been published about social and psychological aspects of the Buffalo Creek disaster and efforts to recover from it.[22] These accounts are presented at length in widely read books by a journalist, an attorney, a psychiatrist, a number of psychologists, and a sociologist. Tom Nugent is a freelance journalist who covered the flood for the *Detroit Free Press*. Gerald Stern was an attorney for the law firm of Arnold & Porter who was assigned to lead the lawsuit against the coal companies on behalf of hundreds of plaintiffs. The three other sets of authors were hired as consultants by Arnold & Porter to help document psychological and social damages to the plaintiffs. Goldine C. Gleser, Bonnie L. Green, and their associates reported on psychological damages to the plaintiffs. Robert Jay Lifton reported on psychiatric damages to the plaintiffs and social damages to Buffalo Creek as a community, as did his colleague at Yale University at the time, sociologist Kai

Erikson. In reviewing and commenting on the work of these authors, we will pay particular attention to what the experts wrote about how the flood and its aftereffects influenced the social relationships of the more than 4,800 survivors with their family, friends, and neighbors.

Was the Buffalo Creek disaster utterly exceptional?

Was it a "total" disaster? Was "everything" destroyed—and destroyed so thoroughly that it never could be rebuilt, recovered, or re-created?

What efforts were made by survivors, their neighbors, networks of survivors, churches, and outside agencies to recover and rebuild Buffalo Creek in the years immediately following the disaster?

Tom Nugent: A Journalist's Account

> And so the 5,000 people of Buffalo Creek slept on through the rainy night. At Lorado and Lundale and Stowe Bottom; at Crites and Pardee and Accoville; in double rows of houses laid out between the state highway (W. Va. 16) and the railroad tracks which carried the coal away, they slept and passed the long winter night. And in the reservoir at the top of the hollow, behind an unstable, illegal dam which never should have been built, the rain came slanting down the wind and the water rose inch by inch.[23]

To the best of my knowledge, the only journalist's account of the flood that was published by a major national publisher is Thomas Nugent's *Death at Buffalo Creek: The 1972 West Virginia Flood Disaster*. When the book was published in 1973, Nugent was a twenty-nine-year-old freelance journalist who had covered the disaster for the *Detroit Free Press* from early March to September 1972. His book is mainly a report on his interviews with several dozen of the Buffalo Creek residents— from Three Forks to Amherstdale—whose families and houses were severely damaged in the flood. He also interviewed some of the controversial officials and key witnesses to the flood and its immediate aftereffects. Along the way, Nugent also reports on some of the recovery efforts and the public hearings by various agencies that occurred in the four months following the flood. His account is deeply sympathetic towards most of the Buffalo Creek residents, and it is highly and almost relentlessly critical about Pittston Company, the coal industry, and many of the senior officials in the government agencies who had responsibilities for mine safety and who testified during the hearings.

Of course, we are primarily interested in how Nugent's account can help us understand the impacts of the flood on the well-being of Buffalo Creek's people and Buffalo Creek as a community, particularly in terms of neighboring and the recovery process. Highlights of Nugent's account on these topics will be presented here as Nugent conveys them. However, readers need to be alerted that Nugent provides very little documentation for his facts and his assertions about them, and his facts sometimes contradict his generalizations. For example, in the preceding quotation, Nugent portrays *all* of Buffalo Creek's residents almost as though they were helpless, ignorant babies asleep in their beds and subject to evil designs of the coal companies. And yet, his book presents factual material that reveals that many of the residents of Buffalo Creek—including managers of the coal companies, some of whom lived along Buffalo Creek—were aware that the dams at the coal slurry ponds could collapse and that a disastrous flood could occur. Dozens of Buffalo Creek's residents were outside in the rain, nervously watching the creek. Dozens or perhaps even hundreds more had already relocated downstream in anticipation of the dams collapsing.

Before the Flood

At about 9:00 p.m. on Friday, February 25, the U.S. Weather Bureau in Huntington, West Virginia—about ninety miles from Buffalo Creek—announced a flash flood warning to Logan County and eleven other counties in southwestern West Virginia because of the past two days of heavy rains (see map of Buffalo Creek in the front of the book).

> Of course, dangerous flash floods were nothing new in Logan County, where more than 46,000 people live mostly along unpredictable rivers and creeks which make up the Guyandotte River watershed. Perched high on the western flank of the Appalachian Mountains, about fifty miles south of Charleston, Logan County is

456 square miles of narrow, twisting valleys, jagged ridgelines, and racing creeks where the briefest rain squall can send floodwaters shooting through a valley like bullets through the barrel of a gun. Each year the spring rains bring their usual quota of flooded basements, washed-out roads, and rock slides, and every five years or so the county suffers through more severe flooding which leaves devastated homes and occasional drowning victims in its wake.[24]

A lot of the men have been talking to Jack Kent, and he says the dam is in bad shape. He's been telling people that it may go before daybreak—and that they better be prepared to get to higher ground.[25]

But the miners who lived in the sixteen communities along the hollow were well aware of it. Indeed, many of them had been running from the big dam at Three Forks for years. During periods of heavy rain, families would often pass the word from Three Forks, the first town in the path of the water: They say the dam's about to go, better get ready to run. Some families remembered spending entire nights on hillsides, sleeping under tents and makeshift lean-tos, in order to assure their safety. Once in a while, even, practical jokers would race up and down the narrow road that ran the length of the hollow, honking their horns and shouting that the dam had broken. Remembering the past, then, some families had slept fitfully, or not at all, on Friday night. Again and again, these residents had braved the rain to go outside and take another look at the creek.[26]

Readers might notice that these statements suggest several facts that are sometimes overlooked in accounts of the flood. Many of the people at Three Forks had been helping one another and other residents farther down Buffalo Creek for years by watching the water height in Buffalo Creek and by notifying others about possible dangers. Many of the people were aware of the danger posed to them by dam #3. Some residents had been evacuating their homes for years during heavy rains. And sadly, some people made false alarms that frightened others into evacuating needlessly. This might have reduced their willingness to react to subsequent warnings.

Nugent reports that one fellow who actually witnessed the collapse of the dams (probably the only eyewitness to the event), just after Dennis

Gibson raced away, was miner Johnny Wells. He had just completed his "hoot owl" shift at mine #5 one-half mile above dam #3. As he drove down the muddy access road along Middle Fork on his way home, he rounded a curve 200 yards above the dam.

> [S]uddenly he was watching an enormous explosion cover the impoundment "like an atomic bomb." Stunned, Wells hit the brakes. The car skidded to a stop, and within seconds, its front end was completely covered with a thick layer of black, gooey muck. "I couldn't tell what it was," Wells said. "I couldn't hardly see. It looked to me like the dam had blowed up, and had blowed that dust back up on the hill." Actually, Wells was watching a series of explosions which occurred as the millions of gallons of water, after cutting through the collapsing dam, careened into the 200 foot high, burning gob pile below the impoundment. Like water poured on the glowing coals of a campfire, the surging flow sent clouds of steam and ash roaring hundreds of feet into the air.[27]

From Well's vantage point above and adjacent to what had been dam #3, thousands of tons of rainwater and gob surged through dam #2 and dam #1, gained mass and velocity as they fell 250 feet, and then smashed into the homes and buildings at Three Forks. There they picked up even more mass—broken houses, vehicles, storage tanks, railroad tracks, and equipment—and raced down the seventeen miles of Buffalo Creek, falling another 700 feet, before plunging into the Guyandotte River below Man at about 11:00 a.m. Nugent tried to recapture a sense of the damages that the flood inflicted on each of the coal camps along the way by retelling the experiences of some of those survivors who observed the worst of it.

At Three Forks
At Three Forks, the front wave of the flood—thirty to fifty feet high according to some accounts—shattered the Buffalo Mining Company's garage, "sending huge trucks and other pieces of heavy equipment flying through the air." It tore through the railroad yard and the highway. It swept up the Free Will Baptist Church and knocked down power lines

and transformers, some of which exploded. The noises frightened and alerted some of the families that remained at Three Forks that destruction was on the way. Some of these people called out to other family members. Others tried to warn their neighbors. For example, when the electric power failed, the Lambert family, in the middle of breakfast around their kitchen table, hurried out to their front porch. Their neighbor Freddie Thomason was jumping up and down and waving at them excitedly: "Run for your lives, here comes the church houses!"

That warning saved the lives of all the Lamberts, although they were injured and lost their house and all their possessions. Ester Lambert was severely injured and became hysterical. All of the Lamberts were soaking wet and in danger of freezing because a frigid wind turned the rain into snow. According to Nugent, the Lamberts watched helplessly and alone as, thirty feet below, "Three Forks had broken into a thousand pieces and washed away."[28] However, Nugent also reports that the Lamberts were saved shortly after that by another neighbor, Ossie Adkins, whose own house was unharmed.

> Finally, the agony ended. Ossie Adkins, climbing along the hills above the hollow, found the Lamberts standing together on a hillside, shivering in the wind. He led them back to his own, un-harmed house, to the warmth of blankets and hot coffee and food.[29]

According to Nugent, twenty people from Three Forks—most of them from five families—died in the flood, and "all the homes in the immediate vicinity were gone." As it slashed down Buffalo Creek Hollow towards Lorado, the flood "picked up a set of deadly teeth. Shattered timbers, sections of railroad track, millions of tons of coal-waste debris—they sliced back and forth inside the descending wave."[30] Along the way, it destroyed the farmhouse of Dellie Trent and killed her and all but one of her family members, Herbert. He narrowly escaped by riding a mile downstream on the roof of a house that floated by. Then he limped down to Lorado, where friends gave him dry clothes and shoes. Herbert later told Nugent that some of their neighbors had stopped by the Trent farmhouse several times during the night to coax the Trents to evacuate Three Forks, as had Deputy Sheriff Mutters.

At Lorado

At about 8:00 a.m., miner Billy Aldridge received a phone call from his buddy and fellow National Guardsman, Sgt. Doug Williamson, asking him to drive up to Three Forks and check on rumors that the dam was about to burst. As Aldridge drove through Lorado in his Ford pickup truck, he noticed "a lot of people were up and about in Lorado; that seemed unusual for so early on a Saturday morning."[31] At the south end of Three Forks, Aldridge suddenly was shocked to see the flood wave roaring down the hollow towards him. He turned around his truck, pulled on his truck's flasher lights, and sped back down the hollow, honking his horn to alert families in the houses along the way. His warnings and bravery saved many lives in the little camps of Sandy Bottom, Pardee, and Lorado.

> Racing downhill, Aldridge turned on his truck flashers and kept the horn going. His warnings would be extremely brief, as he fled the front of the wave, and many of those who failed to understand them would die...Two of the families heard Aldridge's racket— his horn and his shouts—raced outside, and escaped.[32]

When Aldridge got to Lorado, he kept honking his horn and yelling at people who were outside their homes to run for the hills. Many of them did so.[33] He stopped at his home, helped his wife escape to safety, and then ran into the house of his neighbors, the Doczis, and helped them escape to the hillside. He continued helping others until the flood swept past him down through Lorado. Then he spent several days helping his neighbors recover from the flood's damage. For this effort, Aldridge was declared one of the local heroes of the Buffalo Creek flood and he received a citation for bravery from the National Guard.[34]

At the Lorado school, all of the evacuees from Three Forks escaped, but they did so just before the flood wave destroyed all of the school except for the gym. Surely, it seems likely that the death toll would have been even higher if Aldridge had not made his courageous "Paul Revere ride" into camp, as the locals fondly called it. It also might have been higher if many of its miners had not already left to start their shift at 7:15 a.m. in the mines, assuming that they would otherwise have slept in on that rainy Saturday morning. Then again, some of them had departed for the mines, only to turn around and return to Lorado because they found that the roads on the hillsides to the mines had washed out.[35]

Nugent reports many other acts of neighborly concern and heroism that involved Buffalo Creek people—usually healthy persons aged twenty to fifty—helping disabled and dependent persons, very young children, and pets to escape. He also reports that many neighbors helped other neighbors immediately after the flood passed—by keeping them company, reassuring them, tending to their wounds, and helping them to stay warm with coffee, food, blankets, and makeshift shelters. However, some of Buffalo Creek's people were less than helpful and others did not take the flood very seriously, even after it passed them by and they narrowly escaped with their lives. Consider the testimony of coal miner Roy Hicks:

> I'm not ashamed to say where I was when the water hit. I was in the bathroom, sitting on the pot. I thought it was a train going by, but I thought it had a wreck. And all at once the door bursted open in my bedroom and before I could get my pants up, here I was with the water clear up to here [pointing to his knees]. I finally waited 'till the water went down. When the water went down, I turned around, took off my clothes and went to bed, believe it or not![36]

At Lundale

The flood wave rushed down out of Lorado and through the little village of Craneco, destroying ten of the twenty homes there, on its way to Lundale, the largest camp in the upper hollow. It had more than 150 houses, including "a row of two story houses which housed the bosses of Amherst Coal," dozens of garages and stores, and more than 500 residents. At least fifty of those residents died in the flood, or because of it, and only about 25 of its 150 houses were not destroyed.[37]

> The Buffalo Creek flood virtually annihilated Lundale, West Virginia. At least fifty of the town's 700-plus residents were killed; most of its homes were washed miles down the hollow. Both the Lundale Free Will Baptist Church and the Island Creek Supermarket suffered heavy damage. Once again, however, a major coal company installation escaped destruction: Amherst Coal's Lundale headquarters were almost untouched by the racing wave, and were soon back in operation.[38]

A number of captivating rumors circulated through Lundale in the wake of the flood. These rumors can help us understand how people regarded their neighbors and families. One rumor, possibly reflecting wishful thinking on the part of some Buffalo Creek people, was that Steve Dasovich, the mining company official in charge of the dam, had a nervous breakdown after he watched the flood race down the hollow through Lorado. Supposedly, he ran up the hollow screaming, "Oh my God, I killed all them people! I killed 'em all." Nugent reports that he could not find any eyewitnesses to the event, but that Dasovich did in fact "go into shock after meeting the flood at Craneco and was hospitalized for several days because of it."[39]

Another rumor actually had some element of truth in it. For years, Lundale's own "Big John" Bailey had been warning news reporters and anyone else who would listen to him that the dam at Three Forks was going to fail someday and cause a disaster of biblical proportions. After he and his family drowned in the flood, Lundale's survivors recalled his efforts at prophecy and made him into something of a local folk martyr. "Nobody listened to his warnings and his reward was death," lamented one of his many friends. The legend of Big John quickly became a rallying point for Buffalo Creek people who believed that the coal company's callous disregard for public safety allowed the disaster to happen.

Other stories inform us about how people helped their neighbors escape the flood and recover from it. Ruth Tomblin's sister was eavesdropping on the telephone party line the night before the flood. She heard one warning after another about the dam breaking at Three Forks.

She overheard one housewife tell her absent husband, "The big dam has cracked, they say it's gonna break." Hearing about this from her sister, Ruth Tomblin had her husband drive the family down to Man, where they remained safe from the flood.[40] In yet another case, widow Cleo Collins was able to move her children from the breakfast table to a hillside only because "a neighbor pulled up in the yard outside, blew his horn, and hollered 'The goddam dam's broke, get out of here!'"[41]

The flood and postflood experiences of one of the most prominent (and historically connected) residents is worth considering. Wayne Brady Hatfield was one of the many descendants of the famous Hatfield clan of the Hatfield-McCoy feud. Wayne provided Tom Nugent with troubling details of how some neighbors reacted to his plight. At the time of the flood, Wayne, his wife Etta Pearl, daughter, and grand-daughter were living in a two-story, seven-room house in Stowe Bottom. He was suffering from black-lung disease and countless other injuries from decades in the mines, and he was drawing $210 a month in social security checks and $150 a month from his miner's pension. He and the rest of the family were sleeping in on Saturday morning when he heard sounds of rushing water. He awoke, looked out the bedroom window, and saw that his house was surrounded by swirling floodwater. He alerted his family and tried to run outside to find a means of escape. "I tried to run through the water, but it was too deep and I had to run back insides. It scared me to death. All I could do was stand in the door and pray and ask God to have mercy on us. 'Cause I knowed they was gone. I knowed they was gonna drown."[42]

Soon his house broke from the foundation and was swept down the hollow, sections falling off as it bumped into other houses and debris. Then the house collided with a large tree and began disintegrating. Hatfield lost consciousness, regained it, and found himself trying to swim in raging, black, oily water. By chance, he was able to pull himself up on an embankment more than a mile downstream.

Unfortunately, Hatfield's premonition turned into reality. When he found the bodies of his wife and daughter (his grand-daughter's body was found later), he asked people nearby to help him move the bodies into a nearby house. He was shocked to hear the people were afraid to touch the bodies for fear that they were haunted. "I begged and cried and prayed, I done everything that could be thought of to get them in the house. But they wouldn't help me."[43] Hours later, National Guard troops arrived and moved the bodies to the makeshift morgue at Man. Hatfield concluded that people had stopped caring about one another.

> Back when I was a boy, growing up, say on a farm, if a man got sick, the folks would come down off of Bend Creek, off Horsepin Creek and Gilman Creek, why, they'd hoe that man's corn, take care of that sick man's farm for him. Somebody would go and see that he had coal carried in to build him a fire. If a man gets sick now—why, let him die![44]

So great was his anger and despair that he became one of the most ardent critics at the many postflood investigations that are summarized elsewhere in this book.

Through the Lower Hollow
The floodwater slowed down appreciably in Stowe Bottom, and even more so as it passed through the less steeply sloped coal camps in the lower half of Buffalo Creek Hollow: Crites, Latrobe, Robinette, Amherstdale, and Braeholm. Still, it destroyed about ten of the twenty homes in Latrobe and killed three people there. Then it destroyed twenty-five more homes and killed three more people in Robinette. Next it damaged about one-half of the seventy homes in Amherstdale, including twenty homes in Proctor Bottom, the same camp that was struck by a collapsed gob pile in 1967 and prompted a U.S. congressman to warn that the people of Proctor Bottom were "living under the gun of threatened annihilation."[45]

The flood's last mortality was James Brunty, an eighty-three-year-old invalid. He was in a coma and dying of black-lung disease in a bedroom of his daughter's house in Braeholm. She and her husband, a middle-aged coal miner, had been warned by relatives that the dam had collapsed and that a flood wave was approaching. However, they had received conflicting reports about whether they needed to evacuate their house. When the flood smashed into the house, they were unable to move Brunty to safety. He drowned.

Coming out of Braeholm, the floodwater slowed considerably as it moved across the slighter slopes in lower Buffalo Creek Valley. Much of the debris from the upstream coal camps—derelict cars, trucks, houses, railroad equipment, and fuel tanks—piled up in twenty- and thirty-foot mounds at the many bridges in the area. When the flood reached Accoville, Crown, and Kistler, it swirled two to ten feet over the creek banks, flooding basements and first floors of many of the stores and houses within one hundred yards of the creek and leaving layers of thick black mud and gob over the roads, yards, porches, and floors. Even then, however, several dozen houses and trailers were destroyed and a few more residents were injured, mainly in Accoville. Finally, the flood washed down through the creek bed in the town of Man and spilled into the Guyandotte River. Most of the floodwater drained out of the valley by noontime, leaving behind it seventeen miles of muck, mud, oil, and house-high mounds of twisted debris that would frustrate recovery efforts for months on end. Of course, the damages were much, much greater than that.

Some Tabulations

All in all, Nugent tabulates that the flood destroyed 507 homes, inflicted major damage on another 273 homes, and did minor damage to 663 homes.[46] One-half of the homes along Buffalo Creek were uninhabitable, according to Nugent, "leaving perhaps 4,000 people without a place to sleep."[47] Six hundred cars and thirty stores also were destroyed in the flood. Ten highway and railroad bridges were unusable. Phone, sewer, water-treatment, and electrical systems were knocked out of service. Federal officials estimated that the property damage exceeded $50 million. The human toll was equally staggering, in Nugent's estimation. Over 125 people had died, more than 500 were injured, and psychological damage was so extensive that it could not be estimated.[48]

Some Observations About Nugent's Account

As best as we can tell from the contents of his book, Nugent gathered information from a relatively small number of people that would be of interest to readers of the *Detroit Free Press*. We should not assume that all or even most of the survivors of the flood are represented by the people Nugent conversed with. We also should be aware that Nugent is unmitigated in his criticism of coal companies and their executives and managers. Yet there is no doubt that Nugent's account provides a number of valuable insights about Buffalo Creek as a residential community before and in the days and weeks immediately after the flood.

1. Some of BMC's managers, including Jack Kent, lived in the coal camps with the other residents of Buffalo Creek close to the creek. The coal companies had several offices along the creek in Lundale and in the other camps. Therefore, they had very personal stakes in the safety of the dams. They had plenty to lose. They were not absentee landlords or remote "masters."

2. Impoundments had collapsed and caused flooding along Buffalo Creek several times in the previous decade, including the collapse of dam #2 at Three Forks in 1967 and a gob pond that collapsed near Proctor Bottom in 1967. Many local residents were aware of these incidents and were warned about them occurring again.

3. Many of the residents all along Buffalo Creek knew of the danger posed by the dams at Three Forks many years before the flood. For years, "Big John" Bailey was known for his prophecies that the dams would collapse. For years, Buffalo Creek's people had been evacuating their homes during heavy storms out of fear that the dams would collapse.

4. It is also true that the people of Buffalo Creek for years had been subjected to false alarms about the dams collapsing by pranksters who drove down Buffalo Creek Hollow blaring the horns on their vehicles and yelling out alarms that the dams had collapsed. Some residents and a few local deputies discounted the danger on

February 25 and 26 because of their past experiences with false alarms.

5. Some of BMC's own superintendents, managers, and laborers were very concerned about dam #3 collapsing. They inspected the dam several times in the twelve hours before it collapsed. Some of them warned residents of Three Forks to evacuate down to Lorado. Many residents did so.

6. There were many instances of residents all along the creek who tried to warn their neighbors of the oncoming flood once the dams collapsed. There were many acts of heroism—not just a few. After that, dozens of survivors quickly started providing first aid, coffee, blankets, and shelter to other survivors in need.

7. Most houses were severely damaged or destroyed in the upper end of Buffalo Creek Hollow—but not all of them, by any means. Some dwellings remained inhabitable, even at Three Forks. Even in Lorado, the camp that was most damaged by the flood, at least 470 of the 500 or more residents survived, and at least 10 of the 125 houses were not severely damaged, although most of them were.

8. Contrary to claims in some books and newspaper articles, a lot of residents were *not* sleeping in their beds when the flood hit. After all, it was 8:00 a.m. on a Saturday morning. Many parents and grandparents with several youngsters in their houses were preparing breakfast while the youngsters watched cartoons on TV.[49] Dozens of miners who had not gone to work on the 7:15 a.m. shift, or who had just returned home from the "hoot owl shift," were out in the streets and alleys watching the creek for signs of flooding.

9. Some survivors were *not* traumatized or even unduly disturbed when the floodwaters surrounded their houses. Roy Hicks went back to bed.

10. Unfortunately, some other survivors were so traumatized, shocked, disgusted, or superstitious that they refused to help their neighbors remove bodies from the debris.

So, in sum, Nugent's account, *Death at Buffalo Creek*, helps us understand that many areas of the valley were damaged suddenly and severely and that statistics alone are inadequate to convey an appreciation of the damages done by noontime on February 26, 1972. Still, I feel obliged to encourage readers to question the validity of some of Nugent's generalizations.

"Most Buffalo Creek residents were completely unaware of the danger they faced on this stormy Saturday morning."[50] Let me suggest to you that Nugent's own reporting indicates that hundreds of Buffalo Creek's residents were so aware of the danger, and concerned about it, that they were outside of their houses, watching the creek, talking to other residents, and trying to decide whether to evacuate their homes and their coal camps. Possibly the only people completely unaware of the danger were very young children and people who were too sick or impaired to have been aware of the flood warnings of the past two days and the considerable amount of talking about the dams at Three Forks that had been going on during that time.

> From one end of the seventeen-mile-long valley to the other, Buffalo Creek looked like it had been bombed. In every direction, shattered homes lay tumbled like the pieces in some insane jigsaw puzzle. Amid such total destruction, little things seemed to stand out: a knife and fork, glinting side by side in the mud.[51]

Nugent was not there on February 26. Neither was I, of course. Yet, let me suggest that Nugent's generalization might hold true for Lorado, Lundale, and some of the other coal camps in the upper half of Buffalo Creek Valley—but some of his other descriptions of conditions in the coal camps contradict his generalization about "*total* destruction" (emphasis added). Even then, it might be said that while Three Forks was almost totally washed away (at least one house was undamaged, according to one of Nugent's accounts), it would not have appeared as though it had been "bombed" so much as that it had been, well, *washed away*.

Obviously, Nugent is compassionate in his account of how the flood damaged Buffalo Creek. However, readers are encouraged to question whether Nugent sacrificed accuracy for sympathy and dramatic affect by implying that everyone was in shock, that no one was able to move or react, and that the entire valley suffered "total destruction." Perhaps it is callous of me to do so, but, for the moment, let us invert Nugent's statistics. At least 4,800 (97 percent) of Buffalo Creek's 4,950 people were still alive. More than one-half of them had not been injured. More than one-half of the homes and businesses were still standing in place, and at least three of the settlements in the lower part of Buffalo Creek Valley were more or less intact and partly operational—although large parts of them were muddy, oily, wet, and without electricity. Surely, this condition constitutes damage far beyond the damages that occur in a "normal" flood. And surely it constitutes a disaster—and a major one at that, by national standards and possibly even by international standards (a subject that I address more fully in the last two chapters of this book). However, in all honesty, it does not, and did not, constitute "*total* destruction." There was still plenty of human life living along Buffalo Creek at 11:00 a.m. on February 26, 1972. There were still plenty of people who were able and willing to help one another. There were still plenty of neighbors. And they were needed more than ever before.

This being said, there is no denying that Nugent's account is well worth knowing—for more than a few reasons, not the least of which is that it helps us to understand the diversity of human experiences in this disaster. It also helps us realize that neighbors, friends, and families often, but not always, helped one another in crucial ways before, during, and after the dams collapsed. And surely, it alerts us to the fact that we must read carefully and somewhat critically what has been published and widely accepted as objective truth about Buffalo Creek.

GERALD STERN: AN ATTORNEY'S ACCOUNT

> The Buffalo Creek disaster destroyed everything, the entire community. There was nothing left to build on, no roots left to grow again.
>
> —Gerald Stern, *The Buffalo Creek Disaster*[52]

Gerald Stern was Arnold & Porter's lead counsel for the Buffalo Creek plaintiffs in their lawsuit against Pittston Company. His book, *The Buffalo Creek Disaster* (1976), was marketed heavily by Random House, its publisher, and is highly regarded as an insider's description of how and why the lawsuit occurred.[53] The book became popular in law school classes because of the size of the out-of-court settlement ($13.5 million) in favor of Stern's clients and because of Stern's candid disclosures of his emotions and his reasoning throughout the legal process. Stern also portrays a colorful cast of characters with fetching names that would be the envy of any scriptwriter of Hollywood films: Pittston Company, Buffalo Mining Company, Harry Huge, I. C. Spotte, Zane Grey Staker, and of course Stern himself. Our interest, of course, is primarily in what Stern's account tells us about the nature of the social community and people of Buffalo Creek in the months and years after the flood. We are also interested in knowing how the lawsuit may have helped Buffalo Creek and its people in the recovery process since then.

Stern reports that his involvement in the case began when he agreed to be the Arnold & Porter lead counsel, on a *pro bono publico* basis, in representing some of the survivors of the flood. As Stern tells it, a Buffalo Creek Citizens' Committee had been formed two weeks after the flood. It included two elected members from each of Buffalo Creek's sixteen coal camps. The committee contacted Harry Huge, a partner at Arnold & Porter who had just won an $11.5 million verdict for disabled coal miners and widows against the United Mine Worker Welfare and Retirement Fund. It invited him to help some of the survivors get compensation from Pittston Company for damages that they suffered in the flood. Huge traveled down to Buffalo Creek, met with the committee, toured the devastation along the valley, and returned to Arnold & Porter's offices in Washington with a recommendation that Arnold & Porter take the case. A few weeks later, only six weeks after the flood, Stern and Huge traveled down to Buffalo Creek to meet with the committee and begin the legal process. Stern describes what he saw at Buffalo Creek in this way:

> Six weeks after the disaster it still looked like a war zone. The National Guard was everywhere, bulldozing destroyed homes

into big piles for burning, directing traffic over temporary wooden bridges, searching the rubble for bodies. The U.S. Army Corps of Engineers had its big machines down in the creek, clearing out the debris and widening the channel. Houses here and there were marked with a large X, meaning they soon would be leveled and burned. The railroad crews were hard at work putting in new rail lines. Black water marks showed everywhere, on stores, churches, houses—even on the side of the hill. There was an eerie nothingness on each side of the road, what was left of it. Where towns had been, there now were only railroad signs, announcing that here once stood Latrobe or Crites or Lundale.[54]

Stern and Huge visited the former dam sites up at Three Forks and then met with over one hundred families of survivors at the Buffalo Creek Grade School. After explaining Arnold & Porter's plans for the lawsuit, Stern drafted a form retainer letter for each plaintiff that established a contingent fee "around 25 percent, plus expenses."[55] During the next four months, Stern visited Buffalo Creek several more times in order to "meet and talk with the people individually."[56]

> Now we were sitting knee-to-knee, and I was beginning to see the serious personal consequences of this disaster. They were crushed. Their whole demeanor demonstrated how overwhelming this disaster had been. It was hard for them to sit up straight or to talk for long periods of time without drifting off in their thoughts or without averting their eyes from my glance. Tears came quickly and often.[57]

Stern presents lengthy summaries of his interviews with several of the plaintiffs (whom he names) who suffered serious bodily injuries and lost family members in the flood. He then provides a number of assertions about the survivors, based on these interviews and on his other endeavors during the next two years until the case was settled out of court on June 26, 1974.

1. "A coal company's massive coal-waste refuse pile, which dammed a stream in Middle Fork Hollow in the mountains of West Virginia, collapsed without warning to the people in the long, narrow

Buffalo Creek Valley below." The flood "devastated Buffalo Creek's sixteen small communities." "There were over 4,000 survivors, but their 1,000 homes were destroyed as well as most of their possessions."

2. "[T]he Buffalo Creek disaster is unique. This time it was not the strong, working male coal miners who died in the mines. That has become so commonplace in coal mining as to be expected. No, this time it was the miners' defenseless wives and children, caught, unprepared for death, in their beds on Saturday morning."

3. "There was absolutely no trace left of Saunders at the mouth of Middle Fork. Its twenty houses and the Freewill Baptist Church were gone."[58]

4. "Many of those who reached high ground gathered together in undamaged houses. The people remember the exact number who crowded together in various houses on the hill after the disaster... There were thirty-seven in Herman Stiltner's house...Nineteen in Charley Walls' house up one of the side hollows."[59]

5. "Many others who reached high ground wandered aimlessly that day and into the night, building makeshift shelters, often huddling with scores of survivors in ramshackle, unheated wooden huts, or just freezing out in the cold next to fires."[60]

6. "In the Buffalo Creek disaster, though, most of the survivors suffered no physical injuries. They had escaped to the hills before the water came down the valley."[61]

7. "The fact that the Buffalo Creek community was so completely destroyed caused serious problems for the survivors for months and years thereafter. As a result, the parents' reactions and the parents' inabilities to reconstruct their own lives had long-range effects on the children, despite the fact that the children might not have even seen the disaster, or been much troubled by it at the time it occurred."[62]

Stern's book also tells us much more about how he conducted the lawsuit. In reviewing some of the major events in the litigation process, we can ask ourselves how these events might have helped or hindered survivors recover their social well-being. In what ways would these events, as well as the financial settlements, help Buffalo Creek's people rebuild their lives and their community? Would these events foster or frustrate neighborly relations and social integration all along Buffalo Creek—given the research, mentioned previously in this chapter, that found that the litigation process sometimes interferes with long-term recovery by victims of disasters?

According to Stern, local newspapers quickly spread the news that a group of survivors had retained Arnold & Porter to conduct a lawsuit on its behalf. Within days, Pittston Company, through Buffalo Mining Company, opened three claims offices along Buffalo Creek and announced that it would meet with survivors who wanted to file claims for wrongful deaths and property damages. "Many of the survivors soon fell prey to claims adjusters who persuaded them to settle their claims against Pittston as expeditiously as possible."[63]

Arnold & Porter decided to bring suit against Pittston in the U.S. District Court for the Southern District of West Virginia. It also decided to include in its complaint against Pittston some claims for damages for mental suffering and "psychic impairment," as well as for wrongful death and property damages. Additionally, it decided to include as plaintiffs the minor children of the adult plaintiffs. Doing this increased the number of plaintiffs to around 450 from the original 200 adults in 100 families.[64] After lengthy deliberations, Arnold & Porter also estimated that the plaintiffs had losses of real and personal property of $11 million and damages for mental suffering that amounted to approximately $20 million. It decided to claim punitive damages of $21 million, based on the fact that Pittston's net income for the previous year was $42 million—a rather remarkable way to estimate punitive damages, some might say.[65] Late in the summer of 1972, as Arnold & Porter was about to file this complaint against Pittston, Governor Arch Moore of West Virginia released to the press some of the findings of the Ad Hoc Commission that he had appointed to investigate the reasons for the flood. Stern was surprised that the commission openly accused Pittston (and much of the coal industry, for that matter) of "flagrant disregard," because some of the commission's leaders had long-standing financial ties to the coal industry. Nonetheless, the commission contended that: "The Pittston Company, through its officials, has shown flagrant disregard for the safety of residents of Buffalo Creek and other persons who live near coal-refuse impoundments. This attitude appears to be prevalent throughout much of the coal industry."[66] The commission also called for a grand jury investigation to determine if criminal indictments should be brought against anyone because of the flood. Subsequently, a grand jury met, deliberated, but decided not to criminally indict anyone.

For the next twenty-two months, Arnold & Porter and Pittston prepared their cases and tried to outmaneuver each other with flurries of depositions, petitions, and postponements. Among the many experts hired by Arnold & Porter to document the extent of mental suffering by their plaintiffs were noted psychologists Dr. Robert Jay Lifton of Yale University, Dr. Robert J. Coles of Harvard University, and a number of psychiatrists from the University of Cincinnati Medical School, led by Dr. James L. Titchener. Tichener's team "sent over sixty psychiatrists, social workers, and psychologists on two trips of two days each to see over 600 people in the Valley. We were going to do in four days what Pittston's doctors at Williamson, Kentucky, had been doing for over six months." From this extraordinary effort, Stern concluded that

> [t]he individual psychiatric interviews confirmed what we had already learned from Dr. Lifton and our sample of psychiatric interviews—no one who survived the Buffalo Creek disaster escaped emotional and mental distress as a result of it. Our psychiatrists individually interviewed 613 plaintiffs. There were only 9 plaintiffs who demonstrated no degree of psychic impairment; 115 plaintiffs demonstrated mild psychic impairment; 301 demonstrated moderate psychic impairment; 182 demonstrated severe psychic impairment; and 6 were psychologically incapacitated.[67]

In addition to these findings, Stern says that Dr. Lifton reported that "the psychological and psychosomatic effects of the disaster resemble those I encountered in Hiroshima. Though a flood experience can hardly be equated with exposure to an atomic bomb, the survivors of both had much in common, which itself is an indication of the extraordinary human destructiveness of the Buffalo Creek disaster."[68] Stern says that Lifton concluded that "no one exposed to the Buffalo Creek disaster escaped the significant psychological suffering associated with patterns and conflicts common to such disasters." From this conclusion, Stern himself concluded that "The Buffalo Creek disaster destroyed every-thing, the entire community. There was nothing left to build on, no roots left to grow again."[69]

At Robert Lifton's suggestion, Arnold & Porter also hired sociologist Kai Erikson to document damages to Buffalo Creek as a community. "When we first contacted Dr. Lifton, he suggested we add Dr. Erikson to our team. He is chairman of Yale University's American Studies Depart-ment." About Erikson, Stern writes:

> He had spent days and days interviewing the people in the Val-ley, plaintiffs and nonplaintiffs. He got to know them as well as any of us. He found that "many of the traumatic symptoms experi-enced by the people of Buffalo Creek are as much a reaction to the shock of being separated from a meaningful community base as it is a reaction to the shock of being exposed to the actual disaster itself."[70]

Stern felt that the combined testimony of all of these experts would give Arnold & Porter a distinct advantage in a jury trial. He was so con-fident of this that he even included within the plaintiff pool people who had been away from Buffalo Creek in hospitals, jobs, and jail at the time of the flood, but who became distraught months later when they learned how their relatives had suffered in the flood.

> Our experts told us that all the survivors were suffering, whether they were in the water or not, whether they saw their family mem-bers die or not. Indeed most of our plaintiffs weren't in the water and didn't see anyone die. Some were not even in the Valley that day. A few were temporarily away, looking for jobs, in hospitals, or even in jail.[71]

In May 1973, Stern finally was able to take depositions from nine of Pittston's principal officers and managers, including its president, Nicholas Camicia; its vice-president, John Kebblish; the president of Pittston Coal Group, I. C. Spotte; and Pittston's vice-president in charge of the Buffalo Mining Company operations, Steve Dasovich. Besides putting considerable pressure on all of these officials, Stern was able to get them to disclose many new revelations that could be to Stern's favor in a jury trial. One of these revelations was that Kebblish, Spotte, Dasovich, and Pittston's chief engineer, James Yates, had flown near the dams at Three Forks and visited mining operations at Buffalo Creek just two days before the flood. While there, they had discussed the danger of the rising water near the top of dam #3. Kebblish even revealed to Stern that he had encouraged Dasovich to install "an emergency overflow" at the dam.[72]

While Stern was collecting evidence and building his case, several additional events occurred that he felt increased pressure on Pittston to settle out of court rather than go to a jury trial. First, Stern essentially received written authorization from the plaintiffs to settle on their behalf, out of court, for what he would consider to be fair compensation from Pittston. In addition to this "vote of confidence," there were other ways in which the plaintiffs indicated that they were firmly behind Arnold & Porter. One of the plaintiffs, Nora Kennedy, proudly named two of her pigs "Arnold" and "Porter." She announced to everyone that she did so because "Arnold & Porter are rootin' for us."[73] Second, another 200 plaintiffs joined Arnold & Porter's plaintiff pool in the suit against Pittston. Many of these new plaintiffs had already settled with Pittston for their losses of property and for wrongful deaths, but they joined in the Arnold & Porter suit in order to sue for psychic impairment. Doing this enabled Arnold & Porter to increase the plaintiff pool to 625 and to increase the total of the claims to $64 million, considerably more than the original claim of $52 million.[74] Third, articles appeared in major news media that portrayed Pittston in unfavorable ways. For instance, as the two-year statute of limitations for the filing of the complete lawsuit approached, *The New York Times* published an article headlined,

"Flood Survivors Sue Pittston Co.—Plaintiffs Ask $64 Million—Seek Damages over 'Survivor Syndrome.'" Stern avows that "[t]he article had its effect. Pittston's management immediately received phone calls from stockbrokers and shareholders wanting to know what this lawsuit was all about, what survivor syndrome was, and why the suit now was $64 million rather than $52 million."[75] Fourth, the state of West Virginia filed suit against Pittston, both in federal court and in state court, for $50 million in punitive damages and for $50 million in compensatory damages for the destruction of bridges, roads, and schools in the flood.[76] Fifth, newspapers also ran stories that were critical of the U.S. Department of Justice for failing to file a lawsuit against Pittston for compensatory damages of at least $7 million for the cost of the disaster assistance loans, educational facilities, food stamps, unemployment compensation, and HUD trailers that agencies of the federal government had provided to Buffalo Creek in the relief effort.

Stern filed a full complaint in the lawsuit against Pittston for $64 million in total damages in February 1974. Both Arnold & Porter and Pittston engaged in a series of nerve-wracking negotiations to determine whether settling out of court would be preferable to the jury trial that was set for mid-July. Pittston's outside counsel, Zane Grey Staker—a well-known, almost mythic figure in West Virginia trial law circles—eventually invited Stern to make a settlement proposal. Proposals and counter-proposals went back and forth for several months. Finally, on June 26, 1974, almost two and one-half years after the disaster, Stern and Staker settled the case during a telephone conversation as they sat in their corporate offices in Washington DC and Charleston, WV, respectively.

> I called Zane after lunch. I told him the firm would not push me to settle for any figure under $15 million. I said I would split the difference with him, between $13 million and $15 million, and settle for $14 million. He immediately offered $13.5 million and then went on to talk about a number of other matters...After we talked for a few more minutes, I finally told Zane I would accept $13.5 million.[77]

In his epilogue, Stern provides some insight as to how the plaintiffs reacted to the settlement:

> The plaintiffs were overjoyed with the $13.5 million settlement. The division of the money, which we proposed and they accepted, provided them with full replacement value of their homes and possessions. This was more than their market value, the usual measure of recovery in West Virginia for these items. We also evaluated the wrongful-death cases at more than the $10,000 standard Pittston often used. This division of the $13.5 million provided approximately $5.5 million for property and wrongful-death damage payments, with approximately $8 million for the psychic-impairment, "mere puff and blow" claims. Thus, the 600 or so plaintiffs who sued for their mental injuries recovered an average of about $13,000 each.[78]

In some ways, these claims by Stern may be considered to constitute "lawyers license." To his credit, he also discloses that these terms refer to gross compensation. He goes on to state that the "net recoveries for the plaintiffs were somewhat less, after deducting the expenses and legal fees of the case." In fact, he acknowledges that the legal fee in the case amounted to "almost $3 million." As a result of that legal fee and deductions for expenses, Stern claims that the plaintiffs recovered "almost $5.5 million for their psychic-impairment claims" and that the 226 children would collect about $2 million for mental suffering through a trust fund that would dispense their shares to them as each of them turned age eighteen. Stern indicates that all of the plaintiffs accepted Arnold & Porter's formula for distributing their share of the monetary awards to them. He does not disclose the formula. He indicates that the plaintiffs were "overjoyed" with the outcome but that they generally regarding it as a "bittersweet victory." He explains this by quoting one of the plaintiffs, Doris Mullins: "The money can help us live an easier life, free from some of our problems, but it can never put our minds completely at ease, because nothing but death can stop our minds from going back to that morning."[79]

Some Comments on Stern's Account

Stern's account helps us understand several aspects of the flood and its aftereffects beyond the accounts of other experts, although there are some inconsistencies within Stern's account and between his account and those of the others. First, and to his credit, Stern does not assert that the terms of the settlement would enable every one of the plaintiffs to recover fully from the flood. He indicates that the settlement forced the coal company to provide significant compensation to the plaintiffs, that it involved considerable cooperation on the part the plaintiffs, and that the legal system obviously worked for them. We might assume that all of these things were apparent to the plaintiffs and that they took some solace in them, as a result. "And we did some good. We made the coal company pay, and pay well. Maybe the cost of our settlement will make them [*sic*] a little more careful in the future. And we proved that people acting together can have some effect. They can make the legal system work for them."[80]

Stern also quotes some of the plaintiffs in order to indicate that neither this settlement, nor perhaps any monetary settlement, however large, could ever "put our minds completely at ease." This avowal suggests that some of the plaintiffs expected that they would have to endure psychological suffering throughout the remainder of their lives. Certainly, we can understand how this would be true for all or most human beings.

Second, in describing what he saw six weeks after the flood, Stern's account helps us understand why many of the survivors would be perplexed and shocked by what was being done by government agencies to their community and to their former homes. As Stern tells it, the National Guard was "bull-dozing destroyed homes into big piles for burning," and it was still "searching the rubble for bodies." Houses "were being marked with a large X, meaning they soon would be leveled and burned." "Black water marks showed everywhere, on stores, churches, houses." Surely, it is likely that recovery of psychological health would be interrupted, if not reversed, in survivors who saw these actions. Witnessing these conditions might even have diminished what little sense of well-being the survivors had left immediately after the flood.

Third, Stern writes that most of the survivors suffered no physical injuries and that many of those who reached high ground gathered together in undamaged houses where they apparently were invited in and cared for by the owners of those houses, often for several nights and even for weeks at a time. This suggests that some survivors were very willing and able to help their less fortunate neighbors. They shared their households, food, and privacy with them. This also suggests that Stern might have gone too far in asserting that the Buffalo Creek community was so completely destroyed. It was not so destroyed that survivors could not and did not help one another.

Fourth, Stern contends that "many survivors soon fell prey to claims adjusters who persuaded them to settle their claims against Pittston as expeditiously as possible." If so, this indicates yet another probable source of psychological damage to some of the plaintiffs beside the flood itself. This new source of damage could slow the recovery process in many of the survivors.

Fifth, Stern indicates that the investigatory commission that was appointed by Governor Arch Moore accused Pittston Company of "flagrant disregard for the safety of residents of Buffalo Creek and other persons who live near coal-refuse impoundments." The commission also recommended that a grand jury investigate the disaster in order to consider criminal indictments against persons and parties that were responsible for the collapse of the dams. We might speculate as to whether news of these events would help or hinder survivors in the recovery process, yet it seems likely that many survivors would at least take some satisfaction in knowing that they were not being blamed for their plight. As indicated previously, Governor Arch Moore settled West Virginia's lawsuit against Pittston Company for $1 million before he left office in 1977.[81]

Sixth, Stern indicates that Arnold & Porter arranged to have "over sixty psychiatrists, social workers, and psychologists" sent to Buffalo Creek to assess psychological impairments to more than 600 of the plaintiffs. These professional health workers were engaged in assessment, rather than in rendering therapy. Nonetheless, their contacts with the plaintiffs might well have had salutary effects on the plaintiffs by providing them with a sense that their plight was of concern to many other people, including scores of health care workers. This contact might have made it easier for plaintiffs to seek mental-health–counseling services in Logan County. Then again, the activity might have aggravated their anxieties by asking them to recall, yet again, their experiences in the flood and by exposing them to embarrassment about their current living conditions and state of health. Inadvertently, the visits might have disrupted social relations within the households, and they might have created distrust between those households that were and those that were not visited.[82]

Taken as a whole, these revelations by Stern indicate that the residents of the valley were not being ignored by outside agencies or by governments at the county, state, and federal levels. Plenty of outside help was coming into the valley and was being put to good use.

At the same time, however, Stern's account bears a few dubious assertions and some inconsistencies that are by no means minor. For example, Stern writes that the coal-waste refuse pile "collapsed without warning to the people," that it "devastated Buffalo Creek's sixteen small communities," and that "1,000 homes were destroyed." Yet, as previously mentioned, he also writes that radio stations had been issuing flash flood warnings to the Buffalo Creek area, that a number of residents had evacuated Three Forks the night before the flood because they had been warned by other Buffalo Creek people that the dams were about to collapse, and that most of the survivors "had escaped to the hills before the water came down the valley." How would so many of these people have "escaped" if they had not been warned ahead of time? Stern also writes that many survivors spent the night after the flood in the undamaged homes of neighbors, and that some of them spent many days and nights after that relying upon neighbors for their sustenance.

Also consider that Stern seems to have exaggerated the incidence and severity of emotional and mental impairments in the flood's victims, as a whole. Quoting Dr. Lifton and other experts hired by Arnold & Porter, Stern repeatedly asserts or implies that no one escaped impairments and that many survivors were severely and permanently impaired. And yet he also tells us that "[o]ur psychiatrists individually interviewed 613 plaintiffs" and determined that nine plaintiffs demonstrated "no degree of psychic impairment, 115 plaintiffs demonstrated mild psychic impairment" and, in fact, only "6 were psychologically incapacitated." Again, at the risk of sounding callous about human suffering, let me suggest to you that a more devastating disaster than the one at Buffalo Creek would leave more than 1 percent (6 of 613) of the plaintiffs psychologically incapacitated. It would produce considerable amounts of psychic impairment in *all* of the 613 plaintiffs, and it would leave all of the *survivors* impaired, not just the plaintiffs.[83]

Nonetheless, Stern's account also is of great value because he informs us that the 613 plaintiffs were neither the most nor the least inundated, physically injured, and materially deprived victims of the flood. They were somewhere "in between." They were not representative of all of the survivors. Possibly they were not even representative of most of the survivors. As Stern tells it, the most severely damaged survivors already had hired local lawyers to conduct lawsuits on their behalf, or they were still too upset to do so. On the other hand, many of the survivors who had suffered relatively little damage in the flood already had filed standard claims for compensation of property damages at the claims offices that were established for them by the state of West Virginia. In contrast to these other survivors, many of the plaintiffs who hired Arnold & Porter had lost their homes or property, but most of them did not lose members of their families. Most of them had not been in the floodwater. Most of them had not seen anyone die. Stern contends that "The Buffalo Creek disaster destroyed everything, the entire community. There was nothing left to build on. No roots left to grow again." As indicated in my analyses of Nugent's account and of the accounts of Lifton and Erikson that follow, *assertions of "total destruction" such as this are very compassionate and sincere, but they are of questionable validity, to put it mildly.* They might have some validity if they are restricted to some portions of some of the coal camps at the upper end of Buffalo Creek Hollow such as Three Forks, Lorado, and Lundale. Stern's own account often mentions houses and family households that were not destroyed in the flood and which served as refuges for survivors whose own houses had been destroyed. Stern often tells us that survivors who were left homeless were aided by survivors who were not homeless. So, it seems fair to say that, contrary to Stern's interpretation, Buffalo Creek had not been destroyed as a residential community.[84] There would not have been any survivors to interview if the flood had destroyed everything in the sixteen coal camps that were said to have comprised Buffalo Creek. Or, if there were some survivors, they would have been so impaired socially and psychologically that they would have been unable to help one another survive long enough to form a Citizens' Committee, to initiate a lawsuit, and to use the settlement money to try to rebuild homes along Buffalo Creek. Yet, many of the survivors, including many of the plaintiffs, have tried to rebuild Buffalo Creek, and with considerable success—as we will see in part 2 of this book.

Accounts by Psychologists: The Gleser-Green Team

> [B]oth adults and children showed clear-cut improvement from the first to the second decade following the disaster. There were some differences between the samples over time, however. The adults continued to be more impaired than their non-exposed counterparts with regard to symptom levels.
>
> —Green et al., *Clinical Disorders and Stressful Life Events*[85]

As indicated previously, Arnold & Porter used many experts to help prepare its case on behalf of the plaintiffs against the coal companies. A clinical team from the Department of Psychiatry at the University of Cincinnati, headed by psychiatrist James L. Titchener, was hired to establish the extent of psychological and behavioral impairments in each plaintiff. That team was then augmented by a research team that included the late Goldine C. Gleser and Bonnie L. Green, a psychologist who now is professor of psychiatry at Georgetown University. Since 1981 Gleser, Green, and various coauthors have published a book—*Prolonged Psychosocial Effects of Disaster: A Study of Buffalo Creek*—and more than six research papers about how the plaintiffs and other people from Buffalo Creek have adjusted to the flood and its aftermath since 1972.[86] These works report on intricate studies that Gleser, Green, and their colleagues conducted in 1974, 1986, and 1989. Arnold & Porter paid for the interviews by the clinical team in the first study, while the National Institute of Mental Health funded Gleser and Green's research team via competitive grants.

We will give considerable attention to the Gleser and Green reports on these studies (for convenience, we will just mention Green's name because the reports have varying and numerous coauthors, as indicated in the endnotes and the bibliography) because these are the most detailed studies of psychological impairment suffered by some of the survivors of the flood. Familiarity with these reports can help us understand the levels and types of impairments at Buffalo Creek at various points of time and among various subgroups including men, women, children, and some nonplaintiffs. This will also set the stage for examination of the various forms of original data that I collected at Buffalo Creek and that I present in part 2 of this book.

Green's Research Methods

In 1974 Green's research team analyzed the clinical data that had been collected at Buffalo Creek regarding symptoms of traumatic neurosis from 381 adult plaintiffs and 207 child plaintiffs (adults provided the relevant information on the behalf of the younger children). Members of the clinical team, or interviewers trained by them, had interviewed these 588 plaintiffs first with their families in their residences and then later in individual interviews. A report was dictated for each plaintiff based on these interviews. Interestingly, Green's research team also incorporated into its study other reports on these plaintiffs that were produced by a psychiatrist, Dr. Russell Meyers, of Williamson, West Virginia, who was hired by the coal companies to examine the plaintiffs for symptoms of gross stress reaction. Members of Green's team then rated the symptoms from their reports and the defense psychiatrist's reports using a standard instrument in psychiatry called the "Psychiatric Evaluation Form"

(PEF). According to Green, "this instrument allows ratings of nineteen symptom dimensions (e.g., suicide, depression, anxiety, alcohol abuse) from the written reports, as well as overall severity" (289). The team used coders to rate the reported symptoms in each plaintiff's case report as to overall severity, alcohol abuse, and three empirically derived "clusters" of symptoms:

> These clusters were Depression (from depression, suicide/self-mutilation, social isolation, daily routine impairment, and retardation/ lack of emotion); Anxiety (from agitation-excitement, anxiety, and somatic concerns); and Belligerence (from suspicion-persecution, belligerence, and antisocial attitudes and acts).[87]

Green's team also analyzed information from the plaintiffs regarding extent of exposure, including loss by death in the disaster, proximity to floodwaters, extent of warning, extended trauma in the form of exposure to the elements and other experiences, and displacement from the original home site. In the case of reports on the child plaintiffs, family atmosphere was estimated as to violent, irritable, depressed, and/or supportive. The team also used a "Hopkins Symptom Checklist," at times, and did some additional interviews on small samples of plaintiffs in 1975 and 1977.

In 1986 Green's team conducted a "14-year follow-up study" (to the flood of 1972) that was much more complex than the original study in 1974, two years after the flood. It consisted of three samples: (1) 120 of the original 381 adult plaintiffs (the other 261 original plaintiffs either had died, moved away, refused to participate, or were omitted in other ways), (2) 80 original victims of the flood who were not plaintiffs, and (3) "a comparison sample from a culturally and demographically similar area that had not been exposed to the event."

There was also a seventeen year follow-up study, conducted in 1989. In it, Green's team interviewed 99 of the 207 plaintiffs who were children in 1974. The instruments used in the 1986 and 1989 follow-up studies included a "Symptom Checklist 90R," an "Impact Event Scale," and a module for assessing Post Traumatic Stress Disorder (PTSD), as well as the "Psychiatric Evaluation Form" (PEF).

In reading about research findings about mental illness, it is prudent to keep in mind that, historically, estimates of mental illness in the general population usually vary from 15 to 30 percent. They are even lower for specific types of illness such as post-traumatic stress disorder.[88] Furthermore, to the best of my knowledge, there has never been a credible research study that has found levels of mental illness to come close to approximating the extremes of either zero or 100 percent in any sample of the general population. So, it should not surprise us to learn that Green's team found that more than 15 percent, but considerably less than 100 percent of the plaintiffs manifested symptoms of psychological impairment, especially of impairment at moderate to severe levels. Of course, it is also possible, if perhaps unlikely, that all persons who experienced and survived the flood were immediately and severely impaired by their experience, but that their symptoms diminished so quickly that the Green team "missed" much of it by the time the team arrived at Buffalo Creek and conducted its first study, which started in the month of June 1973. Most of the data were collected in March and April 1974, a little more than twenty-four months after the flood.

Estimates of Impairment in the Plaintiffs in 1974
Green's team estimated that 66 percent of the adult men and 70 percent of the adult women plaintiffs had "moderate to severe" impairment when they were studied in 1974. The defense psychiatrist's estimates were 29 percent for the men and 42 percent for the women. In other words, the estimates of impairment by Green's team were more than twice as high for the men plaintiffs than the expert for the defense (66 percent versus 29 percent) and considerably higher for the women plaintiffs (70 percent versus 42 percent). Green's team indicates that the major reason for these lower estimates was that the defense psychiatrist found fewer symptoms of depression. Both "sides" estimated that impairments were more frequent in the women than in the men plaintiffs. Regarding the specific kinds of impairments, Green's team found that the women plaintiffs manifested more depression, anxiety, and "overall severity of symptoms," while the men manifested more belligerence and alcohol abuse.

Concerning the risk factors that were correlated with these levels and kinds of impairments, Green's team found that impairments were higher in the adult plaintiffs who: (1) lost close relatives and friends in the flood, (2) nearly lost their own lives, (3) were displaced to temporary housing in a new neighborhood (4) were not able to "clean-up and restore their houses" (this was especially damaging to the men plaintiffs), and/ or (5) were couples between the ages of twenty-five and fifty-five.[89]

Green also found that spouses were similar in terms of the extent and kinds of problems they faced. Taken as a whole, however, all of the risk factors that were measured by Green's team accounted for only 30 to 40 percent of the variations in the impairment scores for the adult plaintiffs. In other words, Green's team might not have discovered the most important risk factors that contributed to the impairments of the adult plaintiffs. Then again, it is possible that the team did discover the most important risk factors, but that there were many other undiscovered risk factors, such as chronic substance abuse preceding the flood, each of which would account for very little of the unexplained variations in impairment scores. Also worth noting for our deliberations in later chapters of this book is that Green's team found that nonplaintiffs and plaintiffs manifested similar levels of impairment. In Green's own words, "A sample of 40 exposed non-litigants from the area showed nearly identical scores on the symptom checklist." This is a rather remarkable finding in that it suggests that *all* Buffalo Creek adults who were exposed to the flood, regardless of whether they were litigants or nonlitigants, manifested similar levels and kinds of impairments only two years after the flood. Green's team interprets this finding to mean that the litigation process itself did not exacerbate impairments within the plaintiffs.[90]

Of the child plaintiffs in 1974, Green's team found that the older children (ages 8–15) manifested more symptoms of impairment than the younger children. As with the adult plaintiffs, girls manifested more anxiety, depression, and PTSD (measured retroactively). Boys manifested more belligerence. Children who had witnessed loss of lives, who had parents who were impaired, and who lived in homes with poor "atmosphere" manifested higher levels of impairment. These risk factors accounted for about "30% of the variance in overall severity and PTSD scores," according to Green. So, it appears that child plaintiffs were less likely to become moderately to severely traumatized if their parents were able to avoid becoming traumatized and maintain relatively positive and stable home environments for their children.

Estimates of Impairment in the Plaintiffs After 1974
Green's team collected data on small samples of plaintiffs in 1975 and 1977 that showed some "decreases in pathology after the settlement of the lawsuit." By 1986, in the fourteen-year follow-up, they found much more significant decreases for women and men in all of the symptoms except alcohol abuse, which they said "was relatively low to begin with." The percentage of men and women plaintiffs who manifested PTSD decreased from 32 to 23 percent and from 52 to 31 percent, respectively. Even with these decreases, the adult plaintiffs in 1986 "continued to show significant impairment in the areas of anxiety and depressive symptoms"[91] when compared to a small sample of nonexposed people who lived in a similar area. On the other hand, as in the 1974 study, the litigants did not manifest more impairment than did a sample of eighty exposed nonlitigants who had similar exposure to risk factors after the disaster.

The child plaintiffs of 1974 were ages nineteen to thirty-three at the time of the seventeen-year follow-up study in 1989. Green's team found that PEF scores declined in general for this sample and that the other symptoms, including anxiety and belligerence, decreased significantly. The only exceptions were for substance abuse and suicidal ideation, which had not been present in the original sample in 1974 but were now significant.

Among the child litigants, PTSD and major depression decreased from 32 to 7 percent and from 33 to 13 percent, respectively, between 1974 and 1989. Green mentions that these percentages in 1989 were "higher than norms", but that they were "quite similar to those found in the comparison community."[92] Despite the significant decreases in symptoms of impairments over the seventeen years, it was the older former juvenile plaintiffs who continued to manifest higher levels of symptoms than the younger children, although most of the differences were not statistically significant. The females continued to manifest higher levels of impairment than the males in terms of anxiety, social isolation, and self-reported PTSD symptoms.

The Green team summarized its findings of all three studies this way:

> [B]oth adults and children showed clear-cut improvement from the first to the second decade following the disaster. There were some differences between the samples over time, however. The adults continued to be more impaired than their non-exposed counterparts with regard to symptom levels. Further, while gender differences by type of symptom were found in both samples at two years, the gender differences were no longer evident in the adult sample by fourteen years, but continued in the child sample at seventeen years.

From these observations, Green then concluded that "the specific impact of the disaster was no longer detectable in the subjects."[93] This conclusion is particularly noteworthy and will be worth remembering when we deliberate these topics in the final chapters of this book.

Some Comments on the Green and Gleser Research

In trying to draw inferences from these studies, we should keep in mind that, like so many studies in the social sciences of disasters, there were no baseline data of note before the disaster, and there was considerable attrition of the original interviewees in the follow-up studies. In essence, the Green studies tried to determine the levels of psychological impairment in about 12 percent of the survivors (i.e., 600 plaintiffs from among the estimated 4,825 survivors) sixteen to twenty-four months after the flood, and then fourteen years and seventeen years later.[94]

Even with these caveats in mind, it seems fair to say that the research done by Gleser and Green's team produced many findings that are credible and valuable, even if their final conclusion might be somewhat overstated: "[T]he specific impact of the disaster was no longer detectable in the subjects." After all, their own findings for the litigant interviewees in

1986 and 1989 indicated that psychological-impairment levels were still somewhat higher than for nonexposed interviewees. They also found that former juvenile litigants still had higher frequencies of "substance abuse" and "suicidal ideation" than did the general population. Additionally, they also found that PTSD frequencies had decreased for men from 32 to 23 percent and for women from 52 to 31 percent by 1986. Let us note again that PTSD levels of 31 and 23 percent are very high relative to national averages, which are generally around 7 percent. Furthermore, Gleser and Green found levels of impairment for anxiety and depression that were significantly higher for litigants than for residents in a "similar area" that had not been exposed to the flood.

For these reasons, I believe that Green and Gleser were somewhat inaccurate if they were concluding that the surviving litigants who were interviewed in 1986 and 1989 were no longer different than the rest of the U.S. population in terms of psychological impairment, regardless of the causes of those impairments. And yet, our primary interest in this book is to determine what has happened to Buffalo Creek and its people since the flood—rather than to focus on lingering damages or to critique the research literature that was published long ago. It is well worth knowing that Green and Gleser's extensive psychological studies establish that, for as many as 12 percent of the flood's 4,825 survivors who had lost a lot of material goods, one-third to 70 percent of them manifested some psychological impairments twenty-four months after the flood, and that many of them were considerably less impaired by the late 1980s. Surely this suggests that they had regained or re-created a considerable amount of psychological well-being. As such, the social re-creation perspective has at least as much validity as the social destruction perspective in this regard. In less than twenty years after the flood, hundreds of the survivors were less impaired than they had been only two years after the flood. Also consider that, only two years after the flood, hundreds of survivors were not so impaired that they could not voluntarily consent to participate in Green and Gleser's research. Doing so might have even helped some of these survivors re-create social well-being in their lives and in their community. Fortunately, there is no evidence that it damaged them further—although, as indicated earlier in this chapter, subsequent research by other scientists on places other than Buffalo Creek has found evidence that some survivors of disasters are damaged by their participation in the "litigation process." Let us keep in mind that the earliest phase of Green and Gleser's research was part of the litigation process that was partially paid for by the law firm of Arnold & Porter. Chapter 4 presents interview data from some survivors of the flood who attest that they refused to participate in the Arnold & Porter litigation process because they feared that the process might cause undue stress to their children. It also presents interview data from some other survivors who attest that their participation in the Arnold & Porter lawsuit did not cause additional stress to them or to their children.[95] However, in the absence of compelling evidence to the contrary, it seems fair to believe that Green and Gleser's team credibly established that much of the psychological damage suffered by about 12 percent of flood survivors (i.e., the litigants in the Arnold & Porter lawsuit) diminished considerably in the seventeen years after the flood. Among other questions, we might ask ourselves: How could this have happened if *everything*, or almost everything, was destroyed in the flood or because of its aftereffects? And how could this have happened unless most of these litigants were able to re-create relatively satisfying social lives?[96]

ROBERT JAY LIFTON: A PSYCHIATRIST'S ACCOUNT OF BUFFALO CREEK AS "TOTAL DESTRUCTION"

> The totality of the Buffalo Creek disaster, then, encompasses this communal breakdown as well as the survivor conflicts described earlier. Both in fact merge in a final common pathway of individual suffering.[97]

Robert Jay Lifton is one of the most famous scholars to have written about the Buffalo Creek disaster. When he published the results of his study in February 1976, as the lead article in the esteemed journal *Psychiatry*, he was Foundations' Fund Research Professor of Psychiatry at

Yale University School of Medicine. He had been elected as president of the American Psychiatric Association, was known as a cofounder of the Center for Study of Human Violence and—along with Bruce Mazlish and his former teacher, Erik Erikson (Kai Erikson's father)—had founded the Wellfleet Psychohistory Group. He had already published a number of widely read books, including a study of survivors of the atomic bomb attack on Hiroshima, Japan, *Death in Life: Survivors of Hiroshima*. The title of his research article, "The Human Meaning of Total Disaster: The Buffalo Creek Experience," readily conveys his thesis that the disaster at Buffalo Creek constituted a *total* disaster to its survivors and to Buffalo Creek as a social community, at least according to his criteria.

A subsection of his article (coauthored with his research assistant, Eric Olson) affirms the findings of Dwight Harshbarger, a psychologist at West Virginia University who was one of the first researchers to present a report of his findings:

> Totality of communal destruction. The Buffalo Creek disaster was unique in its combination of suddenness, destructive power within a limited circumscribed area, and resulting breakdown of community structure. Harshbarger has stated the matter well in comparing Buffalo Creek with other disasters and explaining his use of the term "total loss disaster."[98]

They quote Harshbarger as follows:

> I...feel that the Buffalo Creek disaster was, while smaller in the value of property lost, a more intense disaster than the later floods of hurricane Agnes, or other large disasters. It takes a considerable amount of searching to find this combination of *total loss*, i.e., of lives, properties, and the basic structure of social fabric of communities themselves. The San Francisco earthquake and the Chicago fire are reminiscent of larger, but comparable, *total loss* disaster. While there may be more recent examples, none come to mind (Rapid City [South Dakota, where a large flood took place], while comparable in some ways, retained its basic community structure; Buffalo Creek did not).[99]

It is worth noting that Lifton was hired by Arnold & Porter "to consult on the psychological effects of the flood disaster," as was Dr. James L. Titchener and many of his associates, including Gleser, Green and associates. Lifton also recommended that Arnold & Porter contact his colleague at Yale, Kai Erikson, regarding the prospect of documenting damages to Buffalo Creek as a social community. Lifton wrote that he and his research assistant, Eric Olson, "worked closely with Erikson and Titchener throughout."[100] All of them presented research papers about Buffalo Creek at meetings of the American Psychiatric Association in May 1975.[101] Also worth noting is Lifton's statement of his research methods:

> In connection with our consultation in the case we made, together and individually, five trips to Buffalo Creek between April 1973 and August 1974 and have conducted a total of 43 interviews involving 22 Buffalo Creek survivors. In addition we have talked with several ministers and volunteer workers in the area, and read through the extensive documentation of the disaster compiled by a variety of observers and professional consultants working with the survivors.[102]

Based on these research methods, Lifton and Olson reported that the psychological impact of the disaster had been so extensive that "no one in Buffalo Creek has been unaffected." Everyone exposed to the disaster "had experienced some or all of the following manifestations of the general constellation of the survivor: 'death imprint and death anxiety,' 'death guilt,' 'psychic numbing,' and 'counterfeit nurturing and unfocused rage.'"[103] They also believed that everyone was suffering part or all of the "survivor syndrome" because social relationships had been destroyed and the community had broken down.

> Survivors lack the human structures we all require to maintain orderly rhythms and consistent values in our lives. Since they still live more or less in their pre-disaster environment, it is as if a vast, destructive force decimated the elements of community, totally removing some and shaking up all the others so that they now exist in distorted and incoherent relationship to each other... There can be no doubt that this communal breakdown results in

severe stress and contributes greatly to a wide variety of medical and psychiatric illnesses and disorders.[104]

Lifton and Olson's article is particularly relevant because it repeatedly asserts that the disaster at Buffalo Creek was "*total*" (emphasis added) in its destruction of the psychological well-being of the survivors and the crucial social relationships that had existed in the community before the flood. The article repeatedly states that the disaster at Buffalo Creek was as "total" as any disaster known to the authors, including the "disaster" that the atomic bomb wreaked upon Hiroshima, Japan. The article also contends that even after thirty months, there was no reduction in the impairments suffered by the survivors and no reduction in the damages suffered by the community. Furthermore, it reports that the psychological impairments, despair in particular, have been passed on to the children of the adult survivors, even to children born years after the flood.[105]

> There is, in fact, mounting evidence that the effects of disaster can extend over generations, and that adverse effects of significant proportion can occur in children of survivors, even when the children are born some years after a particular disaster...There was evidence of a similar phenomenon in Hiroshima, and while one cannot as yet speak of future generations at Buffalo Creek one can certainly observe many families to be "a collection of severely disturbed and traumatized individuals" who could well transmit various disaster-related conflicts to subsequent generations.[106]

In sum, Lifton and Olson's article provides no direct evidence or assertion in support of the social re-creation perspective, thirty months after the flood. The authors mention no rebuilding of any kind along Buffalo Creek. It is almost as though they visited Buffalo Creek one hour after the flood had passed on February 26, 1972—not in April 1973, fourteen months after the flood. In fact, Lifton and Olson's article constitutes a near perfect example of the social destruction perspective as presented earlier in this chapter. Their article uses and affirms the words "total" and "totality" more than eighteen times in eighteen pages, including the title of the article. It repeatedly claims that Buffalo Creek was destroyed socially, and its survivors were destroyed psychologically. None of this destruction had been undone even thirty months after the flood. Surely, this article is an example *sine qua non* of the social destruction perspective in its line of argument—if not in the persuasiveness of the evidence that it presents.

In chapter 6, I reconsider Lifton and Olson's work in light of my own research along Buffalo Creek, as reported in chapters 3, 4, and 5. Before turning to the research reports of another expert, Kai Erikson—who was a colleague of Lifton's at Yale during the time of the studies—consider the importance that Lifton and Olson attribute to the disaster at Buffalo Creek, to "holocausts," and to "contemporary existence."

> In all of these ways, Buffalo Creek epitomizes the tenuousness of so much of contemporary existence—our combination of survival of old and anticipation of new holocausts, and our struggles, equally inadequate, to confront that death-dominated precariousness as a source of new vitality and of transformation.[107]

And yet, there is very little sense of "new vitality" and of "transformation" along Buffalo Creek, as reported by Lifton and Olson. In fact, these terms only appear in *that*—the final sentence of their article.

KAI ERIKSON: A SOCIOLOGIST'S ACCOUNT

> Kai Erikson's contentions that Buffalo Creek constituted a total disaster and produced a second disaster (collective trauma) has had far-ranging and continuing influence, even among research scholars who have made their names questioning commonly held beliefs about disasters.[108]

> It was as if every man, woman, and child in the place—every one—was suffering from some combination of anxiety, depression, insomnia, apathy, or simple "bad nerves," and to make matters worse, those complaints were expressed in such similar ways that they almost sounded rehearsed.[109]

Kai Erikson's account is particularly important to us because it focuses on topics that are of greatest interest to us—community, neighbors, neighboring, well-being—and on how these are damaged by disasters. It is also important because it has had so much influence on sociology, psychology, and disaster studies. Erikson's work has won prestigious awards and has stimulated my own research and writing for years. This book obviously is a case in point. For these reasons, I will give a detailed rendering and critique of Erikson's work. In order to understand and appreciate Erikson's work fully, I will start by describing how he got involved in studying Buffalo Creek, as well as the methods he used in his study.[110]

How Erikson Got Involved

Erikson was a well-regarded sociologist in his forties at Yale University when he was contacted by Gerald Stern at Arnold & Porter in early 1973 (about one year after the flood).[111] Prior to that, he had done research in the medical schools at the University of Pittsburgh and Emory University. Erikson also was known for an intellectual and social heritage that links him to Sigmund Freud. He is the son of the late Erik Homburger Erikson, a renowned Harvard psychologist, author of the controversial neo-Freudian monograph, *Childhood & Society*, and a former participant in the celebrated psychoanalytic circle of Sigmund and Anna Freud in Depression-era Vienna, where he apparently was a favorite student of Anna Freud. Erik Erikson was widely considered to be a leading candidate for a Nobel Prize.[112] At any rate, Gerald Stern asked Kai Erikson to suggest the name of a graduate student in sociology who would document the flood's damages to the social life of the plaintiffs who had hired Arnold & Porter to seek compensation from Pittston Company. Erikson decided to visit Buffalo Creek for himself. He was so astounded by what he saw there that he volunteered his own services to Arnold & Porter. From that point on, Erikson visited Buffalo Creek an unspecified number of times, talked with passersby, and asked questions that came to mind. At other times, he attended meetings that Arnold & Porter held with the plaintiffs in order to take depositions, answer questions, explain details, and develop the legal case against Pittston.

Erikson wrote that he was able to get an unusual amount of relevant information and sociological insight about Buffalo Creek because he was a member of the Arnold & Porter team. As such, he was welcomed and immediately trusted by the survivors of the flood—in contrast to their reaction to many other outsiders and to the reactions that social scientists often experience when they try to do field research.

Erikson's Methods and Sources of Data
As a member of the Arnold & Porter team, Erikson had access to hundreds of legal depositions, psychiatric evaluations, and personal letters from the plaintiffs. Erikson also reports that he was able to interview dozens of the plaintiffs and that he conducted his own survey of the adult plaintiffs.[113] He also had access to materials from other consultants to Arnold & Porter, including Robert Jay Lifton, Eric Olson, and psychiatrist James L. Titchener (whose associates included Goldine C. Gleser and Bonnie L. Green, as described in the previous section of this chapter), as well as to documents that were filed in court on behalf of the plaintiffs and on behalf of Buffalo Mining Company and Pittston Company. These materials became the basis for his book, *Everything in Its Path: Destruction of Community in the Buffalo Creek Flood.*

What Erikson Found

> The case can be stated flatly: Everyone on Buffalo Creek has been damaged by the disaster in one way or another.[114]

Notice that Erikson wrote that his research at Buffalo Creek in 1973 and 1974 convinced him that "*Everyone*" (not just the plaintiffs in the Arnold & Porter case against Pittston Coal) "has been damaged by the disaster in one way or the other."[115] "It was as if every man, woman, and child in the place—every one—was suffering from some combination of anxiety, depression, insomnia, apathy, or simple "bad nerves," and to make matters worse, those complaints were expressed in such similar ways that they almost sounded rehearsed."[116]

Erikson provided one, fourteen-page illustrative case of how the flood produced a "syndrome" of these complaints and others in "Wilbur" and "Deborah" (pseudonyms created by Erikson).[117] This case constitutes Erikson's longest and fullest description of flood survivors.

Wilbur and Deborah as Survivors

Wilbur was a fifty-year-old former miner on a disability pension who suffered from black-lung disease. He and his family had lived along Buffalo Creek for twenty-three years. Wilbur was smoking a cigarette in his kitchen in Lorado as the flood approached his home. His wife Deborah and their four dependent children were sleeping. "For some reason, I opened the inside door and looked up the road—and there it came. Just a big black cloud. It looked like twelve or fifteen foot of water. It was just like looking up Kanawha River and seeing barges coming down four or five abreast."[118]

Wilbur said that he screamed for his wife and kids to get out of the house fast. Somehow they managed to do this before the house was hit full force by the first wave. They were almost swept away in the raging floodwater before they were able to splash their way up to some higher ground behind their home. From there, they watched in horror as their house and other houses in their neighborhood floated away or were shattered in place. Fourteen of their neighbors drowned as a result, several of whom called out to Wilbur for help as they swept by. "But I didn't give it a thought to go back and help her. I blame myself a whole lot for that yet. She had her baby in her arms and looked as though she was going to throw it to me. Well I never thought to go help that lady. I was thinking about my own family. They all six got drowned in that house."[119]

Soon a neighbor came over and helped Deborah move Wilbur to his car. They wrapped Wilbur in a blanket or quilt because he was poorly dressed and soaking wet in the rain. That night, Wilbur and his family stayed with neighbors in their home on a slope above Lorado, along with three other people, two of whom were badly injured in the flood. The next day, an acquaintance invited Wilbur to move his family to a little, one-room washhouse on his property, where they stayed for nineteen days.

So we stayed in that man's wash house, six of us, for nineteen days—a one-room wash house about twelve by twenty. We would eat cold cereal for breakfast of a morning, do without dinner, and then we would go walk about a mile over to the high school and get us a hot supper. We had a little gas-burner stove in that wash house, but we had nothing to cook in.[120]

By the time Erikson met Wilbur and Deborah, they had moved from a trailer in one of the HUD trailer camps to a new home on a hillside above Man that overlooked Buffalo Creek. In their interviews with Erikson, they said that they were suffering many psychological problems because of the flood: numbness, nervousness, insomnia, frightening and reoccurring nightmares of the flood, depression, guilty feelings, memory loss, suicidal thoughts, and neglect of each other, their children, and their own personal well-being.

What I went through on Buffalo Creek is the cause of my problem. The whole thing happens over to me even in my dreams, when I retire for the night. In my dreams, I run from water all the time, all the time. The whole thing just happens over and over again in my dreams.

My nerves is my problem. Every time it rains, every time it storms, I just can't take it. I walk the floor. I get so nervous I break out in a rash. I'm taking shots for it now.

I don't know. I'm just a different person. I just don't want to associate with no people. It bothers me. It makes me nervous.

Deborah described her many problems in complaints like these:

I'm neglecting my children. I've just completely quit cooking. I don't do no housework. I just won't do nothing. Can't sleep. Can't eat. I just want to take me a lot of pills and just go to bed and go to sleep and not wake-up.

I haven't told anyone this before, but at one point, on a Saturday morning, I was so depressed that I just didn't want to live. I just took a notion that I'd end it. I got the car keys and stepped out the trailer door, but my husband and my oldest daughter at home,

they had been watching me, I reckon.... I had intended to put that
car over Kelly Mountain with me in it. So they drug me back out
of the car and took me back in the house and gave me some nerve
medicine.[121]

Wilbur and Deborah also told Erikson they felt that they had lost
forever the kind of close-knit and caring home, family, neighborhood,
neighbors, and community that they had in Lorado, specifically. They
were convinced that they would never again be able to achieve that kind
of social cohesion.

> Now I've moved around from place to place in my time, but there
> was nothing like this. When I moved to that community, I had
> neighbors the very next day. The things we did up there, the whole
> community, we played horseshoes, we went to church together,
> we would group up when they had holy revivals, and then on
> Sunday evenings, maybe even on Saturday evenings, we'd come
> back from service and have our sports.
>
> Back before this happened, you never went up the road or down
> it but what somebody was ahollering at you. I could walk down
> the road on a Saturday morning or a Sunday morning and people
> would holler out their door at me, and maybe I would holler back
> at them, maybe go sit down and have us a cup of coffee or a ciga-
> rette or something. And there'd be half a dozen families would
> just group up and stand there and talk. But anymore you never see
> nobody out talking to one another. They're not friendly like they
> used to be. It's just a whole different life, that's all.[122]

Before leaving Erikson's portrayal of Wilbur, we might note that Wilbur suffered black lung and other ailments that forced him to retire and
draw disability income before the flood occurred. Is it possible that some
of his postflood complaints and ailments actually had their origins in
conditions that Wilbur suffered before the flood? Is it possible that the
same thing is true for his wife Deborah? Additionally, let us keep in mind
Wilbur's own testimony that he helped only his family members—not
his neighbors—once the flood appeared at his doorstep. And yet, at least
one of his neighbors and one other member of the community provided

crucial support services to Wilbur and his family in the hour and the day after the flood. One neighbor led him to a vacant car, wrapped him in bedding, and helped him get warm and dry. The other person came up to Wilbur and invited the entire family to stay in his one-room washhouse, without charge. They lived there for nineteen days. Is it possible that Wilbur was never as good a neighbor as his neighbors were to him? He did not seem inclined to try to help others. Perhaps this was because of his personality, rather than the flood.

Kai Erikson reported that every survivor he talked to, or almost everyone, complained about suffering the same kinds of psychological and social damages as Wilbur and Deborah, although often to a lesser extent. He also reported that he was surprised to find that, even two years after the flood, the damages were so severe and profound that Buffalo Creek no longer existed as a social community. "Even the closest family groups had trouble maintaining their old intimacy in the wake of the flood." Without close, caring neighbors, there was no "meaningful community."[123]

Neighbors and Neighboring Along Buffalo Creek
According to Erikson, before the flood, neighbors and neighboring had been unusually strong all along Buffalo Creek. They had been instrumental in providing many services to Buffalo Creek's residents, such as child care, house security, condolences in times of death, and many types of sports and recreation. They were the foundation of community cohesion and of a sense of communality. None of this was true after the flood, according to Erikson. As in the case of Wilbur and Deborah, Buffalo Creek's people had been "neighbor people."[124] Neighbors were not just the people who lived in the houses close by: they were dear friends or even "family" that were readily included in almost all of the activities and events of importance to one's own family and household. Erikson contends that neighbors and neighboring made Buffalo Creek into a highly cohesive community akin to Robert Redfield's "folk" communities, where most of the residents had essentially the same tasks, jobs, resources, responsibilities, values, and goals. When Erikson asked them

what "neighbors," "neighboring," and "community" meant to them, they responded:

> What's a neighbor? Well, when I went to my neighbor's house on Saturday or Sunday, if I wanted a cup of coffee I never waited until the lady of the house asked me. I just went into the dish cabinet and got me a cup of coffee or a glass of juice just like it was my own home. They come to my house, they done the same. See?[125]

> Before the disaster, the neighbors, we could look out and tell when one another needed help or when one was sick or something was disturbing that person. We could tell from the lights. If the lights was on late at night, we knew that something unusual was going on and we would go over. Sometimes I'd come in from work on a cold day and my neighbor would have a pot of soup for me.[126]

> You'd just have to experience it, I guess, to really know. It was wonderful. Like when my father died. My neighbors all came in and they cleaned my house, they washed my clothes, they cooked. I didn't do nothing. They knew what to do. I mean it's just like teamwork you know.[127]

From testimonies like these, Erikson concluded that, at Buffalo Creek, a neighbor used to be "someone you can relate to without pretense, a familiar and reliable part of your everyday environment; a neighbor is someone you treat as if he or she were a member of your immediate family."[128] He also determined that neighbors and neighboring had become the primary source of communality. He defines it as "a state of mind" and a "network of understandings" in which there is "a constant readiness to look after one's neighbors, or rather, to know without being asked what needed to be done."[129] Erikson makes a provocative observation to the effect that communality was so strong at Buffalo Creek before the flood that neighbors did not erect fences—barrier fences, in particular. They did not want to have any barrier to communications and visiting with neighbors. They did not need fences to protect their property. Neighbors would do that for them.[130]

After the flood, and because of it, communality was so damaged that Buffalo Creek ceased to exist as a community: "the whole community more or less disappears, as happened on Buffalo Creek."[131] Survivors repeatedly told Erikson that, when they lost their trusted neighbors, they were no longer able to be neighborly and to practice neighboring. They could no longer experience communality. The community had been lost. It was as though neighbors, neighboring, community, and communality were so tightly intertwined and interdependent at Buffalo Creek that they were inseparable.

> We did lose a community, and I mean it was a good community. Everybody was close, everybody knowed everybody. But now everybody is alone. They act like they're lost. They've lost their homes and their way of life, the one they liked, the one they was used to. All the houses are gone, every one of them. The people are gone, scattered. You don't know who your neighbor is going to be. You can't go next door and talk. You can't do that no more.[132]

Other Disruptions

Erikson returned to Buffalo Creek several times over a period of several years before his book was published. He came to believe that the flood itself was not the only source of the psychological damages to the survivors—to the individuals and to the community as a whole. Additional damages had been caused by the conditions of life in the trailer camps, the permanent loss of homes and homesites, the low levels of reimbursements for property losses, and the belief that the coal companies were not doing enough to help survivors cope with their losses.

Many of the survivors had been relocated to temporary trailer camps that were built on cleared lots along Buffalo Creek and in other hollows along the Guyandotte River. Some survivors remained in the trailer camps for more than one year, under conditions that some of them found to be appalling, demeaning, and alienating. The thirteen new trailer camps provided by HUD were filled on a first-come, first-served basis. "No effort was made to group people according to old neighborhood patterns, and as a result most people had to look across the narrow spaces dividing their new quarters at relative strangers."[133] The trailers were so small and cramped that some families could hardly eat their meals together or entertain neighbors, as they were used to doing in the former coal camps. Among many other complaints, the trailers were so poorly insulated that they were cold in winter, hot in summer, and failed to buffer conversations and sounds. Conversations inside the trailers too often became public knowledge and gossip. Passing cars, squabbles between neighbors, and other external sounds penetrated the trailers, which were packed close together with their front doors facing other front doors only thirty or forty feet away. "Family quarrels could be heard five or six doors away, and such everyday sounds as bedsprings moving or glassware breaking, or toilets flushing were broadcast not only to everyone in the trailer itself but to half the neighbors as well."[134]

Many of the trailer camp residents also complained about the absence of parking places, porches, yards, and play areas in the camps. Utilities were inadequate, as were safeguards against rodents and insects. Some of the HUD employees who managed the camps were unresponsive. Others were overbearing. Erikson reported that "in every day conversations the trailer camps were likened to 'concentration camps' and the mobile homes to 'prisons' or 'sweatboxes'." One resident complained, "we are all like animals in a cage."[135]

The flood had washed away or damaged a considerable amount of the utility and transportation infrastructure of Buffalo Creek, including major sections of Route 16 that twisted and turned its way up through the coal camps of Buffalo Creek, the crosscutting alleyways in the coal camps, the rail lines and rail yards, and the many bridges over Buffalo Creek and dozens of its tributaries. What the flood did not destroy it packed with huge piles of debris in the form of broken wood-frame buildings, busted vehicles, railroad ties and rails, trees, boulders, and gravel. West Virginia state agencies decided that it would be much more efficient to build a straight modern transportation and utility conduit up the length of Buffalo Creek Valley rather than rebuild it in trace of the old lines, which had originally been built piecemeal and in haphazard fashion. In order to make these improvements, state agencies confiscated hundreds of houses and house lots from Buffalo Creek's homeowners. Many of these people learned that they were being bought out just as they were struggling to adapt to the trailer camps and were eagerly waiting to move back to their homesites along Buffalo Creek.

Many survivors also were shocked and bitter about what they believed to be callous disregard for their plight on the part of the coal companies and by the level of compensation offered to them by Pittston Company for their losses of personal property. They felt that the compensation they received for their confiscated property was not sufficient to allow them to acquire replacement property in or around the valley. "The coal company set up a claims office shortly after the disaster, offering to repay survivors for the actual value of property destroyed, but many people thought that they were being treated shabbily by the company attorneys and turned elsewhere for relief."[136]

Although Erikson had no prior experience as a disaster researcher, his visits to Buffalo Creek led him to believe that all disasters produce various kinds of damages, including psychological damages (which Erikson calls "individual trauma") to individual people who experience the disaster. However, only a relatively small fraction of disasters extensively damage the social relations and social life of the community as a whole (which Erikson calls "collective trauma").[137] He came to believe that, in most disasters, individual trauma subsides fairly quickly as material resources are mobilized and services are restored to the human settlements. He felt that this did not occur at Buffalo Creek because collective trauma was just too intensive, extensive, and enduring.

An Aside on "Individual Trauma" and "Collective Trauma"
Erikson uses the term "individual trauma" to refer to the generalized psychological "state of shock" and to one or more specific psychological impairments that survivors suffered immediately and many months after the flood.[138] He writes that the psychiatrists hired by Arnold & Porter examined 615 of the survivors who were plaintiffs eighteen months after the flood. They determined that "at least 570 of them, a grim 93%, were found to be suffering from an identifiable emotional disorder."[139] Erikson also writes that the physician who examined these plaintiffs for Pittston Company "found a similar incidence of disorder" but "thought

that the disturbances he was noticing could not have been a result of the flood."[140] He was prepared to argue that many of the plaintiffs must have had these emotional disorders before the flood. Erikson then writes that

> most of the survivors responded to the disaster with a deep sense of loss, a nameless feeling that something had gone awry in the order of things, that their minds had been bruised beyond repair, that they would never again be able to find coherence, that the world as they knew it had come to an end.[141]

To Erikson, these outcomes are understandable because

> almost everybody who survived the disaster did so by the thinnest of margins, and the closeness of their escape, combined with the relentless savagery of the water, left them feeling numbed and depleted, almost as if the rush to safety had consumed most of their energy and the sheer force of the waves passing below them had somehow drawn off what reserves were left.[142]

All of these feelings were so pervasive, severe, and crippling—even two years after the flood—that Erikson eventually concluded that the flood alone could not have produced them unless it also destroyed the community, particularly the essence of community, which he calls "communality." By this he means "a constant readiness to look after one's neighbors, or rather to know without being asked what needed to be done."[143]

During the first months of his study of Buffalo Creek, Erikson indicates that he sent "a questionnaire to some five hundred persons asking for a few brief answers to a few crisp questions," including "What do you miss most about the old community?"[144] From the responses that he received, and apparently from the many other sources of data that he had access to, Erikson learned about what neighbors, neighboring, community, and communality meant to the people of Buffalo Creek and how these had changed since the flood. "We did lose a community, and I mean it was a good community. Everybody was close, everybody knowed everybody. But now everybody is alone. They act like they're lost."[145]

Erikson determined that all of these aspects of social life had been destroyed. He decided to refer to these kinds of damages to the community as a whole as "collective trauma"—as distinct from the kinds of trauma that are suffered by individual people, or "individual trauma."

Erikson also reported that some kinds of survivors—including women and former residents in the upper part of Buffalo Creek Hollow around Three Forks and Lundale—reported greater damages to Buffalo Creek as a community than did the other survivors. Erikson speculated that many adult men still experienced a sense of community in the mines and their other workplaces, whereas many of the adult women were unemployed housewives who knew very few of the other people in the trailer camps and found themselves wiling away lonely hours each day. Residents of the upper hollow, in the coal camps of Three Forks and Lorado, for example, felt a greater loss of community because the flood left few buildings standing in those camps, and most of the residents who were not killed were relocated to the thirteen different trailer camps. Yet, despite these differences, Erikson writes that these differences were slight. "Everybody on Buffalo Creek, regardless of his or her exposure to the black water, was implicated in the loss of communality, and in that regard, at least, all were hurt in much the same way. This does not appear to have become a new basis of community."[146]

This assertion by Erikson is noteworthy not just for its substance, but also because it counters often heard clichés such as "misery likes company," "adversity forges common bonds," and "no pain, no gain." Erikson writes that he found no evidence that the destruction of community motivated or allowed Buffalo Creek's survivors to band together in order to overcome adversity and to reestablish the deep communal bonds that they once had. Of course, this is one of the many ways in which Erikson's report is more congruent with the social destruction perspective than with the social re-creation perspective. Actually, it is hard to find anything in Erikson's interpretation of what happened after the flood at Buffalo Creek that supports the social re-creation perspective—at least not until Arnold & Porter distributed to the litigants their shares from the settlement of the lawsuit. Erikson seems to portray even that event as being rather inadequate in terms of recovery.

The devastating combination of individual and collective trauma, in turn, produced a welter of long-term adverse consequences. Alcohol abuse, interpersonal violence, child neglect, marital estrangements and divorces, theft, larceny, and disturbances of the peace increased. Survivors also came to believe that these deviant behaviors and social problems increased appreciably, and they reported this to Erikson.[147]

Demoralization and Immorality

Given the loss of neighbors, communal bonds, communality, and increased loneliness, it is hardly surprising that Erikson found "a state of severe demoralization"[148] and plenty of talk about rampant misbehaviors— which sociologists often refer to as "deviant behavior." Quite possibly, many survivors were no longer able or willing to abide by traditional moral codes and social norms. Other survivors might have become unable or unwilling to enforce those norms when other people deviated. Still other survivors might have lost the ability and energy to tell the difference between what was and was not immoral behavior in themselves or in others. Several respondents admitted to Erikson that they were unable to explain why they themselves started drinking uncontrollably many months after the flood. One retired miner told Erikson, "I did acquire a very bad drinking problem after the flood which I'm doing my level best now to get away from. I was trying to drink, I guess, to forget a lot of things and get them moved out of my mind."[149] Others reported seeing or hearing about increases in vulgar language, fist fights, thefts, infidelities, marital quarrels, abuse, separations, and divorces.

> The use of alcohol, always problematic in mountain society, has evidently increased, and there are rumors spreading throughout the trailer camps that drugs have found their way into the area. The theft rate has gone up too, and this has always been viewed in Appalachia as a sure index of social disorganization.
>
> Adolescent boys and girls appear to be slipping away from parental control and are becoming involved in nameless delinquencies,

while there are reports from several of the trailer camps that younger wives and husbands are meeting one another in circumstances that violate all the local codes.[150]

One widow lamented to Erikson her difficulties in controlling her teenage daughter and in other aspects of her social life:

> And then she started running with the wrong crowds. She started drinking. She started taking dope. And feelings wasn't the same between her and I. Before the flood it wasn't like that at all.[151]

> My husband and I, we was happy before the flood. We got along real good, other than just a few quarrels that never amounted to nothing. But after the flood we had fights, and it was constantly we were quarreling about something or other. We had fights. He would hit me and he would choke me and he would slap me around.[152]

> Well, living there [in the trailer camps] was an intolerable situation for me because my children were exposed to people that I didn't want my children to be around. There were drunkards. There were fights, vulgar language. And all of these were situations to which my children had never been exposed. This is not the type of home life we have nor our friends and families have. Even the small children used language which I didn't approve.

While Erikson says that "there is no question but that 'immorality' is on the rise,"[153] he also notes that some of the reports of increases in misbehaviors must be discounted because they are based on rumors and exaggerations. He mentions that many people have a tendency to say that a behavior like drinking or swearing is deviant if a stranger does it, but that they would overlook that same behavior in one of their neighbors because they have seen it so often that they consider it to be harmless.

Erikson's Conclusion

These, then, are Erikson's major findings and explanations about the damages that were done to the people and the community of Buffalo Creek by the flood and its aftereffects. The psychological and social conditions that he observed were so grim that he concluded his book saying that he was uncertain whether recovery could ever occur. He feared that many of the survivors were regressing into behavioral patterns that he felt had historically hampered well-being in Appalachian mountain culture: "household disorder," "fatalism," and "dependency."

Near the end of his book, Erikson wrote that "this report ends at the very moment it might have begun, for the main task of restoration is still ahead."[154] In many ways, this book that you are now reading is my response to Erikson's call. It is an effort to estimate the extent and nature of what he calls the "restoration," to describe how it occurred, and to suggest the prospects for Buffalo Creek's people in the years ahead.

Some Comments About Erikson's Account

It would be hard to overstate the influence that Erikson's book has had on sociology in the United States, on social scientists worldwide who study disasters, and on the many people who have taken sociology courses which highlight Erikson's view of the Buffalo Creek disaster. His book is mentioned prominently, and almost always in glowing terms, in every major reference work I have ever read about disasters.[155] A strong case can be made that his book did more than any other to establish "Buffalo Creek, West Virginia" in the public conscience and lexicon of the United States. For example, as mentioned earlier in this chapter, Thomas Drabek published a massive inventory of the most important research done by social scientists concerning disasters. In it he repeatedly refers in reverential terms to Erikson's work and to the work of other experts we have just reviewed in this chapter:

> [T]he single natural disaster that has produced the most evidence of negative impacts occurred in Buffalo Creek, West Virginia in 1972. This flash flood had many atypical qualities. It was a horrifying event that struck a population already stressed, and there was evidence of culpability. These qualities were developed brilliantly by several scholars, most especially Lifton and Olson (1976), Erikson (1976), Titchener and Kapp (1976), and Gleser, Green, and Winget (1981, 1978).[156]

Of course, Erikson's astounding influence is the reason why we have spent so much effort here in reviewing his work. And so, before moving on, let us review some of the highlights of Erikson's account. Among its many other attributes, Erikson's writing style is so creative and compelling that he helps us understand the many different ways that survivors can suffer and have difficulty recovering for years on end. He also helps us to understand that well-intended reactions to disasters can be just as damaging to survivors as the immediate physical destruction inflicted by the disaster itself—possibly even worse. Of particular relevance (and inspiration) to this book, Erikson, more than any other author then and since then, describes how the flash flood impacted social factors, including social relations among survivors, their families, friends, and neighbors. He goes further than any other author in trying to explain how and why neighboring, community, communality, and social integration changed as a result. These are singularly important achievements.

Nonetheless, the many merits of Erikson's work should not force us to accept all of his findings and arguments without reservation. Recall that his account was influenced by an unspecified number of visits that he made to Buffalo Creek from early 1973 to August 1974. This means that he started his interviews and observations there about one year after the flood and completed most of his observations there less than three years after the flood, given that his book was published in 1976. It seems fair to say that Erikson did not witness the worst of the flood's immediate, short-term, secondary effects. The last event along Buffalo Creek that he mentions in his book is his visit there in August 1974 for Arnold & Porter's distribution to the plaintiffs of their shares of the $13.5 million that was won from Pittston Company and Buffalo Mining Company. There is no doubt that many of the plaintiffs were still struggling, even after they received their shares of the settlement money.

> That evening, most of the adult participants in the suit gathered in the local school auditorium to hear a few announcements and to mark the end of the long ordeal. People shuffled awkwardly into the hall to the sounds of country music being played by a band (provoking more than one complaint that the moment was too

solemn for such festivities) and then listened to a few speeches delivered from the stage, the speakers looking pale and remote in the glare of the television lights...The gathering was too subdued to count as a joyous occasion, although it was affectionate and warm. A stranger might very well have mistaken it for a graduation exercise.[157]

Poignant recollections like this support Erikson's belief that, as part of Arnold & Porter's legal team, he had easy access to many of the adult plaintiffs and that they were very friendly towards him. He reports that he collected short surveys from about 500 of the plaintiffs, possibly including juveniles. But he does not provide us with much information about the social characteristics of the plaintiffs he talked to in terms of age, education, gender, occupations, and the locations of the residences before and after the flood. Based on his anecdotes, he seems to have talked primarily with middle-aged men who were retired or disabled coal miners, much more than with women, juveniles, unmarried men and women in their twenties, and active coal miners. He does not tell us how many people he talked with in total, how many of them were nonplaintiffs, how many of them were officials for the coal companies, government agencies, and relief agencies, or how many of them—if any—were unresponsive, skeptical, contrarian, or antagonistic towards Arnold & Porter or towards some or all of the plaintiffs. Of course, it is possible that, as a consultant to Arnold & Porter, he did not feel that it was appropriate or necessary to talk with any people who belonged to "management" of the coal companies, although a considerable number, probably dozens, of the supervisors and managers for the coal companies lived along Buffalo Creek at the time of the flood, as mentioned in chapter 1. Going further along this line, he does not tell us how the nonplaintiffs reacted towards him when he approached them. Is it possible that he was recognized as a member of the Arnold & Porter team and treated with suspicion by some survivors? Could his role as a consultant to Arnold & Porter have limited his access to some nonplaintiffs? Could it have distorted the information he received from nonplaintiffs? Is it possible that significant numbers of nonplaintiffs were jealous of the plaintiffs, or bitter about them?

"Human nature" being as surprising and varied as it is, is it not likely that some nonplaintiffs would avoid members of the Arnold & Porter team, for any number of reasons? Perhaps they did not want to help the plaintiffs get "more than their fair share." Perhaps they were waiting for settlements of their own lawsuits and believed that the Arnold & Porter lawsuit might compete with theirs.

There also is the possibility, already mentioned several times in this chapter, that many of the plaintiffs whom Erikson, Lifton and Olson, and Green and Gleser's team relied upon were in the throes of the "blaming and bitching phase" of disaster recovery. Is it possible that many of these litigants were involved in a phenomenon such as a "litigation response syndrome"?[158] If so, the data that Erikson collected from these litigants could have been distorted by the litigation process they were involved in—possibly by Erikson's own official role as a consultant to Arnold & Porter. As a compassionate interviewer, Erikson might have been unwittingly influencing, distorting, biasing, and contaminating "his own data"—the data that he was trying to collect from the litigants in order to help their cause.[159] This would be ironic as well as unfortunate, given that Arnold & Porter, Erikson, and the other consultants were trying to help the litigants.

Furthermore, is it possible that Arnold & Porter, the Citizens' Committee, or other parties had intentionally or unintentionally "rehearsed" many of the plaintiffs before Erikson arrived at Buffalo Creek to begin his work? Perhaps the plaintiffs had learned and practiced common rhetoric, themes, and lines of testimony. And, perhaps the same thing was true of the consultants hired by Arnold & Porter.[160]

Regarding Erikson's general conclusions, we might wonder how and why he concluded that virtually everyone who survived the flood was psychologically impaired when he visited Buffalo Creek more than a year later. This conclusion seems exaggerated, if not erroneous, in light of the facts that Arnold & Porter's own psychiatric consultants did *not* find evidence of impairment in 34 percent of the male plaintiffs or in 30 percent of the female plaintiffs. Pittston's own psychiatric consultants found even less evidence of impairment. Seventy-one percent of the male litigants and 58 percent of the female litigants did *not* manifest symptoms of impairment. How, then, was Erikson able to leap so far from these empirical findings to the general conclusion that all *survivors—* everyone—were psychologically impaired in one way or the other?

Hardly less puzzling is Erikson's sweeping conclusion about the totality of the loss of social community at Buffalo Creek. Why did he go so far as to conclude that "everything" was destroyed along Buffalo Creek, including communality—the essence of every social community? After all, the title of his book asserts that this is exactly what happened there: *Everything in Its Path: Destruction of Community in the Buffalo Creek Flood.* Surely, this title, and so much of Erikson's interpretation of what he found at Buffalo Creek, exemplifies and advances the social destruction perspective. And yet, there is frequent evidence within Erikson's own account that some forms of social re-creation were occurring along Buffalo Creek even before Erikson arrived there. Hundreds of the survivors already had received thousands of dollars each in compensation through the state of West Virginia for their losses in property. Some of the survivors had formed the Citizens' Committee. That committee went out and hired Arnold & Porter. More than 200 survivors had joined in the lawsuit against the coal companies. Most of Buffalo Creek's children were back in schools, some of which were along Buffalo Creek. Most of the miners were back at work in the mines along Buffalo Creek. And, according to Erikson's own account, many, most, or perhaps nearly all of the survivors were able and willing to converse with Erikson about their experiences. Could Erikson have witnessed any of these things if the flood had destroyed "*everything* in its path"?

These are some of the questions that remain about specific aspects of Erikson's work, derived from what he does and does not address in his book. Let us keep them in mind as I report on my own research work along Buffalo Creek, many years later, in the chapters ahead.

SUMMING UP THE ACCOUNTS OF THE EXPERTS

In this chapter, we have reviewed very influential accounts by authors and teams of experts about the psychological and social consequences of the flash flood at Buffalo Creek. Four of the five accounts (by Nugent, Stern, Lifton and Olson, and Erikson) contend that the flood and its aftereffects were exceptionally overwhelming and destructive—so much so that virtually nothing had been left to build upon, let alone to be re-created, by the time that these accounts were published as highly acclaimed books. In many ways, these accounts not only fit within the social destruction perspective but they also exemplify it. They exemplify it with their claims about the flash flood becoming a "total disaster" where "everything" was irreparably destroyed. They more or less ignored the facts that the vast majority of Buffalo Creek's people survived, were still living near Buffalo Creek if not along it, and were still intending to move back as soon as they could. These authors also seemed to discount the fact that many of the survivors already had received considerable attention, care, and monetary compensation for the damages that the flood had inflicted upon them.

The other set of accounts, by Green, Gleser, and their various associates, did not contradict the other four accounts so much as it simply found evidence of considerable levels of recovery from psychological impairments by hundreds of survivors in 1981 and, even more so, in 1984 and 1987. Their accounts did not explain why these improvements occurred as they did. The authors seem to assume that the improvements were part of a natural healing process that gradually benefits many victims of traumatic events.

Still, none of the five accounts reported that, as a social community or as sixteen contiguous communities, Buffalo Creek was rebuilding, was recovering, or was being re-created in any way.

Was it too soon for any evidence of recovery to appear? Were the authors of these accounts overlooking something? If not, then what has happened to Buffalo Creek and its people since then? After all, our primary purpose is to describe and explain what has happened to the people of the Buffalo Creek Valley since the authors departed so many years ago—rather than to find fault with their reports. Chapters 3 to 5 are meant to serve this primary purpose.

ENDNOTES

1. Charles E. Fritz, "Disasters," in *International Encyclopedia of the Social Sciences*, vol. 4 (1968), 204.
2. Robert Jay Lifton and Eric Olson, "The Human Meaning of Total Disaster: The Buffalo Creek Experience," *Psychiatry* 39 (February 1976): 1. I inserted the word "syndrome" in parentheses because that word seems to have been omitted due to a typographical error in the copy of the article that I read. Throughout the remainder of the article, Lifton and Olson often use the phrase "survival syndrome" and assert that all residents of Buffalo Creek who survived the flood suffered at least some "manifestations" of the survivor syndrome: "death imprint and death anxiety," "death guilt," "psychic numbing," and "counterfeit nurturing and unfocused rage." Years before Lifton published this article about Buffalo Creek as a "total disaster," he had become famous for his book about the "survivor syndrome" in the victims of the atomic bomb destruction of Hiroshima, Japan, *Death in Life*. Lifton's article is considered at some length later in this chapter.
3. Thomas E. Drabek, *Human System Responses to Disaster: An Inventory of Sociological Findings* (New York: Springer-Verlag, 1986), 298.
4. On the history of disaster studies, see Charles E. Fritz, "Disasters," in vol. 4 of *International Encyclopedia of the Social Sciences*, ed. David Sills (New York: The Macmillan Company & The Free Press, 1968), 202–207; Allen H. Barton, *Communities in Disaster: A Sociological Analysis of Collective Stress Situations* (New York: Doubleday, 1969); Enrico L. Quarantelli and Russell R. Dynes, "Response to Social Crisis and Disaster," *Annual Review of Sociology* 3 (1977): 23–49; Thomas E. Drabek, *Human System Responses to Disaster: An Inventory of Sociological Findings* (New York: Springer-Verlag, 1986); Henry W. Fischer III, *Response to Disaster: Fact Versus Fiction and Its Perpetuation: The Sociology of Disaster*, 2nd ed (Lanham, MD: University Press of America, 1998); and Gary A. Kreps, "Disasters, Sociology of," in vol. 6 of *International Encyclopedia of the Social and Behavioral Sciences*, ed. Neil J. Smelser and Paul B. Baltes (Amsterdam: Elsevier, 2001), 3718–3721. These same sources, among others listed in the bibliography, are used extensively in my rendering of the research literature on the sociology and psychology of disasters.
5. See Douglas Brinkley, *The Great Deluge: Hurricane Katrina, New Orleans, and the Mississippi Gulf Coast* (New York: William Morrow/Harper-Collins

Publishers, 2006); and Susan Blackhall, *Tsunami* (Surrey, U.K.: TAJ Books, 2005).

6. Fritz, "Disasters," 204.

7. Ibid., 206. Readers are advised that Fritz's portrayal occurred in 1968 and was based on studies of the previous twenty years. Many of these studies, and Fritz's writing as well, were imbued by the "functionalist" theoretical perspective that was very popular after WWII among sociologists in the United States. The functionalist perspective generally portrays human societies and groups as normative, consensual, equilibrium-seeking systems that are able to adapt to almost any kind of problem or disruption, including disasters, given enough time. Since the 1970s, however, many reviews of research on disasters, including those of Drabek (1986) and Kreps (2001), have been more circumspect about the frequency of uniformly positive and quick recoveries from disasters by most communities and survivors who suffer them. A strong case can be made that this countermovement was based in part on the accounts of the Buffalo Creek disaster that are reviewed in this chapter, Erikson's account in particular.

8. Interestingly, Drabek rarely if ever mentions "neighbors" or "neighboring" in his analysis of hundreds of studies of disasters, although he systematically considers many other levels of social organization including families, communities, counties, societies, governments, businesses, and nonprofit organizations. This apparent "gap" in the research literature is one of the reasons my research has focused on "neighbors" and "neighboring" at Buffalo Creek, as well as on Buffalo Creek as more than one community.

9. Drabek, *Human System Responses to Disaster*, 179.

10. Ibid., 181.

11. Ibid., 256.

12. Ibid., 293–295.

13. Ibid., 295.

14. G. A. Kreps, "Disasters," 6:3720.

15. J. Steven Picou et al., "Disaster, Litigation, and the Corrosive Community," *Social Forces* 82, no. 4 (June 2004): 1495.

16. Elements of various sociological theories of societies and of disasters are integrated into these two perspectives. The social destruction perspective includes elements from conflict theory, social disorganization theory, social control theory, and some aspects of social/cultural evolutionary theory. The social re-creation perspective draws upon structural-functional theory, resource mobilization theory, and theories of collective behavior. On the theoretical bases of these perspectives, see various papers in

Gary A. Kreps, ed., *Social Structure and Disaster* (Newark: University of Delaware Press, 1989); especially Thomas E. Drabek, "Taxonomy and Disaster: Theoretical and Applied Issues," 317–329. See also Randall Collins, *Four Sociological Traditions* (Oxford and New York: Oxford University Press, 1994); Enrico L. Quarantelli, *What Is a Disaster: Perspectives on the Question* (London: Routledge, 1998); and Gerhard Lenski, *Ecological-Evolutionary Theory: Principles and Applications* (Boulder, CO: Paradigm Publishers, 2005).

17. *Encyclopedia Britannica*, vol. 18 (Chicago and London: Encyclopedia Britannica, Inc. William Benton Publisher, 1975), 54, 212–213.

18. This is how the site of Pompeii was described to me by *Wall Street Journal* columnist Deborah Ball in December 2006 after she visited the site.

19. On the concepts of "corrosive community" and "risk society," see William R. Freudenberg's "Contamination, Corrosion, and the Social Order: An Overview," *Current Sociology* 45 (1997): 19–40; "Risk and Recreancy: Weber, the Division of Labor, and the Rationality of Risk Perceptions," *Social Forces* 71 (1993): 909–932; and "The 'Risk Society' Reconsidered: Recreancy, the Division of Labor, and Risk to the Social Fabric," in *Risk in the Modern Age: Social Theory, Science and Environmental Decision-Making*, ed. by Maury J. Cohen (New York: St. Martin's Press, 2000), 107–120. See also Ulrich Beck, Risk Society: *Towards a New Modernity* (London: Sage Publications, 1992); and Picou et al., "Disaster, Litigation, and the Corrosive Community," 1493–1522.

20. Picou et al., "Disaster, Litigation, and the Corrosive Community," 1496.

21. Re-creation is especially likely to occur in areas of politically stable nations where the people, businesses, and other organizations have the means and the inclination to risk successive disasters that are believed to be far more "natural" than "technological" or "human-caused." For these reasons, we can expect extensive re-creation to occur for many of the communities that were devastated by the Indonesian tsunami in 2004, Hurricane Katrina in 2005, and Hurricane Wilma in 2005.

22. In addition to these five very influential accounts, more than a dozen scholarly articles were published about some of the social and psychological aspects of the disaster, most of them in the first few years after it occurred. Most of these scholarly articles address the kinds of psychological impairments that survivors suffered or were expected to suffer in the years immediately after the disaster. Taken as a whole, these articles are consistent with the accounts by Nugent, Stern, Lifton, and Erikson as to how exceptional and utterly devastating the flash flood was to the well-being of the people of

Buffalo Creek. See, for example, J. Church, "The Buffalo Creek Disaster: Extent and Range of Emotional and/or Behavioral Problems," *Omega* 5 (1974): 61–63; "Disaster at Buffalo Creek," symposium presented at the meeting of the American Psychiatric Association, Anaheim, CA, 1975, proceedings published in the *American Journal of Psychiatry* (March 1976): 133; C. J. Newman, "Children of Disaster: Clinical Observations at Buffalo Creek," *American Journal of Psychiatry* (1976): 133, 306–312; and James L. Titchener and Frederic T. Kapp, "Family and Character Change at Buffalo Creek," *American Journal of Psychiatry* (1976): 133, 295–299.

23. Thomas Nugent, *Death at Buffalo Creek*, 31.
24. Ibid., 20.
25. Ibid., 22.
26. Ibid., 37. Rather curiously, after Nugent mentions this information, he claims that the 5,000 residents of Buffalo Creek slept through the night of February 26: "And so the 5,000 people of Buffalo Creek Hollow slept on through the rainy night" (31). Readers also should note that Nugent's estimates of population sizes of various coal camps do not always agree with the "official" figures that are presented in chapter 3.
27. Ibid., 60.
28. Ibid., 62, 72, 75.
29. Ibid., 75–76.
30. Ibid., 76.
31. Ibid., 83.
32. Ibid., 84.
33. Ibid., 85.
34. Ibid., 87.
35. Ibid., 99.
36. Ibid., 102.
37. Ibid., 104.
38. Ibid., 113.
39. Ibid., 105.
40. Ibid., 107, 115.
41. Ibid.
42. Ibid., 122.
43. Ibid., 123.
44. Ibid., 124.
45. Ibid., 144.
46. Nugent does not tell us how many homes were undamaged. Based on my six research trips to Buffalo Creek, I estimate that at least one hundred houses,

yards, and commercial properties were not touched by any floodwater. Many of these properties were (and are) on steep hillsides that are at least forty feet above the banks of Buffalo Creek.

47. Ibid., 146.
48. Estimations of the psychological and social damages are presented in the following sections of this chapter.
49. Chapters 3 and 4 present testimonies to this effect from people I interviewed along Buffalo Creek.
50. Ibid., 113.
51. Ibid., 147.
52. Gerald Stern, *The Buffalo Creek Disaster*, 115.
53. See chapter 1, endnote 21, regarding edition information for the book, *The Buffalo Creek Disaster*.
54. Stern, *The Buffalo Creek Disaster*, 28.
55. I could not find in Stern's book very much information about how he and Arnold & Porter enrolled, selected, or vetted the original pool of about 200 plaintiffs or about who they were, other than that they were survivors. He does not report on how many of them had already received some compensation from Pittston for their damages, other than to say that many of them "had not yet recovered anything for their own property losses because they had sued Pittston rather than settle" (206). Stern also wrote that, of the first 200 plaintiffs, "most of the people seeking our help had lost their homes or property, but no members of their family. In general, those who had lost family either had gone to lawyers in Logan County or were still too upset to even consider talking to lawyers about their claims" (22). Stern also indicated that most of the plaintiffs were not in the floodwater, and they did not see anyone die (122). As noted later in this chapter, almost two years after the flood, Arnold & Porter added another 200 plaintiffs to the lawsuit. Many of these new plaintiffs "had already settled with Pittston for their property losses or for wrongful deaths of members of their families but we felt they still could sue for their own psychic impairment." This is about all we know about the plaintiff pool from Stern. Based on this limited amount of information from Stern, it seems that the majority of the original 200 plaintiffs he represented were neither the most damaged nor the least damaged of the survivors of the flood. Most of them had lost their homes or property, but they had not lost family members, they had not been in floodwaters, and they had not seen anyone die. While it is not possible to determine whether these same attributes were true of the 4,000 survivors as a whole, it seems likely that they were common attributes of many of the nonplaintiff survivors

in that most of these survivors would not have been among the estimated 300–400 survivors who lost members of their families of origin in the flood.

56. Stern, *The Buffalo Creek Disaster*, 41.
57. Ibid.
58. Ibid., ix–x, 46.
59. Ibid., 47.
60. Ibid., 49.
61. Ibid., 65.
62. Ibid., 232.
63. Ibid., 21.
64. Ibid., 67.
65. Ibid., 68.
66. Ibid., 70.
67. Ibid., 230, 233. While it might be considered to be a minor discrepancy, notice that Stern's conclusion here, "no one...escaped emotional and mental distress," is not obviously consistent with the fact that "nine plaintiffs demonstrated no degree of psychic impairment," unless it was also established that these nine plaintiffs were distressed without being impaired. Stern does not clarify this matter.
68. Ibid., 112.
69. Ibid., 115. Readers might notice here, and throughout this chapter, that Stern, Lifton, and Erikson use very similar words, phrases, and arguments in reaching some of their conclusions, including the conclusion that the flood directly or indirectly destroyed "everything."
70. Ibid., 237.
71. Ibid., 122.
72. Ibid., 147.
73. Ibid., 211.
74. Ibid., 115, 206.
75. Ibid., 116.
76. Governor Arch Moore settled West Virginia's lawsuit against Pittston Company for $1 million just before he left office in 1977, see "Buffalo Creek Report," http://www.marshall.edu/speccoll/VirtualMuseum/Buffalo Creek/HTML/depositions.html. This I-net site is maintained by the Special Collections Department of the Marshall University Library system. It includes copies of depositions of several of the survivors of the flood, a copy of the report of the governor's investigatory commission on the flood, and a chronology of mining activity since 1947 in the Buffalo Creek area.

77. Stern, *The Buffalo Creek Disaster*, 299.
78. Ibid., 302.
79. Ibid.
80. Ibid.
81. Ibid., 28, 58, 70.
82. Ibid., 230. Consider that a growing body of research published in the past twenty years has found that survivors can suffer additional stress because of the interviews, diagnoses, treatments, and depositions they participate in after a disaster. Increasingly, these kinds of stresses are referred to by experts in the research literature as "litigation response syndrome," "litigation stress," "forensic stress disorder," and "survivor stress syndrome." In fact, J. Steven Picou, Brent K. Marshall, and Duane A. Gill conducted research in the village of Cordova, Alaska, three years after the Exxon Valdez oil spill in 1989, in order to determine which factors interfered the most with the recovery process for Cordova's residents. In a peer-refereed article titled "Disaster, Litigation, and the Corrosive Community," *Social Forces* 82 (June 2004): 1493–1522, the authors found that residents who were participating in litigation against Exxon had considerably higher levels of stress than those who were not doing so, even when many other factors were taken into consideration (i.e., "statistically controlled") including occupation as a commercial fisherman, marital status, and gender. The authors concluded that "litigation is a critical characteristic of technological disasters that precludes timely community recovery and promotes chronic social and psychological problems and impacts how well the inhabitants had recovered" (1519).
83. Ibid., 233. The accounts of Green and Gleser, which follow, indicate that Stern is mistaken in claiming that "our psychiatrists individually interviewed 613 plaintiffs." What actually happened, according to Green and Gleser, is that the psychiatrists hired by Arnold & Porter derived their determinations of "psychic impairment from the clinical notes and codings of social workers, psychologists, and graduate students who were sent to Buffalo Creek to interview the plaintiffs." Bonnie L. Green et al., "Traumatic Events over the Life Span: Survivors of the Buffalo Creek Disaster," in *Clinical Disorders and Stressful Life Events*, ed. Thomas W. Miller (Madison, CN: International Universities Press, Inc., 1997), chapter 13. *See esp.* p. 289.
84. Stern, *The Buffalo Creek Disaster*, 115. Considerable evidence is presented throughout this book that questions whether Buffalo Creek ever constituted a *single* community or should have been referred to as such by social scientists. For example, chapter 4 presents evidence that residents in different

coal camps identified more strongly with their own coal camp than with Buffalo Creek as a whole. Some of the interviewees even testify that, before the flood, they did not trust residents of any coal camp other than their own coal camp. They were alarmed to find residents of other coal camps in the HUD trailer camps to which they relocated after the flood. Animosities and "turf battles" occurred in the HUD camps among residents of different coal camps as to which coal camp had exclusive rights to a particular area of a HUD camp.

85. Green et al., "Traumatic Events."
86. These works include: Goldine C. Gleser et al., *Prolonged Psychological Effects of Disaster: A Study of Buffalo Creek* (New York: Academic Press, 1981); Bonnie L. Green et al., "Buffalo Creek Survivors in the Second Decade: Stability of Stress Symptoms," *American Journal of Orthopsychiatry* 60:43–54; Bonnie L. Green et al., "Children and Disaster: Age, Gender, and Parental Effects on PTSD Symptoms," *Journal of the American Academy of Child Adolescent Psychiatry* 30:945–951; Bonnie L. Green et al., "Children of Disaster in the Second Decade: A 17-Year Follow-Up of Buffalo Creek Survivors," *Journal of the American Academy of Child Adolescent Psychiatry* 33:71–79; Bonnie L. Green et al., "Buffalo Creek Survivors in the Second Decade: Comparison with Unexposed and Non-litigant Groups," *Journal of Applied Social Psychology* 20:1033–1050; Bonnie L. Green et al., "Age Related Reactions to the Buffalo Creek Dam Collapse: Second Decade Effects," *Aging and Posttraumatic Stress Disorder*, ed. P. Ruskin and J. Talbott (Washington DC: American Psychiatric Press, 1996); and Green et al., "Traumatic Events."
87. Green et al., "Traumatic Events," 289. All quotations in this section about Green's reports are from this 1997 report, unless noted otherwise.
88. Ronald C. Kessler et al., "Lifetime and 12-Month Prevalence of DSM-III-R Psychiatric Disorders in the United States: Results From the National Comorbidity Survey," *Archives of General Psychiatry* 51 (January 1994): 8–19; Ronald C. Kessler et al., "Posttraumatic Stress Disorder in the National Comorbidity Survey," *Archives of General Psychiatry* 52 (December 1995): 1048–1060; Richard A. Kurtz and H. Paul Chalfant, *The Sociology of Medicine and Illness*, 2nd ed. (Needham Heights, MA: Allyn and Bacon, 1991), 33–39.

It is worth noting that Kessler and his many collaborators conducted an often cited study of the prevalence of psychiatric disorders in the United States by surveying a national, stratified, multistage probability sample of 8,098 noninstitutionalized persons aged fifteen to fifty-four in the early 1990s. Kessler's team reported that "nearly 50% of the respondents reported at least one lifetime disorder, and close to 30% reported at least one 12-month disorder," and that "most disorders decreased with age and with higher socioeconomic status" (1994: 8). The most prevalent specific disorders were depression (17 percent lifetime, 10 percent in the past 12 months) and alcohol dependence (14 percent lifetime, 7 percent in the past 12 months). In a second study, Kessler and a team of collaborators surveyed post-traumatic stress disorder (PTSD) in a representative sample of 5,877 noninstitutionalized persons aged fifteen to fifty-four. This study is especially relevant to our study of Buffalo Creek because many psychologists accept the guidelines of the current Diagnostic and Statistical Manual of the American Psychological Association (DSM-III-R) regarding the nature and symptoms of PTSD. Persons are considered to have suffered trauma if they respond affirmatively to the following question with any of the following items:

Did Any of These Events Ever Happen to You?

1. You had direct combat experience in a war.
2. You were involved in a life-threatening accident.
3. You were involved in a fire, flood, or natural disaster.
4. You witnessed someone being badly injured or killed.
   ....
11. Other (any other terrible experience that most people never go through).
12. You suffered a great shock because one of the events on this list happened to someone close to you.

Surely we would not be surprised to learn that most people, if not all people, who witnessed or experienced the flood at Buffalo Creek on February 26, 1972, responded affirmatively to at least one of the items in this question in the days immediately after the flood. The items are so inclusive that almost any adult can believe that he or she has had "a terrible experience that most people never go through." Possibly, they would still respond affirmatively to these items more than thirty-five years later, given that the question is so broadly worded. It asks if any of the events *ever* happened to you (or to someone close to you)! In doing so, its proponents assume that these kinds of events are inherently "traumatic" to everyone and anyone who experiences them.

As a professional social scientist, I feel obliged to state that I find these assumptions to be dubious, if not invalid. As a former Marine Corps infantry officer who was wounded in an ambush by Viet Cong forces in Viet Nam, February 11, 1966, I avow that the experience did not traumatize me in any way. Quite the opposite. It provided added value to my military service and it enabled me to be a better officer and leader in future combat operations. However, I will also admit that, had I been severely and permanently paralyzed or handicapped by the experience, probably I would have become psychologically impaired. Even then, the psychological impairment probably would have resulted from the physical paralysis and handicap more than from the combat experience itself.

This personal testimony is provided because I feel obliged to call into question the all too casual assumption that is made by many researchers and writers: that anyone who experiences a disaster like the flood at Buffalo Creek in 1972, or combat in war, necessarily is traumatized by it. In chapter 4 of this book, I present several cases of people who experienced the Buffalo Creek flood without being traumatized by it even on the day that it occurred. And earlier in this chapter (chapter 2), we read about one survivor who testified that he went back to bed and went to sleep after he watched the flood surround his house. He gave no evidence or claim of being traumatized in any way by that experience.

I believe that this is one of the many important corrections that this work can contribute to our deeper understanding of disasters and other events that can be tragic. That they are tragic does not necessarily mean that they are traumatic to everyone who experiences them.

89. Of course, it is possible that the men and women of Buffalo Creek generally had these rather stereotypical symptoms even before the flood in 1972. These are rather typical gender differences in manifestations of psychological impairment in the U.S. population.

90. Green et al., "Traumatic Events," 291. It might be worth pondering whether being excluded from the litigation process, or deciding not to participate in it, might have increased the levels of impairments among the forty exposed nonlitigants to nearly the same level as the litigants. Also consider the possibility that the simple fact that the litigation was underway and was public knowledge might have increased impairments in *both* the litigants and nonlitigants. This might have been the case if, per chance, the forty nonlitigants did not want the burden and worry of being part of a "court fight," and yet they also worried about losing out on the reparations that might be forthcoming or about being treated as though they did not support the litigants.

91. Ibid., 293. This statement about alcohol abuse being low to begin with is at odds with portrayals of Appalachian coal-camp subcultures by respected authors including Harry M. Caudill and Jack E. Weller. It also is at odds with Erikson's frequent assertions that alcohol abuse might have been high before the flood and that it might have increased dramatically because of the flood. Of course, it is possible that increases in alcohol abuse after the flood were not qualitatively severe enough to constitute psychologically pathological alcohol abuse. It is also possible that increases in alcohol abuse attributable to the flood had subsided by 1986. Some of the case data that I present in part 2 of this book indicate that postflood alcohol abuse was severe enough that it led to a number of marital separations and divorces.

92. Ibid., 299. Readers might ponder Green's finding that substance abuse and suicidal ideation were not present in the child litigants of 1974, only two years after the flood. While substance abuse and suicidal ideation tend to be rare in the general population until children reach adolescence, is it possible that these impairments could have been considerably more frequent than reported at Buffalo Creek after the flood because parents and guardians were too distracted and impaired to detect these problems in their children and because parents were too embarrassed to disclose such intimate and disturbing information?

93. Green et al., "Traumatic Events," 294.

94. Ibid. Green's team clearly recognized that the plaintiff sample does not represent the "community at large." It also stated that adults in the fourteen-year follow-up and the children in the seventeen-year follow-up "had suffered significantly less personal loss through death in the disaster than those who refused to participate" (292). When we read about the findings of Green's team, we should keep in mind that the 588 plaintiffs who participated in the 1974 study probably suffered more damages in the flood, and more psychological impairments as a consequence, than most of the more than 4,000 other survivors of the flood who did not become plaintiffs. We might speculate that, if this were not the case, most of the nonplaintiffs probably would have joined the lawsuit as plaintiffs in order to seek additional reparations beyond the reparations that had already been mandated by the state of West Virginia. On the other hand, we might also assume that the plaintiff sample in the fourteen-year and seventeen-year follow-up studies probably suffered less damage in the flood and less impairment consequently than did the plaintiff sample in 1974. If nothing else, the plaintiffs of 1974 who suffered the most damage in the flood, and the most impairment consequentially, probably were the ones who were most likely to die, move away

from Buffalo Creek, and be unable or unwilling to participate in the follow-up studies.

95. See the cases of Sam Chance and Lonnie McCain in chapter 4. In the absence of compelling evidence to the contrary, I believe that Arnold & Porter, and the many consultants whom they hired, did a very credible job of gathering depositions, other legal testimony, clinical data, and survey data from the litigants without directly causing undue stress to most or to all of the litigants.

96. Unfortunately, Green and Gleser do not tell us what percentage of their interviewees remained in the Buffalo Creek Valley or the percentages who returned to the valley during the study period. Nor do they tell us whether interviewees who remained in or returned to the valley had less success in recovering from psychological impairments than did interviewees who moved away permanently.

97. Lifton and Olson, "The Human Meaning of Total Disaster," 12.

98. Ibid.

99. Lifton and Olson's citation here is to Dwight Harshbarger, "Draft of Research and Intervention Based on the Buffalo Creek Disaster," 10. Noting the dates of citations to Harshbarger, Lifton and Olson, and Erikson, it is possible that Harshbarger was the first of these experts to claim that community structure was destroyed by the flood at Buffalo Creek and that the flood produced and essentially constituted a "total disaster." Of course, we might question how Harshbarger, writing in 1972, could claim that it was a "total loss" disaster in terms of "lives, properties, and the basic structure and social fabric of communities themselves," when more than 4,800 of the 4,950 residents of Buffalo Creek survived the flood, at least 1,000 of them were not forced to leave their homes even for one night, and several of the larger coal camps—including Kistler and Accoville, at the lower end of the valley—were relatively undamaged by the floodwaters when compared to Three Forks, Lorado, and Lundale.

100. Lifton and Olson, "The Human Meaning of Total Disaster," 1.

101. Ibid.

102. Ibid. Chapter 6 discusses the adequacy of research methods used by the experts who have studied Buffalo Creek, including Lifton and Olson's. However, at this point, let me call attention to the fact that this quotation from Lifton and Olson's article presents the only information in his article about his research methods. Readers are left to wonder about questions such as these: How many of the five trips included Lifton, rather than just his research assistant, Eric Olson? Of the more than 4,800 survivors of the flood, why did Lifton and Olson only interview twenty-two

of them—and how did they select these twenty-two interviewees? Whom did they represent? Some of the litigants? All of the litigants? The more than 4,000 nonlitigants as well as the litigants? Since Arnold & Porter had hired Lifton and the other consultants, why did Lifton and the other consultants not interview far larger (and more representative?) numbers of survivors and explain to us the selection process? Were all of these interviewees litigants who had hired Arnold & Porter to represent them? Were the interviewees the survivors who were most impaired? The least impaired? The most willing to be interviewed? Were any of them hospitalized at the time? Why did Lifton and Olson only talk with "several ministers and volunteer workers in the area"? Why did they not interview these ministers and social workers rather than just "talk with" them? What did they talk about? Why did Lifton not interview many other people in many other occupations who had direct, lasting, and relevant contact with the survivors—such as health care workers, nurses, physicians, policemen and fireman, and "first responders?" And how about managers and employees of Buffalo Mining Company and Pittston Company? Of course, it would be worth knowing more about the nature and content of the "interviews." How and where were they conducted? What questions were asked, if any? How did Lifton and the other consultants avoid biasing the questions? How were the responses recorded? While all research methods and reports have limitations, Lifton and Olson's report would be much more valuable if it had answered more of these questions.

Furthermore, of course it would be worth knowing more about the "extensive documentation" by the other consultants that Lifton and Olson "read through." What was the "documentation"? When did Lifton read through it—before, after, or during his own interviews with the twenty-two survivors? How did Lifton guard against some of the many kinds of biases that can dog research methods in the social and behavioral sciences, including "groupthink"—a distortion that was popularized by one of Lifton's own colleagues at Yale, Irving Janis, and whose contribution to the Buffalo Creek studies has been acknowledged by some of the other consultants, including Kai Erikson in his introduction to his own book, *Everything in Its Path: Destruction of Community at Buffalo Creek.*

103. Ibid., 1–7.

104. Ibid., 8, 12. One of the more intriguing passages in Lifton and Olson's article is this one:

It is felt not only that one's natural surroundings no longer sustain life but that they have been permanently impaired by the disaster. One of the plaintiffs spoke of 'snakes coming back now, many more snakes than before the flood, black snakes and rattlers.' Many other survivors had similar impressions, and a number have observed that unusual matings between different species of poisonous snakes have been taking place. (11)

105. Ibid., 1, 12. Readers might note that these findings by Lifton and Olson are not consistent with the findings of the Green and Gleser team that are recounted in the previous section of this chapter.
106. Ibid., 14–15.
107. Ibid., 17.
108. Fischer, *Response to Disaster*, 42.
109. Erikson, *Everything in Its Path*, 136.
110. Unless stated otherwise, all references to Erikson's work are based on his original hardback edition of *Everything in Its Path*, and on conversations that I have had with him over the years, for which I am most grateful. I also spent a few days with him along Buffalo Creek during the thirtieth anniversary memorial ceremonies in February 2002.
111. As mentioned previously, one of Erikson's colleagues at Yale, psychologist Robert Jay Lifton, already had joined the Arnold & Porter team as an expert consultant regarding psychological damages. Lifton recommended Erikson to Gerald Stern.
112. For a fascinating account of these social and intellectual linkages by Kai Erikson's sister, see Sue Erikson Bloland, *In the Shadow of Fame: A Memoir of the Daughter of Erik H. Erikson* (New York: Viking, 2005), 62–77.
113. Erikson, *Everything in Its Path*, 14.
114. Ibid., 136.
115. Ibid. It is worth noting that Erikson wrote that he conversed with many survivors along Buffalo Creek, not just those who had become plaintiffs in the Arnold & Porter case. Usually he uses the term "survivor" rather than the terms "plaintiff" or "litigant" when he refers to his respondents. Often he generalizes his findings to include all or almost all of the survivors at Buffalo Creek—not just the plaintiffs. Erikson reported that he found a remarkable uniformity of complaints among the survivors regarding the psychological and social impairments that they were suffering more than a year after the flood. He says that these complaints constitute a "syndrome," which he defines as "a group of symptoms that occur together and affect whole populations of individuals similarly" (254).

Furthermore, Erikson occasionally uses the concept of "disaster syndrome," which he attributes to Anthony F. C. Wallace, the author of an influential book on disasters, *Tornado in Worcester*. The major "symptoms" of the "disaster syndrome" include "numbness," "apathy," "insomnia," and "depression" (164, 198, 199, 202, 203, 273, 283).

116. Ibid., 136.
117. Ibid., 137.
118. Ibid., 138.
119. Ibid., 140.
120. Ibid., 142.
121. Ibid., 145.
122. Ibid., 146–147.
123. Ibid., 145, 146, 203.
124. Ibid., 187.
125. Ibid., 188.
126. Ibid., 190.
127. Ibid.
128. Ibid., 188. See the glossary for definitions of "neighbor" and other key terms. Let me suggest that the interviewees whose quotations are presented here were trying to tell Erikson how "good neighbors" typically behaved along Buffalo Creek and they were avowing that many of their neighbors were "good neighbors" before the flood.
129. Ibid, 190.
130. Erikson's assertions are intriguing about how fences are barriers to neighboring. However, as with so many of his intriguing assertions, it is not clear how he determined that few fences existed along Buffalo Creek before the flood. I was so intrigued by this prospect that I attempted to determine the percentages of dwellings in four of the former coal camps of Buffalo Creek (Lorado, Lundale, Braeholm, and Kistler), Elk Creek, and St. John, Washington, that have "barrier" fences (i.e., fences that are so tall, long, and dense as to preclude neighbors being able to converse with each other across them. While my methods were rather rudimentary, I tentatively determined that "conversation-barrier fences" are infrequent (i.e., less than 10 percent of the dwellings have them) in all three locales. However, fences that mark boundaries and that can restrain small pets and small children are somewhat more common (i.e., about 40 percent of the dwellings have them) along those areas of Buffalo Creek's four former coal camps, where the dwellings are close to Highway 16, than they were at Elk Creek or at St. John, Washington. From these observations, I generally conclude that "conversation-barrier fences" are not more common between and among neighbors along Buffalo Creek than they are

at Elk Creek or St. John, Washington. Buffalo Creek's residents are not less neighborly in this rather symbolic regard than are the residents of the other places.

I also noticed that very few dwellings at Buffalo Creek have fences that separate the dwellings from the creek itself. Possibly, the absence of fences of this nature suggests that very few people who own property along the creek are afraid of having people fall into the creek from their property. This speculation on my part is in keeping with my more general finding that, except in two cases that are presented in chapter 4, residents of Buffalo Creek whom I encountered or observed did *not* seem to be afraid of the creek itself. Rather, most residents seemed to ignore the creek, except for young boys who would throw rocks into the creek, fish in it, or float objects in it, and a preacher who sometimes baptized converts in it.

131. Erikson, *Everything in Its Path*, 194.
132. Ibid., 196.
133. Ibid., 149.
134. Ibid., 150.
135. Ibid., 152.
136. Ibid., 153. I learned through my interviews with survivors that some of them received one-time compensation from the West Virginia Mine Workers Assurance Fund for the loss of some of their personal property in the flood. Compensation varied from household to household, but never exceeded the maximum specified by law, $8,000. Many survivors felt that this amount of compensation was woefully inadequate. Additionally, I learned that some of the survivors were shocked and dismayed by what they believed to be negligent and self-interested responses to their plight by Pittston Company and Buffalo Mining Company. They said that officials did not visit the disaster site, nor offer condolences or any aid, in the days immediately after the flood. Some of the mines continued to operate in limited ways, digging and piling up coal reserves by using their own sources of power. They could not ship out the coal until the rail lines were repaired. Some survivors also felt that first priority in the cleanup efforts by government agencies went to the needs of Buffalo Mining Company for new rail lines and gondola cars, rather than to the miners and their families.
137. Ibid., 153–154.
138. All of the material in this section is derived from chapter 7 of *Everything in Its Path*, unless noted otherwise.
139. Erikson, *Everything in Its Path*, 156.

140. Ibid., 157. Readers might notice that Erikson's descriptions of the findings of the psychiatric teams on both "sides" of the legal case differ somewhat from the descriptions of the Gleser and Green team in the preceding section of this chapter. For example, contrary to Erikson's assertion that psychiatrists for both sides found about the same incidence of psychological impairment in the plaintiffs, Gleser and Green reported that the psychiatrist for Pittston Company found that the incidence of disorder was much lower (i.e., 29 percent for the male plaintiffs and 42 percent for the female plaintiffs) than the incidence of disorder that was reported by the psychiatrists for Arnold & Porter (i.e., 66 percent for male plaintiffs and 70 percent for the female plaintiffs). By the way, by obverting these statistics we realize that both the psychiatrists for the prosecution and for the defense found that at least 29 percent of the plaintiffs were not psychologically impaired.
141. Ibid., 159.
142. Ibid.
143. Ibid., 190.
144. Ibid., 197. I am not at liberty to report any more information about Erikson's effort to survey 500 persons.
145. Ibid., 196.
146. Ibid., 203.
147. Ibid. In his book, Erikson at times seems to waffle on whether these social problems actually increased appreciably, in an objective sense, or whether they just seemed to increase in the minds of survivors. In several conversations that I had with him over the years, he seemed to back away from the observation that these social problems actually had increased, in favor of the position that survivors only came to believe that they had increased. I spent a considerable amount of time, without success, trying to collect documentary evidence that would allow me to determine whether these social problems actually had increased among survivors and in the Buffalo Creek Valley after the flash flood. I strongly encourage other researchers to look into this matter.
148. Ibid., 204.
149. Ibid., 206.
150. Ibid., 205.
151. Ibid., 205–206.
152. Ibid., 220.
153. Ibid., 208–209.
154. Ibid., 249, 251.

155. On the other hand, there has been an undercurrent of criticism of Erikson's work about Buffalo Creek, although the criticism has been overlooked for the most part. For instance, in 1978 a book review by noted sociologist Russell R. Dynes questioned Erikson's research methods, particularly his reliance upon depositions taken from plaintiffs by the law firm that hired him to testify on their behalf. Another book review published in 1978, by Dwight Billings and Sally Maggard of the Appalachian Center at the University of Kentucky, commended Erikson's ability to describe the terrible ways the victims suffered for many months after the flash flood. However, the authors rejected as "absurd" what they believed to be his reliance upon long-standing stereotypes of Appalachia and its people as ignorant, backward isolationists who are prone to deviance, welfare dependency, and manipulation by outsiders.

Far more scathing in its condemnation of Erikson's work (and of Erikson himself, for that matter) is an article by Lynda Ann Ewen and Julia A. Lewis that was published in *Appalachian Journal* in 1999. Like so many specialists in "Appalachian studies," they seem to believe that they are the only ones who can write anything valid about Appalachia and its people. They complained that the mindset and culture of the people of Buffalo Creek cannot possibly be understood by someone like Erikson—a Yale University professor they dismiss as an elitist White Anglo-Saxon Protestant. They bitterly denounced his research methods and his portrayals of Buffalo Creek as being contaminated by his reliance on Arnold & Porter's legal depositions and on a theoretical perspective that they deemed to be utterly obsolete—functionalism.

156. Drabek, *Human System Responses to Disaster*, 256.

157. Erikson, *Everything in Its Path*, 248.

158. Picou et al., "Disaster, Litigation, and the Corrosive Community," 1520; and Paul R. Lees-Haley, "Litigation Response Syndrome," *American Journal of Forensic Psychology* 6 (1988): 3–12.

159. Distortions of this type have long been recognized, and feared, in scientific research in which researchers are in direct, personal contact with the people whom they are studying, or the researchers are able to manipulate the environment in which the research occurs. Errors of this type sometimes are referred to as "obtrusive measures," "researcher reactive error," "research effect," "research distortion," and the "Hawthorne effect," among other names. See Webb et al., *Unobtrusive Measures: Nonreactive Measures in the Social Sciences* (Chicago: Rand McNally, 1966); Steven J. Taylor and Robert Bogdan, *Introduction to Qualitative Research*

Methods: The Search for Meanings, 2nd ed. (New York: John Wiley & Sons, 1984), 117–118; Earl Babbie, *The Basics of Social Research* (Belmont, CA: Wadsworth Publishing Company, 1999), 176, 214; see also Robert I. Levy and Douglas W. Holland, "Person-Centered Interviewing and Observation," chap. 10 in *Handbook of Methods in Cultural Anthropology*, ed. H. Russell Bernard (Walnut Creek, CA: AltaMira Press, 1998), 346–351. While solutions to these problems are not easy, there are a number of techniques for reducing this kind of error and for measuring it. One way to reduce this kind of error is to carefully train and use several different interviewers in collecting both observational and interview data. For example, at Buffalo Creek, rather than just asking litigants if they have trouble sleeping when it rains, members of the research team can become customers in cafes and coffee shops in the morning. As customers, they can observe, as unobtrusively as possible, whether litigants, compared to nonlitigants, are much more likely to drink a lot more coffee, to complain about sleeplessness, and to complain about the rain, the mornings after nights of heavy rains. Incidentally, I tried to employ this technique in my own research at Buffalo Creek on a number of mornings and in several cafes. I did not observe obvious differences between several former litigants and several former nonlitigants in this regard (several of whom I interviewed days later). For that matter, I did not detect any other differences between former litigants and nonlitigants that I could attribute to their former litigatory status, although my observational techniques were very rudimentary and my study of Buffalo Creek was not intended to determine whether former litigants behaved differently than nonlitigants more than thirty years after the flood. However, it seems as though, more than thirty years earlier, the research that Erikson and the other experts conducted at Buffalo Creek would have been more valuable if these kinds of concerns had been addressed more thoroughly.

160. Having mentioned these possibilities, I should say that, as indicated in chapter 4, I did not focus on these kinds of issues when I conducted my own research along Buffalo Creek. I also should say that only a few of the dozens of people I interviewed at length (including "Sam Chance") mentioned that they believed that litigants had been more or less "coached" to provide responses that would favor their side in the lawsuit. None of these people revealed to me highly credible and verifiable evidence that "coaching" took place. Nor did I try to get them to do so.

PART II

SINCE THEN

CHAPTER 3

REBUILDING THE INFRASTRUCTURE SINCE 1972[1]

[T]he fabric of community life had been irreparably destroyed.
—Robert Jay Lifton and Eric Olson,
"The Human Meaning of Total Disaster:
The Buffalo Creek Experience," 1976

Buffalo Valley residents have the will to come back strong. If we all work together in the spirit of friendship and cooperation, Buffalo Valley will be rebuilt more beautiful than before with a better life for everyone.

—Arch A. Moore, Jr.
Governor, State of West Virginia,
Buffalo Valley Redevelopment Plan,[2] July 1973

The Governor and the State did a good job...it took some time, of course. The Federal government helped a lot also, with money and help from agencies like that HUD agency that came in with the trailers and all that.

—A respected minister and longtime resident
of Buffalo Creek, 2005

So it's taken years, and it hasn't been straight progress all of the way. But I'd say it's kind of a miracle today, when you think about it. To see it rebuilt like it is now up in the Valley with all the houses and manufactured homes in different colors, styles, and all that. They got good roads and bridges, too. Some people from the flood are still coming back here to retire.

—A respected businessman in Man, 2006

KEY QUESTIONS

- What does Buffalo Creek look like today?
- To what extent has the infrastructure been rebuilt? Modernized?
- How was it rebuilt, by whom, and at what cost?
- How involved were the flood's survivors in the rebuilding process?
- How have they responded to it? Do they appreciate it?
- Has the rebuilding been done in such ways as to enhance social relations, social integration of the community, communality, and the social well-being of the residents?

These are the primary questions that are addressed in this chapter. First, I summarize the major efforts taken by citizens groups, government agencies, and private organizations to plan for rebuilding infrastructure to support the people who remained in residences along Buffalo Creek and people who intended to move back whenever possible. We give considerable attention to an informed and ambitious document, the *Buffalo Valley Redevelopment Plan*, that served for a number of years as a blueprint for much of the rebuilding that was funded by federal and state agencies. Second, we describe rebuilding efforts that fulfilled the recommendations in this plan and the rebuilding efforts that occurred outside of this plan and, at times, despite the plan. We also consider some of the promises that have not yet been fulfilled as yet, unfortunately. Fortunately, some of these promises still can be fulfilled—and they would be very beneficial to the people of southwestern West Virginia. Along the way, we describe how ordinary citizens and community leaders regard the rebuilding that has and has not occurred.

Then

At the time of the flood, Buffalo Creek's sixteen coal camps were estimated to have about 4,950 residents in 1,800 dwellings.[3] As shown in table 3.1, there was considerable variation in the population size, buildings, and services available in each of the camps.

Some of the camps, such as Pardee and Three Forks, had fewer than 150 residents and few services, save for a small church. In contrast, a few of the larger camps such as Lorado, Amherstdale, Accoville, and Kistler had at least 500 residents, 120 dwellings, and an array of services including offices of physicians, banks, hotels and boarding houses, cafes, pharmacies, garages, cobblers, hairdressers, barbers, tailors, laundries, stores, churches, and industrial sites for the coal companies and railroads. Coal tipples and load-outs were operating at Three Forks, Pardee, Lorado, Lundale, Amherstdale, Fanco, and Kistler. At least five coal mines were operating in the steep ridges on both sides of the valley. As documented in chapter 4, which follows, current residents recall that many of the camps along Buffalo Creek provided their residents with most of the services that were needed on a daily and weekly basis. Most of the adult residents only traveled down to the town of Man a few times a month—if that—usually on Saturdays and Sundays, to socialize, attend events at the high school, and shop for large consumer goods such as appliances and vehicles. Adults traveled to the county seat, Logan (thirteen miles from Man), perhaps once a

TABLE 3.1. Buffalo Creek then and now: Some demographics.

	1970	2007
Three Forks	70 residents, church, rail depot.	15 residents in six dwellings.
Pardee	100 residents, 3 churches, repair shops, coal tipple.	30 residents in ten dwellings, new tipple and coal-loading facility.
Lorado	500 residents, many stores and services, 2 working mines, tipples, 3 churches, school.	375 residents in 150 dwellings, 2 churches, water-pump plant, post office, small community building.
Craneco, Lundale	500 residents, many stores, services, hotel, hospital, 2 working mines, tipples, shops.	250 residents, 100 dwellings, 1 church.
Stowe	200 residents, several stores, church.	110 residents in 40 dwellings. 1 home-heating service.
Crites	150 residents, company store, 2 churches.	25 residents in ten dwellings. Small playground.
Latrobe	100 residents, church, store.	25 dwellings and 30 units of subsidized housing. Playground.
Robinette, Amherstdale	1,500 residents, dozens of shops, stores, hotel, offices, and repair shops, coal mine, tipple, railroad depot, school, clinics.	800 residents, 320 dwellings, and home for handicapped citizens, 3 churches, gas and convenience store, post office, senior center, keno parlor, abandoned primary school.
Becco, Fanco	300 residents, coal mine, tipple, several stores, shops, and services.	70 residents, 20 dwellings, 2 churches, tipple and coal load-out, public service district office.
Braeholm	200 residents, tipple, repair shops and loading docks.	60 residents, 20 dwellings.
Accoville	500 residents, dozens of shops, stores, offices, hotel, warehouses, churches.	250 dwellings, 600 residents, several offices, grocery store, post office, churches, elementary school, home for handicapped citizens, garage, warehouse, pizza shop.

(continued on next page)

TABLE **3.1.** (*continued*)

	1970	2007
Crown	330 residents, shops, stores, garages.	90 dwellings, 250 residents, hardware store, churches, recycling center, warehouses, church.
Kistler	500 residents, 2 company stores, 10 shops, 2 churches, many other services.	160 dwellings, 400 residents, 3 carry-outs, gas station, 3 churches, pool room, keno parlors, grocery store, 40 units of subsidized housing, playground, disaster memorial.
TOTAL	4,950 residents, more than 1,800 dwellings, 100 businesses and services, 5 working mines, 4 schools, 30 churches, 5 hotels, 2 hospitals, 3 theaters.	About 3,100 residents, 1,200 dwellings, 25 businesses and services, 2 mines, 1 school, 15 churches, 2 homes for handicapped persons, 80 units of subsidized housing, 4 keno parlors.

Sources. For 1970: *Buffalo Valley Redevelopment Plan*, p. 43, based on 1970 U.S. Census data; for 2007: Logan County Commissioner's Office, the Buffalo Creek Public Service District Office, and estimates based on community leaders and on personal reconnaissance.

month—if that—and to Charleston (about eighty miles away) only once or twice a year, at most. Many children who were born along Buffalo Creek never traveled beyond the town of Man until they were in high school. For many native-born residents, Buffalo Creek and the town of Man constituted their entire social, cultural, and economic universe— augmented, of course, by access to TV, telephone, and radio.

Buffalo Creek's sixteen coal camps had been built where the valley floor was wide enough, sometimes only 200 feet across, to allow rows of miners' houses to be built adjacent to the three "avenues" that curved and crossed their way up the length of the valley, often competing for the limited space on the valley floor: the creek itself, Route 16, and two or more railroad tracks. Probably 80 percent of the dwellings were located within the very narrow and sharply delineated floodplain, often within 100 or 200 feet of the creek, and often only five or ten feet above the normal surface height of its water. Most of the other dwellings were located in narrow side hollows along small streams that branched up and away from the creek.

Taken collectively, Buffalo Creek's sixteen camps had more than one hundred shops, stores, and services, three theaters, thirty churches, four schools, five hotels and boarding houses, two small hospitals, four volunteer fire departments, and even a Boy Scout camp. They also had more than forty industrial buildings, most of which were associated with the coal companies and with the Chesapeake & Ohio Railroad.

This is our best estimate of the Buffalo Creek Valley's demographic and services profile as of 7:59 a.m. on Saturday morning, February 26, 1972. As described in chapter 1, only three hours later, by perhaps 11:00 a.m. that same morning, the flash flood had disrupted, displaced, damaged, and destroyed perhaps as much as 90 percent of that profile—which is when the gruesome tasks of rescue and recovery began.

FIRST STEPS: RESCUE, EVACUATION, SECURITY, AND DAMAGE ASSESSMENT

As indicated in chapter 1, for the first five days after the flood, government agencies concentrated on emergency activities: rescue, evacuation, relief, recovery, and damage assessment.

Of course, the most crucial emergency activity was to help the people of Buffalo Creek recover bodies, rescue stranded and homeless survivors, and transport injured survivors to the hospitals at Man, Logan, and Charleston. Civil Defense helicopters and National Guard MEDEVAC units provided assistance the first few days, but they were in demand throughout southern West Virginia because flooding had been widespread. A morgue was set up in the gym at Man High School. Route 16 had to be reopened in order to evacuate the hundreds of injured victims and the thousands of people who needed shelter and food. Concurrently, access to the constricted valley had to be controlled as thousands of relief workers, worried relatives of survivors, reporters, politicians, and curious spectators poured into the area. This is the troublesome "convergence factor" that is so common in disasters and that is documented so well by disaster researchers.[4] State agencies from Charleston took the lead in these efforts, in part because none of Buffalo Creek's sixteen coal camps were incorporated and there were no offices of county or state agencies along Buffalo Creek. Flooding had occurred throughout southwestern West Virginia, not just along Buffalo Creek, and the only direct road to Man from Logan (twenty miles northwest) and from Charleston (eighty-nine miles north) did not provide easy access to Route 16 and to Buffalo Creek. On Saturday afternoon, February 26, 1972, only hours after the floodwaters rushed out of Buffalo Creek Hollow and into the Guyandotte River, Governor Arch Moore ordered his Office of Federal/ State Relations to establish an emergency office in the town of Man. That office would coordinate the rescue and security efforts of more than 800 National Guardsmen, ninety state troopers, and dozens of police, firemen, and emergency medical technicians from counties and towns throughout southern West Virginia. The West Virginia Department of Health quarantined the entire valley as a safety precaution.[5]

Rammie Barker, a local reporter at the time of the flood and a fixture in West Virginia political circles since then, recalls Governor Moore's direct involvement this way:

> Moore appeared at the scene numerous times, talking to victims, to workers, to see what more could be done, showing his compassion for them. His "ambassador for disasters," Norm Yost, appeared daily for two months, "as a sign of respect as much as anything," according to Yost...Governor Moore provided the kind of strong emotional leadership that Mayor Rudy Giuliani did in the wake of 9-11 in New York. It may have been his finest hour. And I was a Rockefeller supporter at the time. The people of Logan County appreciated Governor Moore.[6]

Preliminary Assessment of Direct Damages Due to the Flood
Within days, the governor's office determined that the flood had immediately caused the following damages to Buffalo Creek's population and
infrastructure:

Public Health: 125 residents had died and about 650 residents suffered injuries that required hospitalization. Many others suffered shock,
lesser injuries, and respiratory and digestive disorders because they
ingested toxic floodwater and had been overexposed to the cold, wet
weather. And yet, fortunately, "no communicable diseases broke out."[7]

Utilities: Water, electricity, and telephone systems incurred damages
of about $250,000.[8] Electricity and phone services were knocked out in
all of the coal camps and in much of the town of Man for at least four
days. Prior to the flood, about one-half of the water was supplied by
individually owned wells and pumps. The other half consisted of water
systems built over the years by local coal companies and sold to a private company, Cashion Water Works. The governor's office determined
that "all existing systems received some flood damage."[9]

Economic: It was estimated that the flood had destroyed at least $40
million in private and public property, had destroyed at least thirty commercial buildings, and would cost millions of dollars in revenues lost to
industries and businesses in the Buffalo Creek Valley, millions of dollars in lost tax revenues to the state of West Virginia, and thousands of
dollars in wages that would be lost by gainfully employed workers who
resided in the valley.

Housing: Between 500 and 1,000 homes were destroyed by the flood.
Of the 834 that remained, "198 are in sound condition, 390 are deteriorating, and 246 are dilapidated. Many of the dwellings left standing had
no sanitary facilities."[10]

Transportation: Most roads and alleys in the valley were badly damaged. "Nine miles of road were completely washed-out, and six more
miles were damaged. Twelve bridges were demolished or needed
replacement."[11] Heavy losses of privately owned vehicles occurred. Estimates ranged from 600 to over 1,000 vehicles destroyed. "Fifteen miles

of railroad track were destroyed or needed repair. Two railroad bridges needed to be replaced."

Schools: Four primary schools were located along Buffalo Creek at the time of the flood, but one of these was not in use. The school at Lorado was "completely destroyed."[12] The other two schools remained in service.

Natural environment: "Most vegetation in the Buffalo Creek Valley flood plain was destroyed and extensive damage to the landscape has occurred."[13] A "black substance derived from the sludge and slag of mining operations covered the entire Valley."[14]

NEXT STEPS:
SERVING DISLOCATED SURVIVORS, CLEANUP, AND SALVAGE

By the middle of the week following the flood, emphasis shifted from rescue and security to feeding, sheltering, clothing, and providing health care services to about 3,500 survivors who were still displaced from their homes; to clearing out debris from roads, railroads, and public facilities; and to salvaging as much of the infrastructure as possible. The Army Corps of Engineers and several local coal companies brought in heavy equipment to clear debris and open the main roadways and railways. Much of the relief and cleanup work was done in March, April, and May, although some of it continued for many months after that. Dozens of federal, state, and county agencies were involved in these activities. State agencies that were heavily involved in this work, as directed by the Governor's Office of Federal/State Relations, included the Department of Finance and Administration, the Department of Highways, the State Fire Marshall, the Department of Agriculture, the Department of Welfare, the Department of Health, and the Department of Employment Security. Governor Moore also arranged for free legal services to be offered to the victims of the flood. These services were to include information on how the victims could file for bankruptcy.[15]

The U.S. Office of Emergency Preparedness oversaw the activities of seventeen federal agencies in the human services, cleanup, and recovery efforts. For example, the Army Corps of Engineers removed 300,000 cubic yards of debris and created several sanitary landfills. It prepared homesites for hundreds of mobile homes at seven locations and built eight temporary bridges up through Buffalo Creek Valley. The U.S. Department of Labor assisted the West Virginia Department of Employment Security in processing hundreds of claims for "Disaster Unemployment Assistance" and hundreds of job applications for Buffalo Creek's survivors. The Department of Agriculture issued food stamps to more than 1,000 Buffalo Creek families. The Department of Housing and Urban Development provided temporary housing for hundreds of families and supplied about 600 mobile homes to thirteen temporary camps that would house homeless families from Buffalo Creek, as well as from some of the other residential communities in Logan County that had been flooded. These dwellings were provided for one year, free of charge, to qualified disaster victims. The Internal Revenue Service counseled more than 500 of the survivor families concerning tax-deduction disaster credits and procedures for filing tax-loss claims. The Environment Protection Agency assisted state agencies in determining the damages to water and sewage systems and in designing and installing twenty-seven "package sewage-treatment plants" throughout the County.

The town of Man served as the base of operations for many of the state and federal agencies that established temporary offices near Buffalo Creek. The town helped the agencies find office space. It made space available in the high school and in other public buildings as temporary housing for dislocated survivors and for dozens of relief workers who were hired under the Emergency Employment Act.

Logan County government created a new public service district for the Buffalo Creek Valley in order to speed up the funding for temporary and for new water- and sewage-treatment facilities. It also created a new public housing authority for the valley and adopted floodplain zoning ordinances that would make rebuilding safer and more insurable.

Private businesses and large corporations also contributed a variety of services. Some of the coal companies loaned small heaters and stoves to families whose homes were without heat. The companies also sent drivers and earth-moving equipment into the coal camps to help with the cleanup operations. Reportedly, Sears Roebuck Company and some other merchandisers forgave debts of their customers whose homes were destroyed in the flood.

A number of private organizations provided direct assistance each day, and for many months, to the floods survivors along Buffalo Creek, in the town of Man, and at other locations in Logan County. The American Red Cross brought more than seventy recovery staff workers and 400 volunteers to Buffalo Creek for the relief effort. It spent more than $8 million in direct services to more than 1,000 families. It operated four "mass care shelters" that served about 1,500 survivors. Fifteen months after the flood, the Red Cross was still providing long-term rehabilitative counseling, at no cost, to dozens of Buffalo Creek survivors. The Salvation Army operated seven mobile canteens with sixty-seven officers and more than 250 volunteer workers from seven states. The Seventh Day Adventists joined with the Salvation Army in providing clothing, bedding, and more than 200,000 meals to people in need and to volunteer recovery workers. The Mennonite Disaster Service had sixty-eight volunteers assist survivors in repairing their homes by doing plumbing, electrical, and carpentry work.

Not to be overlooked was at least one grassroots organization, The Buffalo Creek Citizens' Disaster Committee, Inc., which is credited with providing "a great deal of valuable information (to the governor's Office of Federal/State Relations) regarding the feelings, attitudes, and opinions of the local citizenry."[16]

And so, it is obvious that extraordinary efforts were made by many government and nonprofit agencies to help the people of Buffalo Creek recover and maintain their physical well-being and to remain in Logan County, near Buffalo Creek, for many months after the flood. Of course, we should not overlook the less visible and less well-documented efforts that individual citizens, families, friends, and neighbors made in recovering and in repairing, restoring, and rebuilding what might be called their own infrastructure—the roads, utilities, dwellings, churches, and other institutions that were closest to them. Chapters 4 and 5 provide evidence that some of the flood's survivors helped to rebuild some parts of the infrastructure closest to their homes, as best they could.

PLANNING THE REBUILDING AND MODERNIZING OF BUFFALO CREEK

In mid-May, Governor Moore announced that a master plan for the rebuilding of Buffalo Creek would be prepared by his Office of Federal/State Relations in conjunction with the Federal Regional Council for Region III. Costs for preparing this plan, the Buffalo Valley Redevelopment Plan, were to be paid by the federal government through the Office of Management and Budget. Table 3.2 provides a chronological overview of the major events in the rebuilding of the valley's infrastructure. A full-time staff of administrators and planners from state agencies and the Federal Regional Council established an office in Charleston. During the next year, the staff worked for a newly appointed Federal Planning Task Force, assembled relevant data, and conferred with dozens of experts in federal and state agencies and in private sector businesses and associations. Among dozens of other organizations, these included the Federal Highway Administration, the Office of Emergency Preparedness, the Economic Development Administration, Environmental Protection Agency, and many offices of the Department of Housing and Urban Development, including its Buffalo Creek Disaster Field Office. Other agencies included the Appalachian Regional Commission, the West Virginia Department of Employment Security, Department of Health, and Departments of Commerce, Education, and Civil and Defense Mobilization. The Logan County Board of Education, the Town of Man, the West Virginia Home Builders Association, Bank of Logan, Appalachian Power Company, Logan County Coal Operators' Association, West Virginia Grocer's Association, and the Buffalo Creek Citizens' Disaster Committee, Inc., also were acknowledged for their contributions to the planning process.

In July 1973, the plan was approved and signed by Governor Arch Moore and Theodore R. Robb—chairman of the Federal Regional Council III—and released to the public. It promised that "Buffalo

TABLE **3.2.** Some notable events in rebuilding the infrastructure of Buffalo Creek since 1972.

1972	*May:* Governor Moore announces that a comprehensive Buffalo Creek Redevelopment Plan will be prepared with, and funded by, the federal government.
1973	*July:* Governor Moore and the Federal Regional Council III approve the completed Buffalo Valley Redevelopment Plan that calls for more than $44 million in federal funding to modernize the infrastructure of all communities along Buffalo Creek. *August:* A citizens group, The Buffalo Creek Memorial Committee, erects a small Memorial Park in Kistler. *September:* The Buffalo Creek Public Service District is formed by the Logan County Commission.
1975	The Buffalo Valley Community Health Foundation is established.
1976	The Buffalo Creek Public Service District opens the new water system and the new wastewater (sewage) system for the Buffalo Creek Valley, costing more than $16 million and funded by the federal government. A six-room outpatient clinic, the Buffalo Creek Memorial Health Center, is built at Crites and opens to serve low-income people. Eighty units of subsidized housing for low-income people open at Kistler and Latrobe.
1977	A group of residents in the upper Buffalo Creek Valley fund and build a four-room community center at Lorado. *December 31:* Governor Moore leaves office.
1978	The long-awaited, modern, two-lane, concrete highway (Highway 16) opens from Crown to Pardee to replace the former Route 16 that was battered in the flood.
1979	A vocational-training center opens and job-training programs begin at Three Mile Curve Industrial Park, ten miles from Buffalo Creek.
1980	A referendum to incorporate Buffalo Creek's former coal camps is defeated.
1985	The state of West Virginia opens two small residential facilities at Amherstdale and Accoville for mentally handicapped people. The Chesapeake & Ohio Railroad closes down the rail line above Braeholm after years of declining production of coal along Buffalo Creek.
1988	Citizens of Logan County, including Buffalo Creek, approve a number of referenda to enable the Logan County Commission to consolidate schools, fire-response, and emergency rescue services throughout the county with some financial support from the state of West Virginia. (The consolidation process continues to the current time.)

(*continued on next page*)

TABLE 3.2. (continued)

1995	The Buffalo Creek Memorial Health Center at Crites closes. The elementary school at Amherstdale closes.
1998	State of West Virginia appropriates $10 million to begin modernizing Route 10 from Logan through southeastern West Virginia. It will bypass the town of Man and the long-standing juncture to Highway 16 and the Buffalo Creek Valley. Work begins on this project, which will take many years to complete.
2000	The Appalachian Regional Hospital in south Man closes. The state of West Virginia appropriates $2 million for developing a Hatfield-McCoy Historic Trail system that includes Logan County and several sites near Buffalo Creek.
2001	Increasing national demand for steam coal and relaxed federal environmental standards boost the production of steam coal and the opening of new mines in southwestern West Virginia.
2002	Dozens of new trails are opened for recreational use of all-terrain vehicles (ATVs) in the hills around Buffalo Creek and the town of Man. Over the next few years, more than a dozen businesses open in and around Man and south Man to accommodate tourists and ATV enthusiasts.
2003	The Appalachian Fuels LLC of Kentucky announces plans to open new mines in Logan County including at least one large "mountain top" surface mine on Laurel Ridge and a new loading facility at Pardee for coal trains.
2005	The new coal mine above Pardee starts producing hundreds of tons of steam coal each day that are transported by coal trucks down Highway 16 through the Valley.
2006	*March:* The Chesapeake & Ohio Railroad reopens the rail line from Fanco to a new coal-loading facility at Pardee and starts hauling out thousands of tons of coal each day. *September:* The state suspends indefinitely further work on modernizing Route 10 from Logan to Man because of budgetary problems and faulty construction to date.
2007	Appalachian Fuels LLC extends the rail line from Pardee to Three Forks, clears roads to the old coal mines above Three Forks, and expands its mining operations along Laurel Ridge above Buffalo Creek.

Sources. Most of this information was provided by the Logan County Commission and the Buffalo Creek Public Service District Office. Some of the dates presented here are estimates based on interviews with residents of Buffalo Creek because official records were indefinite or contradictory.

Valley will be rebuilt more beautiful than before with a better life for everyone.[17]

We will give a considerable amount of attention to the plan for several reasons. It is a very informed, detailed, and ambitious plan that includes several rather surprising features, including a provision to try to preclude trouble from veterans of the war in Vietnam. Apparently, it was supported by many interest groups and by many of Buffalo Creek's people. There seems to have been relatively little public opposition to it, probably in part because it called on the federal government to provide more than $44 million to fund the modernizing of the infrastructure of Buffalo Creek. The plan includes very specific guidelines as to how the federal government should spend millions of dollars on more than a dozen programs that it recommends. Considerable efforts were made by many agencies and organizations to implement many of the recommendations in the years immediately after its release. Unfortunately, interest in the plan seems to have diminished rather quickly after Governor Arch Moore left office in 1977. Nonetheless, a great deal was accomplished through it.

The Buffalo Valley Redevelopment Plan
Consider the clarity and the ambitiousness of the plan:

> The main objective is to provide for Buffalo Valley residents a better quality of life than they had prior to the disaster. If the plan is fully implemented, it will be possible for them to reside in moderately priced new homes free from environmental hazards, such as mining operations and pollution, and insured against flood damage. The homes will be located in areas most receptive to new construction located out of the flood plain. The clustering of housing will enhance the beauty and value of the individual homes and provide better flood protection for more people than the previous patterns of development which stretched from one end of the Valley to the other prior to the disaster.

The Planning Task Force determined that the vast majority of Buffalo Creek's infrastructure prior to the flood had been crammed into the middle of a very narrow floodplain (less than 400 feet wide, on average) that would continue to flood severely, at least several times each year, unless drastic measures were taken. It also concluded that the flood was "equal to forty times that of a flood occurring naturally every fifty years."[18] In order to avert more disasters, the floodplain would have to be altered rather drastically. Any rebuilding would have to be located away from the floodplain or many feet above it. The planners also determined that Buffalo Creek's infrastructure prior to the flood was so obsolete that it needed to be radically modernized—not just rebuilt.

Some General and Specific Recommendations

The central recommendation in the plan is to build a modern highway the length of Buffalo Creek Valley in such as way as to allow new residential communities to be located at the safest places above a newly designed floodplain.

> To develop attractive new communities[19] that are safe from future disasters, the proposed new State Highway 16 (formerly Route 16) and the stream itself will be realigned to attain maximum space for new development. In addition, the highway and railroad, which mostly run next to each other, will border rather than divide the new housing development. In certain areas, the highway, which will be built above the 100-year flood plain, will act as a buffer against future flooding. Fill many be added as needed to bring the land used for new construction up to the 100-year flood plain. Additional safety precautions will be proposed by flood prevention studies now underway.[20]

The most notable recommendations in the plan are summarized below. Many of these recommendations include estimates of the costs to implement them, the agencies that should apply for the funding that was necessary, and the agencies that should share the costs of funding each recommendation. For example, the Federal Planning Task Force suggested that the West Virginia Department of Highways should apply to the Federal Highway Administration for the estimated cost of $11.25 million for rebuilding and modernizing a new Highway 16 from Man to Pardee.

Flood Prevention

1. "State and local governments should design a coordinated program of flood plain management which includes proper enforcement of land use regulations and controls to guard against future problems."

2. Detailed studies of all factors "affecting the entire watershed" are needed.[21]

3. Residents of Buffalo Creek Valley should be made aware of the flood insurance programs available to them so that they can recover appropriate settlements for property losses now and in the future.

Environment

1. Strict controls should be established on land use and wastewater discharge into Buffalo Creek Valley, with emphasis on "reducing surface run-off and loading sediment into Buffalo Valley."

2. "Utility lines in the new community areas should be placed underground and coal mine operations should be screened or controlled."[22]

Community Facilities

1. A new "complete water works should be installed to serve the entire disaster stricken area from Pardee to Man."[23]

2. "Sources of water should be established to serve each new community so as to allow each source to be used in other areas in case of emergency."[24]

3. "A regional sewage treatment facility" should be built "to serve the entire Valley area," and it should provide the highest level of sewage treatment that is now available in terms of technology. This facility should be owned and operated by the Buffalo Creek Public Service District "and should also serve the Town of Man as a customer."[25]

4. "A community center should be constructed to house the operations of the Buffalo Creek Public Service District, the new health care facilities, additional law enforcement equipment, fire trucks

and other activities related to recreation, civic affairs and community cohesiveness.[26] This building should be centrally located
in the Valley."[27]

Transportation

1. "The Valley should be provided with a modern highway that
    extends the length of the Valley. This highway, Highway 16,
    should eventually be connected to Route 85, providing easy
    access to the East" and to new, industrial sites in the eastern part
    of the state.[28]
2. The county should form a transit authority to serve Buffalo Creek
    Valley. Facilities to house and store the equipment for the tran-
    sit service should be located in the valley. The system should
    include "a minimum of five to six mini-type buses" to operate in
    route assignments in the valley. Bus shelters should be erected in
    the valley "in such a way as to prevent a stop-go effect for traffic
    movement along the valley floor."[29]

Economic Development

1. A feasibility study should be conducted for a "massive sanitary
    landfill and recycling program that would bring in solid waste or
    sludge from one of the major metropolitan areas and fill in some
    of the recesses and hollows...thereby creating new level land for
    industrial, residential, or recreational use."[30]

    New wealth would be brought into the Valley if two million tons
    of solid waste was brought in each year, the fee collected from
    the cities would be $8 million a year. Earnings from the proj-
    ect could be used for community improvement projects or other
    public purposes. Recycled material could also be sold to man-
    ufacturers for profit, while local employment situations would
    be improved by the need for machine operators, safety inspec-
    tors, sanitary technicians, truck drivers, managers, accounting
    clerks, etc.[31]

2. The Department of Employment Security should "coordinate among the contractors who will build the new houses, highways and water/sewer systems so that maximum utilization of local manpower is achieved."[32]

3. Implement a new "training program" to enable unskilled and unemployed workers to get trained and employed in "the immediate future and in the immediate vicinity" to increase the tax base and to attract new industries into the area.[33]

4. Fund "retraining programs for the approximately 140 veterans from Viet Nam" to reduce their unemployment "as well as possible social unrest."[34]

5. Fund and build a vocational-technical center at the Three Mile Curve Industrial Park to provide skilled labor for Logan County.

Housing

1. All of the new, high-density housing should be built "above the level of the 100-year frequency of the intermediate regional flood."[35]

2. Between 500 and 776 new permanent dwellings are needed to serve Buffalo Creek flood survivors who intend to move back to Buffalo Creek Valley.[36] Federally subsidized low-income housing (both rent- and mortgage-supplement types) should be made available for at least 267 low-income families. At least twenty-five units of subsidized housing should be built for low-income elderly residents of Buffalo Creek.

3. Three new communities are recommended for future construction:

    a. The area including Accoville and Right Fork to Perry Farm
    b. The area from Becco to Latrobe including the HUD trailer parks north of Robinette
    c. The area including the towns of Craneco and Lorado.

4. Housing construction in the valley should be coordinated by the Builders' Emergency Housing Corporation, a nonprofit organization that was established by the West Virginia Home Builders'

Association in order to expedite housing construction in the valley.[37]

Health and Public Safety

1. Quality of healthcare should be improved for all Buffalo Creek residents. This should include a new outpatient clinic affiliated with the Appalachian Regional Hospital in Man, "but located in a central location in Buffalo Creek Valley."[38]
2. *Law enforcement:* "A corporate body should be established...to develop and support Valley-wide police protection." This should include "a specific agency to serve the Valley."[39]
3. *Fire:* The valley should be provided with a new firehouse, fire truck, and equipment. The current volunteer fire departments should be upgraded and reorganized into a comprehensive system of fire protection for Buffalo Valley.

Education

1. The (destroyed) school at Lorado should be replaced.
2. (See the recommendation to build a vocational-training center at the Three Mile Curve Industrial Park.)
3. *Adult education:* The new vocational training center and new manpower training programs should be maintained and expanded to meet the needs of the Buffalo Creek Valley for economic redevelopment and diversification.

Recreation

1. A new organization should be created to manage all public recreation in the Buffalo Creek Valley.
2. A master plan should be prepared to integrate all proposals for outdoor recreation areas in the Buffalo Creek Valley.
3. "A three-unit regional park should be created, preferably at the area designated as Camp Buffalo."[40]
4. Play lots and mini-parks should be built near all new housing areas.

IMPLEMENTING THE PLAN:
SOME SUCCESSES; MANY INCOMPLETES

To the best of my knowledge, there has been no published "after action" report on how well the Buffalo Valley Redevelopment Plan was implemented or on how the infrastructure (roads, utilities, government services, businesses, and other institutions) of Buffalo Creek was rebuilt since the flood. In order to fill this gap, I interviewed more than a dozen longstanding leaders in state, county, and local government, and dozens of longtime residents of Buffalo Creek about their reactions to the efforts that have been made to rebuild Buffalo Creek's infrastructure by any and all parties.[41]

Only a few of the community leaders recalled the plan, and none of them claimed to have much familiarity with it. They did not express strong emotions about the plan, although they generally supported it. They did not recall strong objections towards the plan by the public or by public interest groups in the 1970s or since then. These leaders generally were of the opinion that some parts of the plan had considerable influence and were implemented within a few years. Sadly, the plan's influence dissipated rapidly during the 1980s. One current community leader, who recalled he was "a young boy eatin' cornflakes and watchin' Superman on TV when the flood hit," had this to say about what he has seen in the rebuilding of Buffalo Creek since the flood:

> I don't think that any one person is an expert on how Buffalo Creek was rebuilt. I looked over that Plan years ago. I thought it was okay. Some parts of it were followed pretty well. Like the rebuilding of Highway 16 as a straight, fast, concrete, two-lane up to Pardee and the water system and waste water treatment system that we have for the entire Valley. These have worked pretty well, I think. Of course we've had to upgrade them since they were built. We are upgrading the water system right now, again, so that we don't have to rely on surface run-off for drinking water. A lot of those parts you mention in the Plan—they just haven't been done. Some of them could still help us a lot. I don't know why they weren't done. Maybe the politicians behind them died or just lost interest. Maybe the State ran out of money for them.

A different point of view was offered by a well-respected journalist who worked along Buffalo Creek as a teenager, before the flood, and who has visited friends along Buffalo Creek many times since then: "Unfortunately people are sort of fatalistic down there, and in much of this State. A lot of apathy sets in about whether conditions can be improved, unless some leader in State government gets their attention and finds a way to get enough money and political support to get things rolling again."

At least one prominent businessman and community leader was more impressed by the amount of reconstruction that has occurred over the years:

> A lot of Buffalo Creek was rebuilt in maybe the first five to ten years, as far as roads, bridges, and things like that. Plenty of people moved back along the creek. Of course, we've had some slow times in the coal industry since then. They set us back some. Like ten, fifteen years ago things were pretty sad around here. So it's taken years, and it hasn't been straight progress all of the way. But I'd say it's kind of a miracle today, when you think about it. To see it rebuilt like it is now up in the Valley with the houses and manufactured homes in different colors, styles, and all that. They got good roads and bridges, too. Some people from the flood are still coming back here to retire.

A lapse in redevelopment probably occurred for at least three reasons. First, most of the survivors of the flood who wanted to remain or move back to Buffalo Creek did so and were busy rebuilding their own properties. They found that living conditions along the valley had improved in terms of roads, bridges, and basic utilities to the point that they had relatively little to complain about compared to the deprivations they had suffered in the months immediately after the flood. For the most part, these improvements in material conditions defused the limited activism and advocacy that had emerged among some of the survivors who felt that they had almost been imprisoned in the HUD trailer camps. So, they did not press for further implementation of the plan's recommendations—if they were even aware of them. The coal economy was also generally weak and erratic during the 1980s. Three or four of the biggest mines in the ridges above Buffalo Creek closed down. The Chesapeake & Ohio

Railroad stopped running coal trains beyond Fanco. The coal companies and related businesses lost interest in Buffalo Creek. Partly as a result of this, federal and state economic-development efforts shifted away from southern West Virginia towards the center and northern end of the state, as was the case in the funding and building of the Senator Byrd Interstate Highway (I-79) from the northern border with Pennsylvania, south to Charleston and the "High Technology Corridor" that straddles part of that interstate. It was not until the early twenty-first century that significant improvements in the local economy started again around Buffalo Creek, probably because the coal economy was revived by rising prices per ton for steam coal, and federal regulations shifted in favor of the mountaintop removal method of coal mining. A number of new federal tax breaks and incentives also became available that encouraged big coal producers—including Massey Energy and Arch Coal Company—to open new mines throughout the region.

Rank-and-file residents of Buffalo Creek whom I spoke with had even less recall of the plan than community leaders, and they were even less certain about when and how improvements were made to the infrastructure of Buffalo Creek. Many of them agreed that the roads, bridges, water and sewer systems had been improved substantially within five or six years after the flood. They also were of the opinion that many other elements of the infrastructure had not improved and, in some cases, might even have worsened since the flood. Among these less-than-satisfactory elements are the quality of services that involve police, drug enforcement, traffic-law enforcement, littering, code enforcement on abandoned and deteriorating commercial and residential buildings, and poor access to medical services, shopping, recreation facilities, and public transportation, and the absence of modern highways to the eastern and southern parts of the state. One of the senior, native-born residents told me,

> To be honest with you, I don't remember that Plan you're talkin' about. Some of those suggestions you just mentioned have been done okay. Like the road out here (Highway 16). It's a lot straighter and faster than it used to be. Maybe it's too fast for safety—the way the coal trucks and drinkers and 4-wheelers speed up and down it at all hours of the day and night. Most of us

have the same water and sewers now. The monthly fee ain't too bad. But most of them other things are news to me: a big building for our own police force, new plants for people to work in, busses, playgrounds for the kids, and brand new towns with plenty of homes for poor folks. If those things are around here they are hiding them from me.

Another native son of Buffalo Creek told me,

We still don't have our own police like they called for in that Plan you mentioned. If you call the Sheriff in Logan it seems like it's days before they show up. Sometimes they don't ever show up. We lost most of our schools and stores and doctors and conveniences up here in the Valley in the flood. Then the places they were at were bulldozed for the new highway. Some small stores tried to come back; but most of them didn't make it. Now we got to drive down to Amherstdale just to get gas, bread, and coffee. We got to drive all the way to Logan for most things, even to bowl.

As to the major recommendations of the plan, community leaders and ordinary citizens provided a variety of assessments, augmented by my own observations during my visits to Buffalo Creek over the last seven years. As might be expected, community leaders were more informed about changes in the infrastructure, and they were more positive about the current state of the infrastructure than were residents of Buffalo Creek who were elderly, were less than thirty years old, or were renting their dwellings.

EVALUATIONS OF INFRASTRUCTURE DEVELOPMENTS SINCE 1972

Flood Prevention

In general, the residents I spoke with were uncertain as to whether the recommendations for flood prevention had been implemented according to the plan.

Some interviewees pointed out that flood-control measures were installed when Highway 16 was modernized. Elevations, embankments, dikes, and drainage ditches were built in many of the places that had flooded most severely. Efforts were made to place sections of Highway 16 between the creek and tracts of land where the largest clusters of new homes were expected. People observed that there has not been another flood of Buffalo Creek anywhere near the magnitude of the flood in 1972. They doubted that another flood of that magnitude could occur again because they have heard that the old gob ponds have been drained and that newer gob ponds are much smaller and have diversion pipes that will keep them from overflowing and collapsing.[42]

However, people report that the small streams that feed into Buffalo Creek often have flash floods. They believe that this is because of excessive clear-cutting of timber on the ridges along the valley and on top of the mountains. Several community leaders added that the flooding also occurs because the creek has filled with silt and debris over the past thirty years, since it was rerouted after the flood, and that it needs to be cleaned and deepened. People report that flash floods of sidestreams often wash over road surfaces, leave fallen timber and large rocks on road surfaces, flood basements, and sometimes wash away fences, yards, gardens and porches. A seventy-year-old resident reacted this way when I read to him the plan's recommendations for flood prevention:

> All of that sounds pretty good to me, but I don't know whether they did all of those things. We don't have gob ponds like that any more, so we can't have a flood like that one. But we still get washouts, and some peoples' places flood-out when it rains heavy. A few weeks ago some cars washed-away down the hollow and a woman got three or four inches of flood water in her kitchen.

Flash floods can be even more damaging than this, however. For example, during one of my visits to Buffalo Creek in May 2001, a young couple and small child drowned when they tried to drive across a ford at a swollen branch of Buffalo Creek at Robinette.[43] When I spoke with local residents about this the next morning, some residents in their teens and twenties were neither alarmed nor very sympathetic. They blamed the driver and suggested that some people are too ignorant, careless, or "hardheaded" to avoid situations that are obviously so dangerous. Some older residents were more sympathetic, but they were not alarmed. Nor were they critical of any person or agency for disregard of public safety. One of these people said to me, "if you live *along* the creeks you gotta live *with* the creeks."[44]

Only a few of the older, longtime residents I spoke with were aware of flood insurance programs and how they could recover settlements for property losses due to flooding. They did not have flood insurance. The Buffalo Creek Memorial Library in south Man did not have information like this, nor did the town hall at Man when I checked on the matter. I phoned several insurance agencies in Logan County before I found one that sells flood insurance. I was told that there were no special policies or programs for property owners in places like Buffalo Creek that had suffered catastrophic damages in previous floods. Rather, I was told that all insurance is sold by private insurance companies and the prices are standardized by federal law. When I passed this information on to several older residents, they said that the information was new to them and that they doubted that they could afford to purchase flood insurance. In contrast, several Buffalo Creek residents who are employed in government service jobs and who were very active in community affairs told me that flood insurance is relatively inexpensive for properties within five miles of a fire station and that state law requires all properties that are mortgaged to have flood insurance. They were of the opinion that the only residents without flood insurance were tenants, renters, and old-timers who paid off their mortgages long ago or who inherited their property when their parents died.

From my very limited perspective as a nonengineer, it appears that less than 40 percent of the dwellings in the Buffalo Creek Valley currently are located on land that has some man-made barriers to flooding and that places the dwellings at least fifteen feet above the normal water surface level of Buffalo Creek. Most of the larger clusters of dwellings now are located across Highway 16 from the creek. Some of these clusters are protected by earthen embankments that are at least fifteen feet high. And yet, there are dozens of dwellings that do not have these protections. In fact, one can see dwellings that are less than twenty years old which are located on lots that are immediately adjacent to the creek, without flood barriers, and are less than fifteen feet above the normal water level of the creek.[45]

Environmental Protection

Many of the leaders and the residents of the Buffalo Creek Valley whom I spoke with conceded that laws regarding land use and wastewater discharge have gotten much stricter, and appropriately so. They believe that land use and wastewater discharge by property owners have improved, but that too many offenses still occur along the floor of the valley and, much more so, up on the hillsides and in the side hollows, usually by "outsiders," young people, and tenants who rent cheap housing on a short-term basis. The streambed of Buffalo Creek itself is cluttered in many places with metal debris, broken glass, discarded tires, and appliances. As one resident said:

> Well, it's no where near as bad as it was years ago. Most people along here don't dump their garbage in the creeks anymore, or burn it in their back yards, or just toss it in empty lots. Some people do— mainly people who are renters and don't want to pay the monthly fee to the company that hauls most of our garbage. Most people here don't use land that's not theirs anymore for whatever they want, like for storing their old trucks or cutting firewood and all that. Some still do. Too many still do. That's true. It could be a lot better. There's a lot of littering, I admit. But it could be a lot worse.

The plan's recommendations for placing underground the utility lines for new communities and for screening coal-mine operations do not appear to have been enacted. Electric, phone, and cable TV lines are very visible at housing areas, both old and new. The coal tipple and loading dock at Fanco are readily visible from Highway 16. A coal conveyor crosses thirty feet above the highway to the tipple at the rail depot. The new mine on Laurel Ridge (Kelly Mountain) above Pardee is not visible from the floor of the valley. One elderly resident in the upper valley told me:

> I don't think any of that stuff was done. Maybe they wanted to bury it all underground so it wouldn't wash away if another flood

come along. It seems to me that the utility lines is everywhere: electric, telephone, and now that cable TV. You see transformer boxes everywhere. And if they put screens around the mining operations, then those screens are invisible to me. I can't see any screens. You sure can see and hear the coal trucks and the coal train. You can see the tipples and conveyors at Fanco when you drive by. But they don't bother me none. I don't mind seeing any of that stuff. It's always been here. It's what Buffalo Creek is all about.

Public Works

In keeping with the plan's recommendations, the Public Service District was created in 1973 for all sixteen of the coal camps in the valley. This was a significant achievement whose ancillary benefits should not be underestimated. By creating this entity, Logan County and the state of West Virginia were able to quickly apply for and receive authorization from the federal government to build state-of-the art water and sewage systems for the entire valley. These were completed in December 1976, funded fully by the federal government through the Appalachian Regional Commission for more than $16 million.[46] The new water and sewage systems have been upgraded several times at considerable expense since 1976. Millions of dollars worth of improvements are planned for the next few years. Residents differ as to whether the monthly fees are reasonable ($25 to $75 per month depending on usage rates and the number of members in the household). Some residents are not satisfied with the quality of the water or with the reliability of the sewage system. In the words of one retired miner who lives in the upper end of the valley:

> It works okay, mostly. Costs me maybe $35 to $40 a month. But the water quality isn't up to par. The water tastes bad. And it irritates my skin when I wash in it. I got to drive down to Logan for bottled water at Sam's Club…As far as the sewer goes, it works good most of the time. But sometimes it backs up in the main lines when it rains. Then you smell it up here plenty. But it's better than what we had. Outhouses and the woods.

The new community center that was called for in the plan has never been built, and there is no reason to believe that it will be built. It was to have been centrally located in the Buffalo Creek Valley so as to enhance "community cohesiveness." It was to include new offices for the Public Service District, a new health care facility, a new fire truck, equipment for a new police department, and rooms for social activities. Some of the elderly residents of Buffalo Creek told me that none of these plans materialized, to their way of thinking.

> None of that happened. Nothin' was built like that. We pay our water and sewer bill at the PSD office at Fanco. It's an old, two-room building. The volunteer fire department is in that old garage down at Amherstdale. It's our only one, now. We used to have four of them up and down the Valley. Now, to keep it going, the volunteers pass around cans and buckets for donations at ball games.

Several of these beliefs by "ordinary citizens" are mistaken, however, according to community leaders with whom I spoke. They told me that fire and ambulance services were modernized in the early 1990s when Buffalo Creek was included in the consolidation of these services throughout Logan County. Citizens approved a "fire and ambulance levy" on home owners' insurance premiums that has resulted in Buffalo Creek getting a new fire station at Amherstdale, four modern fire-and-rescue vehicles, and plenty of other new equipment and training for the firefighters. Volunteers still run the fire department, but it is well funded by the Logan County Commission and the state of West Virginia rather than through "pass-the-hat donations from the people at ball games."[47]

Another community leader was of the opinion that a comprehensive community center probably never will be built, and is not really needed, because of aspects of the local culture. He provided me with a very sociological explanation for this: "Buffalo Creek and Logan County families are clannish via religion and socio-economic factors. So community centers don't function as intended in this culture. People get together when they need to at a family home, a local church, or a school-house near someone in their clan."

Transportation

Only one of the several recommendations in the plan for improving transportation was implemented. Many sections of the old, irregular Route 16 that twisted and turned its way up through the coal camps were replaced with a modern, well-banked, concrete, two-lane highway (#16) from Crown to Pardee. Many residents indicate that this highway is a major improvement in terms of speed and visibility, but they complain that the speed limit (40 mph in many places) is poorly enforced and that coal trucks often drive out of control on it. Some residents still complain that too many homes and businesses were confiscated by the state in building the new highway. Some residents also complain that the lower two miles of Highway 16 from Crown to Man have not been modernized (and the speed limit is only 15 mph as the road twists through Kistler and Man), and that the highway was supposed to be four lanes wide but was reduced to two lanes when the federal government balked at funding all four lanes. Almost every resident and community leader I spoke with lamented that Highway 16 has not been extended from Pardee, over the mountains, to Route 85 so as to connect with Bolt and Beckley, as called for in the plan.

> Sure, they did that first part. They modernized Highway 16 from down at Crown up to Pardee. It works good enough. It's fast and straight enough. But they never extended it beyond Pardee over the mountain. They should. It would be only fifteen miles at most to Bolt and on to Beckley. That would save us at least an hour of driving all the way down south.

Very few residents are aware that the plan also calls for forming a transit authority that would operate "a minimum of five or six mini-type buses" to serve the valley and to be housed at a new facility in the center of the valley. When I mentioned this recommendation to them, several old-timers said that a public-transit service such as this would reduce their sense of isolation and make them and their friends and neighbors less homebound. Several community leaders said they were guardedly optimistic that, with a few more years of economic growth from revived coal mining, a mass-transit system would be extended to serve the entire valley and that the Highway 16 would be extended eastward over the mountains to Bolt and Beckley. Nevertheless, quite a few adult residents who have their own vehicles and are healthy tell me that they do not mind driving an hour to a decent-paying job in Charleston or to go shopping at the nearest megamall on the far side of Logan.[48]

Economic Development

The plan is very ambitious and specific regarding economic development. Unfortunately, only one of the several major recommendations has been implemented—the funding and building of a vocational-technical center at the Three Mile Curve Industrial Park between Man and Logan. Several residents said that they had relatives who had benefited from job retraining programs at this center. Some of them also remarked that the courses at the center were expensive and that graduates usually had to leave the Buffalo Creek area in order to find gainful employment that used their newly acquired skills. One Buffalo Creek resident said, "They train people down there to be welders, mechanics, and security guards—things like that. But I don't know that they bring new industries into the area or help us cut down on our taxes."

None of the people I spoke with remembered that the plan called for retraining "approximately 140 veterans from Viet Nam," and no one recalled whether Viet Nam veterans had been socially disruptive in the 1970s around Buffalo Creek, or that they had benefited from any of the recommendations in the plan.[49]

Community leaders did not know if any effort had been made to develop a "massive sanitary landfill and recycling program" that is given a lot of emphasis in the plan. Some leaders thought that this would still be a very promising project, while others doubted that it would contribute very much to the local economy. They said that building projects in the Buffalo Creek area rarely result in many jobs going to residents of Buffalo Creek. For example, when I informed a longtime Buffalo

Creek resident that the plan called for "maximum utilization of local manpower," he said:

> Well, a few local people got jobs when they built the new highway here in the Valley and when they put in the new water and sewer lines. Those jobs didn't last very long, though. Then the local boys were out of work again. My son worked for a road crew for a few months. Then the job was gone. So it wasn't a big employer of local people. Like the new mines up above Pardee right now. They are supposed to hire local people to work up there to drive trucks and all that. I don't know more than a few boys who got a job up there yet.

Then again, several community leaders told me that, as of January 2007, dozens of Buffalo Creek's young men, and a few young women, had gotten jobs at the new coal mine above Pardee. They also mentioned, however, that some of these newly employed residents already had been laid off, possibly because of some recent downturns in coal the coal economy.

Housing

Most of the people I interviewed liked the plan's many ambitious recommendations for new housing in the valley, but they said that, from what they could see, only a few of the recommendations had been implemented, and those were only partially completed. They doubted that most of the housing that had been built since the flood was "above the level of the 100-year frequency of the intermediate regional flood" ("whatever they mean by that"—said one resident). They said that, as you drive along Highway 16 up through Buffalo Creek Valley, you can see that several dozen new homes had been built at various places on the hillsides more than thirty feet above the valley floor. These were not in high-density clusters, however. These were the homes of the more wealthy residents who wanted considerable distance from the creek and from other houses. They wanted privacy from neighbors, as well as safety from any future floods. Most new housing, including about eighty units of apartments for low-income and elderly residents, has been built on the floodplain or on moderate elevations of earthen fill, perhaps ten to twenty feet above it. Often these elevated areas are located in place of the housing that was destroyed in the flood. As noted previously, new housing in the floodplain often is separated from the creek by embankments and by Highway 16. Nonetheless, dozens of houses, manufactured homes, and some of the subsidized housing units have been built less than twenty feet above the normal water surface level and less than one hundred feet from the creek. To quote one senior citizen who is well regarded throughout the valley:

> A lot of the new places are just above the high water level of the creek. I don't know why they are allowed to do that. Like the apartments they built for low income people at Latrobe. They don't seem very safe to me. Maybe the people who built them and the people who live there weren't around for the flood.

A disabled miner in his fifties remarked:

> I doubt that most of us are above a flood that comes along every hundred years. A lot of places are just about the water level of the creek right now. Some people up in Latrobe, Crites, and Stowe can just about jump off their porches right into the creek. Sometimes their trucks get flooded-out if they park too close to the creek the night before it rains. And there are places along the road out here (Highway 16) where you can drive right into the creek if you aren't paying attention. It's almost even with the road and there's no barriers to stop you.

Some leaders and residents point out that a considerable amount of subsidized housing has been built for low-income families and for elderly people at two or three places in the valley. They say that they guess that the total number is about eighty units rather than the more than 260 units that were called for in the plan.

> I don't know that we need that much housing anymore around here. The population has shrunk a lot over the years. A lot of the young people leave the area after they graduate. When the old people die-off their places stay empty if they are older places like the houses the mining companies built many years ago or trailers

that are in poor shape. Then they just fall apart or they burn down from kids playing around in them.

Probably the most ambitious recommendation in the plan for housing is the recommendation for building three entirely new communities at Accoville to Perry Farm, Becco to Robinette, and Craneco to Lorado. Leaders and residents alike had no recall of this recommendation, nor did they recall any concerted effort by government agencies, nonprofits, or by private developers to build these three new communities.[50] They said that, as best as they could recall, the Army Corps of Engineers cleared, filled, elevated, and graded fairly large tracts of land at or near each of these places. Since then, however, building on these tracts has been rather quite haphazard—rather than financed and managed by professional developers or agencies. Usually, what happened was that survivors of the flood who wanted to relocate to these places bought one or two lots there and either built a house or moved a mobile home onto the lots. Other people relocated to these places by renting a lot, moving a mobile home onto the lot, and then living there for months or years on end. This kind of piecemeal resettlement was most obvious at the area of Accoville referred to as the "Right Fork to Perry Farm." Some knowledgeable residents of Buffalo Creek told me:

> The only place I'd call a "new community" is up where Mac Perry had his farm years ago. I don't think the government had much to do with it. Mac had a pretty big farm up there and, after the flood, he started renting-out places up there for people to put their HUD trailers on. Some of them bought-out their lots after a time. So they ended up with a lot of trailers back there. They haven't grown that much since then, though.

> Even down there at Perry Farm it isn't what I'd call a development. People rented or bought land there for their HUD trailers and mobile homes. Most of them ended-up with double lots when they could afford it. They bought the old HUD trailers and put them down there. Over the years they upgraded them. At other places along the creek the government had the land graded for houses. A lot of that land is still vacant, for the most part. There

are some apartments at Accoville that the State built. I wouldn't call it a new town or anything like that.

The HUD camps at Latrobe were dissolved. There are a few newer houses and mobile homers there, but not many. Some of the people up there built a kind of recreation area alongside the creek up there. That's all.

Up at Craneco and Lorado people just moved back on the land after it was graded. They built whatever they wanted there. It wasn't built for them by the government or anyone else that I know of. Not that many people wanted to locate that far up the Valley anymore. So they didn't need to build a whole new town up there.

No one I spoke with considered any of the new clusters of new homes to constitute "new communities," nor did they consider any of these clusters to be "high-density" clusters. Several residents mentioned that there are no new names for the places where people reside along Buffalo Creek—something that might be expected if entirely "new communities" had been created. One resident commented:

We still got signs on the highway out there for most of the sixteen coal camps we had years ago. Only thing is that some of those signs aren't where the camps were. Some of the camps were on the opposite side of the highway from where they are now. And there isn't much left of the coal camps at some of those places, like Braeholm, Becco, and Crites. Some of them are mainly just signs now, it seems.

Most of the people I spoke with also doubted that the housing that had been constructed since the flood had been coordinated by a "Builder's Emergency Housing Corporation" that was created in order to expedite housing construction in the valley. One flood survivor told me:

I don't remember nothing like that. You had to do it all on your own. Go find a lot where you wanted to move your family if the place you had before the flood wasn't available any more. Like if the State took it for the highway they was building on it. Then figure out what you were going to live in and how you could afford it. Sometimes you had relatives or friends that had already done it and could help you figure it out. It took a lot of us years to figure it all out and then get settled-in again. I'm sure glad that's over with.

Public Safety

The Plan calls for major improvements in fire department services for the valley, including a new firehouse, fire truck, and modern equipment. It recommends that the volunteer force should be upgraded into a comprehensive system of fire protection for Buffalo Valley. As reported earlier, some "ordinary citizens" were unaware that major improvements have been made in fire-and-rescue services since the early 1990s—not because of the plan, but because Buffalo Creek has been included into a consolidated system of fire-and-rescue services for Logan County. While the fire station still relies on volunteers, it has received two modern Class A pumpers, a new rescue vehicle with a "jaws of life" metal-cutting device, and other major upgrades in equipment, as well as the training to operate that equipment. Several community leaders and volunteer firemen I spoke with attested that fire-and-rescue services now are funded very adequately by Logan County and the state, and that the services were very up-to-date and reliable. And yet, several elderly residents complained that there were far too many "firetraps" around their own homes—dilapidated and abandoned old houses, garages, and other buildings that were easy targets for vandalism and arson by local children and young adults "who got nothin' better to do" and are "lookin' to make some mischief." These residents told me that some fires spread quickly from house to house before the fire-and-rescue units arrive.

The plan recommended that a corporate body should be established to develop and support Valley-wide police protection. Thirty years later, most people tell me that Buffalo Creek still does not have adequate police protection, let alone its own police force, as called for by the plan. As indicated in many of the interviews that are presented in chapter 4, many residents of Buffalo Creek blame inadequate police protection for the kinds of crimes that they believe are far too common along Buffalo Creek: arson, breaking and entering, larceny, vandalism, speeding, driving while under the influence of drugs, littering, and the sale and abuse of illicit and of prescription drugs including cocaine, crystal methamphetamine, ecstasy, marijuana, Oxycontin, and codeine. As was the case before the flood, police protection for the valley is supposed to be provided by the Logan County Sheriff's Department, headquartered in Logan, and supplemented by the state police. A deputy sheriff from Logan occasionally operates out of a "satellite station" along Buffalo Creek, from time to time, with uncertain results, according to various residents. Some people report that the police department in Man can render emergency assistance in cases of reported homicides or similar felonies. Some residents said that the sheriff's office is supposed to have one deputy patrol Buffalo Creek on a regular basis. Others said that they doubt whether this actually happens. In general, people I interviewed reported that police protection and responses to calls were unreliable and that they might be flawed by favoritism and corruption. One old-timer who has lived in Lorado for most of his life told me: "I guess it would help to have our own police force if they hired people you could trust. It doesn't do any good if you can't trust them to do what they're supposed to do or if you got to be related to them to get any results or get a fair shake."

Possibly as a result of this belief, "No Trespassing" signs (and signs with more threatening warnings) are nailed to an appreciable number of front doors and garage doors in the valley. This is particularly frequent in the upper end of the valley, in the side hollows, and where a dwelling has few other dwellings close to it. A lifelong resident in the middle of the valley expressed his sentiment this way: "I got my son living with me here. My dogs and one of my neighbors look after the place when we aren't around. After that, I rely on my shotgun—not the Sheriff down in Logan."

Public Health

The plan called for major improvements in health care for all Buffalo Creek residents to include a new outpatient clinic affiliated with the Appalachian Regional Hospital in the town of Man, but centrally located in the Buffalo Creek Valley. Sadly, by many accounts, the quality of health care that is available in the valley has deteriorated significantly—except for one major improvement that lasted from 1979 to about 1995, but then closed, for reasons that no one could ascertain. A nonprofit "Buffalo Valley Community Health Foundation" was established in 1975 in order to improve access to health care in the valley. One of its first successes was in arranging funding (in part by a contribution from the law firm of Arnold & Porter, according to some reports) to build a single-story brick building in Crites and to establish an outpatient clinic there for low-income residents. Several people who have lived in the area for many decades told me that the clinic seemed to be popular and important until the 1990s. Now it stands abandoned, vandalized, and derelict—one of the sorriest looking buildings in the valley.

> I don't know why that clinic there in Crites was closed down. Now it's empty and trashed. I never used it myself. I think it was for low income people. It helped miners who had black lung, too. It seemed to be doing a lot of business for years. There were cars in the parking lot. People were coming and going in and out. You could see them from the road. I don't recall any complaints about it. Then it just closed down and never opened again.

Also lamentable is the fact that almost all other health care services and offices have disappeared from the valley except for two small residential facilities at Amherstdale and Accoville for people with emotional handicaps. The two small hospitals that operated at Lundale and Accoville before the flood never reopened. The offices of physicians and dentists also have slowly disappeared from the upper valley, although in Man, there are a number of small pharmacies and offices of physicians, rehabilitation therapists, and other health care providers. The medical facility closest to Buffalo Creek is an outpatient clinic in south Man, across the Guyandotte River and adjacent to the now closed Man hospital, operated by the foundation. In reviewing the situation, one community leader said,

> They created that Community Health Foundation right after the flood. It did some good work for years. It kind of seems to have fallen apart in recent years though. Then the hospital in south Man closed down. Then doctors moved their offices down to Logan. Now we have to get down to Logan or Charleston for most of our problems: exams, tests, doctors, dentists, chiropractors, surgery, clinics—you name it. That's not easy to do in bad weather or if you can't drive or don't have a car.

Education

One of the plan's recommendations has been fulfilled regarding education. Some others have gone wanting. A new vocational-training center and several new manpower training programs were established at the Three Mile Curve Industrial Park soon after the flood, as called for in the plan. People I spoke with felt that these have been fairly successful in helping local men and women gain vocational skills or retrain for more technical jobs. Some people felt that graduates have had a hard time finding jobs that can use their newly acquired skills unless they relocate to Charleston or other parts of West Virginia or to other states.

The recommendation to rebuild the primary school at Lorado was not fulfilled. The only schools in the valley now are the Buffalo Elementary School at Accoville, for grades K–4, and a Head Start program that operates out of a one-story community building at Lorado (Davy Hollow) that was built with funds collected by local people. All other schools for Buffalo Creek's students are in or near Man and south Man. Students are bussed to those schools. Prior to the flood, there were two other primary schools in the valley (and, until 1963, two high schools—one for Blacks and one for Whites). These never reopened. Current residents seem resigned to the fact that their school-age children will be educated outside of Buffalo Creek, for the most part. As with fire-and-rescue services, Buffalo Creek's schools became part of the consolidated educational system of Logan County in the early 1990s. As a result of this, funding and educational programs for Buffalo Creek's children have increased considerably since then. An impressive, new, state-of-the-art middle school, said to cost $20 million, opened just outside of Man a few years ago. Several community leaders said that reaction to consolidation of schools is mixed and contentious along Buffalo Creek. Many old-timers oppose the loss of local control over the schools and miss the sights and sounds of schoolchildren playing in schoolyards. Many parents of young children would prefer to have schools closer to their homes. On the other side of the issue are community leaders and parents of teenagers who endorse consolidation as a necessary and progressive change that affords their children with access to state-of-the-art instructional technology, sports facilities, and impressive new buildings.

Recreation

Almost none of the plan's recommendations for recreation have been fulfilled. Residents and community leaders say that they do not believe that a "master plan" for outdoor recreation was created, nor was a new organization created to manage all public recreation in the valley. Also never built was a "three-unit regional park" for the area designated as "Camp Buffalo." One of Buffalo Creek's most senior citizens was baffled when I mentioned these recommendations to him. "Camp Buffalo? Where's that? A regional park? Those are good questions. I don't have a clue about the answers." When I asked whether play lots and miniparks had been built near any areas with new housing, as called for by the plan, another citizen told me,

> Not that I know of. The only thing like that around here is what they call "McCoy Memorial Park" up at Latrobe. It used to be a scout camp. The local people fixed it up after the flood with some help from the County. It's got two picnic shelters there and a few basketball hoops. That's the only place for kids to play except for the postage stamp sized playground at Kistler. Most kids have to drive down to south Man for recreation. There are ball fields and an outdoor swimming pool down there that they can use. There's not a whole lot for them up here except for trails for four-wheeling.

*   *   *

In sum, despite the best intentions of the drafters of the Buffalo Valley Redevelopment Plan, only a fraction, perhaps 30 percent, of the plan's recommendations for infrastructure development have been implemented. The recommendations that have been implemented certainly have been worthwhile, although they are not without complaints from some local citizens. And yet, it is also true that a number of the needs that prompted various recommendations in the plan have been met by including Buffalo Creek's former coal camps in the consolidation of public services throughout Logan County. In effect, Logan County and the state of West Virginia have largely taken over and funded the public education and the fire-and-emergency–rescue services for the people of the valley. Most residents I spoke with seem to be resigned to these changes, if not indifferent to them, rather than enthused about them as evidence of progress having come to the Buffalo Creek Valley.

By way of commentary, let me suggest that the modernizing of Highway 16 probably was a mixed blessing. As in so many other rural areas of the United States, the new highway has reduced the insularity of the former camps at the upper end of the valley—from Latrobe to Curtis—for residents who can drive. Now it is quicker and easier for them to get to the stores and services in Man and Logan. The new highway also makes it easier for drivers who are employed to use the valley as a home base as their *residence*—if not as a residential community, in the full sense of the term. At the same time, however, the new highway makes it more difficult for most residents to watch others drive by, wave, and exchange pleasantries when they sit on their porches and walk, work, and play in their yards. It no longer serves as an easy avenue for gesturing and social exchanges—kind of a "town square" that Kai Erikson referred to in one of the quotations in chapter 2. It also makes it much harder for the few remaining local stores and businesses in the valley to monopolize trade with local residents. Combined with ready access to cable TV and other in-home electronic entertainments, the highway makes it easier for Buffalo Creek's residents to ignore local community life and their neighbors along Buffalo Creek—a subject that we address at considerable length in chapters 4 and 5.

OTHER CONSIDERATIONS REGARDING INFRASTRUCTURE

As suggested in table 3.2, there have been other events, both positive and negative, that have impacted Buffalo Creek's infrastructure development, besides events that were spawned by the plan and changes that occurred since the early 1990s when Logan County included Buffalo Creek into all of its consolidated service districts.

The Roadside Memorial Park and Historical Marker

In 1973 a group of residents created a Buffalo Creek Disaster Memorial Committee, raised about $20,000 through local donations, purchased a small parcel of land adjacent to Highway 16 in Kistler—only sixty feet from the creek—and built a modest Memorial Park there in honor of the 125 residents who perished in the flood.[51] The park has a small, open-sided portico and a few benches. Across the road from the park, and immediately adjacent to the creek, stands a simple, six-square-foot, metal marker that the West Virginia Division of Archives and History erected in 2005. It reads as follows:

BUFFALO CREEK DISASTER

> One of (the) worst floods in US occurred here 26 February 1972, when Buffalo Mining Co. impoundment dam for mine waste broke, releasing over 130 million gallons of black waste water: killed 125; property losses over $50 million; and thousands left homeless. Three commissions placed blame on ignored safety practices. Led to 1973 Dam Control Act and $13.5 million class action legal settlement in 1974.

This park and this historical marker might seem to be insignificant to outsiders who drive by without any previous knowledge of the flood. And yet, let me suggest that they are very important to some of the older survivors of the flood, not just for their symbolic value, but also as meeting places for reunions and for annual commemorative ceremonies. This also is the only place where visitors can stop anytime—day or night—read about the flood, and record their sentiments on a simple paper notebook on a pedestal under the portico. Many of the visitors are former residents of Buffalo Creek, or their descendants and friends, whose families survived the flood but moved away. Many of these visitors are unable to find any other place in the valley that they can associate with the flood and where they can meet other visitors who are interested in the flood. They exchange names and addresses with other visitors at the Memorial Park. Some of them embrace each other, cry together, pray together, and reminisce together. The Memorial Park thus becomes the most palpable and memorable place at Buffalo Creek for them. Beyond this, memorial ceremonies are held at the park and at local churches each year on the anniversary date of the flood, February 26. Reporters and photographers from newspapers and TV stations in the region provide coverage of these events.

Now, it is true that events and structures such as these are not ordinarily considered to be *infrastructural* aspects of communities. Yet I believe that—at places like Buffalo Creek that are relatively traditional, rural, and "folksy"—these elements are just as important to community well-being as are the more commonly accepted elements of infrastructure: roads, bridges, water and sewage facilities, government services, schools, and businesses. It is for these reasons that all of these elements should be taken into consideration when we think about what has been recovered, rebuilt, and re-created along Buffalo Creek. This point also extends, to some extent, a small, four-room community building that a small number of residents financed and built at Lorado (Davy Hollow) in 1977. This very modest community building has served a number of purposes since then. Currently, a nonprofit organization, Pride, runs a Head Start educational program there for preschoolers. Many of the older residents at the upper end of the valley take considerable pride in having helped build this facility in the years immediately after the flood. One of them told me: "Well, it showed that we could do something on our own. The Governor and the State and the coal companies didn't build a big community center for us down in Accoville, like they was supposed to do. So we built something for ourselves up here."[52]

And yet, as noted previously, some community leaders have told me that it would be a waste of money to build physical structures to serve as community centers. They asserted that this is because the people of Buffalo Creek are so clannish that they would ignore the community centers and would continue to congregate, when they congregate, as clans and as extended families in the homes and churches of other members of their clan.

Religious Groups, Churches, and Church-Related Services in the Valley

A strong case can be made that religious groups, churches, and church-related social services and entertainments are the most common and important forms of institutional life along Buffalo Creek, outside of the family and clan. On a given week, there are probably at least twenty meetings of religious groups and organized churches operating in the valley, and they probably involve at least 700 of Buffalo Creek's 3,100 residents (with quite a few residents participating in more than one service per week). Some religious groups meet and function without a permanent church building of their own. Most of the fifteen churches in the valley are simple, unpretentious chapels of one to four rooms, without offices or living accommodations for preachers or ministers. And yet, in the course of a week, more residents of Buffalo Creek assemble at these churches than at any other place or kind of place along Buffalo Creek. Church services on Wednesday evenings, Saturdays, and Sundays are the most frequent weekly events in the valley. The church services themselves are only a small part of the social and benevolent activities that the congregations participate in. Members of the congregations organize food pantries, clothing drives, raffles, pot luck suppers, and bus and van trips to other churches, malls, theaters, and casinos far from Buffalo Creek. I have been told that the flood destroyed about ten of the more than thirty church buildings along Buffalo Creek. Several of them were rebuilt farther down the valley on land that was designed to be more flood resistant. While it is likely that a much smaller percentage of Buffalo Creek's residents are active churchgoers than was the case before the flood—in keeping with the well-documented decline in church attendance by so many sectors of the U.S. population—there is no doubt that churches and churchgoing are still very salient elements in the social life of many of Buffalo Creek's residents, especially older residents including grandmothers and their middle-aged daughters with preschool and grade-school–aged children.

Failure to Incorporate the Coal Camps
An event that is still controversial and divisive along Buffalo Creek occurred more than twenty-five years ago. Fortunately, it did not involve a flood or any type of natural disaster, although it had major ramifications for Buffalo Creek's infrastructure and for social factors including community cohesion. Around 1980, a referendum to incorporate all of the camps was defeated by a fairly wide margin. Several residents told me that the defeat was attributable to "scare tactics and propaganda" by local coal companies and by some business interest groups in Logan. The local new media were filled with speculations that, if the camps incorporated, the coal companies would no longer be required to pay severance taxes for road maintenance and for other infrastructural support in the valley. Allegedly, citizens would be obliged to pay additional taxes in order to build sidewalks and curbs, to modernize their schools, and to fund their own police force and municipal offices. These speculations worried so many of Buffalo Creek's citizens that they voted against incorporating the camps. Infrastructure development stalled for years after that. Even now, some residents regret the failure to incorporate. They believe that it will never happen because of voter apathy, the shrinking population of the valley, and Logan County taking over many of the public services that Buffalo Creek's people formerly provided for themselves or that were provided for them by the coal companies.

I believe there are at least three other reasons why more than one-half of the adult residents I have spoken with have little interest in the prospect of incorporating any of the villages in the valley. Some of these residents are not aware that residents of hamlets and small villages can try to incorporate. Often these residents know of dozens of other hamlets and villages in southwestern West Virginia that are not incorporated, and they more or less assume that this is the way things are meant to be. Other residents are of the opinion that all governments and most elected leaders cannot be trusted. They are corrupt, more or less, or they will become corrupt in short order. It is assumed that adding another level of government—becoming a town, in this case—would just increase the amount of corruption that citizens already have to deal with at the county and state levels. There also are a considerable number of residents of the valley who oppose just about any change in any aspect of government, particularly more government at the local level, out of fear that it will encroach further on freedoms that they relish as "mountaineers" and in keeping with the motto of the state of West Virginia—"*Montani Semper Liberi*" ("Mountaineers are always free").[53] More than a few of these people have indicated to me that the nearest government is so far away (in Logan—only thirteen miles from Man, but often a hazardous drive of more than thirty minutes on the narrow twists and turns of Route 10) that they do not have to worry about whether they are breaking any laws. A few of them burn trash outdoors, accumulate lots full of junked vehicles, let their chickens, goats, and dogs run free, make as much noise as they care to make, and allow their helmetless youngsters to drive motorized vehicles with reckless abandon on public roads. Incorporation of the villages in the valley is not what they are looking for—nor is enforcement of "nuisance" laws.

Three Recent Economic Boosts:
The Hatfield-McCoy National Historic Trail,
Trails and Tournaments for Drivers of All-Terrain Vehicles,
and the Resurgence in Coal Mining
At least three economic boosts have occurred since 2000 in and around the Buffalo Creek Valley. A Hatfield-McCoy National Historic Trail System has been created, funded, and advertised nationally. It is based on the famous feuds between the Hatfield and the McCoy clans at the turn of the twentieth century that were popularized in many newspaper articles, novels, films, and songs since then. The trail system includes dozens of sites throughout southwestern West Virginia and eastern Kentucky where the Hatfield and McCoy clans lived and battled each other, as the stories go. These sites are identified by distinguished-looking roadside markers and descriptive plaques, several of which are within

a few miles of Buffalo Creek. In fact, the administrative offices for the trail system and a tourist attraction with a fetching name, "The Bear Wallow," are less than ten miles from the Buffalo Creek Valley.

In addition to these attractions, agencies of the state of West Virginia have collaborated with local business interests in co-opting or creating hundreds of miles of recreational trails across the mountains for drivers of a bewildering array of all-terrain vehicles (ATVs) with any number of axles, wheels, and tracks for a sport generically referred to as "four-wheelin'." Many of these trails connect abandoned coal mining sites in the ridges above the valley. Each year local business groups sponsor dozens of rallies and tournaments to attract four-wheelin' enthusiasts from around the country. Reportedly, some enthusiasts have traveled from as far away as Japan and Germany to ride the trails above Buffalo Creek. If so, advocates of globalization might gleefully claim that Buffalo Creek has joined the "global village."

Local leaders claim that the growing popularity of the McCoy-Hatfield Trail and the four-wheelin' trails brings thousands of visitors and millions of dollars of revenue into the Buffalo Creek area each year. They also say that this revenue has resulted in the opening of at least ten new service-oriented businesses within a few miles of the lower end of the valley. These include franchises of convenience stores, gas stations, fast food outlets, tobacco outlets, drug stores, dealers and repair shops for all-terrain vehicles, package stores, and bed and breakfast operations. Slot machine gambling, keno, and lottery ticket sales are popular at many of these new businesses, and they thrive at some of the old ones. Community leaders are uncertain about the net effects of these new enterprises on the people of Buffalo Creek. One former owner of a small business in Man told me,

> Well, I don't know how much those new stores are helping the people up along Buffalo Creek. Most of those new places are down near the new section of Route 10 outside of Man. I don't know that those places are creating that many jobs, or many good jobs. And, if the Buffalo Creek people drive all the way down to the new stores, it might hurt the few stores that are still up along the creek.

A resident of Lundale also was uncertain of any direct benefits from the new businesses to the people of Buffalo Creek.

> It's a mixed situation, seems to me. It's nice to have some new stores down there so we don't have to drive all the way to Logan so often. But it's still pretty far for us to drive; maybe further than before for some things. A few months after that big new drug store opened outside of Man, a little drug store we had for years right in Man closed down. So now we got to drive four miles further just to get our prescriptions filled.

In terms of economic activity, the most dramatic and visible change along Buffalo Creek in many years is the reopening of the railroad line from Fanco the new coal-loading dock at Pardee. The line opened in March 2006, and the first coal train to pass through Lorado and Lundale reportedly was cheered on by some of the residents from their porches and yards. One lifelong resident of Lundale who survived the flood and is now in her seventies had this to say about the reappearance of the coal trains in the upper valley:

> Them new coal trains sure make the rudest noises you ever heard, all day and night, when they come to the road crossings and the curves in the tracks up here. They got engines at both ends now so the trains don't have to turn around. It's kind of weird to look at—but it works. I'm glad to see them runnin' again after all these years. I sit out here on my porch and wave at them when they go by. Them conductors probably think I'm crazy or something. But you know what? Some of 'em even wave back!

For many of the older residents, the reappearance of the coal trains is welcome evidence of a resurgence in the coal economy and that Buffalo Creek is not forgotten. It gives some of them hope that employment prospects will improve for young men and women along the Creek who might otherwise have to leave the region in search of jobs.

The opening of the rail line to Pardee was the latest event in the boom in the coal economy in southwest West Virginia that began about 2001.

Until then, only one large mine was operating in the immediate vicinity of Buffalo Creek. It is on Laurel Ridge ("Kelly Mountain") a few miles from Fanco. Its coal is sent down the mountain on a metal-roofed conveyor belt to the old loading dock at Fanco, where it is sorted and stored until it is shipped out by one or more eighty-car coal trains per day. As the market for steam coal grew in the early 2000s, Appalachian Fuels Corporation of Kentucky invested heavily in the coal fields of Logan County and announced that it would start major new mining operations on Laurel Ridge above Pardee, near the head of the valley. Residents I spoke with generally had mixed opinions about the increased traffic from the coal trucks. While they were glad that the coal economy was expanding, they were annoyed by the speed of the coal trucks and by the amount of noise and dust they made in speeding down the valley. And so, it is no wonder that these residents said that they were glad when, in March 2006, the rail line reopened and coal trains replaced many of the coal trucks.

Taken all together, we should not be surprised if these three economic boosts have created a new sense of excitement and pride along Buffalo Creek among a considerable number of the residents, particularly those who have benefited financially from them, or hope to do so in the future. A widely respected, retired, local businessman had this to say about these recent changes:

> I'd say it's fundamentally better now than it was before the flood. The people are happier now because the economy has brought wealth to many. There are modern conveniences for just about everyone. Sure, we have some homeless people and people with drug problems. But every place has that. Now the economy is booming. Not just the coal mines, either. There are machine shops, mine suppliers, and all sorts of new businesses going up. New houses are going up along the Creek. One of them is a fancy place that probably cost maybe a half million dollars. That McCoy-Hatfield tour and the four wheel trails are bringing in the business too. Local people set up four or five lodges just for the ATV riders that come in on the weekends. Those riders don't cause many problems.

Most are business people and retired people who just come in to
ride. We call them "OMTs" not ATVs—old men's toys.

SOME OBSERVATIONS AND A LOOK AHEAD

To conclude this chapter, let us return to the questions that opened it.

What Does Buffalo Creek Look Like Today?

Writing as objectively as I can and admitting that I am forever an "outsider," allow me to tell you how the Buffalo Creek Valley appeared to
me the first time I drove through it from the town of Man, at 9:00 a.m.
on a Saturday morning, March 1, 2000. This was the same time of day,
a Saturday, and the same time of the year, late winter, that the flood
occurred, twenty-eight years earlier. It has not changed dramatically, at
least not to the naked eye, since I first drove through it.

As I drove, I could not help but look for physical evidence of that terrible flash flood that occurred here on February 26, 1972. How many of
the former coal camps still existed? Were there obvious but strange, barren stretches of land along the creek that would somehow reveal where
the coal camps had been? Were there still piles of debris and rubble from
the flood that had not been removed, for whatever reason? Were there
black watermarks on the sides of rocks, cliffs, and buildings? Were
there monuments and other public testimonies about the flood? Were the
inhabitants of the valley up and about on that Saturday morning? Were
they looking and behaving differently than the people I had seen in so
many other coal camps, hamlets, villages, and towns in Appalachia?
Were they living near the creek? Were they avoiding it? Was there some
sense of menace about the creek? And, of course, I was looking for *the*
place, at Three Forks, where the dams collapsed on that fateful day so
long ago. Was it inhabited again? Was it commemorated in some way?
Was it still dangerous?

But, alas, as indicated in the preface of this book with the anecdote,
"Gunner McGruff and Ground Zero," the answers were not obvious to
many of these questions. I could not readily identify more than a few of

the former coal camps as I drove along. I did not see any black water-marks anywhere. I did not see old piles of rubble or broken and aban-doned buildings that I could attribute to the flash flood of so long ago. And I do not believe that I even saw the little Buffalo Creek Memorial Park at the side of the road in Kistler until I drove back down through the valley hours later, and after Gunner McGruff told me to keep an eye open for it.

What I did see on that first trip up the valley, and what I continue to see there each time I visit, is a narrow valley that twists and turns its way for more than seventeen miles beneath two very steep, heavily forested ridges. Except for Kistler, the former coal camps are off to the side of the highway, usually down in low-lying bottomland. They are not clearly delineated by boundaries, road signs, or other markers. Occasionally, I see glimpses of the creek, brown and shallow for the most part, run-ning swiftly at some places, drifting at others. Except for late mornings on Saturdays and for early evenings, May to October, few people are outside. Those who are outside seem oblivious to the creek.

Kistler, Crown, and Accoville seem very much like other former coal camps that I have seen elsewhere in Logan County. Each one has a few convenience stores, churches, and other buildings for commerce of some sort or the other. Most of the dwellings are much older than forty years old. Some of them date back to the 1920s. Some have been modern-ized. Some are tidy but are in their original form. Some are dilapidated. Some are for rent. Many are occupied by short-term renters rather than by their owners. More than a few appear to be abandoned. A few of these have been vandalized. From here on, it is hard to determine where the highway crosses over from one side of the creek to the other because the bridges are short, without superstructure and demarcations, and they are flush with the road.

Braeholm is difficult to recognize as anything more than a cluster of dwellings in bottomland. The same thing would be true of Becco except that a large church and a substantial hardware store are visible from the highway. Fanco is distinguished by a steel-roofed coal conveyor that crosses thirty feet above Highway 16 to a coal tipple, a few three-story heaps of shiny black coal, and a coal-loading station for trains. With one large, red-brick church, a smaller one of white concrete blocks, and about thirty modest houses and trailers, it appears to be more of an actual coal camp than the other former coal camps in the valley.

Amherstdale and Robinette appear as creekside villages with a few convenience stores and churches, a few buildings that may or may not be in use for industrial purposes, and a mixture of older and newer houses and manufactured homes. Then again, Amherstdale does have a substantial-looking grocery store in a modern-looking industrial building. It also has some of the newest and most expensive-looking homes in the entire valley, several of which are built on elevations at least fifty feet above the creek. The most impressive of these is located on three acres of handsomely landscaped, level land at the entrance to Accoville hollow, on the other side of the highway from the creek. It features an impressive mansion and several other sprawling, red-brick buildings with tall, white columns.[54]

From this point on, about midway up the Buffalo Creek Valley, there are long stretches along the highway without any buildings or evidence of human activity other than an occasional coal truck or passenger vehicle. When driving at forty miles per hour, Latrobe, Crites, and Stowe appear to be little more than quiet hamlets with no industry or commerce.

Lundale appears several miles farther on along a straight, gradually inclining half-mile stretch of the highway. It seems newer than the other former coal camps that we have passed so far. Most of the dwellings closest to the highway appear to be about twenty to thirty years old. And yet, there are also several large two-story wooden homes that would seem to have predated the flood by many decades.

Lorado is similar to Lundale in its topography, size, and the relative youth of most of its dwellings that border the highway. It has a compact and newly painted U.S. Post Office in what appears to be a double-wide manufactured home, fronted by an asphalt parking lot. Other than that, the absence of stores and other conveniences in Lorado gives the impression that it essentially is a quiet, rather remote roadside hamlet of about one hundred and fifty residences and two small churches. And, like Lundale, Lorado also has a number of much older, rather large two-story homes that surely predate the flood by many years.

Above Lorado, the valley narrows and steepens appreciably. It is here that several obvious changes have occurred in the past few years—for this is the gateway-access area to the massive new coal mine that is operating out of sight on the ridgeline above Pardee. The railroad line that runs very close to the highway has been cleared, repaired, and cleaned. There is no vegetation or debris near it. The steel rails shine brightly. The railbed has new gravel. The cross ties are of reinforced concrete—not creosote-soaked hardwood. Highway 16 and the railroad abruptly fork to the right as they follow the main branch of Buffalo Creek. To the left is a mud staging area with a half dozen grimy coal trucks, several huge, yellow "Caterpillar" earth-moving machines, and a guard shack. Signs are posted on the guard shack and in the nearby trees: "Appalachian Fuels LLC," "Limited Access," "No Trespassing."

The right fork of the road brings us past a line of seven humble dwellings that some folks refer to as Pardee.[55] A few manufactured homes less than twenty-five years old are located farther along the road, at least 500 yards below what was once the epicenter of Three Forks (Saunders)—the uppermost Buffalo Creek coal camp and the first one to be smashed by the flash flood of 1972. Other than for a widening of the floodplain and a small, debris-choked waterfall about twenty-five feet high, it is easy to overlook this place that once constituted the coal camp of Three Forks, and to continue driving another mile up the unpaved road, covered with loose gravel, until reaching another former coal camp, Curtis. It is so remote and obscure that it is not usually referred to as part of Buffalo Creek.[56]

*   *   *

Looking back, then, and from an "outsider's" roadside view, Buffalo Creek appears to be a rather heavily forested and tranquil rural valley that includes an uncertain number of sparsely populated hamlets and villages that date back to the 1920s. Unless we encounter coal trucks on the highway, or see one of the several coal trains that move up and down the valley each day, there is little evidence of industry or of the economic base of the valley except for the coal tipples and railroad load-outs at Fanco and Pardee. This view obviously is decidedly different from the views that we had of Buffalo Creek in chapters 1 and 2—back when it was a bustling, coal mining community, and then, when it was so badly devastated by the flood.

To What Extent Has Buffalo Creek Valley's Infrastructure Been Rebuilt? Modernized?

It seems fair to answer that the valley's roads, bridges, and utility systems have been not only rebuilt, but they also have been modernized. They are well maintained, and at little cost to Buffalo Creek's residents. The same is true of the valley's fire-and-rescue services. Considerable improvements have been made in the safety of the floodplain in the valley. Many of the dwellings that have been built or installed since the flood appear to be protected from all but the most extreme floods of the main creek that might occur rarely, if ever. A considerable amount of new and renovated housing has been erected or installed since the flood, mainly by survivors of the flood and their descendants, on small parcels of land at Accoville, Amherstdale, Lundale, and Lorado. And yet, the valley only has about 3,100 residents now—about 60 percent of the population size at the time of the flood. It is estimated that, since the flood, owner occupancy of dwellings has decreased from about 90 percent to less than 70 percent—especially in the lower valley where much of the housing that survived the flood is more than fifty years old and is occupied by short-term renters. The infrastructure is less modern in the lower valley—at places including Crown and Kistler—because the flood was much less destructive there. It is also for this reason that most of the relatively few industrial buildings that remain in the valley are in the lower valley. Very few industrial buildings remain in the valley above Amherstdale except for a water pumping plant at Lorado, and the tipples and load-outs at Fanco and Pardee.

Countywide consolidation of the schools has removed all but one public school from the valley. Very few stores and consumer services remain in the valley above the town of Man, and those that remain are mainly at Kistler and Accoville at the lower end of the valley. Almost no medical and health care services remain in the valley now except for two small residential facilities for people with mental retardation.

While churches usually are not considered to be part of the physical infrastructure of communities so much as an element of their social structure, churches are still abundant in the valley, and they provide important social outlets and support services for quite a few of the valley's residents—beyond the spiritual services that they provide to the members of their congregations.

How Was the Infrastructure Rebuilt, by Whom, and at What Cost?
To the extent that the physical infrastructure has been rebuilt, much of the rebuilding was done in the first five years after the flood—1972–1977— for more than $20 million, primarily in federal funds. This rebuilding was done more or less according to the Buffalo Valley Redevelopment Plan under the direction of various agencies of the state of West Virginia, including the Office of Governor Arch Moore. Since then, infrastructure modernization has occurred sporadically and through initiatives of the Logan County Commission, the state of West Virginia, private businesses, and business-interest groups. The total costs for these more recent and ongoing efforts have not been tabulated, but they probably exceed $30 million.

How Involved Were the Flood's Survivors in the Rebuilding Process?
The vast majority of the rebuilding and modernizing of the roads, bridges, and utility systems was by agencies of federal, state, and Logan County agencies, often with contracts to private associations and businesses. It appears that relatively few of the flood's survivors were involved directly as employed planners, managers, and laborers in the modernizing process. Only one voluntary association of citizens, the Buffalo Creek Citizens' Committee, seems to have been "consulted" by the Federal-State Task

Force about the rebuilding process. It is not apparent that either the committee or unaffiliated flood survivors had very much influence on the rebuilding and modernizing of the valley's infrastructure. As indicated in chapters 2, 4, and 5, many survivors wanted to "go home again" to the same homesites they had occupied before the flood. They hoped that schools, playgrounds, and a wide variety of shops and stores would return to their former communities and that these places would be all-purpose and satisfying communities once again. They were stunned and saddened as they came to realize that this would not be the case. Rather than move away forever, or form interest groups and protest aggressively, hundreds of the survivor families gradually decided that they would try to make do with what would be available to them in the valley as government agencies oversaw the rebuilding of the infrastructure. They did this on their own, more or less individually, rather than collectively or in consultation with a number of different outside agencies.

Seen in this light, the rebuilding of the major elements of Buffalo Creek's infrastructure was not attributable to the "social capital" of its survivors. For, if we define "social capital" as the "civic engagement, participation in voluntary organizations, networks of interaction, and the organizational and physical settings for such interaction,"[57] then it does not appear that Buffalo Creek's survivors had much social capital. It was primarily because of political leadership and the financial resources and cooperation of county, state, and federal agencies that the physical infrastructure of the valley was modernized—in conjunction with large constructive companies from outside the valley.

How Have They Responded to It? Do They Appreciate It?
Chapters 4 and 5 provide many recent testimonies by the people of Buffalo Creek about these questions. I believe it is fair to say that the responses by many of the survivors have been mixed. This is especially true of the adult survivors who have not been able to reachieve the kind of homelife and community life that they cherished before the flood. At the same time, many of these people appreciate the improved roads, housing,

and utility systems in the valley, the low cost of living, and the absence of local government interference in their lives. Most of them realize that living conditions could be considerably worse than they are in the valley. They also realize that the way of life they had in the old coal camps probably would not have lasted until now, even without the flood in 1972.

And so, it seems fair to say that there is a moderate level of acceptance and appreciation of the positive aspects of the rebuilding and modernization of Buffalo Creek's infrastructure, even among the residents who lament the loss of schools, stores, services, and jobs. Many of these people have come to realize that similar changes in infrastructure, both positive and negative, have occurred to so many coal camps, villages, and towns throughout southwestern West Virginia—throughout Appalachia, for that matter.

Having said this, however, with some reluctance I must admit that there are at least two elements of Buffalo Creek's population that do not appreciate the rebuilding that has been achieved. The first element consists of survivors who were so damaged by the flood that they could never respond favorably to anything that followed the flood, possibly even if this involved some magical retransformation of Buffalo Creek back to pre-flood conditions. The second element consists of persons in a variety of situations who have little or no knowledge of the flood and its immediate negative aftereffects and who are unable or unwilling to respond positively to much of anything, let alone appreciate anything. Included here are persons who are extremely ill and others who are bitter and alienated because they are residing along Buffalo Creek more or less involuntarily. Many of these people are low-income, short-term renters of the aging housing stock in the lower valley that was not destroyed in the flood. Some of these people have no other resources or places to live. Others are heavily addicted to drugs. Some have little or no idea what happened to Buffalo Creek years ago, or since then. Some could care less. Some are just mad at the world. Then again, let me say that I have found variations like these among the inhabitants of many other places in the United States, not just along Buffalo Creek.

And yet, even with these caveats, I must admit that some of the people who respond most favorably to what has been rebuilt at Buffalo Creek, and appreciate it the most, are people who lived at the lower end of the valley, as well as people who were not living at Buffalo Creek at the time of the flood. These people toured the valley in the hours, days, and weeks after the flood. They were aghast at how badly it was damaged. To quote one of them, a respected businessman and longtime resident of Man who was born at Kistler many years before the flood had this to say:

> So it's taken years, and it hasn't been straight progress all of the way. We've had some slow times in the coal industry since then. There's been changes and problems in the government in Charleston, too. They set us back some. Like fifteen years ago things was pretty sad around here. But I'd say it's kind of a miracle today, when you think about it. To see it rebuilt like it is now up in the Valley with all the houses and manufactured homes in different colors, styles, and all that. They got good roads and bridges, too. Some people from the flood are still coming back here to retire.

Is It More Beautiful Than Before?

Given the widely held belief that "beauty is in the eye of the beholder," I am obliged to say that I have never heard anyone say or imply that Buffalo Creek was, or is, "beautiful" or a "beautiful place to live," either before or since the flood. As indicated in chapter 4, I have heard more than a few survivors say that Buffalo Creek was a "wonderful" place to live—*before* the flood. Sadly, I have never heard anyone say that Buffalo Creek is or has been "wonderful" since the flood. Then again, as we might expect from tried-and-true "Mountaineers of West Virginia," some survivors have told me that they regard as "wonderful" and "beautiful" the many mountains around and above their homes at Buffalo Creek. And so, I must conclude that Buffalo Creek has not been rebuilt "more beautiful than before" to anyone other than the person who was quoted above.

**Has It Been Rebuilt in Such a Way as to Enhance
Social Relations, Social Integration of the Community,
Communality, and Social Well-Being of the Residents?**

The Buffalo Valley Redevelopment Plan does not use these terms. It *does* use the term "community cohesion" several times in such ways as to indicate that community cohesion is a goal in rebuilding Buffalo Creek. Chapters 4 and 5 present data that help us to determine the quality of contemporary social relations and these other social factors along Buffalo Creek. In the meantime, let me suggest that some of the ingredients in the rebuilding of Buffalo Creek could readily enhance social relations. For instance, the modernized roads, bridges, and utilities could make it easier for people all along the seventeen miles of the valley to visit with one another, communicate with one another, remain healthy, and reduce the sense of isolation from and conflict among the former coal camps. These changes could break down some of the social barriers that existed between and among the former coal camps. Survivors who had been displaced by the flood and who decided to move back to Buffalo Creek after the flood had considerable freedom to choose where they would locate and rebuild and thus, to some extent, freedom to choose their neighbors. People with enough resources built new homes or purchased manufactured homes that were new or were fairly new.

There are other ways in which rebuilding and modernizing the infrastructure of the valley might have improved social integration and social well-being for many of its people. A highly respected minister, whom I will refer to as Reverend Ezra Lighter, explained these to me as follows, and testified that the rebuilding of the infrastructure was not the only reason that a lot of recovery has occurred along Buffalo Creek:

> What helped Buffalo Creek recover the most, I believe, is that people down here turned back to God after the flood. It was so bad that they were willing to pull together. The ministers of the churches worked together and encouraged people to overcome

their problems. Many people down here have low self-esteem.
They don't look to the future very much, except maybe for some
of the ones that get good educations and don't move away. And
the coal companies discourage activism in people. You got to
challenge them and convince them that they can do it. They can
overcome problems if they work together and believe together.
That happened for a few years after the flood. People kind of
became activists, believe it or not.

Reverend Lighter explained how these changes helped in the recovery of community.

It probably sounds strange to hear this, but that flood destroyed
some of the things that kept people passive and set in their ways.
It kind of forced them to open their eyes and see beyond their
own little coal camp. Before the flood people kind of stayed in
their own camps and didn't trust the people in the other camps.
There was ill-feelings and distrust among the camps. Competition too. Most of them had their own stores, teams, and interests.
They were self-sufficient—or they thought they were. Not many
of those stores and services came back after the flood. So people
in the camps had to get out more; travel up and down the Valley,
to Man, and to Logan to get what they needed for their homes
and families. They got more of a sense of belonging to Buffalo
Creek as a whole community rather than to just their own camp.
And they had more things in common too, of course. They had
survived the flood. They decided to move back. They were with
other people who did the same thing.

Reverend Lighter also believes that the flood helped to break down
racial barriers in education, housing, and church membership that already
were weakening before the flood.

The flood helped integrate the races in some ways. There was a
lot more segregation before the flood. Buffalo Creek High School
in Accoville is where the Black kids went to school. Man High
was for the Whites. Now the kids go to the same schools. Housing
is more integrated, too. People can live where they want. Some

still prefer to live with people of their own race, of course. But it's voluntary, now. The same is true of the churches here. There are still some churches that have mainly Black or White congregations. But it's more a matter of choice now. The congregations get along well. The ministers work together on projects for the good of the Valley as a whole.

However, it also is likely that the consolidation of schools outside the valley, and the loss of stores, shops, and services in the valley, would reduce the opportunities that many residents have for seeing and conversing with other residents of their localities on an informal, daily basis. And so, it seems that it is prudent to suggest that Buffalo Creek's physical infrastructure was rebuilt and modernized in ways that inadvertently required Buffalo Creek's survivors, as well as newcomers to the valley, to create new forms of social relations, communality, and social well-being. Chapters 4 and 5 can help us determine whether they have succeeded in doing so.

Of course, it is also possible that rebuilding the infrastructure has helped the recovery of almost everyone *except* those people who were most traumatized by the flood. This is the opinion of more than a few knowledgeable leaders in Logan County, including one of the county commissioners. During an interview of more than one hour with me in his office, he very thoughtfully expressed his belief that the standard of living and quality of life have improved appreciably for most of the people of Buffalo Creek. Then he quickly added that these improvements are not and could not ever be enough to overcome the devastation they suffered in the flood.

> The general reputation is that the clean-up of the damage to Buffalo Creek took a few years but went pretty well. Many of the projects to modernize the Valley went well too. Those new housing developments have a lot of amenities, and it seems safer down there. They have some new recreation areas too. In many ways many of the people down there are better-off than they were before the flood, as far as housing, water, sewers and those kinds of things are concerned.

> But, I don't think that the people who were caught in the flood have been rehabilitated. The devastation level was just too great. Even the best plan and implementation couldn't have been a success in making them feel whole again. The mental costs and damages of the displacement were too great. I know families who dealt with it by leaving. Some of them moved here to Logan rather than stay back there. They won't go back ever again because it was too severe a loss for them. The psychological aspects could never be the same. I've gone to some of the memorial services down there. I spoke at the monument they built. So I don't think that they will ever be permanently rehabilitated.

Observations like this one imply that even a total and perfect rebuilding of the infrastructure would have been insufficient for the recovery of social well-being in some of the survivors of the flood. With this thought in mind, we should be prepared to find in the chapters ahead evidence that some survivors are not thriving. We should not be surprised to learn that community life is less than comforting to some of them.

ENDNOTES

1. This chapter benefited from conversations that I had with leaders in Logan County and in state government agencies in Charleston, West Virginia, including F. Rammie Barker, Buffalo Creek public service district supervisor David Crawford, and Logan County officials Arthur Kirkendoll and Roscoe Adkins, as well as many longtime residents of Buffalo Creek.

2. *Buffalo Valley Redevelopment Plan*, prepared by the Office of the Governor [of West Virginia], Federal/State Relations in Conjunction with Federal Regional Council (III), Charleston, WV, July 1973. This plan is the official report on how federal, state, and local government agencies conducted relief and recovery efforts and then planned and began rebuilding of the infrastructure of Buffalo Creek's sixteen coal camps from the day of the flood, February 26, 1972, until the report was issued in July 1973. This document serves as the primary source for the information in the first few sections of this chapter.

3. The principal source of statistical information presented in this chapter is the Buffalo Valley Redevelopment Plan (referred to henceforth as the plan in the chapter text; in the endnotes, as BVRP), supplemented by other sources noted throughout this chapter.

4. See Fritz, 1968.

5. In thinking about the timeliness of these reactions to the flood, readers should keep in mind that two days of heavy rains had produced flooding at many other hamlets, villages, and towns in southwest West Virginia, besides Buffalo Creek, although the flooding was not so disastrous as along Buffalo Creek. Also, as indicated several times in chapters 1 and 2, destructive flooding of residential communities by heavy rains was frequent in this area of West Virginia. Flooding caused by the collapse of gob ponds also was fairly common. State and county agencies had plenty of experience responding to floods of this nature—although probably not to floods of the magnitude of the Buffalo Creek flood.

6. Readers are advised that the source of this quotation, Brad Crouser, is an ardent admirer of Governor Moore. See Crouser's biography, *Arch: The Life of Governor Arch A. Moore, Jr.* (Chapmanville, WV: Woodland Press, LLC, 2006) 311.

7. BVRP, 26.

8. Ibid., 25.

9. Notice that this assessment does *not* claim that all water supply systems were destroyed. Dozens of households in the side hollows of the valley had their own wells or had water lines connected to small springs up on the hillsides. Personal inverview with David Crawford, Manager, Buffalo Valley Public Service District, July 2004.

10. BVRP, 25. It is worth noting that 834 of the estimated 1800–1900 homes along Buffalo Creek were *not* destroyed by the flood, according to the BVRP. Unfortunately, the plan does not specify whether the "deteriorating" and "dilapidated" homes that remained were damaged by the flood. However, the fact that 198 of the homes (approximately 10 percent of 1800–1900 homes) were in "sound condition" clearly establishes that the flood did *not* destroy "everything in its path" insofar as that metaphor is applied to all of the housing that constituted Buffalo Creek before the flood.

11. Ibid.

12. Ibid.

13. Ibid.

14. Ibid.

15. Reportedly, none of the flood victims ever filed for bankruptcy, despite the services that were offered through the office of the governor. Also, according to newsman F. Raamie Barker, one of the young attorneys who was sent to Buffalo Creek to provide free legal services to the victims was a future congressman and governor—Bob Wise (see Crouser, *Arch*, 319).

16. BVRP, 28. According to several of my informants, this is the same organization, led by the late Charlie Cowan, that hired Arnold & Porter to conduct the now famous lawsuit against The Pittston Company and Buffalo Mining Company on behalf of hundreds of survivors.

17. BVRP, 21. The Buffalo Creek Citizens' Disaster Committee, Inc., is the only "grassroots" citizens organization among the more than fifty government and private-sector organizations that is mentioned in the acknowledgments section of the plan. I have found no evidence that other citizen's groups, or that unaffiliated members of the public, were included in the planning process. It is also interesting that the plan does not mention the participation of labor unions. And yet, Rammie Barker, a highly respected news reporter who covered the flood and its controversies for years, told me that "Representatives of the United Mine Workers had heavy input in the Plan to rebuild Buffalo Creek."

18. BVRP, 7, 24.

19. Notice that this statement in the BVRP explicitly calls for the development of attractive "*new communities*"—not just for the rebuilding of former

communities or of communities that still existed. It thereby envisions more than one community, and the communities that it envisions are to be new ones.

20. BVRP, 7.
21. Ibid., 20.
22. Ibid.
23. Ibid., 21.
24. Ibid. Notice the phrase "each new community" and similar phrases through-out the plan.
25. Ibid., 21.
26. Note the phrase "community cohesiveness"—implying that this was one of the qualities that the task force wanted to preserve or to achieve by having the plan implemented. This topic is of particular interest in chapters 4 and 5.
27. BVRP, 22.
28. Ibid., 19.
29. Ibid.
30. Ibid.
31. Ibid.
32. Ibid.
33. Ibid., 18.
34. Ibid., 19. At no time in my seven years of research along Buffalo Creek did I hear anyone mention that they recalled any "social unrest" or chronic unemployment in the Buffalo Creek area regarding veterans of the war in Vietnam.
35. Ibid., 18.
36. Ibid., 13, 18.
37. Ibid., 18.
38. Ibid., 21.
39. Ibid.
40. Ibid., 20.
41. The government leaders include former and current elected and appointed officials of the state of West Virginia, Logan County, and the town of Man. Community leaders include prominent local leaders in business, education, and religious organizations in and around Buffalo Creek. The Buffalo Creek residents are in addition to the more than ninety respondents whose accounts of neighboring and social well-being are analyzed in chapters 4 and 5.
42. Chapter 7 includes some of my observations about whether these beliefs by some of Buffalo Creek's current residents are well-founded and whether gob ponds no longer pose a serious threat to them. At this point, let me

simply say that I have walked some of the hills above Buffalo Creek. I have visited some of the old gob ponds and some of the new ones. While I am not a civil engineer, and I certainly do not want to be an alarmist, I can foresee conditions under which some of these former ponds could pose a threat to small numbers of dwellings at certain places along Buffalo Creek and, more directly, to dwellings along streams that feed into Buffalo Creek.

43. One resident of Robinette told me that volunteers "stretched a net across the creek to try to catch the bodies," but failed. One body was found at Accoville, and one body was found days later in the Guyandotte River at Logan. The other body has not been recovered.

44. Flash floods are still all too common in Logan County and surrounding counties. For example, in mid-April 2007, the U.S. Weather Service issued flash flood warnings for Logan County. Heavy rains caused mudslides over highways and houses and flooded some commercial districts of Logan with two to three feet of water. Some businesses were closed for more than two weeks because of damage from the floodwaters. Buffalo Creek overflowed Highway 16 at Kistler, but did relatively little damage to dwellings. Yet flooding was so severe that the Federal Emergency Management Agency declared a "state of emergency" for much of southwestern West Virginia.

45. This fact alarms me and concerns me from the standpoint of public safety. I have not been able to determine from public officials how or why these dwellings were allowed to be built so close to the creek.

46. Without these two new systems, it is doubtful that more than a few hundred families who were displaced by the flood could have moved back to the Buffalo Creek Valley. Only the two or three hundred families who had their own water sources and cesspools and who had not been displaced by the flood could have remained living in the valley.

47. One former volunteer fireman told me that the fire department has one "tag day" each year when it distributes "treats" to local children and accepts monetary donations from citizens. He quickly added that these donations are not a significant source of revenue for operating the fire department.

48. Over the years, I have not met residents of Buffalo Creek who indicated concern for energy conservation or the cost of fuel. It is almost as if they subconsciously assume that they have a right to consume inanimate energy with reckless abandon because their area of the United States is producing a lot of inanimate energy. Many of the people I visited at their homes have rather staggering numbers of vehicles and machines with gasoline-combustion engines in their garages and yards. One kindly grandfather, a

retired coal miner, had four ATVs chained together under his porch ("One for each of my grandkids"), three trucks, two cars, three riding lawnmowers, and countless "weed-whackers," snow-blowers, generators, and chain saws. When he noticed my amazement at his impressive collection, he responded with a laugh: "I can't seem to get them all runnin' at the same time."

49. A political insider in Charleston told me that Governor Moore made sure the plan included programs to help veterans of the war in Vietnam. He told me that Governor Moore was a veteran of WWII who had been awarded a Purple Heart and a Bronze Star and that he was very interested in veterans affairs and issues. "It was part of his vision for West Virginia."

50. While entirely "new communities" have not been built, there is evidence that a coalition of federal, state, and private agencies assisted hundreds of survivors in acquiring new lots and building new homes in the valley, starting as early as November 1972. The primary process through which this occurred apparently had the U.S. Department of Housing and Urban Development providing grants to the Builders' Emergency Housing Corporation of the West Virginia Home Builders' Association. These agencies then determined the sites where hew housing could be built safely above the floodplain. The agencies coordinated the installation of utility services at these sites and assisted prospective homeowners in purchasing land and in financing the building of their homes (HUD News, "Looking Ahead," November 1972, May 1973. Janet Dunn, editor. Office of the Department of Housing and Urban Development, Man, WV).

51. I hope that, within the next few years, the people of Buffalo Creek will see to it that a much larger memorial with a disaster-education center is constructed close to the source of the flood at Three Forks. A facility like this can educate schoolchildren and the general public not only about the flood, but also about how the people of Buffalo Creek struggled to recover from the flood, and how they were helped by so many external agencies and by so many "outsiders" who really cared about them.

52. Several community leaders told me that Arnold & Porter set aside some of the settlement money for the large community-center building that was called for in the plan. I could not confirm this information.

53. In keeping with this motto and a general distrust of governments, one native-born son of Buffalo Creek proudly reminded me that, during the Civil War in the 1860s, "my ancestors seceded twice—once from the Union, and again from Virginia."

54. This home clearly is the most expensive and visually impressive home in the valley. Its market value easily exceeds $1 million, even in Logan

County, according to one realtor I spoke with. Its owner-occupier, who is in the construction business, is well known to many of the older residents in the valley. They do not disparage his good fortune or his status symbol. As one resident told me, "He's one of our own (a native of Buffalo Creek). We're just different branches from the same tree. Besides, he's usually willing to help out whenever we need help around here."

55. As of May 2007, a brand new tipple and load-out was operating along the road and railroad tracks about 300 yards beyond this cluster of homes in Pardee, just below Three Forks. Coal trucks were bringing newly excavated coal down from the massive new mine on Laurel Ridge to the tipple for processing and storing until the coal was loaded into railroad gondola cars and transported down Buffalo Creek Valley through Man to Logan, and eventually to the Kanawha River near Huntington, WV. There also was a lot of brush clearing going on along the old railroad tracks and the roads to the old mines at Three Forks.

56. In fact, the first time I drove up the Buffalo Creek Valley, in March 2000, I inadvertently passed through the former coal camp of Three Forks and passed by the site of the failed dams until I found myself in the tiny, former coal camp called Curtis. When I stopped there for directions to Three Forks, one fellow informed me that I had "missed it by more than a mile."

57. This definition of social capital is derived from William W. Falk et al., eds., *Communities of Work: Rural Restructuring in Local and Global Contexts* (Athens, OH: Ohio University Press, 2003), 424. This book also provides a skeptical view of the utility of the concept of social capital as it might apply to understanding small, rural communities.

CHAPTER 4

BEING WITH PEOPLE OF BUFFALO CREEK

Some people went away to mental hospitals. Maybe I should have, too. I had counseling. But a lot of people got closer after the flood. They learned how quick life can go. People did talk to each other and help when they could. I don't agree with those experts about how people couldn't help themselves or their families anymore—how they couldn't even try. People stuck together a lot. Helped me a lot.

—Sam Chance, flood victim and retired coal miner

Everyone knew you got to put the round peg in the square hole. You knew what they wanted you to say. Some people told lies thinking they would get more money… . The kids had money to buy beer, drugs, cars, and whatever they wanted. So they didn't want to work or anything. They got into trouble, arguments, and fights… . That's why there were fights and divorces afterwards. It took maybe ten or fifteen years for things to settle down.

—Lonnie McCain, flood survivor and hard-working miner

It's a good neighborhood for us and for the kids…I'm real thankful that I got good neighbors, even though I'm not very sociable. Mainly I just stand and talk with them over the fences and along the road when it seems right. We respect each other. That's what's important—respect each other and each other's property.

—Arnie Canfield, disabled coal miner and patriarch
of the Canfield clan

It was just a little old coal miner's house when we got it…We also liked meeting all the new neighbors in the neighborhood. They really accepted us and made us feel real welcome. We'd go swimming in the pond down there in the Creek with all the other little kids.

—Becky Canfield Pollins, third-generation resident of Buffalo
Creek, speaking from her late grandparents' cottage
that was almost destroyed by the flood

*   *   *

Let us now consider how some of the people of Buffalo Creek feel about their current situation, about their past, and about the future. How important are neighbors and neighboring activities to them? Do they have a strong sense of social community and do they feel socially integrated into the community? Do they have a strong sense of their own well-being? Looking back over their lives, how do these people react to assertions by authors regarding the social conditions of Buffalo Creek before, during, and after the flood? Were the people totally unprepared for the flood? Did the flood destroy not only their dwellings but also their sense of well-being, their sense of community, their ability to care for others and to be cared for by others? Were these people hurt more than helped by the aftereffects of the flood: relocation to the HUD trailer camps, involvement in (or exclusion from) compensatory lawsuits against the coal companies, permanent loss of their homesites when the state of West Virginia built new roads and utility systems along Buffalo Creek? Were these people witnesses to, victims of, or participants in waves of substance abuse, interpersonal violence, marital infidelities, theft, and other forms of deviant behavior that were rumored to have occurred after the flood—and because of it? These are the questions at the core of this chapter.

We address these questions by describing what it has been like to meet, talk with, and socialize with twenty-two people who currently reside along Buffalo Creek, or who recently resided there until they passed away.[1] The first one is Molly Good. Molly often is referred to along Buffalo Creek as "our own goodwill ambassador" (to enhance privacy, all names have been altered and other kinds of identifying information have been altered or omitted, when deemed necessary, unless the people requested full disclosure). Molly was one of the first and most frequent respondents over the years. Then we will meet a number of people who had various experiences in the flood, generally presented from extremely severe to less severe, according to their own accounts. These include Sam Chance, Tina and Buck Miner, Goldie and Buddy Cummins, and Lureen and Jake Albro. Towards the end of this chapter, we will meet a few of Buffalo Creek's residents who had no direct experience in the flood, either because they were away from Buffalo Creek at the time of the flood, or because they were born after it. Included here are three generations of the Canfield family and Darren Service, a bright young college student who relishes his Buffalo Creek heritage. These people provide us with insights as to how members of the younger generation are getting along as neighbors and as inheritors to the legacy of the flood, even though they had no direct experience with it. Do they differ appreciably from the flood's survivors in their sense of well-being, neighborly relations, and attachments to Buffalo Creek as a social community?

Near the end of this chapter, we compare these people in terms of the levels of social well-being, neighborly relations, and social integration into the community. Doing this systematic comparison paves the way for the next chapter—chapter 5. It presents more quantitative and comparative analyses of purposive sets[2] of residents of Buffalo Creek, Elk Creek, and another fascinating and important social community in America, St. John, Washington. These analyses can help us estimate how well Buffalo Creek is doing as a social community—and, perhaps, how far it has to go. To start, let us meet some more of Buffalo Creek's good people (in addition to the encounter that we had with "Gunner McGruff" in the preface) and learn more about their perceptions, beliefs, social relations, and experiences. In doing so, we also can gain some intriguing insights into the nature of social life in the "coal country" of Appalachia and thus in a significant part of rural America.

MOLLY GOOD:
A HEART, SOUL, AND SPIRIT FOR BUFFALO CREEK

"You come on up for Sunday dinner. The whole family is gonna be here." So goes my introduction to Molly Good, sometimes called "the lady ambassador of Buffalo Creek," although Buffalo Creek has no ambassador or any elected officials of its own. "You gotta talk to Molly," so many people have told me. And they are so right. Molly Good is a sturdy, loving, and engaging widow in her sixties, with five grown children, at least a dozen grandchildren "and countin'," and hundreds of friends. She is a near perfect respondent: friendly, informed, connected, thoughtful, and entertaining. While I sit at her kitchen table, sundry children walk in and out of her double-wide trailer through the back door and circulate unimpeded through the rooms. Some are hers, some are "theirs," and all of them are welcome, at least until the place gets too chaotic. Then Molly scoots some of them out the back door with feigned irritation and a laugh. "Now you go tell your Momma hello for me. Don't tell her 'bout that cookie you got. Hear?" Her phone rings regularly with inquiries from their mothers and with news from friends up and down the Buffalo Creek Valley. Molly handles them all with patience and rapport, obviously gained from decades of experience. "Well, I'll be! Isn't that something now? Why don't we talk more about that tomorrow?"

Over the years of visiting Buffalo Creek, I have been fortunate to talk with Molly dozens of times and meet some of her legion of family members, kin, and friends. I attended church services with her. I drove around the coal camps with her while she gave me "Molly's tour." More often than not, we just sat around the table in her dining room or in her kitchen drinking coffee in her well-furnished and colorfully decorated, new double-wide trailer. She had it installed on the lot where her parents' home once stood at the gateway to this side hollow. Often Molly and her friends would start by making a few self-deprecating jokes about child rearing, before we turned to "biz'ness."

> Before you name your new baby, go out on the porch and holler the name three times. If the chickens come a runnin' you better try some other name.

> For the first two years you teach 'em to walk and talk. After that you try to get 'em to sit down and shut up.

> Thar ain't much time for no traveling salesmen when you got a houseful of young'uns. And Jehovah's Witnesses knowed they better stay clear of the house.

Molly often supports many of the assertions of the experts regarding social conditions before the flood and in the three years after the flood. She says that most people along Buffalo Creek did not realize that a flood of such magnitude could happen to them, and that hundreds of the survivors never really recovered their sense of well-being before they died in old age. However, she also states that a few of the most sweeping assertions "went way too far." Molly emphasizes that even though she personally knew dozens of the deceased persons and hundreds of the people who were relocated because they lost their homes, the flood was much less damaging for her, and for most or all of her family, than for most people, particularly for those who were relocated to trailer camps. Her former house was never damaged. It sat just across the road on the bank of a small brook. Nor was there much flood damage to this little hamlet. It is considered to be part of Lorado, but it runs back a ways from Buffalo Creek proper at an acute angle and into a steep ravine. Currently, the creek is on the other side of the single railroad track and the road, but less than one hundred meters from the closest dwellings of this hamlet. "The flood kinda bounced against the other side of the mountain over there and more or less missed us over here in the hollow. It was just a freak kinda thing that it did."

Molly and her husband, who died a few years after the flood (apparently from occupation-related diseases), already had their family of five children. They were comfortably situated, both socially and financially. He worked in a mine close by. Molly had a choice job as a school bus driver. She loved that job because it allowed her to supplement her husband's paycheck from the mine, make good wages for part-time work, and still be an active and important part in the life of the community. "Everybody knows the school bus driver around here. And I kinda know just about everybody along the Creek, their parents and their children, too." Molly appreciated her job even more after the flood. Many of the victims could not work or find ways to occupy their days in the trailer camps. Molly did her best to cheer them up and help them get along as best she could.

> So for me it wasn't so bad because we still had our family all together here in the hollow with our closest neighbors and all. Of course we lost hundreds of our neighbors in the rest of Lorado and more than that along other parts of the Creek. It was harder on my kids. They seen so much of the damage walking around with their friends and going to school and all.

Molly uses Lorado as a whole as her referent, not just this side hollow, when she reacts to findings of some of the experts. She says that this hollow was an exception. She agrees that it was a highly integrated community before the flood. "The community here was like a big family. Everybody had the same background. Most people knew one another. If there was sickness or a need, even the teenagers would go door-to-door to borrow food or whatever was needed."

Molly agrees that communality and neighbors were as the experts described them before the flood "for maybe 90% of the people, if not all people. Most people were ready to look after their neighbors when there was a need." He "hit the nail on the head," especially as to how it was in places like this hollow and the rest of Lorado. Neighbors treated you as if you were a member of the family. She adds that they "suffered when you suffered and were happy when you were happy." Molly is reluctant to talk about any exceptions to this kind of communality but, when asked, she admits that some families were less neighborly than others, some spouses had difficulties avoiding alcohol abuse and other temptations, and "some folks just don't know how to get along. I guess they never will, no matter what."

At the same time, however, Molly offers qualifications to some assertions about the immediate impacts of the flood. "He was kinda right about the flood leaving nothin' to build-on along most of the main road down to maybe Becco. That's less right about some parts along the Creek and the side hollows like this one." She then recounts several examples of both cases from her daily runs up and down the creek as a school bus driver. She agrees that, for many of the people who were relocated from the coal camps to the trailer camps, there was a feeling of uprootedness, and that it took months to recover. Those who could not recover "moved away from Buffalo Creek a second time and never come back." She says that many of the people, "maybe a large percentage—over 50%," might have lost their ability to console one another for a while, but that this was mainly in the trailer camps when people found themselves located next to strangers whose habits and personalities were new to them and who might have seemed more different or deviant than they really were. She gives examples of how it could be more alarming to hear people cursing, gambling, drinking, and arguing in the trailer camps, because you did not know whether they were really angry and prone to violence; whereas, "you knew what all this meant in the coal camps." Molly also agrees that probably there were some real increases in misbehaviors in the trailer camps, not just rumors about increases in fighting, alcohol and drug abuse, theft, juvenile delinquency, marital infidelity, divorce, and teen pregnancies. "It might have happened in some of those trailer camps, but I don't recall it happening up here in the hollow or where people could stay put." Molly also mentions a few instances of teenage boys stealing cars, even cars from their neighbors. She quickly adds that they were stopped by other neighbors or by the county sheriff.

When I ask her about what she saw and heard while driving the school busses in the years after the flood, she says that "it isn't clear to me that all that nasty behavior was happening like they said. You heard rumors about all that going on. Course, you heard rumors going on about every-thing. There's kinda always rumors going on around here."

At one point in our conversations, Molly's daughter, Dolly, joins in and helps us realize some of the ambiguities about life in the trailer camps. Dolly says that one of her friends "still lives in the HUD trailer camp down in Green Valley. That poor girl still has to live down there. That Green Valley is still trouble." Molly then goes on to repeat the often told accounts of how miserable and decadent life was in the trailer camps after the flood. Dolly, however, takes some exception to this. She tells us that some of her close friends lived in the camps, and that she visited them there, and still does from time to time. She does not recall that their experiences were as awful as rumored. When I ask Molly to describe her direct personal observations in the camps, she has trouble doing so.

> Well, I drove my bus only through the HUD camp at Latrobe (about five miles away). I can't really say that I recall seeing people drinking heavy or fighting and all down there—not in the streets anyways, or during the daylight when I was down there. I can't say I saw people gettin' beat up, stealin', gangs fightin', drugs being used, or crimes like that. I don't remember any in particular. There was some burned-out trailers down there some-times. I don't know how they happened. Maybe it was problems with the gas stoves or something. I know there was more fighting by the kids on my bus. It was mainly the small kids who didn't know each other. Their families come in from different coal camps that was washed out. HUD put them into the trailers at Latrobe and they didn't know each other. They couldn't figure out how to get along livin' near people they didn't know.

Based on ambiguities like these, I ask Molly and Dolly to help me meet some of the people who lived in the HUD camps and had direct experi-ences of what occurred in the camps. They readily agree to do this.

After Dolly leaves, Molly says that, while she believes that many people in the trailer camps distrusted their new neighbors who were strangers, she does not believe that they also had what some experts have referred to as a deep distrust even of old neighbors—except, perhaps, in the cases of a few teenage boys who were fatherless and who turned to auto theft until the neighbors and police intervened. "It was the old neighbors that helped people get through. We never had distrust for our old neighbors."

Yet, Molly's greatest disagreement with some of the experts is over their contention that people could not even take care of their own families or of themselves because of the flood. Molly insists that this just was not true of people, not just the people in her family and friends, but also for the many people she knows and that she knew back then.

> We helped each other a lot, and we still do. I heard about what some of them books said about us. When I heard about you coming, I told myself to tell you that some of that stuff that they wrote about us was just plain wrong. We were always able to take care of ourselves, and each other, and we always cared about our neighbors too. Lots of people here take exception to what they wrote about us not stickin' together no more.

Molly returns to this topic repeatedly, and it is the only topic on which she comes close to revealing anger.

Molly is not able (or willing, perhaps) to give examples of families who survived the flood only to disintegrate totally as families in the next few years. Rather, she contends that families often struggled for years but that they eventually "pulled through pretty good." Sadly, this was not necessarily true of all of their members, however. She acknowledges that some families lost some members to illnesses, tragedies, and desertions while the family itself was recovering.

> Sometimes maybe one or two of the teenagers got so disgusted with the situation here after the flood that they kinda left their families and moved away and tried to forget about Buffalo Creek. Some came back. Some didn't. Some who stayed here pretty much tried to ruin themselves doing crazy things with cars, drugs, and other people like them. Some others just give up, I guess. Older folks, mainly. Just quit. Lost hope.

Not surprisingly, Molly's responses on the survey form reveal her to be highly integrated into many aspects of Buffalo Creek as a social community: family, friends, neighborhood, church, schools, this hollow, Lorado, and Buffalo Creek as a whole social community. Of course, it is worth noting that many of her family members (at least twelve) live near her in four of the twenty dwellings in this hollow. One child of hers just built a home on an adjacent lot. Molly indicated that three of the things she likes best about Buffalo Creek are: "We recognize most people, we can converse with most people, and we can lie down at night to sleep without fear." What she likes least are: "We have to travel too far for employment, and the jobs are low wages." Molly has sixteen close relatives in Buffalo Creek, twenty-five elsewhere; eleven close friends in Buffalo Creek, and four elsewhere. Her best job was "twenty-eight years as a school bus driver." Lorado is the best place she ever lived (she was born in a different coal camp) and it is also the community that she feels closest to. Her happiest years were: "met my husband, 15 years old. We married when I was just at 16 1/2 years." She also lists 1957, when her first child was born, and 1976 (only four years after the flood) when her first grandchild was born. Molly adds, "Also the births of my other children, grandchildren, and great grandchildren only added to my joy." What does she miss most about the "old community" (the way it was years ago)? "There were more people with the same goals in life and they had the time to share them with one another."

As to neighbors and neighboring, Molly says that she has ten neighbors (defined as "the people who live in the homes and households close to your home in your community.") She answers "all" to the questions about how many she would recognize anywhere she saw them, how many she says hello or good-bye to, how many she knows by name. She says that she talks with any of her neighbors "whenever we meet." She has friendly talks fairly frequently with about four of them.[3] Her neighbors exchange or borrow things from her (and vice versa) "whenever we need to." She has been in the homes of all of them. She and her neighbors visit "whenever we feel the need to, and we talk on the phone two or three times a week."[4] Molly wrote that the most important quality of "a good neighbor" is "[j]ust being there through the good times and bad." Particularly memorable is her response to the question about how important neighbors are to her: "They rank up there with God and Family. They are essential in making me the person I am."

In a lengthy, heartfelt, self-initiated letter to me (and explicitly for you, the reader), she wrote that all of us should remember that the Buffalo Creek community was prospering in the years before the flood. "Wages increased enough that some people could afford air conditioning. Everybody had TVs. Some people had two cars and trucks and sometimes both of them even run." Survivors of the flood reacted in one of three ways, according to Molly. Some people withdrew from their own feelings and from dealing with other people. Some people became self-indulgent, "not realizing you can't really make yourself happy alone—only when you are making some other people happy, too." Others "reversed their ways. They become more free speaking. They started takin' more chances in life, maybe feeling you only live once, make the most of it. And don't be afraid to try to change things for the better."[5]

In weighing Molly Good's reaction to what some experts have had to say about Buffalo Creek, we should keep in mind that Molly drove a school bus up and down the coal camps of Buffalo Creek for many years before and after the flood. This afforded her daily observations with all sixteen of the coal camps, along with other places including Curtis (a remote hamlet of about thirty households that is about two miles above the point where the dams collapsed) and the town of Man. Molly agreed that the people in the upper coal camps were damaged badly by the flood and that it was a tragedy beyond words for many of them. However, Molly also allowed that this was not the case for her and for many of her neighbors. Molly also agreed with the experts that postflood recovery was especially difficult for some of the survivors who were relocated to the HUD trailer camps. And yet, contrary to some of the experts, Molly steadfastly and repeatedly asserted that survivors who remained along Buffalo Creek and were not forced to relocate never lost their ability and willingness to care for one another, their families, and their neighbors in the coal camps that they identified with.

As to the present time, Molly Good convincingly portrayed her situation as being neighborly enough for her and for many of the people she knows. She even went so far as to avow that some survivors of the flood became much more socially conscious and active in community affairs than they were before it. As to individual well-being, Molly often acknowledged that, while life has never been especially easy for her and for those she loves—either before or since the flood—she feels blessed to have been able to see it through.

SAM CHANCE:
"GETTIN' ALONG OKAY NOW, MOSTLY."

Sam Chance walks unhurriedly into the Hardee's fast food outlet a mile from the juncture of Buffalo Creek and the Guyandotte River. It is mid-morning and raining heavily. I wave to him from my table across the dining room. He acknowledges me with a nod. Then he stops at a table near the entrance and exchanges hellos and easy banter with seven retired or disabled "good ole boys," in work clothes and polyester baseball caps with logos of local equipment companies. They are idling away the morning, like most mornings, with coffee, cigarettes, and gossip. Sam is a compact, trim, gray-haired fellow in his midfifties. He looks more like a retired schoolteacher on his way to a round of golf than a former coal miner, now on workers' disability, who lost his wife and child in the flood.

Sam has lived in this area of Logan County all of his life, but he has not lived along Buffalo Creek since the flood. "I don't go up there except sometimes to visit my brothers and sisters." Several of his siblings still live along Buffalo Creek in former coal camps at the upper end. They are "gettin' along all right," although Sam says that one brother "struggles with the past" more than he does. Sam does not elaborate on this point and I am reluctant to probe any further. When I see him grow a little uncomfortable with this topic, I remind him that I am focusing on how the people of Buffalo Creek are doing *now*, as neighbors. Sam tells me that most people along the Creek seem to be doing pretty well, especially now that coal prices have gone from $25 to $65 a ton in the last five weeks, and the mining companies are hiring plenty of young fellows as mine workers, albeit at nonunion wages. When I ask him about community life, he responds:

> People are basically the same everywhere, seems to me. Not everyone gets along, but you don't expect to. Most neighbors are friendly enough, and they will help you if you need help. They just aren't as close as they used to be. There was a lot more socializing in _____ (coal camp) when I was living there and when I was growing up in _____ (coal camp).

Sam goes on to explain that neighbors are busier now in going places in their cars and watching TV. He says that this is the case everywhere, not just along Buffalo Creek. Most neighbors are good people. You just do not see them as much or talk to them as often as when he was growing up.

During the next hour, our conversation ranges far and wide. We talk about the severity of the winter weather, the popularity of all-terrain vehicles among the locals, corruption in local politics and the unions, and some of the content in the psychology and sociology courses Sam has taken at the local community college. He mentions that he has read "some of those books about Buffalo Creek." When I ask his opinion of them, he replies, "Some of it was pretty much right, some of it maybe not." He glances at me and adds, "People knew what the lawyers were looking for. We knew what the sides were. We knew what was going on."

Then Sam starts talking calmly, quietly, and in measured sentences about his work history and his efforts to come to terms with the changes that have occurred recently. Eventually, he mentions the day of the flood. He tells me how devastating the flood was to him and how his life has taken many surprising turns since then. Sam was just waking up with his wife, pregnant with their second child, and their son, a toddler, when the flood hit his small home around 8:20 on that Saturday morning. Sam does not recall any warning of the flood. Suddenly, he was being swept away in waves of black, oily water and debris, clasping his son to his chest. The palm of his son's hand dug so deeply into the side of his neck that he sometimes still feels it there. Sam cannot recall how or when his son became separated from him—only that people were pulling him out of the raging water.[6] He recalls waking up in a hospital and spending many months trying to recover from his physical injuries. He points to deep scars on his upper lip, around his head, along his neck, arms, and chest. Slivers of black coal and slate are embedded beneath his skin in several places. He says that it must have been at least three years before the shock of what had happened to his first family and home really hit him. In the meantime, he was relocated to a HUD trailer camp. He started working again in the mines. He "talked to the psychiatrist they sent from Cincinnati," and he married his current wife and started another family. Sam says that he received "some money from one of the lawsuits against the coal company." Then he hesitates, glances at me for a moment, and adds, "Of course some people got more than they deserved. Some got less. They gave me less because my wife wasn't working at the time. She was home pregnant and taking care of our son." Then Sam remarks that "some of them got into more trouble after the flood than in the flood itself. They overspent what they got. Spent like there was no tomorrow. Got into debt and all sorts of trouble."

Sam and his second wife have raised two boys, now in their twenties, who are "doing well in skilled jobs out-of-state." Sam talks at length about the good jobs he had as a unionized worker in the mines for nearly thirty years. Then, a few years ago, union jobs got scarce and the on-the-job injuries he had suffered over the years left him with disabling chronic ailments. He felt compelled to seek permanent disability status with the state a few years ago. Now he is enrolled in a rehabilitation program that includes job retraining courses at the community college in Logan. Sam says that the stresses of college courses, chronic illnesses, being unemployed, and disagreements with the state about his disability and retraining benefits led to a heart attack and bypass surgery. Still, he cautiously estimates that he is recovering "pretty good. I'm getting along okay now, mostly."

I ask Sam about the recoveries of other people in regards to published accounts by experts who spent time at Buffalo Creek. Speaking slowly, carefully, and with obvious feeling, Sam says that he agrees with some of their findings more than with others. He acknowledges that many people, himself included, suffered heavy losses of family, friends, and possessions. It took many people years to come to terms with what they had lost.

> Sure, I had to quit work for awhile. I had to figure out what was going on and how to get along. But I don't think I changed that much. Some people just left everything and moved away. Some people who got a lot of money (through the lawsuits) went overboard spending and became worse-off than before. Some people went away to mental hospitals. Maybe I should have, too. I had counseling. But a lot of people got close after the flood. They learned how quick life can go. People did talk to each other and help when they could. I don't agree with those experts about how people couldn't help themselves or their families anymore—how they couldn't even try. People stuck together a lot. Helped me a lot. All my neighbors made it out alive. Some of them sort of dropped their heads when they were around me sometimes, maybe out of guilt about what happened to us. Lots of people resented the coal company opening the mines right away and calling us back to work in a few days. People had troubles and complaints. But they didn't stop trying to get along.

Sam also takes issue with experts' claims that social controls broke down and that many survivors turned to substance abuse, violence, property crimes, and other immoral behaviors.

> No. I didn't see all of that afterwards: drinking, arguing, playing around, fighting, and stealing. There was always some of that going on—just like everywhere. Fact is some people always drank heavy on Friday nights. They were sleeping in on Saturday morning and got caught when the flood came down. Nobody wrote about that going on. And down in Gilbert and at Hart's Creek people were worse than the people on Buffalo Creek in drinking and fighting and carrying on. We never shot each other at least. Maybe a few people here tried marijuana. Most of them would have tried it anyways. It was going around everywhere. Most people here were clean and took care of their places. You could eat right off of the floors in their places, even if some of the trailers that we got from the government were filthy when we got them. Fact is, a lot

of people got trailers—new ones—and food and all sorts of stuff that they didn't deserve. Mostly, though, people got along good enough.

Sam then mentions names of other survivors whom I should interview. He gives me several suggestions on how to meet with them and put them at ease. He says that local people are more likely to talk with me, face to face, in their homes, than respond to a phone call or a survey through the mail. "We're always getting bothered by phone calls and mail from people trying to get something from us and lying about it."

I ask Sam if he will fill out and critique a questionnaire that I was thinking about using to survey more people on Buffalo Creek. He takes considerable time doing so while I walk around outside so that he has privacy. When I return, he gives me plenty of useful advice for doing more research along Buffalo Creek. In his written responses on the questionnaire, Sam indicates that in the twenty-six years that he lived along Buffalo Creek, he liked it best for "living close to family and friends" and having his job close to home. He wrote that he has "many" relatives and close friends who live along the creek and "many" who live elsewhere. The best place he has ever lived was in a small village about ten miles away. The happiest years of his life were the year he first married (at age eighteen); the year his first child was born; 1972 (his second marriage, the same year as the flood); and the years that his second child and third child were born (from his second marriage).[7] Sam's response to this question is especially noteworthy because the flood occurred in 1972. Could this response possibly indicate that Sam was able to recover from the damages of the flood well enough to at least continue to form intimate relationships, have children, and find some happiness in the years immediately after the flood, just as he had done in the decades before the flood?

Sam does not evince much interest in his future or in the future of Buffalo Creek. He is glad that his sons are doing well for themselves out of state, but he shows little enthusiasm for topics that interest many of local men in his age cohort: hunting, fishing, "four-wheeling," gardening, grandchildren, buddies, and the latest gossip about mining and miners. His main concern is his declining health and having so much spare time on his hands, just like so many former coal miners in their midfifties who had worked so hard for so many years.

In thinking about Sam's account, we should keep in mind that Sam had direct and tragic personal experience in the flood that cost him dearly. Yet, even while he was recovering physically, Sam was able to work in the mines, remarry, and start a new family. Sam actually listed 1972 and 1973 as being two of the best years in his life. He also was a plaintiff in the Arnold & Porter lawsuit and was examined by one of their psychiatrists. Despite the severity of his losses, Sam's account is similar in several ways to the accounts of Molly Good and some of the other survivors whose accounts follow in this chapter. They agreed partially with experts' accounts about how badly and extensively the flood damaged many people economically and psychologically. Yet these informants said that the experts were too inclusive in their assessments of damages to the ability and willingness of many of the survivors to help one another immediately after the flood, among other points, and on the negative effects of large financial settlements on some families.[8] Sam's account also agrees with some other informants' accounts about how some plaintiffs, possibly even Sam himself, exaggerated their damage claims and feigned the extent of their psychological problems when they submitted written reports to attorneys and government agencies.

Sam Chance's account also raises several allegations of interest that are not in the accounts of the experts. Sam testified that miners typically drank heavily on Friday nights and that some of them were caught in the flood because they and their families were hungover from drinking the night before the flood. Buffalo Creek people were hard drinkers, but they took care of their homes before and after the flood. Considerable numbers of miners were called back to work only a few days after the flood. Some of them, possibly including Sam himself, resented this as being callous on the part of the managers of the coal companies. Many survivors got better trailers from HUD than they deserved, and some plaintiffs got more settlement money than they deserved. More generally, issues about equity and distributive justice among survivors bothered some survivors. Marijuana use became popular in Buffalo Creek in the 1970s, but Sam believes it was part of a national trend, unrelated to the flood. It would have happened even without the flood.

In sum, a strong case can be made that Sam Chance has recovered rather well, for the most part, from the severe losses that he suffered in the flood. Certainly, he was able to function well enough when I met with him in public places like Hardee's. It is likely that his current predicaments are as much a consequence of the long, arduous work life that he had in the mines and his frustrations with the terms of his disability payments as they are the consequence of the flood itself. Sam is relatively well integrated into the hamlets around Buffalo Creek, if not into Buffalo Creek's own hamlets, except for visiting his siblings who reside there. He realizes that the nature of community life has changed in some fundamental ways in many places in the United States, including Buffalo Creek. He has some regrets about decreases in neighboring and communality, but he does not obsess about these changes.

Sam also shows considerable, if incomplete, recovery from the damages that he suffered in the flood. As arduous and controversial as coal mining can be, Sam responded to a question about "the best job you ever had" by writing "coal mine electrician, 1968–97." This leads me to think that his employment in the mines remained as a primary source of sustenance and meaning throughout most of his adult life, including the flood year. His work in the mines enabled Sam to form and to sustain a second family. Yet he has not forgotten the members of his first family and how he lost them in the flood. Overall, then, the account of Sam Chance is complex and provocative. It is an account of tragedies and partial recoveries; of failures and of partial successes. As Sam himself has indicated, he is "gettin' along okay now, mostly." As averred in some of the accounts that follow, the same is true for some of the flood's survivors who still live along Buffalo Creek. Sam is no longer one of them; but he is not far away in person, in spirit, or in memory.

Lonnie McCain:
A Hero's Son and a Legacy of Trust

"My Dad saved us," says coal miner Lonnie McCain, a soft-spoken and modest fellow with the well-proportioned body of a halfback, a blond crew cut, and a few days of stubble on his face. We are sitting on stools at the bar of the "Colonial Supper Club," actually a private gambling club that features slot machines, video games, and pool tables. It is 10:20 on a Thursday morning. Lonnie is trying to wake up with a pack of Winstons and cups of black coffee after working the late shift at the big Acco coal mine in Gilbert, twenty miles up the Guyandotte River.

> I was ten at the time. We were living in _____ coal camp (about one-half the way up Buffalo Creek). My grandmother had just died the night before that. We were supposed to drive over to her place down near Logan. Dad drove down to the Accoville store to buy milk for breakfast while Mom got me, my brother, and sister ready to go to Grandma's. People at the store had just got a phone call from up the Creek saying that the impoundment broke at Three Forks and that the water was coming. Dad raced back-up to our place, past people driving away fast, just in time to get us out of the house and up on the hillside before it hit. Most of the neighbors had heard about it coming and left in a hurry. They didn't try to warn us because they didn't see our car at our house. They thought we had already gone to Grandma's. We turned around when we got up that hillside and just stood there watching that black water come down the valley. It hit our house real hard. Lifted it way up in the air. Broke it in half. Took it all away down the valley.

Lonnie says all of this to me slowly and with surprising equanimity. I wait several seconds to hear if he is going to elaborate. Finally, I remark, "Your Dad was a hero—a real hero. He saved all of you." "That's right," says Lonnie, drawing on his cigarette, "That's just what he did."

After a refill of coffee, Lonnie tells me about how his family moved around several times in the decade after the flood to homes in the hollows farther up the Guyandotte. He and his siblings attended high school in Man with the children from Buffalo Creek. After he grew up, he was not inclined to move back to Buffalo Creek like his brother and sister.

> They moved back to the Creek years ago. They are doing all right up there at _____. They don't seem to mind it. As for me, I won't go back to Buffalo Creek to live. I don't like being around the water anymore. The surroundings aren't the same up there now. Kids aren't much like kids anymore. They just sit around and watch TV. It's not like it used to be.

I ask him if it is because of the flood. Lonnie sips his coffee and pauses. "I'm just not fond of being around water. Scares me. So I won't move back to Buffalo Creek."

I mention some of the experts' assertions about the years after the flood and I ask Lonnie for his opinions. He lights another Winston and thinks for a while. "Well maybe some of that's true about some of the people. But maybe those writers went too far. It really wasn't like that— at least not for me or for most people." Lonnie explains that a lot of people who survived the flood exaggerated when they were interviewed. He says that all five of his family members, himself included, talked with the psychiatrists that were sent in. "Everyone knew you got to put the round peg in the square hole. You knew what they wanted you to say. Some people told lies thinking they would get more money." Then Lonnie adds that the "settlement money made it worse for some people. They found themselves with too much money but no jobs to keep them busy." He says that this was because "some people simply did not want to work" and because the coal economy slowed down during the late 1970s. This was particularly true of the children of some of the survivors who received large settlements. "The kids had money to buy beer, drugs, cars, and whatever they wanted. So they didn't want to work or anything. They got into trouble, arguments, and fights."

Lonnie also takes issue with experts' finding that many adults started abusing alcohol after the flood.

> Miners always drank when they weren't working. That's just what they did. The women just accepted it and took care of the house.

> After the flood the miners just kept drinking like before. It was the boys and younger men who caused problems because they wanted to drink like their dads but not work like their dads. That's why there were fights and divorces afterwards. It took maybe ten or fifteen years for things to settle down.

Lonnie estimates that "maybe ten to fifteen percent of the people are still hurt by the flood." When I ask him if there were any "remarkable recoveries," he answers affirmatively, saying that the flood forced some families to make new friendships with other families—including his own. He talks about the friendships that were formed in the emergency trailer camps after the flood between his family and the Crosby family, which lost one child in the floodwaters.

> We went to church together, shared food and money, in good times and bad, and took care of each other's kids. The older kids took care of the younger ones in both families. Members of both families still call one another almost every day. We are still good friends even if they aren't actually our neighbors anymore.

Then we talk about Lonnie's experiences in the mines and in other villages in the area. He says that he likes his current situation of living here with his wife's family along the Guyandotte River, about one mile upstream from its juncture with Buffalo Creek. He appreciates having his job at the big coal mine down in Gilbert, even though he liked working even more when there were more union jobs with union wages and full benefits. He believes that the coal economy is picking up now because there is a change in the national energy policy in Washington. Still, Lonnie observes that "a lot of the young kids who are starting in the mines don't know what they are getting into. They don't seem to mind taking non-union jobs without many benefits so long as they are making ten or twelve dollars an hour."

It seems to me that Lonnie McCain's testimony indicates that he and his family of origin had stability, good experiences with neighboring, and a strong sense of community before the flood. For the most part, they have been able to maintain or replace old friendships and a sense of belonging since then, despite disruptions and damages associated with the flood and the years of social and economic aftershocks on many members of Buffalo Creek. They lost their house and all of their material possessions, but they were fortified by the fact that their father risked his life to save them and that other members of the community alerted their father to the oncoming flood. The McCains knew that their neighbors had not abandoned them. Probably as a result of this, they have been able to form new, intimate relations that endure to this day.

As a postscript, let me suggest that Lonnie's aversion to water seems rather reasonable and far less severe than what clinical psychologists might diagnose as chronic hydrophobia. Consider that, even as we talked, the Guyandotte River was running muddy, fast, furious, and filled with flotsam—mainly garbage and plastic trash from households—not more than hundred feet from us. It curved around two sides of the barroom, although it was not visible to us from where we were seated. The river was at least six feet higher than normal after a week of heavy rains. I asked Lonnie if he did not mind driving along twenty miles of the river to his job in Gilbert each night. Often the road runs no more than ten yards from the river. Guard rails are few and far between. Lonnie shrugged and said, "I'm not crazy about it. But I've seen worse."

There are several important points to consider when thinking about Lonnie's case, not the least of which is that he is a hardworking coal miner who experienced the flood directly, almost tragically, at a very impressionable age. He lived in the trailer camps and was interviewed by at least one psychiatrist who was hired by Arnold & Porter to support the lawsuit against Pittston Company. He is willing to talk about his experiences without exaggeration or rancor. Recall that he stated that most of their neighbors had at least a few minutes to escape from the flood. They knew that it was coming—and they escaped. Also recall that Lonnie's father was miles away at a grocery store when a telephone call came to the store notifying people that the flood was coming. Yet his father was able to drive back to his home, against oncoming traffic of people escaping down the road along Buffalo Creek, and return home in time to move his family up the hillside to safety. Also recall that Lonnie made a point of mentioning that their neighbors would have warned them of the oncoming flood if they had realized that his family was still in the house, waiting for his father to return from the grocery store. The neighbors already knew that Lonnie's grandmother had died the night before, and the neighbors assumed that the McCains would leave first thing in the morning to go over to the deceased grandmother's home near Logan City in order to help prepare for the funeral. Recall also that Lonnie indicated that some of his siblings moved back to Buffalo Creek and were currently residing there—in the very same former coal camp that they were in at the time of the flood. Probably, Lonnie's aversion to water was much stronger than was theirs. He does not deny that the experts' accounts fit the experiences of some of the victims. However, he takes issue with some elements of those accounts, based on his own firsthand experiences.

Lonnie said that some people, probably his family included, made remarkable recoveries from the flood. His own family made lifelong friends with other families in the trailer camps. Excess drinking was not a new problem in the families of miners and among other people who continued to work after the flood. But excess drinking, fighting, and other misbehaviors increased in families that received such large financial settlements that the men and adolescents no longer cared to work. In Lonnie's words, "the boys wanted to drink like their dads but not work like their dads." He estimated that it took these families ten to fifteen years to recover appreciable stability and that most (85–90 percent) survivors who have not passed away since the flood have recovered appreciably by now. Lonnie also claimed that many people, possibly including some of his kin, exaggerated their claims of damages, and they feigned psychological impairments in order to maximize their chances of getting large settlements. "Everyone knew you had to put the round peg in the square hole." So, it seems that it is fair to say that Lonnie and his family did what they had to do in order to recover as best they could. In closing, we might keep in mind that Lonnie and members of his family of origin seem to be competent people who have remained in and around Buffalo Creek because they choose to do so. As best as I can tell, the way they are living their lives is not radically different than the way they would have been living their lives even if the flood had not happened, other than that Lonnie probably would still be living along Buffalo Creek rather than a few miles away.

WANDA AND WOODY MERCER: CARETAKERS OF THE MEMORIAL

Woodrow "Woody" Mercer and his mother, Wanda, and I are sitting in oversized rocking chairs on his porch, getting acquainted. America's Memorial Day is more than two weeks away, but the porch is already festooned with red, white, and blue bunting and miniature flags. Woody's neatly painted, white-frame house is perched on a steep incline, almost as precariously as a Navaho cliff dwelling. One side of the porch offers a panoramic view of a quarter mile of the village of Kistler alongside Buffalo Creek, now swollen with surging muddy water after last night's sudden storm. Down there, not more than 200 yards away from this house, is a small parcel of fenced-in land with a small portico—the "Buffalo Creek Memorial Park." Wanda was instrumental in creating it in 1992 with a dozen other Buffalo Creek people. They oversee that memorial each day, both figuratively and literally. They have been officers in the Memorial Association. While their lives have been closely intertwined, they have had very different trajectories since their experiences with the flood so many years ago.

Wanda, a slender and self-confident woman with a perm of bright-orange hair, seems much younger than a great-grandmother in her mid-seventies. She has spent her entire life living along the creek. Since 1965 her home has been here in Kistler. It is the modest, white, wood-frame dwelling adjacent to the porch on which we are sitting. Neither her house nor Woody's was touched by the floodwaters, which had diminished greatly in height and velocity by the time they reached Kistler. But her father-in-law (Woody's grandfather) and at least one other relative died in the flood in ways that still haunt some of the family members.

We converse easily about various topics before I read to them some of the experts' assertions about the aftereffects of the flood. Woody waits politely while his mother responds, taking time to think through her

answers before she responds slowly and carefully. Wanda says that some
of the findings are more correct than others. She explains that the worst
thing about the flood was the 125 lives that were lost, including Woody's
grandfather. She nods towards Woody with sympathy. Then she looks
over to me. "My son had to see his Granddaddy's dead body." After a
brief pause, she says that some flood survivors have never recovered.
For some of them, "things won't ever be the same." Then again, many
of the survivors who have not died in the years since the flood seem to
be "getting along better than others. Some are doing okay. Some aren't.
Some of them are moving back to Buffalo Creek as they are getting
older." (Wanda is not able to name any of them when I ask for names).
Wanda then recalls that in the early 1970s, before the flood, Buffalo
Creek "was a boom town. The men were working two and three shifts
in the mines and they had enough money to buy cars and whatever they
needed." After the flood, however:

> The problem was too much money for some people. They went
> kinda wild, spent too much on everything, and took years to come
> back to normal. That was years ago. Now a lot of places along the
> Creek have been rebuilt. Of course, there may be only about one-
> half as many people as before the flood. Some people have new
> homes. Many of the survivors are doing pretty good.

Wanda conscientiously reads and responds to the questionnaire that
I ask her to fill out and critique. She is glad to elaborate on her responses
when I ask her to do so. For her, the best things about living along the
creek are "good friends and neighbors (fifty or more), people are caring,
helpful in time of need, love the environment. It's home." She also indicates that about twenty of her relatives live along the creek (more relatives live along Buffalo Creek than elsewhere), that her best job was as
a "store manager, 1955 to 1985," and that the happiest years of her life
were when her children and grandchildren were born in the 1950s and
1970s, and "the year we got married—1945."

During our time together, Wanda is very cooperative and supportive
of my work. She is glad to tell me about the plans of the Memorial

Committee for future commemorative events for those who died in the flood and for fundraising events. She mentions that maintenance of the memorial park costs about $8,000 per year. We discuss ways to increase funding for the park and my plans for interviewing more Buffalo Creek people. She encourages me to talk to other survivors face-to-face and she gives me the names of several prospects. She also invites me to the anniversary ceremony next February 26.

All the while, Woody has been listening to our conversation politely, if a little nervously. He enters in only when I ask him a question directly. He is a pleasant, soft-spoken fellow with a light crop of orange hair and sunken eye sockets. Combined with his slender frame, hunched forward at the shoulders, his appearance suggests chronic physical pain. I assume that he is a bachelor in his thirties until he reveals that he has several grandchildren and is retired. At first, we talk about the view from his porch and the plant and animal life around his house. He seems to take some pleasure in telling me about the American chestnut trees that have survived blight long enough to bear a bag full of nuts last summer (some of which are in his freezer), about the black bear that came down from the steep ridge at our flank and into his yard last week, and about the family of foxes that lives under the porch. He says that the vixen often appears at about this time of the afternoon to scrounge the yard for the table scraps that he tosses out for her and the pups. It is clear that Woody cherishes this place dearly.

I tell him about my walks up in the hollows, looking at the remains of the old mines, the tipples, the impoundments, the rail lines, and former coal camps. Woody responds by telling me about his twenty years of experience operating heavy dozers up in those hollows, including excavation work around the sites of the failed impoundments at Three Forks that unleashed the flood. He describes how dangerous it was and the techniques they used to secure the impoundments and to close up the mines once they were abandoned, pumping huge quantities of water into them. He says that the impoundments are mostly dry now and that it is unlikely that another flood could occur that would be as devastating as the one in 1972, even with so many homes rebuilt so close to the creek.

When I observe that he seems to miss the work, he nods in agreement, telling me that chronic ailments have forced him into early retirement. He seems more inclined than his mother to lament the changes of the last thirty years, nodding in agreement when I mention the experts' finding that people did not feel as close to their neighbors after the flood as they did before it. He does not seem inclined to address the topic, however, so I leave it alone.

Woody seems reluctant to fill out a survey form. I notice that his hands are twitching a little. I tell him that a lot of us have some "shakes" from time to time. Eventually he acquiesces, probably out of respect for his mother and as a courtesy to me. I excuse myself and go for a walk around the neighborhood. When I return, we discuss his responses and his reactions to the survey.

I ask Woody why he wrote that "1971, before the flood" was the happiest year of his life. He answers slowly and matter-of-factly: "More people lived here. Life was better. It's not the same now." He elaborates by telling me that the flood occurred when he was a senior in high school. He had many friends in school whose families were severely hurt by the flood. (At this point, Wanda mentions again that Woody's grandfather died in the flood and that Woody unintentionally saw the body before it was recovered). Woody then recalls the day before the flood. One of the young girls at school gave him a glass of Kool-Aid to drink. The next day, she drowned in the flood. Even now, he often thinks about her and that glass of Kool-Aid. And yet, he has never really thought about leaving Buffalo Creek. "This is my home. It's where lots of my relatives and close friends live."

A little while later, we go into Woody's living room and look through the log books of visitors to the Memorial Park and some of the records of the Memorial Association. Woody tells me about how a company from out of state sent a crew to film some of the flood survivors discussing their experiences. The meeting was filmed right here in his living room. He offers no interpretation, reaction, or further comments, other than that he has a copy of the tape of the filming that the company sent to him, although he cannot find it at the moment.[9]

Reflecting back over my conversations with the Mercers, it seems that Wanda had already had such a fulfilling life with her family, job, and community before the flood that she was able to help many of the people who suffered much more than her. She gains solace from being able to continue to do so. For her, Buffalo Creek always has been and always will be a cherished community to live in because it is full of people whom she loves. They need her and appreciate her. This is why she is able to live so close to the Memorial Park and correspond each day with flood survivors, their descendants, and with interested persons, such as me. Woody, on the other hand, seems to remain somewhat depressed by his memories of the tragic effects of the flood on other people, particularly on the young girl who gave him a drink of Kool-Aid the day before she perished. And yet, after talking and corresponding with Wanda many times at considerable length over a period of seven years, I believe that neither she nor Woody is unduly obsessed or handicapped by what happened so many years ago. Their behaviors do not appear to be compulsive or distressed in this regard. Their expressions are not out of context with the topics that we have been discussing. There is little evidence of conflict, dysfunction, or avoidance in their social relationships with other residents of Buffalo Creek. They do not seem to harbor bitterness or abnormal levels of "survivor's guilt." They do not fantasize about how their lives or Buffalo Creek could have been better. Certainly, they are able to take care of themselves, their families, and the Buffalo Creek Memorial that they were instrumental in creating.

The thought occurs to me that Woody's negative memories probably are magnified by the physical pain and disability that he has to live with each day, by daily challenges he has in his own family household, and by the surplus time that he has each day due to his unexpected, involuntary retirement. It also seems as though he does not get much enjoyment out of his day or out of his involvement in the Memorial Association. It is almost as though he is doing it for his mother's sake. He does not mention his children or grandchildren by name—or anyone else, for that matter. And yet, this might be attributable to shyness and a deep sense of privacy on his part.

On the questionnaire, in response to the request that he list at least three things that he likes best about living along Buffalo Creek, Woody simply wrote one word: "people." I did not feel comfortable in pressing him to elaborate on this point because of painful memories he had already recounted to me. My sense is that the flood caught Woody at a very vulnerable time in his life and it has permanently stunted his ability to enjoy his life as fully as he would have enjoyed it without the flood experience. Nonetheless, he appears to be an integral part of Buffalo Creek as a social community, and he is appreciated for his efforts to sustain the collective memory of those who perished in the flood.

Woody and I leafed through the logbooks for visitors to the Memorial Park, as I was about to leave his home. Along with the thousands of signatures of visitors from across the United States, I noticed so many heartfelt comments, including these:

> "Thanks for the fine effort. Long overdue."

> "I love this valley."

> "This is a wonderful place. Thanks so much."

> "As you are, I was. As I am, you will be."

> "You have brought us a sense of peace, at last. God bless you. God bless Buffalo Creek."

MABEL CHURCH:
"LIVING WITH WHAT THE LORD GIVE ME."

"I try to live with what the Lord gives me," says Mabel Church, an independent, contented, and sturdy woman in her seventies. She wears her silver hair tied back in a bun, along with glasses, sneakers, a blouse, and a long skirt. My wife and I sit with Mabel for a pleasant hour in the evening sunset on the front porch of her 1960s-era trailer. Its faded tan aluminum siding is surrounded by beds of bright summer flowers and small plots of sprawling, green tomato and pepper plants that Mabel dotes upon. "Them's night lilies over thar. They was bloomin' last night. Then they fold up and sleep during the day." A handsome old apple tree in the front yard hangs heavy with healthy green fruit and promises a bountiful harvest this fall. "That tree thar's almost as old as me, I reckon," comments Mabel with a soft smile.

Before the hour is over, Mabel matter-of-factly describes experiences that sometimes are at odds with the experts' accounts, just as we had been told by some of her many good friends in this hollow. After some small talk, she tells us her story—slowly, factually, and without embellishment. She starts by telling us that as a young girl, she used to "work out as a domestic in rich people's houses down in Man many years ago." In the mid-1940s, she moved up to Three Forks. A few years later, she married her husband, who was the preacher up at Saunders Free Will Baptist Church.

> We was living up at Three Forks right where the water come down. My husband was pastor at that little church that was up there. Night before it come down, some fellow from the coal company come by our place. It was raining real hard that night. He told us not to worry. Told us everything was alright up there where the dams was. But some of the neighbor men was watching the dams and worrying about them at the same time. Roy Chamberlin was one of them. A good man. Some people up thar wasn't so good. Not real neighbors. Most was. Those was our real neighbors. Anyways, Roy come by and warn us about the dam. So me, my husband and our boy packed up what we could and rode on down to Lundale to stay the night with friends. Course, we done that many times before, too. Always was talk of them dams breaking. Once one of them did, too, a few years before the big flood come down. When morning come, we packed-up again and rode back up to Three Forks. We was stopped at Lorado school by some people there. They lived there. Told us the dam was broke and water was coming down the holler. They done saved us, is what they did. We went up on a rise behind the company store. We just stood up there and watched that water come down. It washed away Lorado School and most of Lorado. Then we went down and started helpin' people get out of there. Done what we could all day.

Mabel then tells us how she and her family learned that their church, house, and much of Three Forks had been washed away, and how they eventually moved into one of the HUD trailer camps at Green Valley, along Huff Creek. Green Valley had a reputation for being a depressing and notorious trailer camp. This is not Mabel's experience, however.

> We lived over there in Green Valley for maybe fifteen months. It was first come, first serve. You had to take what the HUD people give you. What we got was pretty good. The trailer was in good shape, but not exactly new. We had two bedrooms, bath, kitchen, living room, and all the furnishings. Pots, pans, some blankets. I liked it good enough. And I liked it over in Green Valley. We got in there kinda early—before it got crowded. We knowed a lot of the people there, too. Maybe six to seven families or more. (Mabel then names each of the families and a number of their family members, including at least one Black family that she was fond of). Some was our neighbors from Three Forks and some was our friends from Lorado and Lundale and other places along the Creek. So we had neighbors we knowed across from us, besides us, around us. It was a nice enough place. Quiet enough. I don't remember any trouble there. I heard tales of trouble after we left it—fighting, and drinking, and all that. But I didn't see none of it. Fact is, I wanted to go back to Green Valley after we moved back up here. I never did care for it much up here. I never cared much for living at Three Forks. My husband decided on it. He wanted to keep pastorin'. So we moved back up here when they rebuilt the church for him right here along the Creek. Then, when he died years ago, I figured I might as well stay here. I got good friends and neighbors here.

We ask Mabel about how they decided to move here to this coal camp and into this particular trailer.

> Well, we didn't know HUD would sell us our trailer in Green Valley for only a thousand dollars. Maybe they didn't start sellin' them till after we left. I don't recall. Anyways, when the first settlement money come in from the coal company we got about eleven thousand dollars. My husband only asked for thirteen thousand for the house we lost at Three Forks and all our belongings. He said that was enough. They give us eleven thousand. So he went out and bought this here trailer. Maybe it was December 1972.

Paid eleven thousand dollars for it.—just what we got in the settlement. It had an air conditioner. He didn't want that. Said there weren't no need for something like that. Had it took out.

We ask Mabel how they decided to locate here, on this land.

Well, my husband decided against taking the one thousand dollars the coal company offered us for our land up there in Three Forks where our house was. He said we ought to take replacement land instead. The man at Pardee Land Company showed us replacement land all along Buffalo Creek. They treated us fair. No problems. Some people bought out the other side of the Creek over there where all them houses had washed out. Then they sold them old lots and made lots of money off people who was movin' back. I didn't want to go back up to Three Forks. Never liked it much up thar. We looked at lots in Oceana, Gilbert, and other places. But, as I say, my husband wanted to come back up here so he could pastor his church where they was rebuilding it. So we settled on this land right here. Nothin' was ever here before. So we had them put the trailer right here where it is now. Maybe it was June 1973. Then our son got old enough and moved away.

Mabel also told us about her experience with Arnold & Porter in the lawsuit against Buffalo Mining Company and Pittston Company.

After we moved in here, Charlie Cowan come up with some of the other people for a visit. They told us about that law case they was doing. They told us about the lawyers. Said it could help out everyone to be in it. Told us every little bit of settlement money would help. My husband made the decision about that. I don't remember much. Maybe one meeting we had with the lawyers down in Amherstdale, maybe. I think maybe my husband filled-out some of them papers they had. I don't remember much of what they told us. My husband took care of all of that. All I remember is maybe a year or two after, we each got a few thousand dollars from them lawyers. Ever little bit helped.

In sum, Mabel Church's account is noteworthy not only for what she revealed and the uniqueness of her experiences, but also for her equanimity and contentedness. Mabel never complained, exaggerated, or tried to interpret her own experiences. She did not condemn or praise anyone. Substantively, she testified that neighbors helped her family escape the flood twice, that her family's house at Three Forks was totally destroyed in the flood, and that she never cared for living up at Three Forks (or the upper end of Buffalo Creek, for that matter). She also avowed that Green Valley trailer camp was amenable to her and that she would have remained there rather than move back to the upper end of Buffalo Creek. She had neither complaints nor compliments about the Arnold & Porter lawsuit against the coal company. She revealed no bitterness about the flood, and she made no mention of any lingering problems from the flood. Mabel seems content to live out the rest of her life right where she is, not more than 150 yards from the streambed of Buffalo Creek, which is just across the railroad track and Highway 16 from her home.

As we are saying our good-byes, Mabel mentioned that she cannot drive very far or at night anymore, but that she has good friends and neighbors whom she could rely upon. She named the neighbors in the three houses closest to her and assured us that they are there if she needs them. All the while, a little boy pedaled his red bicycle back and forth past Mabel's home, without paying any attention to us, even when we waved to him. I could not help wondering whether the neighbors are close enough to Mabel to know if and when she needs help. In departing, we thanked Mabel and commented again on the songbirds, flowers, and trees that enhance the tranquility of her place. "I'm just livin' with what the Lord give me," said Mabel, softy and without affect. And so she is.

EMMA SUE KINSLEY:
"WE WAS EXCITED TO GET THAT BRAND NEW TRAILER AND ALL THEM OTHER THINGS."

We meet Emma Sue in the basement social room of Saunders Free Will Baptist Church, which was relocated to Lorado and rebuilt soon after the flood. Sundry children, friends, and relatives mingle around us, playing games and cleaning up after an "ice cream social and flea market" on a Saturday afternoon. We are seated around a rough-cut pine picnic table getting acquainted with Emma Sue and her very extended family. It takes little time to realize that she is extremely informed about Buffalo Creek's past and present.

Emma Sue is a merry, ample-sized grandmother in her forties, wearing glasses and a loose-fitting cotton housedress. Very plainspoken and modest, she tells us that she is a substitute teacher and an active participant in many church and community affairs. She says that she is so busy in so many activities that "I don't have much time for worrying." Like so many people we interviewed, over the course of our conversation, Emma Sue often mentions highlights of her experiences in the flood even though we ask her mainly about her experiences in the HUD trailer camps and along Buffalo Creek since then.

> Well, I can tell you we was excited to get our own place up there in Green Valley. There was Ma, Pa, and us four kids: me, my sister and two brothers. I just turned thirteen. They give us a new trailer with all the furnishings. It had three bedrooms, living room, kitchen, and a bathroom with everything in it. It had a gas stove, gas heat—everything was gas. The silver tanks was out back. We was kinda scared at first cause we never had gas before. Course, the beds was kinda flimsy. Just metal frames and mattresses. Our old place up at Lorado was only four rooms. No bathroom. So we was excited to get that brand new trailer and all them other things. Then the Red Cross come along and give us vouchers for household goods, clothes, towels, utensils, and all that. Give us vouchers for beans, taters, and groceries that done us up for a month.

Emma Sue goes on to explain that her parents lost at least seven relatives in the flood, but that she, her siblings, and her parents had escaped just in time, thanks to neighbors who came by their place and warned them that the dam had broken. Her family lost the house ("was just washed away") and all possessions. She and her family were evacuated the day of the flood down to the high school in Man. They lived there for twenty-one days with twenty other people in one converted classroom.

We was all in there together. In there was people who we didn't know before. They was from Gilbert (about twenty miles from Buffalo Creek) and other places that was washed out in the rains. Some people forget that Buffalo Creek wasn't the only place flooded-out in them rains back then. You couldn't trust all of them other people in there. My Daddy give me a dress and a Bible book. He bought them in town with money the Red Cross give us. He wanted each of us to have something of our own. Made me real happy. But someone in that room stole them while we was down having our meal in the cafeteria. Stole the only things I had for myself. What kind of people steal a Bible book?

The negative experiences Emma Sue and her family had while living in the schoolroom crammed with so many strangers made it much easier for them to accept their situation in the HUD trailer camp after that.

So we was real happy when Daddy moved us up to that new place they give us in Green Valley. It was all new for us. Nothing was up there before they put the trailers in there. We got a good place up aways from the creek. We knowed the neighbors in front and behind us (Emma Sue names the families and the children). We knowed other families up there too. Maybe five to six families with kids from up and down Buffalo Creek that we knowed before the flood. Went to school with them.[10]

We ask Emma Sue to tell us about life in the trailer camps and why her family finally departed.

Well, it was good for a while. They didn't have no recreation for us to speak of up there. No playground. No swings. But you could walk wherever you wanted. You could ride bicycles. You could play with the other kids on the streets they had. Go down to where the power station was for the electricity and play there. There was a kind of pond there, too. Someone drowned in it, as I recall. I didn't see it, though.

We was there in Green Valley over a year. At first is was okay. People tried to settle in. Then more people come in. It got kinda crowded. Not much privacy. Tensions built up, mainly between the kids that didn't know each other. Kids of strangers. Maybe six to eighteen years old. They would fight over nothin'. Just fight. Even the girls. Like Patti Lou Tyson (pseudonym) just jumped on my back one day. Over nothin.' But then her family moved out.

We asked if there was fighting among the adults; Emma Sue answers,

No. I don't recall that there was. Parents got along well enough. They would try to stop the kids from fightin'. But the kids and women was kinda stuck up there in Green Valley when the men went off in their trucks to work in the mines. It wasn't near any-place you could go to. So the kids and women were kinda stuck down there all the time. The parents got along okay, though. They was neighborly. They watched each other's trailers when they needed to. They tried to get along okay. I don't recall no killings or bad things like that. There was some drinkin' and yellin' and carryin' on at night but it wasn't all that bad, like you sometimes hear tell. People still live down there in Green Valley. You hear about how bad it is, but I don't see it when I visit friends down there.

Fact is, I would of stayed in Green Valley if I could till I graduated high school. When my family moved back up here along Buffalo Creek they made me come back with them. I didn't want to move back. I was scared of it up here after the flood and all. I would go back to Green Valley during the days when I could. So we left Green Valley after maybe a year when the settlement money come in. I believe we got maybe one thousand dollars per child. But we couldn't spend it till we was eighteen years old. Ma and Pa got more. Pa took that money he got and built a new house for us up on our old lot in Lorado, plus one-half of a new lot. After he started building he learnt that HUD was selling the trailers to the people in them that wanted them. Real cheap, too. Maybe one dollar. It was too late for us. Pa was already building our house up here. We've lived up here ever since. Now I'm glad to be here. It's home now.

Emma Sue tells us that they were not plaintiffs in the Arnold & Porter lawsuit. She does not know why. She says that her dad still lives with them and that he still draws their drinking water from one of the closed coal mines up on the mountain above Lorado. "He won't drink no other water. Says it's the best. Underground. Pure. He says nothin' can poison it up there in that mine in the mountain."

Emma Sue is enthusiastic about her life, her family, her church, her many friends, relatives, and neighbors, and Buffalo Creek. She believes that "we got just about everything we need right here in Buffalo now, 'cept maybe for enough jobs for the men." She is also optimistic and eager about the future. Although she lives by very modest means, she gives no sense of regret or dissatisfaction about the past, and little sense of apprehension about the future. Her sense of the future is very immediate. She warmly invites us to the next church service, the next baptism (which we attended the very next day at a murky, shallow pool in Buffalo Creek only a short distance away), and to visit with her and her family the next time we are at Buffalo Creek. She mentions her latest grandchild with pride. "We just got us another grandchild. Love 'em all. Bless the Lord."

As we were saying our good-byes, Emma Sue and a few other women who had joined in the conversation suggested that we talk with some other folks whose experiences in the flood might relate to the assertions that were published by the experts. They mention Annabelle Lockhart, one of their friends who still lives up at Three Forks. They say that Annabelle lived there with her family of origin when the flood came through, and that she never left. Emma Sue uses her cellular phone to call Annabelle for us. After introductions, Annabelle says, in a very frail and tired voice,

> Well, to tell the truth, it won't do you much good to talk with me. We never left Three Forks. We never went to the camps. Didn't have to. We was lucky, I guess. Our place was spared in that flood. It was right behind the Church. That flood hit the Church and washed it away. The church kept that flood from hittin' our place. Kinda diverted that water away from us. Only three or four houses was left up here. We was one of them. That's about all I can tell you.

HELEN WOODRUFF:
"I LOVE LORADO. I WON'T NEVER LEAVE HERE."

So says Helen Woodruff. She is a sincere, friendly woman in her midsixties, recently widowed, with adult children who now work in another state. Helen indicates that she is sorry that none of her children are living close to her, but that she is very contented with life in Lorado. She says that she has plenty of other relatives who live in the area and that she can rely on her many friends and neighbors to keep her company and help her whenever she needs help.

> I'm livin' right here where we always lived, 'cept for that time after the flood. I love Lorado. I won't never leave here. We come back soon as we could. Our house was washed off its foundation in the flood. Lost all our possessions. So me, my husband, and six kids moved down to that HUD trailer camp in Green Valley. Was there maybe April to Labor Day, 1972. We did not like that park at all, I can tell you that. They give us two trailers side by side because there was eight of us. One was new. One was used, maybe four or five years old. They was furnished all right. But we didn't like it because we was separated. We didn't like the gas heat for cookin' and everything. Hadn't done that before. We wasn't near anyone we knew from up here in Lorado.[11] Lorado people always stayed together till that flood come along. We was in the middle of that park. We had people all around us that we didn't know nothin' about. Strangers they was. Their kids was always fightin'. We was able to go to church, though. That was okay. The church was nearby us.

I ask Helen about their decision to move back to Lorado.

> Well, soon as we got that settlement money from the coal company we went out and bought us one of them new double wides (trailers). It had everything. Four bedrooms and all. We didn't want to buy one of them HUD trailers. We wanted to be all together again. Then we had trouble gettin' a permit from the county to put it up on this here lot in Lorado where our house was. But they give it to us after a while. So we moved on up here. And here I am. I love Lorado. We had to rebuild again in 1992. Someone broke in while we was

gone and they burned it down. We built this brand new home here ourselves. We wouldn't never leave Lorado no matter what.

I ask Helen if she was part of the Arnold & Porter lawsuit.

> No. We decided not to do that. Some people told us that, if we joined up, the lawyers would make our kids talk to them psychiatrists they had. Said the doctors would make even the little kids, even the ones three to seven, take off their clothes and all for the exams. Our kids was scared of all of that after the flood. So we decided not to do it. Looking back, we just thank God for bringing us through it alright. I knowed a lot of people lost their lives. I lost seventeen of my neighbors. But none of our family was lost. So I can't be nothin' but thankful to God about that.

As I say good-bye, I asked Helen how well Buffalo Creek has recovered since the flood. "Well, we done alright. It's okay now for most people, I guess. I'd say for the most part Buffalo Creek has recovered okay. Most folks I know wouldn't leave, no matter what." Then Helen mentioned that her sister, Loretta Washburn, "was in the trailers too and she was in that other lawsuit too." Helen suggested that I talk with Loretta directly to learn about her experiences firsthand.

LORETTA WASHBURN:
DISLIKED THE CAMPS; LIKED ARNOLD & PORTER

Loretta Washburn, Helen's older sister, adds to Helen's account but has new insights of her own. Noisy children and country music provide a background as I talk with Loretta. She confides that she finished raising one family years ago and now is raising another one (a teenage grandson and an adopted child). The background noise grows deafening. "Hold on a minute, please." She leaves the room for a few moments, then returns, much more relaxed. "Okay now. Now I got me some peace and quiet. What do you want to know?"

I tell Loretta the topics that I am interested in: life in the HUD camps, her experiences with Arnold & Porter, and how Buffalo Creek has fared since the flood. She indicates that neighbors helped them avoid getting drowned in the flood and that neighbors have helped her and her family a lot except for the time that they spent in a HUD trailer camp after the flood.

> Me, my husband, and the kids had our own place before the flood come down. Neighbors told us it was comin' so we got out and got up to the hillside maybe ten minutes before it hit the house. Washed it away. The State quarantined the place for thirteen months. Then they took part of our land for the new road they was putin' in. We was moved to the HUD trailers in Green Valley. How was it? It was terrible. Those camps was horrible.

When I ask Loretta to explain what she means, she gives several answers, not all of which are necessarily consistent. "Well, people was always complaining, squabbling, and fighting about something up there. Never satisfied. We was raised with Lundale people. We was used to Lundale people. There was a few Lundale people at Green Valley, but we weren't close to them." I interrupt Loretta to ask whether her parents, her sister, and other family members were living at Green Valley at the same time.

> Yes they was. But we was used to people from our own (coal) camp. People wanted to be with their own people, from their own (coal) camp. Growin' up, we never went up to Lorado. We didn't like Lorado people. We stayed with our own kind, our neighbors, in our own neighborhood. Green Valley had a lot of Lorado people in it. We didn't like them much.

I ask Loretta for an example of some of the difficulties that they had.

> Well, like when we would go out to play horseshoes. The people from Lorado would start yellin' at us. They said it wasn't our land and all. The manager for HUD would come down and try to make peace. Soon as he would leave, the arguing would start up again. It would really heat up in the summer in Green Valley. Teenagers and the young adults would be fightin'. Lots of the parents didn't care much or do nothing about it. People would break into the

trailers when you was away. Not our place though. My husband saw to that. It sure was easier on the men. They was workin' and all that. So they could get out of Green Valley every day. My husband worked second shift at Island Creek (mine). So I had the kids all day in the park by myself. No car. Couldn't go no place. I guess the HUD people did about as good as they could, considerin' what the situation was at the time. They got us a home and what we needed to live there. Even sold us that trailer we was in. We moved it back up here to Lundale. Engineers for the bank was surveying new lots up here and got us this one. When we got that second settlement money (in the Arnold & Porter lawsuit) we built us a brand new house here and give that trailer back to HUD.

I ask Loretta about her experience as a plaintiff in the lawsuit.

They done good for us. I would recommend them to anyone. They got Pittston to pay for everything. The three kids got __ thousand dollars apiece. Me and my husband got _____ thousand dollars. The people A&P hired to help us was okay too. They treated us good. No, the kids didn't have to take-off their clothes. They didn't go through nothin' bad when they was checked-out.

Eventually, after Loretta describes to me her experiences with her neighbors and her daily life along Buffalo Creek, she tells me that "[t]hings have settled down a lot. Most people are doing okay. As for me, I like it good enough right here in Lundale. I'm busy raisin' another family. So I'm real busy. Seems to me that the people around here are pretty satisfied. They don't worry that much anymore." Loretta talks about how many people she knows who reside along Buffalo Creek and how they have learned how to adjust to the "ups and downs that come along with the weather, coal prices, politics, and things like that." Then she mentions that her brother Arnie's yard flooded last year when Buffalo Creek overflowed yet another time. The floodwater got into her (late) father's car. "People is used to that around here. That's just the way it is when you're livin' along the Creek. We take the bad with the good. I better go now. Kids is raisin' a fuss. If you're down this way again, you stop on by."

TINA AND BUCK MINER:
DIFFERENT VIEWS OF VARYING REALITIES

"He's wrong about that. Buffalo Creek is still here," says Buck Miner, whose name suggests many of his views, despite the fact that he is well into his seventies, has been retired from the mines for fifteen years, and had a life filled with enough tragedy, loss, and illness to fill the lyrics of several country and western songs. "How can he say it destroyed everything? We're still here, barely at times, maybe. But still here. Always have been."

Tina, his wife for decades (although they separated for a while until they reconciled a few years ago), is slumped in a chair, appearing listless and very ill. Suddenly, she comes alert and speaks her mind with surprising force and clarity:

> People here, lots of them, they have more than they did before the flood. Houses, cars, and money. Course, it wasn't that bad just before the flood either. The flood hurt us, no doubt. But the real losers were the people who lost their families and friends in the flood. The kids had it rough, too. Going to school and coming back home on the school bus. They had to look at everything that was all tore up from here down to Man. It took years to clean it up.

Tina points out that it was easier for her, Buck, and some of their neighbors because their houses are up a side hollow a few hundred yards from Buffalo Creek. They did not lose their homes or have to move. Their children suffered more than did Buck and Tina because they were staying with friends down along Buffalo Creek when the flood hit. They watched the relief crews and saw the dead bodies on their way home the next day.

Just then, I hear someone moving around in the next room back in the house, and I smell a burning cigarette. When I glance in that direction I hear Buck say to Tina, "He don't want to come out. Better leave him be."

The three of us are seated on overstuffed, frayed and faded easy chairs in the partially completed addition to the wood-frame, four-room house that the Miners bought from a coal company forty years ago. Around us are countless cats, medicine bottles, blankets, and other accommodations for the illnesses that plague the Miners and have hospitalized them many times. Tina, looking wan and sleepless, is wrapped in sweaters and bathrobes. She is unable to get up from her easy chair without assistance. Buck—lean, compact, intense, and with some nasty-looking old scars on his face and neck—is chronically short of breath, made worse when he tries to talk fast. I offer to come back some other time, maybe later in the day. Tina says, "No. This is alright. You two talk. I'll just listen."

I tell the Miners a little about myself, read to them some more passages from the experts' accounts, and ask them how well the passages apply to Buffalo Creek now and in the past. Both of them take time in forming their responses. Tina often agrees with the experts, for the most part, while Buck often disagrees, sometimes emphatically. For example, Tina agrees that many people felt lost, out of place, "torn from their moorings," and that they could "no longer get together in a meaningful way." Buck adamantly disagrees. "It's not true now and it didn't happen like that at all. Back then most people helped each other a lot. Why even the people who lost family in the flood were helping other people." Tina and Buck also disagree with each other about whether survivors could still care for themselves, whether they had a "deep distrust even of old neighbors," and whether they slipped into deviant lifestyles. Speaking slowly but with conviction, Tina gives some examples about thievery, vandalism, drug abuse, and marital discord. However, most of these examples are from the 1990s, rather than the 1970s and 1980s. Buck counters these claims with contradictory examples. He says that the only real animosities after the flood were directed at the coal companies. He claims that "drugs and ungodly behaviors" came in from Logan County and the rest of the country in the 1980s and 1990s. "It wasn't because of the flood. It was because of what followed it. Drugs come in here from outside. There was too much money around and the young people didn't have to work for it." Having grown exasperated while listening to Buck, Tina blurts out: "Well it wasn't always so great before the flood either. I could tell you stories you don't want to hear." Then, possibly to lessen the discord, Tina tells me why she sees things differently than Buck. She is not a native of Buffalo Creek. She is less sociable than Buck. She is housebound. However, she also believes that she is more realistic than Buck. She says Buck's point of view became much rosier years ago after what happened to him. He was nearly murdered in a labor dispute. "That changed him alright. That's when he found religion."

By way of explanation, Buck reveals that he once was "a hell-raiser and a fighter" who got involved in a lot of labor disputes against the coal companies until he was almost murdered in an ugly confrontation with strike breakers. Hospitalized and near death, "I found the Lord. Now I see things different." He talks about what life was like in the coal camps before the flood. People in the camps had to settle their differences and conflicts among themselves because there was no government, elected officials, or police forces in the coal camps. The managers of the coal companies and the police down in the town of Man would not get involved in conflicts among coal camp residents unless there was a murder or some direct threat to the property of the coal companies. Buck says that Buffalo Creek people were able to keep the peace on their own.

Tina takes strong exception to this. She insists that women often suffered when the miners were away working and when they were drinking after work. She says that housewives were not always safe in their homes from off-shift miners whenever their own husbands were working in the mines. She says that too many disagreements were settled by violence. "You don't know even half of what went on when you was gone. Women had to put up with all sorts of trouble by themselves." Buck tries to dismiss Tina's claims, but she presses the point home with several more examples, a few of which are too personal to disclose here. Their argument escalates in volume and in emotions. I interrupt them and ask about how things have been going since the flood. Buck responds that the mid-1980s were boom times for Buffalo Creek people, economically. "Things was pretty good. You could work double, even triple shifts if you wanted 'em." Tina, still somewhat miffed, mutters that women still had a hard time finding a job that was worth working, other than to get out of the house.

Concordance is considerably stronger among Buck, Tina, and the experts regarding the nature of community before the flood and that it has changed appreciably since then, especially for other people in the larger villages. I read to them passages about how the old community cushioned pain and provided intimacy, morality, and tradition. There was a constant readiness to look after one's neighbor. Tina responds: "Well, I guess you can say that. Most of us lived and breathed our fellowship up until the flood. Now it's only kind of like that. People help each other, but not with the zeal like before." Buck, somewhat mollified, concedes: "Well, I guess there is something to that. I guess it's never been the same since." Then he goes on to try to explain the changes in terms of migration, rather than the flood itself. "Old people keep moving away or dying. New people move in, some for just a few months, and then they move away, too. So the community keeps changing more than it did back then. You just don't know as many people around here as you used to."

Tina and Buck give very different accounts of social life in their own neighborhood, here along a small tributary of Buffalo Creek. Possibly, the differences are the result of Tina's being so housebound with crippling illnesses and Buck's being a native of Buffalo Creek. He spent his adult life as a coal miner and accumulated a wide network of buddies, as well as more than a few enemies. Their hamlet has shrunk by more than 90 percent in buildings and population since the flood. Now the hamlet has only about fifteen occupied houses and trailers, eight units of subsidized housing, and what remains of the former Buffalo Creek Memorial Health Center, which is now deserted and ransacked. Tina and Buck consider the people in the three dwellings closest to them to be their neighbors. They say that their are eight or nine neighbors in those dwellings now (they are not quite certain about the number of people who reside in the house closest to them), but that they would recognize all of their neighbors anywhere they saw them. Buck does much more talking, friendly talking, and exchanging of items with the neighbors than does Tina (who reports that she sometimes prays with one of her neighbors). Buck also visits the neighbors in their homes fairly often, sometimes shooting a game of pool with some of them. Neither Tina nor Buck report that they go places with any of their neighbors. Both of them say that neighbors are "real important" to them, although Tina expects less of them than does Buck. She says that a good neighbor is "someone who will watch out for your house when you're gone," while Buck says that a good neighbor is "a person you can ask for any kind of help day or night." Tina explains that she came from another state and that she lived years ago in a big city up north where "people just didn't socialize with anyone but their family." She admits that Buffalo Creek has always had much stronger social relations than other places she knew, and that she is glad of it, "mainly because it means so much to Buck." Tina then harkens back to her objection that "things ain't as perfect here along Buffalo Creek as Buck thinks they are. He wants to believe everybody is his friend now." Buck holds his ground by giving current examples of good neighboring, as when people visit and bring meals to sick neighbors who are not family members. He says, "we got those kinds of neighbors, too." He searches momentarily for the appropriate phrase, and then tells me, "I guess you got to be a good neighbor to have good neighbors."

Eventually, our conversation turns into good-byes. I wish them well and prepare to depart. Tina slips back into a dormant state, her eyes cast down to her lap, her breathing shallow. At the door, I ask Buck about the dozens of old wooden pens, now overgrown with vines, along the brook and just across from his front door. "I used to raise gamecocks for the fights. That was a long time ago. Now it's not worth fighting no more."

As I walk down the hollow to Highway 16, I pass by the now abandoned and garbage-strewn shell of the Buffalo Creek Memorial Mental Health Center. I cannot help thinking that this little side hollow is one of the saddest and most abandoned places along Buffalo Creek. Just then, a hefty fellow in his thirties walks out of the one new house in the hollow. He glances over at me as he is about to climb up into the cab of his shiny, new, diesel-powered Dodge pick-up truck—as big, gray, and bulbous as a beached whale. I tell him that I was just visiting a while with his neighbors, the Miners. He responds with a heartfelt sentiment: "That old Buck is as good a neighbor as you would ever want." Surely there is little reason to doubt that sentiment. In fact, over the next few years, I met Buck again several times at social gatherings (sadly, Tina did not survive the year). It was always obvious that Buck was trying to be a good citizen and that he was an integral part of the social community of Buffalo Creek, despite his once contentious lifestyle.

Looking back over my time with Tina and Buck, it seems to me that their differing accounts of their lives can help us to realize that the flood of 1972 was *not* the determining factor in the life course of every survivor, including them. This was particularly true for Tina. Her sense of well-being and her integration into the community of Buffalo Creek probably was never particularly strong. The flood was not a turning point in her life. Nor was the flood the turning point in Buck's life. That happened at least five years later during a violent confrontation with other miners in a labor dispute. But the flood might have been the source of continuing distress in the lives of their children, one of whom apparently died years ago of unspecified causes.

Several other points are particularly noteworthy when we consider what the Miners have revealed to us. As often as Tina and Buck disagreed with each other, their combined accounts were somewhat more congruent with the accounts of some of the experts than are the accounts of Sam Chance and Lonnie McCain as to the decline in neighborly relations since then. The Miners also were somewhat skeptical about whether misbehaviors became more frequent after the flood and because of it. Tina insisted that miners often did not realize how much abusive and predatory behavior went on in the coal camps before the flood. She implied that Buck's perspective was unduly tolerant and uncritical because of his broad base of friends, his conversion to religion, and his subsequent commitment to nonviolence.

On an even more somber note, there are reasons to believe that Tina and Buck's children have had little success in recovering a sense of social well-being. There were no photos or family mementoes in the Miner household—in contrast to omnipresence of items like these in the homes of the Mercers and many of the other respondents whose accounts follow in this chapter. Tina and Buck never mentioned their legacy or their children, other than to make a rather ominous reference to one son in a backroom of their house. Of course, it is true that I met with the Miners while Tina was suffering terminal illnesses. I am grateful for the considerable effort that both she and Buck made to help me understand their lives along Buffalo Creek.[12]

LEROY DIGGS:
NO COMPLAINTS ABOUT THE FLOOD,
THE CAMPS, THE LAWSUIT, OR THE YEARS SINCE THEN

It is a sweltering, hazy Sunday afternoon in mid-July. I am talking with flood survivor Leroy Diggs in the backyard of his modest, five-room, 1920s frame house in Kistler. Buffalo Creek runs shallow and slow only two streets away. Leroy inherited this house from his parents when they died a few years ago. Thick green kudzu vines spill down over the sycamores and tulip trees on Kistler Mountain and threaten to swallow up Leroy's garages and his three not-so-vintage Mustang convertibles. One of his summer projects is to cut back the kudzu and remove a few truckloads of the mountain's steep slope that are gradually sliding down on the garage walls. From the looks of it, the odds favor the mountain and the kudzu.

Leroy is a fleshy divorcee in his fifties, without children. Recently, he retired from a thirty-year career as a service technician for a Fortune 500 manufacturer of office equipment. Shirtless, wearing old, baggy pants and black sneakers, Leroy is something of a loner and an eccentric given to conspiracy theories. Besides his unfinished work on the Ford Mustangs, he collects uncounted stray cats that laze about the garages and the Mustangs. When Leroy hears that I am a sociologist who has been visiting Buffalo Creek for six years, he says that he took sociology courses when he was an undergraduate during the 1970s. He is neither eager nor reluctant to talk about his family's experiences in the flood, the camps, the Arnold & Porter lawsuit, and since then.

> We were living in Braeholm at the time of the flood, right along Route 16 and the Creek where the railroad bridge crossed over it. It was just below the Fanco tipple where the Becco rail line is now. Dad was an UMW (United Mines Workers) electrician in the mines. They were all UMW until Massey broke the unions in the 1980s. As usual, I drove home the Friday night before the

flood from college, where I was finishing-up my final semester. My mother left in the morning for her job down in Man. But a deputy sheriff stopped her along the way and told her the dam had broken at Three Forks and the flood was coming down the hollow. She drove back up to our place and alerted me, my Dad, and brother just in time. The black water rushed down through Braeholm as we ran out of our house for high ground. It was up to our waists. It ruined our house. A neighbor from up on Braeholm Hill came down and took us up to his place for three days. He fed and took care of us until the National Guard arrived. The day after the flood I walked back down into Braeholm to try to find my dog, Ernie, a black lab. He was still alive. He was guarding Mom's car right there on the street. Many of the other cars down there had their windows smashed in; but not ours. I saw some people I didn't know, young men, carrying stuffed duffel bags. Looters.

I tell Leroy that this is the first time that anyone has mentioned looters to me. I ask him how he knows that they were looters. Leroy appears to be annoyed by the question. He responds that he is not certain about it, but that it seemed pretty obvious to him that they were looters. I ask him if he reported the looting to the police. He does not seem inclined to respond. Then I ask him about his experiences with the HUD trailer camps.

Maybe a month after that flood, Mom and Dad moved into the new HUD trailer camp at Crites (about five miles from Braeholm along Buffalo Creek). It was brand new with new furniture, beds, and all. They got vouchers from the Red Cross for food, sheets, and other stuff they needed. I stayed with them there whenever I visited on weekends until I graduated. Then I got a job and moved into the hotel in Man. The company couldn't believe that any of its new employees wanted to return to Logan County. But I did.

I ask Leroy how his parents liked living in the HUD trailer camps.

They liked it alright. So did I. It wasn't bad. Dad still had his job in the mines. They knew some of the people in the camp and they were able to get around okay. They lived there for a least a year and a half. Then they moved into a bigger trailer at the HUD camp in Accoville. They didn't complain about either place.

I don't recall seeing the kinds of social problems there that some people talked about: fighting, drinking, drugs, and kids running wild. I had a sociology course at college so I knew about how those problems can occur and how bad they can be. But I didn't see them, or much of them.

I also ask Leroy how and why his parents left the camps.

Well, they intended to move back all along. The first settlement money came in but it wasn't enough to buy or build a house. I think everyone got maybe fifteen hundred dollars for property damage. So my parents joined up in that lawsuit with the law firm from out of state (Arnold & Porter). I don't remember much about the lawsuit though. I think Dad went to meetings and filled out the paperwork for us. When that was settled I think my parents got a five or six figure settlement for the house and property they lost. Me and my brother each got settlement money too. Most people who lost family members in the flood got fifteen to forty thousand dollars for wrongful death. So Dad took some of the settlement money and bought this house here for him and Mom. Dad also bought that HUD trailer they had in Accoville for maybe one thousand dollars. He sold it to me for the same price. I liked that trailer a lot. I lived in it for more than six years and moved it wherever my company relocated me.

It is worth knowing that my wife and I lived beside Leroy's property in a rented apartment for a few weeks. We already knew several of his neighbors and had interviewed two of them several years before that. When we revisited them, they were mildly complimentary about Leroy and his late parents. Leroy also was complimentary about them. He knew them and four other neighbors by name, even though he had only lived in this dwelling for a few years. He had moved in to take care of his mother before she passed away. While he did not borrow and exchange things with his neighbors, entertain with them, or go places with them (keeping to himself as a retired, single divorcé), it is clear that Leroy is moderately and peacefully integrated into a small network of four neighboring households, or at least with one member in each of these households. However, his interest in and integration into the rest of Buffalo Creek seemed to be limited, by his own choice. He had few complaints or compliments about anything. He gave every indication that he accepted Buffalo Creek for what it was, what it is, and what it will be for the remainder of his life.

In sum, Leroy Diggs' account gives us another example of survivors of Buffalo Creek's flood who were helped by neighbors and by the police to avoid the worst of the disaster. His account also complements the accounts of some other survivors who found the HUD trailer camps to be tolerable accommodations for nearly two years (at least in hindsight), who actually liked at least one of the trailers well enough to buy it and live in it for years, who benefited considerably from the Arnold & Porter lawsuit, and who chose to live out their lives along Buffalo Creek— and not more than one hundred meters from the creek that did so much more damage to so many others than to them. There is no evidence that Leroy's life has been fundamentally altered by the flood of 1972. There is no reason to believe that his very subdued sense of well-being or his limited level of social integration into Buffalo Creek as a social community would be any greater, or less, had the flood never occurred.

GOLDIE AND BUDDY CUMMINS:
NEVER LEFT; NEVER WILL. SUSTAINING A CARING COMMUNITY

"It's about back to where it was," says either Goldie or Buddy Cummins, the other one nodding in agreement, as usual. Often their views and comments are so similar that I cannot keep them apart. This is not so surprising when you consider that Goldie and Buddy have been married more than forty-five years and they have lived here, in their comfortable six-room bungalow, since the late 1950s. They are surrounded by mostly friendly neighbors in the heart of Lundale, the former coal camp that many people say was hardest hit by the flood. The three of us are sitting around a cluttered coffee table in their well-worn and commodious living room. Five decades worth of family photos, scrapbooks, trophies, and other memorabilia decorate the walls, cupboards, and tabletops as testimony to Goldie and Buddy's long and fruitful lifetime together.

Belying the stereotype of coal miners in some country and western songs, Buddy is a compact, mild-mannered, and kindly grandfather in his late sixties, complete with white hair, eyeglasses, and a forgiving manner. Goldie is a large-boned, confident, and direct woman with her short red-to-gray hair pulled back into a ponytail. When I first met her at the post office up in Lorado, she simply said that she was "from Lundale long before, during, and since the flood. We never left and we never will." Then she wrote down her e-mail address, handed it to me, and invited me to visit her home and family. That was two months ago. Now I take some time to tell them about my own experiences growing up around coal mines, about my current work, and about the experts' accounts. They listen patiently and with obvious interest.

> Well, what he's saying was true for some of the people. Some people died, no doubt. Some people were hurt so bad that they could never be the same as before. But around here most neighbors are pretty close. When one has a problem, we all have a problem. That's how I feel. Then we all just sort of pull together. We did it before that flood. We did it when that flood come through here. We been doing it ever since.

Without prompting, the Cumminses spill out a series of convincing anecdotes as examples. During the storm the other night, one neighbor phoned from miles way to say she could not get back in time. She wanted Buddy to go down to her house and close the windows from the rain. "She's like us. Only time we lock our doors are bedtime and when we go on a long trip." Coming back from vacations, they find that the neighbors have cut their grass for them. Just the other night, their next door neighbor/ad hoc babysitter came over and put their grandchildren to bed when Goldie and Buddy were a little late returning from a trip to the mall outside Logan city. Buddy hesitates for a moment and then offers a reassessment: "So, I think its better here now than before. We stick together when something happens to one of our neighbors. The community has grown back together." When I ask him about changes, he hesitates for a while. Then he mentions that Lundale and Lorado only have about one-half as many houses and a lot fewer people than they had before the flood. Some people have moved into Lundale in the last few years that the Cumminses do not know very well yet. "Some don't stay long enough for us to get acquainted. It's mainly the ones that rent vacant trailers by the month. But there's also some that just don't want to be neighborly. They stay to themselves."

The portable phone rings on the coffee table while Buddy is talking. Goldie excuses herself, answers it, and converses for a few moments, then closes by saying "See you there tomorrow. Thank you, Lessy Jane." When Buddy finishes, Goldie explains that the phone call was from a friend who told her that "the funeral service for poor old Mrs. Morris" (who also had survived the flood and whose wake I attended that same evening) is tomorrow at 11:00 a.m. at the Freewill Baptist Church in Lorado. Buddy and Goldie mention that Mrs. Morris was a fine lady and that they will miss her.

The Cumminses fondly recount their first years together, how poor they were ("our only wedding gift was two wash cloths!"), and how they bought this house from the coal company for $2,000 "when it was nothin' but four rooms and a path to the woods." They tell me about how they enjoyed the births of their children and adding on to this house, little by little. Soon they are telling me that everybody knew that coal mining was dangerous and that the creek flooded from time to time. They recall that there had been warnings for days or weeks about the unsafe condition of the impoundments at Three Forks due to heavy runoff of water from the snows and rains. And yet, a lot of people just could not get themselves to leave their homes. Goldie recalls that, the night before the dams collapsed, she was phoning folks to get their opinions about what to do. One conversation was with Denny Gibson—the coal company employee who was the last person to examine dam #3, less than an hour before it collapsed, and who raced down the valley in his pick-up truck, blaring on his horn to warn people of the imminent disaster. "He told me it's bad up thar'—real, real, bad." Goldie admits that she overheard other people's conversations on the "party line" phone system that they had back then. "People was worried all right. They was talkin' about who was leavin' and who was stayin'." One of Buddy's friends, a preacher's son, was so worried about the danger that he spent the night with them in this house. When Goldie and Buddy heard the flood coming the next morning, they took the kids and ran up the side of the mountain with the preacher's son and just watched it go by. It surrounded their house with muddy water and debris, two or three feet deep, but it did not damage it too badly (the house sits on a foundation of concrete blocks about four feet above the ground, and it is located on the street that is farthest from Buffalo Creek, about 200 yards away).

It becomes obvious to me that the Cumminses realize that many people and families lost much more than they did in the flood and that they have been fortunate in many ways since then. "It was a terrible time for everyone, I guess. Some people never was the same since." Buddy then mentions two survivors who have not been able to recover. One of them is a father, a coal miner, who lost every member of his immediate family when their house was swept away. The other is a woman who, as a terrified young girl, was caught in the branches of a tree and watched as the entire flood swept by her with drowned bodies. Buddy continues: "A lot of lives was destroyed, not just by the flood, but then by too much money after that. The financial settlements they got, I mean. Some people had more money than they knew what to do with."

Then, much to my surprise, Goldie joins Buddy in telling me about how some survivors lied to the "experts" who came in afterwards. They say that some survivors lied in order to "make themselves seem worse-off than they was so they could get bigger settlements or just to get their names in the newspapers and books." They name some of the survivors whose stories are inaccurate, to their way of thinking, as published in newspapers and in one book that they are unable to identify. Some of those people were part of a crowd of more than twenty-five survivors who stayed with the Cumminses in this same house the night after the flood. Three or four families stayed on for a month or more. Goldie and Buddy provide me with twenty minutes of wonderful anecdotes about the communal living that went on in this house for three or four weeks. The women started preparing food for everyone and tried to keep the house as clean as possible—an impossible task with all the people coming in soaked and muddy. When one family arrived from up the hollow, one of their little boys stepped inside, looked at the confusion and litter, and said to Goldie, "Lady, your floor here sure is muddy. You need to mop up." Goldie and Buddy laugh together, and then tell me that is how everyone reacted at the time. They recall how everyone was willing to share what little they brought with them when they escaped the flood. Even the Cummins children shared their toys and were glad to have so many playmates, "for a few days, anyhow." As darkness fell that first night, the men went out into the valley. They found many survivors who were just wandering around looking for a place to sleep. Some of them were total strangers from farther up the hollow. They brought these poor, wandering souls back to the Cummins' household, fed them, and gave them places to sleep.

Goldie and Buddy proudly introduce me to some of their grandchildren when they walk in for a visit. The kids cluster around us as we talk, not uncomfortable with me, a stranger in their midst. Buddy says that, on the night of the flood, he went to the mine and worked his shift, "keeping the pumps going." The next morning, he brought back a wood-burning stove from the mine so that they could cook for everyone in the house until the electricity was restored, about three weeks later. "Everyone shared as best they could what little they had until the relief supplies come up from down in Man." Days later, the Salvation Army came with sandwiches and blankets. It stayed for weeks, helping people as best it could. A local dairy sent in a truck with fresh milk, which the men kept cool in the brook outside so that their families had milk for more than a week. Hardly any of it turned sour. U.S. Army trucks came over the mountains on mud roads to evacuate homeless survivors from Lundale and Lorado. A lot of the people refused to leave, no matter how much they had lost or how sick they had become. "Most people didn't want to leave Buffalo Creek, no matter what."

Goldie's and Buddy's responses on the questionnaires reinforced the substance of their conversations with me. Buddy wrote that Buffalo Creek was the best place he had ever lived and that "friends," "quietness of the community" (note his choice of the word "community") and "mountains" are the three things that he liked best about it. The happiest year of his life was "when my first son was born," and his best job was as a foreman in a coal mine in 1976 (just four years after the flood). Buddy indicated that eleven of his eighteen relatives live along Buffalo Creek, as do forty-five of his seventy-five "close" friends. Goldie wrote many similar answers (actually, it appeared that Buddy had "borrowed" some of his answers from Goldie), except that she listed "being a Mom, 1958–2001," as the best job she has ever had. She also wrote that her happiest year was "when all our children were home." They also indicated that they felt contented with their place in Buffalo Creek as a community. They realized that they cannot be as active as they once were because of various age-related ailments that they must contend with. They mentioned that they had not yet been able to meet some of the newer residents in their section of Lundale, and they confided that some of these newer arrivals, "renters mostly, don't seem to want anyone to get to know much about them." That is about the only feature of their community that seems to bother them a little.

In conclusion, it seems to me that a strong case can be made that, similar to Molly Good and Wanda Mercer, Goldie and Buddy Cummins personify a very important portion of the people of Buffalo Creek for whom caring, neighboring, community life, and continuity have been lifelong attributes, despite the flood and the other more personal tragedies that they have endured. Probably, this is because they still have so many hundreds of friends and acquaintances with whom their lives are intertwined in agreeable ways. The Cumminses were happily married parents whose family was established in the middle of Lundale long before the flood. Buddy had a good, steady job at the local mines, and he kept it for years after the flood. The flood spared them heavy damage. It actually enabled them to play vital roles as Good Samaritans and cherished neighbors—roles they continue to play each day.

As I was departing, Goldie, Buddy, and several of their progeny stood with me in the bright, May morning sunlight on their front porch. One of their grandchildren snapped some photos of us there as we shared comments about many common interests. They thanked me for the coconut cream pie that I had brought for them. On one side of the house, a large vegetable garden was already bearing impressive stands of tomatoes, peppers, and corn. Nuggets of waste coal glistened in the sunlight in the garden, along the sidewalk, and in the alley. I told the Cumminses how surprised I was that the vegetables were so healthy despite so much waste coal in the soil. Buddy smiled knowingly and claimed that the coal actually helps sustain them in some strange way. "They kinda git use to it. Fact is, they seem to almost like it, after a while." He could have added that he and Goldie have managed to accomplish the same thing over the years—and with a quiet sense of dignity, purpose, and continuity.

In thinking about the Cumminses, it is worth remembering their testimony for so many reasons—only one of which is that their experiences often refute the accounts of experts as to the totality of the flood's destruction of individual well-being and of caring and effective social relations. They knew the flood was coming, as did many of their neighbors. They escaped, as did many of their neighbors. They gave great comfort and caring to many survivors—including total strangers—the day and night of the flood and for many weeks after the flood. After a few days, the Red Cross and other agencies provided essential relief services to many people along Buffalo Creek, but so did local businesses, including a local dairy and one of the coal companies (which provided Buddy with a stove for his house). At least one mine continued to operate on the day of the flood. Buddy worked his normal shift there that evening. The Cumminses avowed that some survivors whom they knew well, and who stayed with them the night after the flood, became plaintiffs and lied to the experts in order to maximize their chances of receiving large financial settlements through lawsuits. The Cumminses also contended that large financial settlements were misused by some of their acquaintances and that this misuse created more problems in the lives of some of their acquaintances.

As to their more recent situation in Lundale, the Cumminses felt that Lundale has been rebuilt rather well. For them, the quality of neighboring and community life in Lundale is just about as satisfying as it was before the flood except, perhaps, for some of the newer residents—mainly tenants—who shun neighborly relations. Acceptance of the status quo by the Cumminses is a very significant disposition because Lundale was damaged as extensively as any coal camp in the flood, if not more so. They knew Lundale intimately before the flood, during the flood, and in all of the years since the flood. They watched the flood hit Lundale. They lost dozens of close friends and neighbors in the floodwaters. And yet, they never considered leaving Lundale or Buffalo Creek, even though they had the financial means to do so. For them, it has never ceased being Lundale. It has never ceased being Buffalo Creek. These are the social communities they love, almost without any reservations. That never changed and, from what I have witnessed, is not likely to change in their lifetimes.[13]

LUREEN AND JAKE ALBRO:
LOOKING BACK ON LONG, EVENTFUL LIFETIMES;
TAKING FREQUENT EXCEPTIONS TO ACCOUNTS BY EXPERTS

For six years, Buffalo Creek people had been telling me that I should get to know Lureen (Lu) and Jake Albro because they have been integral members of Buffalo Creek society for more than five decades. I finally got the chance to visit with them on an overcast, humid, and quiet morning in July. A few years earlier, Jake had completed a questionnaire that was extremely informative. I called him to ask if I could get him to elaborate on some of his answers of two years ago and to informally retest him in order to check on the reliability of the questionnaire.[14]

We sit on the front porch of their well-kept, white, wood bungalow near the upper end of a side hollow that has about thirty dwellings. A three-foot wire-mesh fence, the most common type along Buffalo Creek, surrounds their garage, house, and several sheds. It is the kind of fence that is used to restrict dogs, cats, and small children. For the next three hours, we talk on and on over a wide range of topics. All the while, little kids pass by the porch dozens of times, walking and riding bikes on a one-lane alley that serves the hollow. Occasionally, they pause to listen in. Sometimes, out of idle curiosity, they ask what we are talking about. A few cars and pick-up trucks drive by slowly on their way to the little, white-frame Baptist church at the upper end of the hollow. The drivers nod or wave at the Albros as they pass by.

Jake, is a tidy, well-groomed retiree in sneakers, blue jeans, and a blue tee shirt. He readily vouches that he still loves to "hit the hills in my four-wheeler with my buddies. I might even ride up in there today if it don't rain too hard." He is an Army vet who served overseas in an Airborne unit, and is proud of it. He has direct opinions about the U.S. military forces in Iraq and Afghanistan, but he stops short of preaching or proselytizing, although he seems tempted to keep going. Besides being a soldier, he has been a lineman for a phone company, a coal miner, a Boy Scout volunteer, a representative and elected officer in the local mineworkers union, and a volunteer on many local initiatives. Jake relishes all of those experiences, and he loves telling stories about them.

Jake says that he likes best the "quietness of living here in Buffalo Creek and the friendliness of Buffalo Creek people. I got so many friends here I can't count them, or even try." He does not care much for "people who dump trash in the hills and burn things like wood and trash in the woods." He also is bothered by the amount of drug abuse that has been going on for years, and by "no enforcement" of the laws. Three of his fifteen closest relatives live along Buffalo Creek, as do dozens of close friends. He was born "right here in Lorado," feels closest to Lorado (and to the town of Man), but somewhat surprisingly, says that he was happiest "when I left here." By this he means when he left with his new bride, Lu, to try living and working "up North." Both of them liked their jobs with a phone company up there.

Lu and Jake believe that Lorado was at its best many decades ago when "everything we needed was right here. We even had a pool hall, bar, movie theater, doctor's office, and drug store." Both he and Lu say that Buffalo Creek was happily self-contained and nearly self-sufficient until it changed in the mid-1950s. During the 1960s, Lorado Coal

Company and the other small coal companies had trouble making money as competition increased from well-financed corporations headquartered outside of West Virginia. The local coal companies cut back on local services in order to trim costs. Miners' families bought automobiles and drove to Man and Logan to shop. "The local coal companies were good providers and really cared for the workers up till then," according to Jake, "but they sold off the company stores and sold the housing to the miners." They shifted from being paternalistic, caring companies, with managers living along Buffalo Creek, to budget-cutting and profit-driven businesses. Again and again Jake emphasizes that most of the local coal companies and managers were not evil exploiters of the miners and their families. Jake gives several examples of mining company practices that were benevolent and well received by most miners. Lu vividly recalls the sumptuous food baskets that the coal companies distributed to the miners' families at Christmastime. "They give us hams, turkeys, all the fixin's, fresh oranges, bananas, and red and white peppermint sticks that was big as sausages. We kids just loved them."

The Albros talk for more than twenty minutes about how good life was in the coal camps until Lorado Coal Company was forced into bankruptcy and finally sold everything to Pittston Company in the mid-1960s.

> Lorado Coal really cared. The owners would come down here from Ohio to make sure we was okay. Some of them even lived down here with us. They kept your job open for you if you got sick or you got drafted into the service. When I came back from the Army they had my job waiting for me. They even kept up the payments on my life insurance policy, even when I left to work up North. They got commodities free for us, like government surplus cheese and butter. They bought uniforms for the ball teams in all the coal camps.

When I ask Jake if there were exceptions to this largesse, he hesitates and looks at me for a moment. He then mutters something to the effect that there are dissatisfied people everywhere. He says that some of the miners and their families were just lazy, profligate, and undisciplined. "Some people were always script bound. They wouldn't work a full week. They would overdraw their accounts at the company stores, just like they do nowadays with credit cards at Wal-Mart. They git themselves into trouble; then they blame the company for their troubles." To this, Lu ads, "we really have good memories. We had good people here and a good company. It was safe back then. And you had everything you needed right here in Lorado."

Lu is a quiet, thoughtful woman in her early seventies with a perm of short, reddish hair. Much of her social life revolves around her favorite church, a few miles away. She proudly recalls that Jake was baptized there twenty years ago. She listens attentively to Jake's leading comments, never disputes him, but also makes her own opinions known when asked to do so.

> It was so nice back then. Each community had its own school and place for people to meet. Lorado had 200 kids in its own school, grades 1–6. At the Lorado Community Building we had parties and dances and weenie roasts. We had our own theater, clothing store, ice cream fountain, beauty shops, and everything we needed. Most of that kind of closed down after Lorado Coal sold out. But I still feel closest to Lorado than to anyplace.

Lu notes that she was born "up there where the dam broke—at Saunders (Three Forks)," but that her family moved down to Pardee in the 1940s. She feels closest to Lorado because she has lived here so long. "This is about all I know anymore. It's just home. It's peaceful and quiet; shut off from all the confusion elsewhere it seems." Lu is reluctant to mention any dislikes, but finally tells us how drug abuse of Oxycontin and "meth" disturbs her. She says that it is not just drug abuse by teenagers, either. "Married people in their twenties and thirties do it too. It causes lots of problems. Divorces." Pressed for another dislike, Lu laughs softly and says, "Cell phones." Asked to explain, she says, "They don't work like they're supposed to. Sales people stick you with a year contract. They tell you how wonderful they are. But they don't work good up here in the hollow." She laughs with Jake and me, knowing that this is a minor complaint.

In fact, during our three hours of conversing on their porch, Lu receives several phone calls on her cell phone. Each time, she excuses herself and moves inside her house to answer the call. When she returns after the last phone call, she explains that their daughter, Jenny, just phoned to say that she was driving up from her home in a nearby village with her daughter, Jillie, eleven months old and just recovering from a light case of measles. They join us on the porch after they arrive a few minutes later. The baby, a toddler, socializes readily with each of us. Jenny easily joins into our discussions, at times preempting her parents until they gently remind her to give them first chance.

Neighboring

When I ask the Albros about current neighboring patterns here in the hollow, Jake says that he has twenty neighbors; Lu estimates that she has thirty to forty of them. She says that she stays home a lot more now because of her slow recovery from an ailment. She and many of the women here talk by phone more often than in the past. The Albros' answers to the questions about neighboring indicate that there are subtle differences between them as to how they neighbor with others. Both Lu and Jake say that they recognize, say hello to, and know the names or faces of just about all of the people here. Lu ads that she knows their first, last, and maiden names, too—because "I grew up together with most of them and went to school together." Jake says that he talks with some of the neighbors face-to-face almost everyday, whereas Lu says that it is now only about once a week for her, "Usually when we see our neighbors at church, the post office, at Bob Evans (restaurant), Charlie's Steakhouse, or Wal-Mart" (three places that are more than a twenty-five–minute drive from Buffalo Creek). Then Lu laughs softly and self-consciously renders a few Wal-Mart slogans: "See you at Wal-Mart," "Everyone you know you meet at Wal-Mart." As we discuss neighboring further, Lu says that she talks with many of her neighbors by phone on a regular basis, much more than does Jake. "Jake, well, he spends his time driving his truck around to see his buddies and hittin' the hills in his four-wheeler." Lu also indicates that she has longer and more frequent, friendly talks with about thirty of her neighbors—although, again, these are usually done by telephone because of her slow recovery from illness.

A significant gender difference appears between Lu's and Jake's written responses to the question, "How many neighbors have ever talked to you about their problems or asked you for advice?" Jake wrote, "they usually don't. Maybe two," then he adds, humorously, "I give it anyways" regarding advice. On the other hand, Lu wrote, "at least 10 to 15 of them, I'd say. Many of the younger women ask the older women for advice or talk about their problems." Lu also wrote that she and a few of her female neighbors (she names them) exchange or borrow things like "flowers, milk, cakes, and cookies at least once a week." Jake's response was, "very seldom." Jake wrote that he visits with neighbors "maybe twice a month," while Lu wrote: "not much visiting anymore, only when they are sick." Both Albros indicated that they do not entertain with neighbors anymore, with Lu noting that, "We don't do that much at all—that's only a family thing now or something we do at church." Furthermore, Lu indicated that she does go to church twice a week with neighbors, while Jake noted that he goes to ballgames, church, and four-wheeling maybe two or three times a month with some of his neighbors. Not surprisingly, both Albros are emphatic in noting that neighbors are "very important" and "really important" to them. When I talk with them about these responses, they go on for ten minutes explaining why these are true, and by giving examples. Lu names neighbors who have come running over to her house to help her when Jake is not around. She adds that they are blessed with good neighbors: "They're here when you need them. They don't wait to be asked for help." Jake adds, half joking, "and they don't gossip everything they hear."

Like so many of the other "old-timers" along Buffalo Creek who survived the flood, in the course of answering my questions about neighboring and community life, the Albros—Jake, in particular—made frequent reference to the flood in 1972, although they did not obsess about it. It is only one of several major reference points in their lives. As the Albros talk at length about the flood, it becomes clear to me that many of their observations and opinions differ from the published accounts by the experts.

Some Differences From the Accounts of the Experts
The Albros insisted that, for the first four days after the flood, all of the recovery, relief, and aid efforts in the upper hollow from Lundale to Three Forks were provided by the survivors themselves and by their relatives and friends who drove and walked on dirt roads "from over the mountains" in Boone County, Kelly Mountain, Limber, Oceana, and Wharton. Some assistance also was provided by work crews from the local coal companies. These crews came down from the mines along Buffalo Creek with trucks, bulldozers, and other heavy equipment to clear debris in Lundale, Lorado, and Pardee. Jake recounted how he found bodies and severely injured people, including some of Lu's relatives up in Pardee, the afternoon of the flood. He and other local people moved the injured and dead to "safe houses" in order to protect them as best they could until sheriff's deputies and state troopers arrived days later. Not once did the Albros mention that any of Buffalo Creek's survivors were unable or unwilling to care for themselves or for their family members, neighbors, or others. It was not until the fourth or fifth day that significant help arrived from county, state, and federal agencies and from charitable organizations. "The roads and bridges down the hollow were too tore up and piled up with busted houses and trailers. They couldn't get up here till maybe day four or five. Then they only had one lane open, so it took half a day to get down to Man."

Jake felt strongly about the motives people had for joining in the lawsuit that Arnold & Porter brought against the mining companies. He said that he knew many of the plaintiffs, and there was no doubt that some of them had not been compensated adequately in the first payout from the insurance companies for the coal companies. But he also said that more than a few of the plaintiffs did not suffer much damage and that they exaggerated their damages. At one point, Jake hinted that Arnold & Porter told them to do so. However, when I asked Jake about this a little later, he hesitated and then changed the subject. He said that Lu's dad and many of their relatives had suffered severe damages, including gruesome deaths of family members. "But they wouldn't file suit. They just said that God wouldn't be pleased with it." Jake said that he and Lu would not even talk to the lawyers about the lawsuit. "We didn't lose anything here at our place. It wasn't right to ask for more." Several times Jake acknowledged that, as a coal miner, he not only was an employee of Buffalo Mining Company, but he also was a member of the United Mine Workers union. He had served as its local representative and as an officer. He said, with modesty, rather than with hubris, "I could see things from both sides. Some people never could. They wouldn't even try."

Both Lu and Jake took strongest exception to those assertions by the experts that portrayed the survivors as being helpless and hopeless after the flood. They were especially incredulous when I read to them the passage: "Nothing was left after the flood. It was a disaster that destroyed everything—the entire community. There was nothing left to build on." To this, Jake exclaims,

> What? What are they talking about? Why, even down in Lundale a lot was left. It didn't look too pretty, of course, but it wasn't all destroyed. Most people were still there or they come back down from the hills soon as they could. Of course, the road was all tore up and lots of houses were smashed. And there was dead and injured people down there. But there was plenty of people down there trying to figure out what to do. Other people come back as soon as they could and started cleaning-up and rebuilding as best they could. We was right there with them, helping as best we could. They was our friends and neighbors. Still are.

Lu then reinforced these exclamations with her own: "People got wore-out working so hard trying to clean up. Some got sick and had to stop for a while. We would go down there and try to help them get back. But most people worked as hard as they could when they were able to."

Furthermore, the Albros looked at me in disbelief—almost dumbfounded—when I read to them the passage: "For a long time there was little or no recovery. It was like a foreign land. Along the entire length of Buffalo

Creek people continued to feel that they were lost in a strange and different place…they no longer relate to each other in meaningful ways." After a moment of silence, Jake objected:

> No. No, that just wasn't so—not for most people. That was true only for the people that was hurt the most and for the people who was always looking to fight or complain about something. Some people didn't want to work anymore, doing anything, not just work for Pittston. So they stopped helping anyone. Some of the people was the type of people who would strike every day against anyone just to get anything they could with no effort. They was like that long before the flood. The flood didn't make them that way. It goes back a lot deeper. Some of them people don't help, won't help, or compromise, or negotiate on anything. They never try to find a middle way. They just want excuses and conflict.

Another passage that aggravated Jake and Lu asserts that: "The community no longer has the quality of people caring for each other in times of need, to console each other and to protect each other." To this Lu reacted with a protest tinged with disgust: "No, No, No! Most people kept on trying and helping each other. I don't agree at all with that. It's just the opposite. You draw even closer to those that are left here." Jake seems to be shocked by the assertion when he hears it. He exhales and proclaims: "We were still caring for each other all along. We drew even closer. We pulled together as best we could. And we still do."

Was there "deep distrust even of old neighbors and trusted friends," as claimed in another passage? Both Lu and Jake reacted decisively. Lu said, "That's not true. I didn't distrust no one, much less my own neighbors and friends." Jake concurs, "No. My old neighbors and friends that lived are still my neighbors and friends. They helped me. I helped them. I always will."

Was it true that social controls diminished and misbehaviors increased after the flood? The Albros generally endorsed this assertion, although they add some qualifications. Lu says, "Yes, I agree with some of that. Outside the coal camps in particular the young kids started fighting and there was other problems, too. People was trying to forget their problems after the flood, so some would be drinking and carrying on, even more if they got lots of money in the settlements." Lu then gives an example of some relatives whose house had been washed away. She says, "When that settlement money come in, all five of the kids got large amounts that they cashed in when they turned eighteen. They bought cars and motorcycles and generally got into trouble for a few years. They wrecked them. They drank too much. But most of them settled down in time." She hesitates, glances at Jake, and then mutters that one of the children recently died, possibly intentionally. She does not attribute this to the flood or to the settlement money. Lu then goes on to indicate that parental supervision diminished in general and that a lot of people tried to forget their woes, especially people ages fifteen to twenty-two. Jake listens attentively to Lu about the extent and frequency of misbehaviors that can be attributed to the flood. He contemplates what she has said, but decides that it applies mainly to people who were relocated to the trailer camps.

> I don't know about that. I think maybe what you are talking about was only in the trailer camps. It didn't happen up here the Hollow or with the people who were able to stay in their homes or get back quick. There was more of that down in those trailer camps, I think. Yes, there was drinking and kids fighting and carrying-on down there. But not all the people down there in the camps were from Buffalo Creek. Some come in from Gilbert and other places that had problems long before the flood.

Then Jake tells me something new—something that might have been overlooked by some of the experts regarding factors that could have mitigated social control and provoked deviant behaviors after the flood. Jake says,

> The years right after the flood there was other problems around here, too. In the middle of the 1970s a lot of people was real upset around here about work conditions in the mines and the contracts with the coal companies. The UMW contract was up for renewal and there was a lot of conflict and controversy. It was a bitter time. Tense. I know cause I was a union rep at the mine where I worked.

There was a strike of more than a hundred days. Everyone was angry. So, if those writers was talking to people down here they would hear a lot of complaints about everything and anything in general. It wasn't a happy time, I will tell you that.[15]

The Albros were puzzled by one-half of the assertion that, as of 1976, "the people of Buffalo Creek are now in the process of recovering from two disasters, the flood and the 'gradual deterioration of mountain culture.'" They ask me about the phrase, "the gradual deterioration of mountain culture." I explain it as I understand it. After a few moments, Lu and Jake indicate that they do not believe that people's basic values have changed very much since the flood. Jake says, "I think the people of Buffalo Creek still believe in mountain ways and values. They still believe in being free and taking care of yourself and your family. They still believe in minding your own business and not bothering too much about what happens outside of Buffalo Creek." Lu adds, "I don't think that modern changes like TV and all that have destroyed our values down here. Maybe some of the young people are different, but I'm not so sure about that, once they grow up some." Jake chimes in: "CB radios actually help people communicate down here. Even the cell phones help us get along—when they work!" He mentions that Lorado had a large radio antenna that helped the people communicate after the flood, and that it still helps. "People still like to talk. They still like to know what's going on around here." His general point seems to be that Buffalo Creek people, at least the older people, use a lot of modern innovations to help them maintain their traditional values, rather than change them.

Recovery and Prospects for the Future
When I ask the Albros about the extent of recovery of community and well-being along Buffalo Creek, they both admit that they did not have to recover anywhere near as much as did many of the other survivors. They say that this little hollow did not have to recover as much as did the straightaway part of Lorado. They also indicate that, for them, the essential nature of Buffalo Creek has endured, despite the changes. Jake says, "We all have to live with our memories of what happened

here. Most of us who are still here stayed here because it's still our home. It isn't just like it was many years ago. What is? Logan isn't. Charleston isn't. Anyhow, it's still the "Hollow," Lorado, and Buffalo Creek to us."

Daughter Jenny joined her parents in emphasizing that Buffalo Creek still constitutes a strong social community in that most residents are still willing to help one another in times of need. They give examples of how they, and some of their neighbors, have taken care of the poorest residents of the hollow and Lorado. They have even helped pay for funeral expenses and dig graves for some of the indigent residents who passed away. Jake describes how he and other neighbors went to the home of another neighbor along the hollow in order to check on her well-being. They found that she had expired in her bed. She left no survivors, no estate, and no cash. Jake and his neighbors took care of all arrangements and costs for "a decent funeral and burial. We even dug the grave for her. We was glad to do it." Jenny exclaims proudly, "Dad always helps people if they need it." Jake laughs and then adds that "Sometimes I even help them when they don't want it!"

Towards the end of the three hours with the Albros, I ask them what would help Buffalo Creek the most in the future. At first they seem a little uncertain. Then they join together in developing an earlier theme of theirs. All three Albros agree that Buffalo Creek could use more police patrols to curb the problems with drug abuse, speeding on Route 16, and littering in public places. I ask if incorporating the sixteen former coal camps into a municipality would help in this regard, and why the effort to incorporate failed in the 1980s. Jake answers that he was a strong supporter of incorporation. He was on the commission to do it in 1985. He felt that businesses in Logan and some of the coal companies "used fear tactics to defeat it. They spread rumors telling citizens up here that West Virginia would require them to install and pay for curbs, sidewalks, and street lights up and down Buffalo Creek. Citizens would be forced to cover all sorts of costs that are now covered by coal company severance taxes. New taxes would be necessary just for the people of Buffalo Creek." Jake also felt that the coal companies opposed incorporation because they feared that new severance taxes would be imposed on them by the taxpayers.

By and large, the Albros seem very comfortable with the status quo of Buffalo Creek and with its prospects for the future, with the exception of the problems of substance abuse, speeding, and littering. They certainly are delighted that their daughter and grand-daughter remain so close to them along Buffalo Creek. They give every indication that they are happy and eager to live out their lives right here, where their lives began: this little hollow at the upper end of the Buffalo Creek Valley.

Remembering the Albros

Among the many other insights that can be derived from conversations with the Albros is the realization that Buffalo Creek never ceased to exist as a caring social community to many people like the Albros. If anything, the flood seems to have deepened and sustained their social bonds to Buffalo Creek. The Albros also called our attention to other forces at work in the mid-1970s, in addition to the postflood rebuilding of Buffalo Creek that probably made it harder for many of the flood's survivors to recover psychologically, socially, and economically. And yet, from the perspective of the Albros, recovery has been appreciable. There is still enough social community along Buffalo Creek to sustain them, their children, and their grandchildren, and more than a few of their many friends and neighbors. I dare say that, even with Lu's slow recovery from illness, the Albros have an abundance of well-being, neighboring, and social community at Buffalo Creek—as much as they would have anywhere in the world, if not more so.

THE CANFIELDS:
THREE GENERATIONS OF FAMILY BONDING ALONG THE CREEK

"Here we are—right over here!" exclaims Becky Canfield Pollins cheerfully—and just in time, for my wife and I are standing in a cluttered cul de sac facing a leggy, muscular Doberman pinscher that just glares at us, without barking. Its owner, obviously inebriated on this steamy Saturday morning in mid-July, totters in the open doorway of his dilapidated trailer, staring at our predicament. "That dog won't bite 'less you come any closer."

Becky motions to us from the back porch of her parents' place. It is an often remodeled seven-room cottage, sky blue with white trim, that started out long ago as a coal company's four-room rental for one of its miners. Fortunately, it is surrounded by a three-foot-high, meshed-wire fence, which we promptly use to separate us from the neighbor's menacing Doberman. Now we are in a well-used yard turned children's playground that is strewn with plastic toys, a twenty-foot-wide inflated swimming pool, and a canopied swing. A hand-carved sign is mounted on the crossbar above the swing: "God Bless our Home." Becky, a pleasantly plump young woman with a bubbly personality, calls down to us from the porch: "Come on in. We're all in here waitin' for you."

Inside the cottage, an extended family of Canfields sits around the kitchen table finishing up their breakfasts and waiting for us. Most of them are smiling and yet a little apprehensive, judging from the expressions on their faces. Becky's introduction is a model of simplicity: "This here's my Pa, my Ma, my sister, my boy, and my two nephews." We tell the Canfields our names, shake hands with the adults, and tell the three little boys about the family of mallard ducks that we saw when we parked our car down along Buffalo Creek. Then we describe to the adults how Becky came up to us when we were at the Buffalo Creek Memorial Library in Man reading through newspaper clippings about the flood. She told us about how her late grandma survived the flood and about the photo album her grandma left for the family when she passed away. Then Becky kindly invited us to come up here to see the photos and to meet her folks.

Becky proudly pushes the album across the table to us. As we leaf through it and comment on the clippings of the flood, the Canfields join in telling us about themselves and about their ancestors. Grandpa Arnie Canfield, in his late fifties, is a retired, disabled coal miner: compact, gray bearded, and easy going. He is a teetotaler and a conscientious cigarette smoker—away from the kids—who loves to hunt, fish, and readily tell stories. Grandma Lucie Canfield, in her fifties, is a quiet woman in a simple cotton housedress. Judging from her appearance, she has had more than her share of physical ailments. Francie Canfield Trump is much like her younger sister, Becky: sincere, sociable, and comfortable with her considerable size. All four of the adult Canfields readily defer to one another, respect one another, and clearly love one another and the three young boys who alternately stand beside them and sit on their laps. Eventually, we learn that the two-year-old, Hootie, is Becky's only child "so far." J. J. and Nicky, eleven and eight years old, are the grandsons of Arnie and Lucie and the sons of Becky and Francie's brother who is "trying to start his life again in a new marriage out of State."

We learn that Arnie and Lucie were stationed in Germany with the U.S. Army when the flood hit Buffalo Creek in 1972. Many of their relatives and friends were injured in the flood, although none were killed. Many of their homes were damaged or destroyed. This one was "turned around on its foundation" and heavily damaged. Most of the other twenty to thirty dwellings in this coal camp were also badly damaged. They were (and still are) only 50–300 feet from the bed of the Creek.[16]

The Canfields tell us about the five households of kin that are among the eight households of neighbors who are closest to us. They run through the first names of all of their neighbors and tell us which ones are friendly (most of them), sick and dying (a few), and not so friendly (one old widow, and one couple that is cohabiting in a rented trailer). As the Canfields tell their stories, it becomes obvious that we are encountering them at a transition point in their lives. They have had many challenges, on and off, for decades, and their paternal grandfather (Arnie's father)—who lived in this house for many decades—passed away only a few months ago. They are still adjusting to his passing. This becomes even more apparent when my wife and I interview Becky and Francie out in the yard while Arnie and Lucie tend to the three boys and clean up the breakfast dishes.

Francie Canfield Trump

Francie tells us that she lives with her husband in the adjacent dwelling—hardly fifty feet away—that is almost identical to her parents' cottage.

Francie and her husband work as aides in a subsidized, assisted-living care center a few miles away. She feels fortunate to have the job and she hopes to keep it permanently. "I got it the week after I graduated high school. It's got good benefits. It's close by. And pay isn't that bad considering what's available around here." Francie was born in Germany during her father's (Arnie's) service there in the Army, eleven months after the flood. She says "it was at the same time that John Denver's song about West Virginia was a big hit. You know the one, 'take me home, mountain Mama, West Virginia, take me home.'" Francie recalls how happy everyone was after they moved back to West Virginia. She describes how much fun she had with her parents, sister, and countless relatives and friends. She confides that she has been somewhat depressed by the recent deaths of her grandpa and other close relatives. "We've had thirteen funerals in one year. Can you believe it?"

Regarding life along Buffalo Creek, Francie readily names the things that she likes best: "We know a lot of the people here. It's like a large family, and of course I love being so near to my mother, father, sister, and so many relatives." She goes on and on about the number of family, relatives, friends and neighbors that live close to her here in this hamlet and elsewhere along Buffalo Creek. The distinctions are blurred at times. Often we have to ask Francie whether she is referring to one or the other. "A lot of them are the same," she says with a little laugh. When pressed for another feature that she likes best, she answers, "Well, there isn't really much not to like living here. There isn't really much crime—not the terrible crimes you read about in other places." Francie has even more difficulty naming things she likes least about Buffalo Creek. When pressed on this topic, she eventually mentions a few. "Well, the coal train wakes us up when it passes by at night. But we know that it means people are earning a living, so we really don't mind too much about that." Francie also mentions that some of the newer neighbors (renters, not owners) seem to litter along the banks of Buffalo Creek, and they do not clean up the garbage in their yards. She surmises that perhaps this is because residents of this hamlet now pay a private firm for personal trash pickup service. Pressed for a third dislike, Francie says, "Well, there aren't a lot of recreational activities around here unless you drink or go four-wheelin'."

Francie's extended network of family members, both local and distant, is apparent when she is asked to estimate numbers of relatives and friends who reside here and elsewhere. She estimates that more than twenty of her sixty or seventy close relatives live along Buffalo Creek, as do five of her nine or ten close friends. So, it is easy to understand why Francie responds that "this right here is the best place I ever lived" and that she intends to live out her life "right here. There's no reason to leave." If there is anything she misses about "the old community," it is that "When we first moved here all the neighbors were extremely friendly and we got to know everyone right away and got along real good." Francie then points to the twelve houses and trailers that are visible from our seats in the backyard. She mentions the names of all of the families that lived in those residences twenty years ago. Then she says that she does not know the names of current residents in two of those residences. She also mentions that a few of the older residents, whose names she knows, are not as friendly as in years past. "They got older. They keep to themselves more now. We just don't see them much anymore."

Francie also mentions some things that have not changed. Good race relations are among them. She points out that "we still have a Black church and a White church. They are side by side just like they was when we moved here." She says that race relations have never been a problem, as far as she is concerned. The young kids of both races play together, go to school together, and get along. She mentions that two of the ten households closest to hers have Black residents. She names the families and says, "They are good neighbors to us, just like everyone else is." Coincidentally, as we are conversing, two groups of four Black children come walking by on their way through the neighborhood, talking quietly among themselves. Francie says that these are the grandchildren of some of her older neighbors. "Those kids come down here from the big cities up North to spend the summers with their grandparents."

Francie carefully counts up the number of neighbors and estimates that she has twenty-four neighbors living in the ten dwellings closest to hers. Nine of these neighbors are her relatives. She says that she recognizes, says hello to, and can name all of them. Excluding her family, Francie says that she talks with the other neighbors "everyday or whenever there is a chance," that she has friendly talks with them daily, that about three of them have talked with her about their problems or asked her for advice, and that she exchanges things "maybe every week or two" with neighbors other than her family (and much more often with her family). She has been in the homes of seven of the ten neighbors but does not entertain, visit, or go places with nonfamily neighbors more than a few times a year. Usually, this takes place in the form of "trips to the mall and Mary Kay parties," Francie says with a smile. She also ventures to tell us that she believes "neighbors seem to neighbor more" with one another when they have young children living with them. There are not as many children in the neighborhood anymore, so neighboring is not as extensive, and neighbors do not seem as friendly. As we discuss this observation, Francie is confident that the decrease in neighboring is because of this demographic change, more than because of a change in individual attitudes about neighboring.

In sum, Francie is a sincere and informative respondent who is glad to reside along Buffalo Creek with her loving families and who tries to accommodate her life's blessings and disappointments as best she can. At the same time, my own sense is that Francie would be struggling emotionally if it was not for the affection she receives each day from her mother, father, sister, and nephews. These people love her unconditionally. Nonfamily neighbors are much less salient to her. They were more important when she was a child because many of them had children who were her age-mates and chums. For Francie, her families—more than her neighbors, her job, or any other involvements—remain as the foundation of her well-being, her social integration into Buffalo Creek, and her hopes for the future.

Becky Canfield Pollins
Becky is the younger sister of Francie (by one year) with whom she has an easy and loving relationship. Becky, her husband (a coal miner),

and young son live in an aging trailer on a small lot behind her parents' home. Her responses are similar to her sister's, except as follows. Becky says that what she likes best about living at Buffalo Creek is the clean elementary school in Accoville with excellent teachers and the acceptance and support that the place has afforded to handicapped people in the last fifteen years. Her only dislike is the garbage that litters public places along the creek. Like Francie, Becky also indicates that she feels closest to this hamlet and that, if she misses anything about "the old community," it is that "back then, all of us here were just family and we were safe." As for the best times of her life, she fondly remembers when her family moved from another hamlet to this one in order to live next to her grandparents, who are now deceased.

> We got all the new appliances like the microwave that we didn't have before. Everybody laughed trying to figure out how to use them. Dad (Arnie) got all of us involved in doing the renovations on that house right there. It was just a little, old, coal miner's house when we got it. We also liked meeting all the new neighbors in the neighborhood. They really accepted us and made us feel real welcome. With all the other kids we'd go swimming in the pond down there in the creek. That's what we called it—a pond. It's just a deep part in the creek, is all it is, really. But we sure liked swimming there when we was kids.

Becky's responses to questions about neighboring also are similar to Francie's, except that Becky indicates that her neighbors do not ask her for advice or disclose their problems to her, and that most of the neighboring that she participates in occurs in her parents' home. "They all come to Mom's place—maybe fifteen to twenty visitors and neighbors a day. So I see them all in the kitchen. Mom even cooks for them."[17] Becky says that neighbors are very important to her. "They are everything. They are a safety net for us." She says that trust is the most important quality of good neighbors. "You got to trust your neighbors. This is such a good neighborhood. Why, my husband don't have to worry if he leaves his toolbox out on the porch. No one steals nothing from it."

In sum, both Becky and Francie provide us with two examples of rather young women who are well integrated into the social fabric of

Buffalo Creek, their hamlet, their families, and their neighborhood. Probably, they will remain so for the rest of their lives. They appreciate the fact that many of their relatives experienced the flood of 1972, survived it, and have carried on. They are not haunted by it. Nor are they fearful of it happening again, although Buffalo Creek still floods suddenly after heavy rains at times. The flood of 1972 actually seems to be a positive part of their heritage to them. When we first met Becky at the Buffalo Creek Memorial Library, she exclaimed with pride: "My grandma was a survivor of that flood. We got her photo album with lots of pictures she kept of it. Would you like to come up to our place and see it?" Obviously, we are so glad that we did.

J. J. and Nicky Canfield
When my wife and I visited the Canfields again the next day, Arnie and Lucie said that they would not mind if their two grandsons, J. J. and Nicky, participated in the survey. "They're already talking to you so much that they might as well do it all. Maybe they can learn something from it." And so, the six of us sit around the kitchen table together. We explain to the boys the purpose of the questions and we relate our project to their schoolwork. J. J., eleven, is bright, lively, eager, and talkative. He tries to answer every question first, and at length. Nicky, eight, tends to repeat his older brother's responses or say, "Same for me." So, we sometimes ask him a question first. Arnie and Lucie sit with them and encourage them, but try to avoid answering the questions for them.

The boys had moved to Buffalo Creek from the Midwest a few years ago to live with Arnie and Lucie, their grandparents. The boys say that they like living here a lot and they mention what they like: the family, friends, school, and teachers. Asked what they liked least, they blurted out "the creek don't have enough fish" and "there are too many bridges along the creek that we ain't allowed to go near." Understandably, it takes a while for the boys to count the number of close relatives and friends that they have along Buffalo Creek. They settle on twenty to forty close relatives living along Buffalo Creek and "lots" living elsewhere. They also say that they have about five close friends, "not countin' each other," all of whom are schoolmates. Emphatically, they state that this is the best place they have ever lived, but they have some difficulty deciding on the name of this place. Eventually, they agree to call it ____ (the hamlet's name) rather than on "Buffalo Creek." The distinction seems irrelevant to them. They boys need help from their grandparents in counting the number of nonfamily neighbors before they settle on "nine" as the answer. This estimate includes two boys, ages five and nine, and two girls, ages three and four, who recently moved in across the street. The boys say that they would recognize most of their nine nonfamily neighbors anywhere they saw them. They say hello to all of them whenever they see them. They know the first names of all of them. They have a talk almost every day with one of the neighbors, a woman nearby who "has a pond and lets us play there and catch frogs." They have been in the homes of three or four of their neighbors, and they visit Becky and Francie in their homes almost every day. The boys only exchange things, entertain, and go places (the movies and the mall on the far side of Logan) with their grandparents and aunts. Asked first, Nicky hesitates and then says that neighbors are "real important because we get to see them a lot." He says that it is most important that neighbors "be nice to us, not shove us or hit us, and help us to do things like make a swing near the Creek." J. J. eagerly adds: "Neighbors are real important. We can do tons of stuff with them." He gives some examples of catching tadpoles and frogs with some of the kids in the neighborhood, whom he names. He adds that he and Nicky like to visit one of their neighbors, Donna Lee, because "she is real nice to us and she lets us catch tadpoles in her pond." The boys cannot think of any ways that the neighborhood or the neighbors could be any better, except "if we could go play near the bridges more." To this, Grandpa Arnie comments with a laugh: "These boys would be over there and down at the creek all day long if we let them!"

Arnie Canfield: "Happy the Way Things Are Right Here."
So says Arnie Canfield, an alert, sincere, disabled, retired coal miner in his midfifties. He is now the titular patriarch of the Canfields of this hamlet since his own father (who was his closest neighbor) passed away in April. An average-sized fellow with a mostly gray beard and

sideburns, Arnie often apologizes for not being very sociable. "Tell you the truth, I'm kind of a loner. I'm happy just huntin' and fishin' by myself, if no one cares to join me. I never drank, gambled, or done the things some folks favor. I've always been happy just gettin' along with the way things are. I don't worry much about the future or the past. I'm thankful for what I got."

As Arnie describes key events in his life, it becomes apparent that he has been able to find happiness and comfort in a broad web of family and kinship relations.

> My family moved us to Buffalo Creek here from Kentucky in the 1950s. I been here ever since except for nine months in Kentucky to get my miner's card and two years that me and my wife was in Germany when I was in the Army. We was over there when the flood hit. I remember hearing about it on the radio. So we was spared. We called home and found out that my sisters and their families was alive. The flood hit their houses real bad and killed lots of the neighbors. Wasn't nothin' we could do about it over there in Germany. I sure felt real bad about it.

As we talk, Lucie offers suggestions to Arnie from the kitchen while she prepares biscuits, gravy, and sausages for the kids. We joke with him about being coached by his wife. He laughs and says, "The wife's good at that." Eventually, the subject turns to the neighborhood and his neighbors.

> Let's see now. Well, we moved up here in 1985 to be near my parents. At first my wife was a little scared because she never lived before around Black people. I had, up in Lorado, and they was good people. I told her it was okay. And it is. All the people here get along real good. It's a good neighborhood for us and for the kids. The whole family together rebuilt these here old mining houses. This one for me and my wife. The one beside us, right there, (pointing) is for my daughter and her husband. My other daughter, her husband, and little boy live in that trailer right there beside us. We're gonna build them a house there soon as we can. So we're all here close together where we can help each other.

I ask Arnie if he considers any of the other people in this hamlet to be his neighbors, besides the family members in the three other dwellings adjacent to his. "Sure. Just about everyone around here is our neighbors." Arnie counts fifty neighbors in eighteen houses and trailers. He says that he would recognize about twenty-five of them anywhere he sees them, even many miles away from Buffalo Creek. He greets "any and all fifty of them when I see them, even the little kids, and the ones I don't know too well." Arnie also estimates that he knows the last names of twenty-five or thirty of his neighbors and the first names of twelve of them. He has friendly talks once or twice a week with three or four of the neighbors, and he has been in the homes of five or six of them.

> Only one of my neighbors borrows from me. She's a widow lady. She borrows the lawnmower and stuff like that sometimes. Myself, I'm not a borrower. I will go and buy something new rather than borrow from someone. I don't visit them in their homes or go places with them or entertain them, as a rule. Mainly I just stand and talk with them over the fences and along the road when it seems right. I'm real thankful that I got good neighbors, even though I'm not very sociable. We try to respect each other. That's what's important—respect each other and each other's property. Like when my Dad died. My brother wanted to take down the fences. I said no. Good fences make good neighbors, just like it says in that famous saying you hear.

Arnie likes this hamlet and all of Buffalo Creek, along with his family, relatives, neighbors, and just about everything else that comes into the conversation. Complaining is not his nature. "Oh, I like it fine right here where we are. I like it because it's been home to me most of my life now. The neighbors I have here are decent people. It's quiet and peaceful." Asked what he likes least, Arnie pauses, thinks, and almost blushes.

> Now it's hard to say on that one. I don't have many complaints. I guess the drug situation has gotten kinda rough the last few years. Nerve pills, Oxycontin, crack, cocaine, meth, and all that kind of stuff they use. And it's not just the teenagers, either. You hear about married people, young kids, and even some old people

getting hooked on that stuff. Takes them years to get off of it. It's caused lots of problems. Families just fall apart.

Arnie often mentions that he comes from a huge family and he has at least one hundred blood relatives. He estimates that he has a rather staggering number of "close" relatives ("seventy-five") living along Buffalo Creek and even more of them living elsewhere ("hundreds, at least.") He chortles and then insists that he feels close to every one of them even though he does not see all of them every often. "I know 'em just the same. I know who they are and what they are like."

By contrast, I am caught by surprise by Arnie's estimates of his close friends. "Well as I said, I'm not a very sociable person. I guess you could say I have quite a few acquaintances—but not close friends. I guess you could count one gentleman here along Buffalo Creek that I hunt birds with. But that's about all we do together. As to close friends outside of Buffalo Creek, I guess I got none—except for you." Pleasantly surprised by his gesture of goodwill, I thank Arnie and tell him that I hope we can be friends for years to come. He then asks when I will return to visit him and his family. I tell him I do not know, but that now I have even more reason to do so. We talk about the possibility of doing some hunting together with his Brittany spaniel. I encourage him to bring his children up to New England for a visit so that they can see firsthand famous historical places like Old North Church, Old Ironsides, and the route of Paul Revere's ride through Boston. Arnie listens patiently, smiles, and apologizes bashfully. He tells me that he has a disability from working in the mines that keeps him from driving more than a few hours from Buffalo Creek, at most.

Looking back over what Arnie revealed to us, his accounts raise some doubts about experts' assertions that the flood of 1972 was a total disaster to everyone whose home was damaged by the floodwater and whose friends were killed in it. Arnie's parents never moved away from this hamlet, despite the extensive damage that was done to their home. Arnie, in Germany at the time, was concerned about—but not traumatized by—news of the disaster and the destruction it wrecked upon his parents, other relatives, and many of this friends. He readily moved his family to this hamlet when the opportunity arose years later. He felt very fortunate to do so—not reluctant or fearful. Now he resides in the same cottage that his parents resided in when the flood knocked it off of its foundation and almost washed it away. Arnie makes little distinction between this hamlet and Buffalo Creek as social communities now, or back in the 1970s. These are still caring communities to him. They provide enough of everything he needs to suit him, including good neighbors, except for adequate controls over the use of illegal drugs and possible child molesters. Arnie realizes that, as a parent, he must be vigilant in protecting his young boys from predatory behaviors of strangers. Additionally, there is plenty of evidence that Arnie Canfield is remarkably well integrated into his family and kin groups. He has a strong sense of social well-being, even with his disabilities and early retirement.

As a postscript of sorts, I learned that Arnie and Lucie's cottage was nearly flooded the previous year when Buffalo Creek overflowed its banks in a heavy rainstorm. For many people, this experience would have been especially unnerving because it was this same cottage that was knocked off of its foundation by the flood in 1972 when Arnie's parents resided in it. And yet, Arnie was not unduly anxious or depressed by the damage that occurred to his yard and outside belongings. Characteristically, he just went to work cleaning up the yard and repairing the damages. He told everyone that it was not worth worrying about. As Arnie reminded me more than once, "Things can always be worse than they are. I'm just happy the way things are right here. There's a good side to most everything."

DARREN SERVICE:
THE NEXT GENERATION; "I WENT AWAY FOR A YEAR OF COLLEGE, BUT I NEVER LEFT HOME."

My wife and I are spending a pleasant hour with Darren Service in summer chairs on the front porch of his parents' wood-frame house along a shallow brook, about four hundred yards up a side hollow of Buffalo Creek.

The brook gurgles as it passes by now. Last night a sudden storm flooded it so much that metal barrels for burning trash and rock-walled wading pools for the children in the neighborhood were washed away. Everything seems tranquil now, however. Five stately tulip and gum trees tower above the brook and shade the porch from the heat that is building up fast on this midmorning in July.

Darren is a slender, easy-going, and sincere fellow who has just finished his freshman year at a small sectarian college in another part of West Virginia. We are talking with him in order to get more interviews from the members of the younger generation of native Buffalo Creek residents who have no direct experience of the flood of 1972. We ask Darren how he liked his first year of college.

> I liked it a lot. I did pretty good with grades. I didn't care much for the dorms though. So I came back here most weekends. Maybe I was homesick. I guess you can say I went away for a year of college but I never left home. Some day I'd like to own my own chain of hotels. But I'll always have a place back here in Buffalo Creek. I've lived here all my life. It's home.

Darren tells us that he does not know much about the flood of 1972 except that it did not come up this side hollow very far and that none of the six dwellings within view were damaged. One of his uncles, Dewey Burgess, drove his jeep ahead of the flood wave into Robinette, blaring his horn to warn people of the oncoming danger. Darren responds readily and thoughtfully to our questions.

> Well, I like living on Buffalo Creek because the people are all friendly. Everything is convenient. It's home. There's not much I don't like about it except maybe there is not a whole lot to do and that sometimes people are a little too close (as he laughs) in knowing what you are doing. That's okay some of the time; but I don't like that being the case all of the time.

Darren estimates that fifty of his seventy close relatives live along Buffalo Creek, as do forty of his seventy close friends (and he insists that he is *close* to them, socially, when we ask him about it). "Yes, I have lots of close relatives and friends, here and outside of Buffalo Creek." He says that he enjoys many things about Buffalo Creek: his part-time summer job at a used-car lot, his belonging to a youth group at one of the larger Baptist churches just a few miles from Buffalo Creek, his girlfriend, his younger brother, and the friends he made during his high school years. He says he has not seen any changes of significance at Buffalo Creek as far as social life and community is concerned. "I guess I'm too young yet. It's been about the same all along."

Darren has lived in this dwelling with his mother, brother, and stepfather for a number of years. He says that he has ten neighbors in the four nearest houses. Four of these neighbors, in two of the houses, are uncles and aunts (some of whom have suffered major personal losses recently). Darren says he knows the names of all ten, recognizes all ten wherever he sees them, and says hello to eight of them on a regular basis. He talks with some of them every day, has friendly talks with six of them fairly frequently, and has talked with five of them about their problems (or his). Most of his contacts are with the neighbors who are his relatives. In fact, during one of our visits to Darren's home, we have a five-minute conversation that includes Darren, one aunt, and one uncle who happens to be passing by. After we return to converse with Darren on his porch, the aunt and uncle (from separate households) continue conversing together for another half hour.

Darren says that he exchanges things once or twice a week. "My aunt just borrowed my air pump for her tires." He has been in all of his neighbors' homes, visits with some of them three or four times a week, entertains some of them "maybe once a week at a cook-out here or there," and takes some of his older neighbors "to church services, movies in Charleston, maybe three times a month" when he is not away at college. Darren readily avows that neighbors are "very important to me, and we have good ones here mainly. They are reliable. They are here for us in times of need. And we do the same for them."

In sum, Darren Service is a well-adjusted, sincere, and bright young man who is well integrated into Buffalo Creek. He has no reservations about his lifelong affection for Buffalo Creek, and he sees scant evidence of problems in Buffalo Creek as a social community, or in its individual residents, that might be attributable to the flood of 1972. To Darren, stories of the flood are an integral part of the folklore and heritage of Buffalo Creek, just like stories of remarkable faith healings, eccentric mountain men, the feuds between the Hatfield and McCoy clans, and the Battle of Blair Mountain. Darren neither flaunts nor rejects these tales. Rather, he accepts them with a sense of modest pride in his ancestors and his community. At the same time, however, let me suggest that Darren probably is so busy, optimistic, and positively attached to some other people that he does not pay attention to people, places, and conditions that are unsavory. This is not because he is naïve so much as that he is a hopeful and religious fellow. It seems as though he has told himself to keep focused on his own challenges so that he can succeed for himself. He accepts Buffalo Creek for what it is—and he is the better for it.[18]

Summary: What Have These People Revealed to Us?

What have these twenty-two people of Buffalo Creek revealed to us regarding the social conditions of Buffalo Creek and the psychological states of Buffalo Creek's people immediately before the flood of 1972, immediately after it, and in the last few years? Table 4.1 summarizes my best estimates of what they have revealed to us about these and about other topics.

Explanation of Table 4.1

By way of explaining the estimates that are presented in table 4.1, let us consider the case of Molly Good (the top row in table 4.1) and read across that row from left to right regarding each of the following factors that are listed in the titles of each of the columns, from left to right.

Before Flood

"Very high": In my many conversations with Molly, she indicated to me that she believed that, before the flood, her personal well-being, her neighboring, her neighbors, her level of integration into Buffalo Creek

as a social community, and the communality and well-being of Buffalo Creek as a whole all were "very high" in quality (abbreviated in table 4.1 as "V-high"). Said another way, before the flood, Molly believed that she was very well, that Buffalo Creek was very well, and that her social relationships at Buffalo Creek community were very well.

Flood Damages
"*None*": Molly indicated to me that her dwelling and her other property were not damaged in the flood and that neither she nor any of the other members of her household were in the floodwaters. They did not suffer any direct, immediate physical injuries because of the flood itself.

Impairments or Deviances
"*Some anxieties*": During my many hours with Molly and some members of her family, Molly revealed to me that she suffered some anxieties immediately after the flood that were related to what she and members of her family witnessed along Buffalo Creek in the hours, days, and weeks after the flood. Furthermore, from my time with Molly, I believe that some of these anxieties have remained with her up to the time of this writing. However, Molly did not reveal to me any evidence that, as a result of the flood, she engaged in misbehaviors or what sociologists often refer to as deviant behaviors or deviances, such as excessive use of alcohol and drugs, marital abuse or infidelities, theft, vandalism, or other crimes as a result of the flood.

Relocations, Compensation, Health Care
"*None*": Molly did not indicate to me that she had been relocated from her dwelling to the HUD trailer camps, or anywhere else, after the flood. Nor did she indicate to me that she had received compensation from any government agency, business, or other organization in the form of financial remunerations, health care services, or therapy.

Concordance With Experts
"*Mixed*": Molly generally agreed with the experts as to the suddenness and intensity of the flood and the extent of the flood's immediate

damages to Lorado, Lundale, and some other coal camps at the upper end of Buffalo Creek Hollow. However, she took exception to some assertions by the experts, including the assertion that many survivors were so psychologically impaired that they could no longer care for and about themselves, their families, or their neighbors. She also took exception to the assertion that Buffalo Creek ceased to exist as a social community.

Furthermore, it is important for readers to note that this factor, "Concordance," includes more than just the presence or absence of explicit agreement with the experts' assertions by Molly Good and by other survivors of the flood. Concordance also takes into account whether the objective experiences of Molly and other survivors support, refute, or fail to support key assertions by the experts. For instance, Molly revealed that the vast majority of the residents in her own coal camp did not suffer any property damages directly in the flood or due to it. This testimony of Molly's is credible and it is not in concordance with assertions by some experts to the effect that the flood destroyed virtually everything in its path. Furthermore, according to Molly, she and many of her neighbors immediately went to work aiding the many injured and homeless survivors whom they found in and around Lorado and Lundale. Molly and her neighbors did not wait for outside relief agencies to arrive. Rather, Molly and many others (including Wanda and Wally Mercer, Buck Miner, Goldie and Buddy Cummins, Lureen and Jake Albro) immediately provided essential relief services to many other survivors—friends as well as strangers—for at least four days before members of outside relief agencies arrived in sufficient numbers in Lorado and Lundale to take over the relief efforts. And so, in sum, I used both Molly's *experiences* and her own *reactions to major assertions by experts* in estimating that her account was "mixed" regarding concordance with the experts.

Later Life Events
"Many positive, some negative," (abbreviated in table 4.1 as "Many +, some –"): Molly indicated to me that there have been many positive

TABLE 4.1. Estimates of various factors in the lives of Buffalo Creek people: Before, during, and immediately after the flood—and after 1999. Respondents 1–11, columns A–D.

		A Before Flood	B Flood Damages	C Impairments or Deviances	D Relocations, Compensation, Health Care
1.	Molly Good	V-high	None	Some anxieties	None
2.	Sam Chance	Mod.	Extreme, in water, severely injured	Physical & emotional impairments	HUD trailer camps, comp. from state and A&P, received therapy
3.	Lonnie McCain	High	Severe	Anxieties and A&P	HUD camps, comp. from state
4.	Wanda Mercer	V-high	None	Anxieties	None
5.	Woody Mercer	High	Not directly	Anxieties & other psych. problems	None
6.	Mabel Church	Mod.	Severe	None revealed	Liked HUD camps, comp. from state and A&P
7.	Emma Sue Kinsley	High	Severe	Some anxieties	Liked HUD trailer & camp, comp. from state
8.	Helen Woodruff	High	Severe	None revealed	Disliked HUD camps, comp. from state
9.	Loretta Washburn	High	Severe	None revealed	Disliked camps, got trailer, liked A&P comp.
10.	Tina Miner	Low & mixed	None	Probable impairments to children	None
11.	Buck Miner	High	None	Probable impairments to children	None

Note. V-high = very high   comp. = compensation   A&P = Arnold & Porter
      Mod. = moderate   psych. = psychological

TABLE 4.1. (*continued*) Respondents 12–22, columns A–D.

		A *Before Flood*	B *Flood Damages*	C *Impairments or Deviances*	D *Relocations, Compensation, Health Care*
12.	*Leroy Diggs*	Mod.	High, in water	None revealed	HUD camps, trailers, comp. from state and A&P
13.	*Goldie Cummins*	V-high	Barely escaped, some damages	None revealed	None
14.	*Buddy Cummins*	V-high	Barely escaped, some damages	None revealed	None
15.	*Lureen Albro*	V-high	No damages	Possible anxiety about dead kin	None
16.	*Jake Albro*	V-high	No damages	Possible anxiety about dead kin	None
17.	*Francie C. Trump*	n.r.	n.r.	n.r.	n.r.
18.	*Becky C. Pollins*	n.r.	n.r.	n.r.	n.r.
19.	*J. J. Canfield*	n.r.	n.r.	n.r.	n.r.
20.	*Nicky Canfield*	n.r.	n.r.	n.r.	n.r.
21.	*Arnie Canfield*	High	Damages to parents' home	None revealed	None
22.	*Darren Service*	n.r.	n.r.	n.r.	n.r.

Note. V-high = very high   comp. = compensation   A&P = Arnold & Porter
Mod. = moderate   psych. = psychological   n.r. = not relevant

(continued on next page)

TABLE **4.1.** (*continued*) Respondents 1–11, columns E–K.

	E Concordance With Experts	F Later Life Events	G Neighboring Active	H Neighbors Value	Recent Disposition		
					I Social Integration	J Social Well-Being	K Community Well-Being
1.	Mixed	Many +, some −	V-high	V-high	Max.	High	Mod.
2.	Mixed	Mixed	n.d.	n.d.	Mod.	Marginal	Mod.
3.	Mixed	Mainly +	n.d	n.d.	Mod.	Mixed	Mod.
4.	Mostly	Mainly +	High	High	V-high	Mixed	Mod.
5.	Mostly	Mixed	Ltd.	High	Mod.	Low	Mod.
6.	Limited	Mixed	Ltd.	High	Mod.	Ltd.	Mod.
7.	Limited	Positive	n.d.	n.d.	V-high	High	High
8.	Mostly	Mixed	n.d.	n.d.	High	Mod.	Mod.
9.	Mostly	Mixed	n.d.	n.d.	Mod.	Mixed	Mod.
10.	Mixed	Many −	V-low	High	Low	V-low	Mod.
11.	Mixed	Mixed	V-high	High	High	Mixed	Mod.

Key: n.d. = not determined　　V-high = Very high　　+ = Positive
n.r. = not relevant　　V-low = Very low　　− = Negative
Mod. = Moderate　　Max. = Maximum　　Ltd. = Limited

TABLE **4.1.** (*continued*) Respondents 12–22, columns E–K.

	E Concordance With Experts	F Later Life Events	G Neighboring Active	H Neighbors Value	Recent Disposition		
					I Social Integration	J Social Well-Being	K Community Well-Being
12.	Low	Mixed	Ltd.	Mod.	Limited	Mod.	Mod.
13.	Often refutes them	Many +	V-high	V-high	V-high	High	High
14.	Often refutes them	Many +	V-high	V-high	High	High	High
15.	Mixed, some refutations	Mostly +	V-high	V-high	V-high	High	High
16.	Mixed, some refutations	Many +	High	V-high	V-high	V-high	High
17.	n.r.	Mainly +	High	V-high	High	Mixed	High
18.	n.r.	Many +	High	V-high	V-high	V-high	High
19.	n.r.	Very +	V-high	V-high	V-high	V-high	V-high
20.	n.r.	Very +	V-high	V-high	V-high	V-high	V-high
21.	Doubtful	Many +, some losses	High	V-high	V-high	High	Mod.
22.	n.r.	Many +	V-high	V-high	V-high	V-high	High

Note. n.d. = not determined   V-high = Very high   + = Positive
n.r. = not relevant   V-low = Very low   – = Negative
Mod. = Moderate   Max. = Maximum   Ltd. = Limited

events in her life since the flood. These include the births of many grand-children and great-grandchildren, many new friendships, active participation in memorial committees and reunions, and many years of enjoyable and gainful employment as a school bus driver. Molly also indicated that there were more than a few sad events since the flood, including the premature death of her husband a few years after the flood, the tragic deaths of some of her many friends and relatives, and various chronic illnesses and disabilities to herself and to people she loves dearly. All of these probably have had considerable bearing on her current sense of well-being, her perception of the well-being of Buffalo Creek as a social community, and her participation in a wide range of social relationships and community affairs.

Neighboring: Active

"Very High": This factor refers to how active the respondents are in inter-acting with their neighbors. Compared with all the other people I have interviewed in the United States, Molly is very highly active in neigh-boring. Very few people anywhere do as much neighboring as Molly, in part because quite a few of Molly's neighbors are her blood relatives and because Molly reaches out to embrace many other people unless or until they shun her.

Neighbors: Value

"Very High": This factor refers to how much value respondents place on having good neighbors and on being good neighbors. Molly often told me (and showed me) that "good neighbors are very important—right up there after family and church in importance to me." By the way, I often found that these two aspects of neighboring—"active" and "value"—are somewhat independent of each other, particularly in the cases of people who are shy, housebound, or so fully employed or occupied that they do not have time to participate in very much neighboring. They still can value good neighbors very highly. Notice in table 4.1 that Wanda and Woody Mercer and the late Tina Miner fit this profile.

Social Integration

"Maximum," (abbreviated in table 4.1 as "Max."): As described in the early part of this chapter, my several experiences with Molly Good at public events convinces me that her level of social integration into the Buffalo Creek community is maximal. She is as integral to Buffalo Creek as is anyone. She is as widely known and respected as is anyone. She is aware of, and participates in, an impressive array of social events along Buffalo Creek. Certainly, she is often seen as a goodwill ambassador for Buffalo Creek and a social-event arranger for many friends and relatives along Buffalo Creek.

Social Well-Being

"High": In the six years that I have known Molly, it is abundantly clear that Molly usually has a high (but not optimal) level of social well-being and that she understands and appreciates this. She works at it. Most days she can be found enthusiastically cultivating caring social relationships with many friends, family members, relatives, neighbors, and even casual acquaintances. Her social networks are as extensive and deep as anyone I have met at Buffalo Creek and at any of the other small towns and villages that I have studied. Of special value to her are the many hours that she spends, most days, with her grandchildren, great-grandchildren, and her female friends at her church. Furthermore, Molly is highly satisfied with many of her other social relationships, for the most part—but there are exceptions. She is sad that a few people in her hamlet and along Buffalo Creek seem to resent her popularity and her influence. She also often is deeply saddened by the many relationships that she has lost over the years due to the deaths—often premature, sudden, and unduly tragic deaths—of so many of the people she loved dearly. Certainly, this sadness includes her husband's death to black-lung disease only a few years after the flood.

Community Well-Being

"Moderate," (abbreviated in table 4.1 as "Mod."): Molly is also a pragmatist and a realist, however, regarding the well-being Lorado and

Buffalo Creek as social communities. She does not believe that these places have as much well-being as they had before the flood, in terms of general standards of living, quality of life, serious social problems, community health, and social cohesion. At the same time, however, Molly believes that these places are considerably better in these regards than they were in the months and years immediately after the flood. Molly also believes that these places that are so dear to her have more well-being than do many other places of similar size in Logan County and in southwest West Virginia as a whole. She also realizes that many current residents along Buffalo Creek do not have the same level of well-being as she. This is particularly true of many of the younger people who are struggling to cover their costs of living, independent of their parents.

Some Inferences About Buffalo Creek and Its People, Before and Since the Flood

In order to draw reasonable inferences about Buffalo Creek and its people, let us first summarize the estimates that are presented in the columns of table 4.1, from left to right.

Before the Flood

High to Very High Quality of Life: According to the estimates that are presented in the far left column of table 4.1, 35 percent (6 of the 17 respondents who were residing at Buffalo Creek at the time of the flood) believed that their well-being, Buffalo Creek's well-being, and their social relations at Buffalo Creek were of "very high" quality. Another 41 percent (7/17) believed that these same factors were "high" quality. Combining these percentages, 76 percent of the seventeen respondents believed that their lives and Buffalo Creek as a community were of very high or high quality. Only four respondents did not believe this to be the case. Therefore, it seems appropriate to infer that, before the flood, a strong majority of our respondents agreed with those experts who asserted that, before the flood, most residents of Buffalo Creek were doing rather well, had a strong sense of well-being, and believed that the same things were true of Buffalo Creek as an entire social community.

Flood Damages

Highly Variable: Some Respondents Experienced Extreme Damages: Others Experienced No Damages at All: Regarding immediate damages that were inflicted by the flood on the seventeen respondents who were residing along Buffalo Creek at that time, 35 percent (6/17) sustained extreme or severe damage; 18 percent (3/17, rounded up from 17.6 percent) sustained high-level damages or some damages; 12 percent (2/17) experienced no direct damages; and another 35 percent (6/17) of the respondents sustained no damages at all. Said another way, about one-third of the respondents were severely damaged, a little less than one-third of the respondents had lesser levels of damages, and another one-third of the respondents and their homes were not damaged physically at all. The inference to be drawn from this is that accounts by some experts about the totality of the immediate damages of the flood are overstated to a considerable extent—at least as far as seventeen of our respondents are concerned.

Impairments and Deviances

Highly Variable as to Impairments: No Reports of Household Deviance as a Consequence of the Flood: Concerning physical and emotional impairments that were attributable to damages incurred in or because of the flood, notice that there is considerable variation in the amounts of damages inflicted by the flood. Only one of the seventeen respondents (Sam Chance) reported being extremely impaired by the flood's damages. Another 29 percent of the respondents suffered anxieties or other psychological impairments, while 24 percent might have suffered anxieties because of impairments to their children or because of the deaths in the flood of some of their relatives. However, once again, about 35 percent of the respondents did not reveal any direct impairments related to the flood. Therefore, it once again seems appropriate for us to infer that some experts overstated the extent of impairments that can be attributable to the flood. Also notice that none of the respondents revealed that they witnessed or experienced deviant behaviors in themselves or in other members of their households that they attributed to the flood or to damages or impairments that were incurred in the flood.

Relocations, Compensation, and Remedial Health Care

Considerable Variations in Experiences: Seven of the sixteen respondents (44 percent) who resided along Buffalo Creek at the time of the floods relocated to one or more of the HUD camps. Of these seven people, one of them (Sam Chance) was indifferent or oblivious to the experience, and four of them (Lonnie McCain, Mabel Church, Emma Sue Kinsley, and LeRoy Diggs) either appreciated the camps or had few complaints about them. Emma even said that she would have preferred living at the camp to moving back to her former coal camp along Buffalo Creek. Two people (Helen Woodruff and Loretta Washburn) disliked the camps, but for different reasons. The members of Helen's family disliked a HUD camp because they were residing in two trailers rather than all together in one trailer. Loretta Washburn disliked the HUD camp at Green Valley for most of the reasons that were identified by some of the experts: substandard trailers packed into dense, poorly designed, and mismanaged trailer camps that lacked recreational facilities, privacy, and adequate forces for controlling social conflict and deviant behaviors. Collectively, then, these findings do not provide much support for the unqualified condemnation that most experts directed at the HUD trailer camps.[19] The "camp experience" seems to have been tolerable to people who were among the first to arrive in the first few camps that were erected relatively close to their own coal camps, along with other people from their own coal camps.

Regarding monetary compensation for damages, seven of the seventeen respondents received compensation from the state of West Virginia for damages suffered in the flood. Six of these seven people also received compensation through the settlement that Arnold & Porter accepted on behalf of the plaintiffs from Pittston Company. To the best of my knowledge, none of the other ten respondents sought monetary compensation from any sources. The seven respondents who received monetary compensation generally appreciated the compensation that they received, but none of them claimed that the compensation dramatically changed the recovery process for them or for their families, either positively or negatively. Two of the seven respondents who received monetary compensation (Sam Chance and Lonnie McCain) mentioned some skepticism about the honesty of the claims-making process and about the fairness of the rewards process. However, they were not adamant in doing so. Additionally, six of the respondents who did not seek monetary compensation (the Miners, Cumminses, and Albros) also mentioned some skepticism about the honesty of the claims-making process. And yet, their observations were not so pointed as to indicate that perceptions of dishonesty by some claims-making respondents interfered with anyone's ability to recover from the flood or to engage in positive social relations.

As to remedial health care, at least three of the seventeen respondents who witnessed the flood (Sam Chance, Lonnie McCain, and Loretta Washburn) indicated that they and their families were examined by personnel from the psychiatric team that Arnold & Porter hired to help prepare the lawsuit against Pittston Company. Loretta Washburn had no complaints about this experience. Lonnie McCain and Sam Chance did not complain about the experience so much as they indicated that they had some reservations about the accuracy of the diagnostic procedures. They indicated that they and other plaintiffs knew that they needed to provide evidence of emotional impairment that could be attributed to their experiences in the flood. Sam Chance was the only one of the seventeen respondents to indicate that he received extensive remedial health care for his injuries. Sam also implied that he probably should have undergone much more extensive therapy, possibly including psychiatric hospitalization, for his emotional problems.

Concordance With Experts
Four Respondents Agree, Seven Partially Agree, and Six Do Not Agree:
Concordance is varied between the assertions of some experts and the

accounts of the seventeen respondents who were alive at the time of the flood. Four of the seventeen respondents (Wanda and Woody Mercer, Helen Woodruff, and Loretta Washburn) are most often in agreement with the experts' assertions. The accounts of seven other respondents are mixed in their concordance with the experts' assertions. Often these respondents agree with the experts' assertions that Buffalo Creek was a strong community with vibrant social life before the flood and that many of the residents of Buffalo Creek were caught unawares by the flood. And yet, very often these same respondents do not agree with assertions that the flood rendered the people of Buffalo Creek helpless, hopeless, and alienated from one another. The other six respondents were even less often in agreement with the experts' assertions. For example, Goldie and Buddy Cummins often provided testimony that refuted experts' assertions that the flood caught most Buffalo Creek residents unawares, that managers of the coal companies were oblivious to the dangers at the dams, that they were unwilling to respond to the dangers, and that they were unresponsive to the needs of the survivors after the flood. The Cumminses also provided convincing evidence that many survivors of the flood—themselves included—eagerly served as Good Samaritans immediately after the flood and for many months after that. They were not just "good neighbors" to their less fortunate neighbors. They were saviors to strangers and to neighbors alike. This is *not* the way Buffalo Creek's survivors are portrayed in many of the assertions by the experts whose accounts are presented in chapter 2.

Later Life Events

More Positive Than Negative: Events since the flood have been more positive than negative in the lives of 64 percent of the twenty-two of the respondents, including five respondents who were not born until after the flood. Excluding these five respondents, nine of the seventeen (53 percent) of the remaining respondents who were born before the flood have experienced life events such as jobs, marriages, children, grandchildren, and spiritual and religious events that have been more positive than negative. Probably, the most fortunate of these respondents is Emma Sue Kinsley.

Her accounts of her life since the flood are resoundingly positive, in part because she is such an optimistic, upbeat, and spiritual person.

I estimate that 41 percent of the other respondents who were alive during the flood have had such a mixture of positive and negative life events that it seems most prudent to just label them as "mixed" in this regard. Flood victim Sam Chance is one of these respondents. Since his devastating experiences in the flood, Sam had a long and partially successful recovery from the physical wounds he suffered in the floodwater. He remarried and has two sons, now grown, but living out of state. He was able to work for most of postflood years. However Sam has had many work-related injuries. He was retired on disability and has had experiences since then in job retraining and adult education that have disappointed him and aggravated his sense of being underemployed and underappreciated.

Even less fortunate than Sam was the now deceased respondent, Tina Miner. She had many disappointments in her life, both before and after the flood, but she also realized that many of Buffalo Creek's people have had more difficult lives. Tina had been able to live in her house along Buffalo Creek for all of these years. She and Buck reunited after a separation and years of conflict, probably in part because Buck "found religion" and settled down to a more tranquil and acceptant lifestyle. Life was ending for Tina when I interviewed her, but she seemed to accept it, somewhat grudgingly perhaps, for what it had been for her and for how much worse it was for so many others around her.

In sum, all of the twenty-two respondents, including Tina Miner, had some positive life experiences along Buffalo Creek since the flood. For a few of the respondents, including Emma Sue Kinsley, Becky Pollins, and J. J. and Nicky Canfield, life along Buffalo Creek is highly satisfying. For a slight majority of the respondents, positive life events outweighed negative ones. For at least five of the respondents (Wanda Mercer, Goldie and Buddy Cummins, Lureen Albro and Jake Albro), the flood probably was one of the few highly negative experiences in their lives. And yet, it was not so overwhelmingly negative that it has kept them from having lives of great meaning to them.

Neighboring and Neighbors

Most Respondents Are Quite Active as Neighbors and They Value Their Neighbors and Neighboring: Columns G and H of table 4.1 show that strong majorities of the seventeen respondents for whom neighboring could be estimated were rated to be very high or high on two dimensions of neighboring: their level of activity in neighboring (76 percent) and the value of neighbors to them (94 percent). Only one of the respondents, Tina Miner, indicated that she was very inactive in neighboring. This was primarily because she was suffering terminal illnesses, was bed- and chair-ridden, and often was under heavy medication. And yet, Tina still avowed that neighbors were important to her and that she valued them highly.

Surely, these estimations indicate that most of Buffalo Creek's respondents are quite active in neighboring and that they value good neighbors.

Social Integration

Relatively High for Most Respondents: Column I shows that most (68 percent) of the twenty-two respondents were estimated to be at least "highly" integrated into Buffalo Creek as a social community. These people participated in many aspects of community life, and they had positive social relations with people besides their neighbors and family members. Only one of them (again, the late Tina Miner), was estimated to be "low" in social integration, mainly because her terminal illnesses severely limited her mobility and her ability to communicate with others. Let me add that none of the twenty-two respondents indicated that they felt excluded from any aspect of social life along Buffalo Creek that they were interested in. None of them complained about being socially isolated or discriminated against. None of them indicated that they felt either privileged or marginalized because they had survived the flood or had "missed it" entirely. I believe that this is a particularly surprising finding in my research. I did not detect evidence of a status hierarchy among Buffalo Creek's current and recent residents regarding survivorship of the flood. Terms including "survivor," "victim," "hero(ine)," and "veteran" were not used routinely or reflexively by residents of Buffalo

Creek, regardless of their age or of their experiences related to the flood. And while I do not doubt that some, many, or most of the flood's survivors have special respect for other survivors simply because they *are* survivors, I did not see or hear direct evidence of this.[20] This absence of an obvious status hierarchy based on who did and did not experience the flood of 1972 probably reflects and reinforces the relatively high level of social integration along Buffalo Creek.

Social Well-Being

Varied but Lower Than on the Other Factors: As shown in Column J, there is considerable variation in the evaluations of the social well-being of the twenty-two respondents. What is more, taken as a whole, the evaluations are lower on social well-being than on the other dimensions related to the current or recent disposition of the respondents. Only 50 percent of the respondents were estimated to have at least a high level of social well-being. These people—including Emma Sue Kinsley, the Cumminses, and the Albros, most of the Canfields, and Darren Service—were highly satisfied with the quantity and quality of social relationships and with their social status among Buffalo Creek's people. Unfortunately, this is less true of the other 50 percent of the respondents, although we should not assume that their relatively mixed or low level of social well-being is primarily or solely attributable to their experiences in the flood of 1972.

Six of the twenty-two respondents (27 percent) were estimated to have a mixture of positive and negative aspects of social well-being. Lonnie McCain, for example, indicated that he is grateful that he still has intimate social relations with members of one of the families that his family befriended in a HUD trailer camp after the flood. At the same time, however, Lonnie also indicated that he is not very comfortable with some of his social relationships with former friends who still live along Buffalo Creek, and that his work in the mines keeps him so busy that he has limited time for rewarding social life outside the mines. A number of other respondents, including Mabel Church, were estimated to have limited, low, or very low social well-being.

In Mabel's case, this was because she can no longer drive, many of her friends have died during the past decade, she is a widow, and her only child lives in a distant state.

Overall, then, we cannot conclude that these twenty-two respondents are strong in social well-being. Five of the six respondents under the age of thirty are high or very high on social well-being, whereas only five of the sixteen respondents age thirty or older are estimated to score this highly. I was not able to establish whether this difference between age cohorts primarily is due to the flood, to declining physical health, or to other factors. But the fact that four of the oldest respondents who witnessed the flood (the Cumminses and the Albros) have strong social well-being suggests that neither old age nor witnessing the flood necessarily condemned people to being deficient in social well-being many decades after the disastrous event.

Community Well-Being

At Least Moderately Well by All of the Respondents: In the eyes of the twenty-two respondents, Buffalo Creek is doing rather well as a social community. Column K shows that 45 percent of the respondents indicated that the well-being of the community was very high or high. The remainder of the respondents felt that Buffalo Creek was doing at least moderately well. Even Tina Miner, suffering terminal illnesses and relatively negative on so many other measures, felt that Buffalo Creek was doing at least moderately well, particularly in terms of "houses, cars, and money." Those respondents who felt that Buffalo Creek was doing only moderately well in social relations usually indicated that its shortcomings were not because of the flood, but rather because of factors such as:

- Too few jobs that pay decent wages and benefits
- Too many uncertainties and downturns in the coal mining economy of the region and in the loss of union jobs throughout the region

- Insufficient police forces for Buffalo Creek and too little enforcement of laws to control speeding, littering, and the sale and misuse of recreational drugs and prescription drugs including Oxycontin and methamphetamines
- Too few recreational activities and shopping outlets along Buffalo Creek
- Too many unstable strangers who become short-term renters in the apartments and trailers along Buffalo Creek

Despite beliefs about these and other problems, none of the twenty-two respondents—or, for that matter, the many other people I interviewed and report on in chapter 5—ever made utterly negative remarks about Buffalo Creek. None of them ever said or did anything in my presence that indicated that Buffalo Creek was, in their eyes, a failed, miserable, lost, violent, or immoral place to live. None of them ever said anything to the effect that Buffalo Creek and its people were anti-social or antagonistic. None of them said that they would leave Buffalo Creek if they had the means to do so. Very few of them ever indicated that they would prefer to live elsewhere or that they fantasize about doing so. None of them ever said or implied that Buffalo Creek was destitute, desperate, dissolute, or damned. Quite the opposite is true. As documented elsewhere in this chapter, at least nine of the respondents gave every indication that they were very glad to be spending their lives along Buffalo Creek, despite the challenges of doing so. Surely, this is *prima facie* evidence that Buffalo Creek meets their social needs quite well and that Buffalo Creek is more than adequate as a social community to them.

General Inferences and Conclusions
Now let us consider the some general inferences and conclusions that can be drawn from table 4.1 and the rest of the findings that have been presented up to this point.

Notice that there is considerable variation in the estimates in each of the columns for each of the factors in the table. This amount of variation would not exist if all or most of the respondents had similar experiences before, during, immediately after, and long after the flood of 1972. For instance, this amount of variation would not exist if all or most of the respondents, and Buffalo Creek as a social community, were doing extremely well before the flood, the flood badly damaged most or all of them, most or all of them suffered serious impairments and participated in and witnessed increases in deviant behaviors, were relocated to the HUD trailer camps, and did not receive financial compensation, therapy, and other health care services. Nor would this amount of variation in the estimates occur if most or all of the respondents experienced decidedly overwhelming positive (or perhaps even negative) later life events, and yet they were unable to participate in neighboring, did not value good neighbors, were alienated from the rest of the residents of Buffalo Creek (i.e., they were not in the least bit socially integrated into the community), and they sensed that their own social well-being and the well-being of Buffalo Creek as a social community were minimal, desperate, morbid, or moribund.

Now consider that the *hypothetical* pattern that I have just described is *not* the rather complex but positive pattern that you see before you in table 4.1. On the contrary, the hypothetical pattern that I have just described is the pattern that you would see before you in table 4.1 if the flood of 1972 inflicted overwhelming and decades-long damages on these respondents (and on many other survivors of the flood) and on Buffalo Creek as a social community. And yet, the opposite appears to be true. Notice that most of the estimates in columns H–K of table 4.1 (regarding "Recent Disposition" of the respondents) are quite positive (i.e., "very high" and "high"). Only a few of them (three of them, to be exact) are "low" or "very low." Expressed in another way, the estimates indicate that most of the respondents have been doing rather well along Buffalo Creek in the last few years.

In terms of chronology, the estimates in table 4.1 indicate that most of the respondents were doing rather well before the flood—and so was Buffalo Creek as a social community. Some (six) of the respondents were severely damaged in the flood. Some of the respondents were relocated and received financial compensation for the damages that they incurred in the flood. The respondents vary greatly regarding the valences of their later life events, although about one-half of them (not counting those who are less than thirty years old) have had mainly or mostly positive later life experiences. Furthermore, while the social well-being of the respondents varies considerably, only four of them are estimated to be low, limited, or marginal in this regard. Even more distinctive are the estimates for neighboring and social integration. On these two factors, highly positive dispositions far outnumber highly negative dispositions. For instance, notice that the only "low" estimates are for the late Tina Miner, who was suffering terminal illnesses when I visited with her and her husband. Even then, Tina indicated that good neighbors had "high" value to her. She also indicated that the reason she was "very low" in neighboring was that she was housebound and enervated by her grave illnesses. Finally, in the eyes of these respondents, Buffalo Creek has at least moderate well-being as a social community. None of them portrayed Buffalo Creek as being cursed, doomed, or utterly deficient in social relations.

Therefore, given the frequency of these rather positive patterns, it is reasonable to conclude that all but a few of the twenty-two respondents whom we have gotten to know here in chapter 4 are doing reasonably well, socially, as is Buffalo Creek, more than three decades after the flood. Not one of the respondents indicated that she or he would leave, even if it was easy to do so. Not one of them indicated that he or she regretted his of her life along Buffalo Creek. Not one of them indicated that Buffalo Creek has failed to re-create at least an appreciable amount of community well-being since the disaster of 1972.

*   *   *

Of course, it is possible that the twenty-two people portrayed in this chapter are not very informed about Buffalo Creek and its people. Perhaps they have not provided very accurate information about social life along Buffalo Creek. They might have forgotten what social life really was like more than three decades ago. They might have intentionally misrepresented their experiences. Or maybe they do not "get around much," or enough, anymore. These issues are discussed in chapters 6 and 7. And so, with these considerations in mind, let us now turn to chapter 5 and meet many more of the residents of Buffalo Creek and of two small, rural communities that have been spared disasters like the flash flood of 1972. In doing so, we should gain more confidence in drawing conclusions about whether neighborly relations and social well-being have been lost, recovered, or re-created along Buffalo Creek.

ENDNOTES

1. Appendix A provides more information about the research methods that were used to produce the original data in this chapter and in the other chapters.

2. Appendix A describes and explains the research methods in detail. It is important to note that I used *purposive* selection, insofar as possible—not random sampling. See Delbert C. Miller, *Handbook of Research Design and Social Measurements*, 5th ed. (Newbery Park, CA: Sage, 1991), 60–64; and Bernard S. Phillips, *Social Research Strategy and Tactics*, 2nd ed. (New York: The Macmillan Company, 1971), 93–96. One of the reasons for this is that many informed, longtime residents of Buffalo Creek, Elk Creek, and St. John were only willing to be interviewed at length, in their homes, about the many sensitive topics in this study, if another resident whom they trust introduced us or served as a reference. Interviewing residents in their homes, at length, enabled us to observe how residents lived and how they interacted with other residents, particularly with their neighbors. Another reason for using purposive selection is that it is closer than random sampling to the sampling design that Lifton, Erikson, and some others used in their research—to the extent that they used *any* kind of sampling design.

3. Molly Good did not answer the question about how many neighbors discuss their problems with her, but it is likely that many of them do so because she is so empathetic and accessible.

4. Like Molly, many respondents made no distinction between face-to-face conversations and telephone conversations with friends and neighbors as to the nature and importance of their personal communications. Interestingly, none of the respondents indicated that they communicate with neighbors through the Internet or through other innovative electronic means such as text messaging. To the best of my knowledge, only three of the twenty-two respondents have Internet access through computers in their homes. None of these respondents indicated that they use the Internet to communicate with neighbors.

5. As of 1976, experts' accounts emphasized that shock and withdrawal were the most common immediate reactions of the flood's survivors to their predicaments. Self-indulgent and reckless misbehaviors were common reactions that occurred later, usually after a few months of frustration,

depression, and despair. Experts did not give much attention to "reversing of ways" as an emergent pattern of behavior in survivors. Possibly, the pattern of outgoing activism that Molly mentioned did not become widespread until after the experts completed their writing.

6. With considerable reluctance, I feel compelled to mention that some of the survivors I interviewed did not at any time speak about their former spouses with terms of endearment, despite having many opportunities to do so. Cases like these can alert us to the possibility that some marriages were much stronger than others along Buffalo Creek, just as they are in so many other places in the world. Some survivors of the flood might have recovered more fully and quickly than others because the flood more or less allowed them to form new intimate relationships that were at least as fulfilling as the ones that they lost. Published accounts by experts about Buffalo Creek often overlook this possibility. Extending this observation a bit further, "disaster researchers" tend to overlook the likelihood that disasters can be perceived as entertaining, thrilling, profitable, and even beneficial to some of the people who experience them. For example, an antisocial person who dislikes his neighbors and believes that they are evil people might readily welcome a flood that "washes them away." A person like this might also find justification for such an outcome in various passages in the holy books of various religions. See, for example, The Book of Nahum 1:8 in the St. James version of the Bible.

7. Notice that Sam Chance listed the year of the flood, 1972, and the year after it, 1973, as two of his happiest years because of his new marriage and the birth of his first child in that marriage. These responses are congruent with the argument that I make in the preceding endnote, but I am *not* suggesting that this necessarily pertains to Sam Chance.

8. Possibly, Sam and other survivors are especially correct in asserting that most survivors were mutually supportive in the first few days after the flood. However, it is also possible that many of these survivors became increasingly dispirited—even alienated—as the days turned into weeks, and then into months, and the cleanup, rebuilding, and recovery efforts did not meet their expectations. The misery dragged on too long for them, to the point that they lost hope and any of the euphoria that might have occurred when they first realized that they themselves had survived the flood. Possibly, this is what Erikson observed and recorded when he visited Buffalo Creek in the period sixteen to thirty months after the flood.

9. Months later I viewed a copy of the film at the Buffalo Creek Memorial Library. I have drawn upon relevant material from that film in writing this book.

10. While positive recollections of life in the HUD trailer camps were in the minority, they were not rare and they were not incredible. Some of the HUD camps that were located in the Buffalo Creek Valley, including the camps at Robinette and Latrobe, seemed to have a better reputation than some of the camps outside of the valley. One of the veterans in the HUD trailer camp at Robinette remembered it this way to me: "We lived in that trailer camp HUD built in Latrobe. I guess we were lucky. We had relatives and other Lorado people as neighbors. Our parents and the other neighbors kept a firm grip on us kids. So we didn't have a lot of those problems that you read about in the books...I recall it being a good experience at Robinette, but we wanted to move back to Lorado no matter what. And I'm glad we did."

11. Helen's sister, Loretta Washburn, and Loretta's family also were at Green Valley, as described in the next account in this chapter, but Helen did not mention this.

12. I am sorry to report that Tina passed away only a few months after I interviewed her. And yet, I am glad to report that, when I visited Buck and his adult son at their home in 2007, both of them were gracious and friendly. They had refurbished their home and they indicated that they were very satisfied with their lives in the valley. Said Buck: "Things have settled down now. We got most of what we need right here now. I wouldn't think of leaving Buffalo Creek. No need to."

13. I have been fortunate to be able to keep in touch with the Cumminses and with many of the other people profiled in this chapter. For example, in May 2007, I was able to "ride the hills" with Buddy in one of his beloved ATVs, visit a number of the closed-up mines above the Buffalo Creek Valley, and catch up on the local news and views.

14. Jake Albro essentially gave the same answers in 2003 and 2005 to the seventeen questions about community and to the fifteen questions about neighboring, except for two minor differences. On question #16, Jake originally answered that he felt closest to Man (not Lorado—his home), probably because he misunderstood the question in 2003. On question #15, about the happiest years of his life, he answered in 2003 "when I left here," whereas in 2005, he agreed with his wife when she said that they were happiest "when we was a courtin' in high school."

15. As best as I could determine, the major conflicts over the UMW contract occurred in 1975 and 1976, whereas Nugent, Stern, and Erikson collected all of their data, or most of their data, before 1975.

16. Even now, only riverbanks less than six feet high and a narrow paved road separate the creek from most of the dwellings in this coal camp.

17. Becky had more difficulty than Francie in distinguishing her relations between family and nonfamily neighbors. The distinction is not very important to her.
18. It also is likely that Darren Service is rather exceptional in these regards.
19. There is little if any evidence in the accounts of the experts (see chapter 2) that they personally visited the HUD camps and carefully examined living conditions there. They seem to have relied on what some informants told them about the camps.
20. Absence of an overt status hierarchy at Buffalo Creek based on who did and did not experience the flood would be in contrast to the overt status hierarchies that often exist informally among military personnel based on the amount and ferocity of combat that one has directly experienced. See Theodore Caplow and Louis Hicks, *Systems of War and Peace*, 2nd ed. (Lanham, MD: University Press of America), 126. Privileged status and honor often are afforded to those combatants who were "blooded" in combat. For example, over the years, I have heard some combat veterans of the U.S. war in Viet Nam, 1959–1975, sarcastically reproach other people, both veterans and nonveterans, with comments such as: "If you weren't blooded, you weren't really there," "If you ain't been hit (dinged, nicked), you ain't got nothin' to tell me," "If you didn't put in your time, you're wastin' mine," "If you weren't in the Nam, you don't know nothin' about it." It is remarkable to me that I have never heard comments similar to these by or about survivors of the flood at Buffalo Creek. And for this I am thankful.

Chapter 5

Comparing People of Buffalo Creek, Elk Creek, and St. John

To me, Buffalo Creek hasn't changed, just the people. I left in the 1980s and returned in the 1990s and bought my house here, not far from where I grew up. Sure, I don't know everyone anymore—just the neighbors around me here. Some I know well. One of them I don't bother with. Life goes on. It has to.

—Markay McColl, flood survivor and returnee

Love thy neighbor as thyself. The Bible says it plain and clear. And that's how important neighbors are to me.

—Roger Cline, a longtime resident of Elk Creek

It's more a "Hi" and "Goodbye" kind of thing.
                                    —Van Hegel, a longtime resident of St. John

                    *   *   *

This chapter expands on what we learned in chapter 4 about neighbors, neighboring, social integration, social well-being, and other aspects of social relations along Buffalo Creek from our in-depth interviews with twenty-two of its good people.[1] There are three highly interrelated parts to this chapter.

First, we examine the responses that ninety-five residents of Buffalo Creek provided to us during interviews regarding their attitudes and their experiences along Buffalo Creek during their lifetimes.

Second, we consider whether there are appreciable differences in the attitudes and experiences of these residents according to whether they were victims of, witnesses, possible witnesses, or nonwitnesses to the flood of 1972.

Third, we compare and contrast the respondents of Buffalo Creek to respondents from two places that did not experience the flood of 1972 or comparable disasters. One of these places is Elk Creek, West Virginia. It is a former coal camp in the next hollow up the Guyandotte River, about ten miles southeast of Buffalo Creek. Elk Creek is in many ways similar to Lorado, Lundale, and several of the other former coal camps along Buffalo Creek, except that it did not and has not suffered a flood like the flood of 1972. The other place is a small town very far away from West Virginia—St. John, in Washington State. Well-regarded research has been published about St. John that credibly establishes that St. John is an unusually vibrant rural community with high levels of social cohesion, neighboring, and social well-being.

Throughout this data-rich and challenging chapter, it can be helpful to keep in mind the two alternative perspectives that we introduced in chapter 2 and that we referred to often in chapter 4: the social destruction perspective and the social re-creation perspective.[2]

How well do these perspectives help us understand the differences and similarities among the respondents in these places?

Is there compelling evidence that social relations along Buffalo Creek were destroyed? That they still are destroyed?

If not, have social relations been re-created along Buffalo Creek to a considerable extent, when compared with other places?

With these two competing perspectives in mind, let us now consider what respondents reveal to us about the quality of social relations along Buffalo Creek.

THE RESPONDENTS OF BUFFALO CREEK

During our many visits to Buffalo Creek, we administered the "Community and Neighboring Questionnaire"[3] to ninety-five adults, ages 18–78, who had been residing along Buffalo Creek from Kistler to Three Forks (Saunders) for at least two years. Of these ninety-five residents, special effort was made to meet and to interview residents of the upper valley— particularly the two former coal camps that were damaged so heavily, Lorado and Lundale—who resided there at the time of the flood in 1972. After we received completed questionnaires from fifty of these people, we made a concerted effort to meet and to interview forty-five people, ages 18–40, who had not resided along Buffalo Creek at the time of the flood or who had no obvious direct recall of the flood because they had not been born yet or they were too young to remember it. Our primary purpose in using this selection process was to enable us to compare residents who had experienced the flood with residents who had not experienced the flood, in terms of their perceptions on neighboring and social well-being in their respective residential communities.[4]

Some Demographic Characteristics
Table 5.1 in appendix B summarizes some of the demographic characteristics of the respondents along Buffalo Creek. As described in the table, the average age of the respondents is forty-eight years, 63 percent of the respondents are female, and 44 percent of them have lived along Buffalo Creek their entire lives.[5] Taken collectively, the respondents should be able to tell us about their neighbors, not only because many of them are lifelong residents of Buffalo Creek, but also because 67 percent

of them have lived in their current dwelling for at least ten years. About 34 percent of the respondents have at least ten close relatives and at least ten close friends who reside along Buffalo Creek. Only 19 percent of them have three or fewer of each. So, it is reasonable for us to believe that many of the respondents could have a strong sense of social integration into Buffalo Creek if they choose to interact with their neighbors, close relatives, and close friends in the area. Taken as a whole, the respondents certainly are not isolated in this regard.

Some Attitudes About Buffalo Creek
As presented in table 5.2 of appendix B, most of the respondents (71 percent) reported that they feel closest to their home village (former coal camp) along Buffalo Creek, rather than to any other place. Another 23 percent of the respondents reported that they feel closest to Buffalo Creek in general, or to some other village along Buffalo Creek. Clearly, both sets of these respondents feel attached to Buffalo Creek regarding this aspect of social integration. They are not alienated from it in this regard.

Respondents also were asked to specify three qualities that they liked best and least about living at Buffalo Creek. In general, the respondents indicated that they liked at least two or three qualities (sometimes considerably more) about living along Buffalo Creek, including qualities that involve social relationships, and that they were very favorable about Buffalo Creek's positive qualities.[6] Qualities that involve social relations were mentioned by many of the respondents. Thirty-six percent of the respondents mentioned that their "family is here" or "it's my home." "Friends," "neighbors," and "community" also were mentioned by at least 20 percent of the respondents, as were "quiet" or "quietness," "peace" or "peaceful," and "safe" or "safety." Taken collectively, these response patterns indicate that many of the respondents regard aspects of social relations as being qualities that they like best about living along Buffalo Creek. Nonsocial qualities that were mentioned by at least three respondents are identified at the bottom of the table. These qualities include "scenery," "hunting," and "the mountains"—qualities that are hardly surprising to hear, coming, as they are, from people who identify themselves as proud "mountaineers" of West Virginia.

The respondents reported fewer qualities that they liked *least* about living along Buffalo Creek. Few of the qualities that they specified referred to social relationships. The most frequently reported disliked characteristic was that the respondent's home was "far from" things such as shopping (the most frequent complaint), cinemas, restaurants, and recreational facilities. Thirty-four percent of the respondents mentioned this drawback about living along Buffalo Creek. Another 15 percent disliked some aspect of the local economy such as low wages and scarce jobs. Among the relatively few complaints about deficiencies in social relationships were "nosey" and "rowdy" neighbors and some aspect of the community that is considered to be lacking, such as togetherness. One, but *only* one respondent wrote "the floods" (notice the plural, "floods") in response to this question. While these complaints accounted for less than 10 percent of the responses, they certainly are the kinds of complaints that are particularly relevant to our investigation and they are the kinds of complaints that Kai Erikson and some other authors reported (as reviewed in chapter 2) as being widespread after the flood and because of it. In contrast, 7 percent of the ninety-five respondents reported that they found nothing objectionable about living along Buffalo Creek. These respondents wrote comments including, "I like everything here" and "nothing here to complain about."

And so, it seems fair to say that these response patterns do not indicate that the respondents dislike living along Buffalo Creek. Combined with the response patterns regarding what the respondents like best about living along Buffalo Creek, it appears that the respondents generally like living along Buffalo Creek more than they dislike it. What they dislike ("far from" shopping, etc.) probably is unrelated to disasters and floods in any direct way. After all, the relocation of commercial services from small towns and villages to massive shopping malls during the last few decades now requires many residents of rural America to travel considerable distances in order to shop, to dine, and to be entertained and "serviced" in any number of ways.

As to qualities missed most about Buffalo Creek of years ago, many respondents were momentarily perplexed by this question. Only a few of them had immediate responses to it. Fourteen percent of them reported that they missed the good jobs and wages of Buffalo Creek from years past. Then again, 16 percent of them reported that they miss "nothing" from the past or that they really cannot comment on the past. Often these respondents added that they felt that they were still too young to have a sense of the past along Buffalo Creek. However, 20 percent of the respondents mentioned the word "community" and indicated, usually without much emphasis, that they missed some quality that once existed in Buffalo Creek as a community, such as "things to do," "dances," "spirit," "togetherness," and "cooperation." These respondents generally did not complain about these changes so much as they just indicated that they missed some aspect of social life along Buffalo Creek from years past. Also of interest is the fact that 7 percent of the respondents mentioned that they missed something involving "neighbors" from years past. Usually, they indicated that they missed specific neighbors who had died over the years, that they had fewer neighbors now, or that their neighbors do not socialize with them as much as in the past at "cook-outs" and "porch-sittin'." These kinds of responses are particularly relevant to our investigation, of course, in that they indicate that Buffalo Creek is not exactly the same kind of place as it was years ago as a social community. Whether these reported losses are because of the flood of 1972 or because of other factors—such as aging and the deaths of the respondent's neighbors—is yet to be determined.

Neighbors and Neighboring Along Buffalo Creek
Table 5.3 in appendix B shows us that Buffalo Creek's respondents have plenty of neighbors and that they generally have basic familiarity with all or most of these neighbors. Yet they socialize regularly with only some of their neighbors, and only on a limited basis. They claim that neighbors are "very important" or "real" important to them. The qualities that are important in neighbors include trustworthiness, reliability, and honesty, as well as being friendly. There are some surprising subtleties in their responses, however. For example, the respondents report having a little more than ten neighbors on the average. Forty-eight percent of the respondents report that they have ten or more neighbors,

while another 37 percent of the respondents report that they have five to nine neighbors. Clearly, then, Buffalo Creek's respondents have plenty of neighbors to socialize with. Only 15 percent of the respondents have fewer than five neighbors.

Regarding familiarity with their neighbors, 78 percent of the respondents report that they have basic familiarity with all of their neighbors. These people claim that they can recognize all of their neighbors anywhere they see them, not just when they see them in their neighborhood. They know the names of all of their neighbors. They usually greet these neighbors with a "hello" or other appropriate greetings whenever they see them. They converse at least occasionally with these neighbors. Twenty percent of the respondents report that they have these forms of familiarity with most or with many of their neighbors, and only 2 percent of the respondents report that they do not have one or more of these familiarities with any of their neighbors. Small percentages of respondents (usually respondents who had resided in their current dwelling for less than five years) reported that, while they recognized at least some of their neighbors, they did not know their names or they had not yet conversed with them.

Socializing with their neighbors was much more varied and limited among the respondents than was basic familiarity. As we might expect, respondents were more likely to report that they engaged in spontaneous, casual, and brief forms of socializing (such as having friendly talks with some of their neighbors, having been in the homes of their neighbors, and visiting with their neighbors) than in more time-consuming, planned, and obligatory forms of socializing (such as discussing personal problems with their neighbors, borrowing or exchanging tools or other objects, entertaining with their neighbors, or going places together with their neighbors).[7] Given these considerations, it is perhaps not all that surprising that only 11 percent of the respondents report that they engage in all six forms of socializing with all of their neighbors. However, only 6 percent of the respondents report that they *rarely or never* engage in any of these forms of socializing with any of their neighbors. Taken collectively, then, the respondents are not socially isolated from their neighbors.

The most common patterns of socializing in these six ways are to do so occasionally with more than a few of their neighbors (as reported by 52 percent of the respondents), or to do so infrequently and only with one or a few of their neighbors. Thirty-one percent of the respondents reported this pattern. Thus it seems that Buffalo Creek's respondents are somewhat limited socializers with their neighbors, even though they are quite familiar with them and they regard neighbors as being very important to them.

Three categories of qualities of particular interest to us are identified by substantial percentages of the respondents as being important to them in their neighbors: "trustworthy, reliable, or honest" (identified by 35 percent of the respondents), "friendly/friendliness" (31 percent of the respondents), and "for help in crises and when needed" (20 percent of the respondents). Other positive qualities reported by 24 percent of the respondents are social in nature: "respect," "loyal," "keep company," "compassion," and "nice." It is interesting to note that only 11 percent of the respondents mentioned "friends, intimates, or confidants" as the most important quality of neighbors. Possibly, this means that Buffalo Creek's respondents regard or expect friendliness in their neighbors more than they regard or expect their neighbors to be their friends. Also worth noting is that only 9 percent of the respondents identified the absence of a negative quality in neighbors as being most important to them. "Nosiness" and "gossip" were among the more frequent complaints, although they were not frequent, by any means.

By way of comment, let me suggest that the relatively small percentage of respondents who mentioned "for help in crises or when needed" is particularly interesting. The flood of 1972, and the frequency of dangerous seasonal floods along Buffalo Creek and so many other rivers in southwestern West Virginia (as discussed in chapters 1–3), could be expected to sustain what might be called a "crisis consciousness" along Buffalo Creek. And yet, the majority (fifteen) of the nineteen respondents who identified this quality did *not* use the words "crisis" or "crises," and *none* of the nineteen used the words "flood(s)" or "disaster(s)" in their responses. These facts support the inference that respondents were *not* asserting or implying that the most important quality of neighbors is the assistance that they can provide during a disaster like the flood of 1972. By the way, this percentage (20 percent) is examined more closely in later sections of this chapter when we compare different subcategories of respondents from Buffalo Creek and when we compare Buffalo Creek's respondents with respondents from Elk Creek and St. John.

Overall, then, the respondents of Buffalo Creek report patterns of neighboring that do *not* seem to be obviously deficient, disadvantaged, or damaged—at least not in an absolute or intuitive sense. Neighbors are common along Buffalo Creek—and they are valued highly. Basic forms of neighboring are extremely common among the respondents, although intense socializing is not so frequent or widespread. If neighboring was severely damaged in the flood of 1972, it certainly seems to have been re-created to a considerable extent in the past three decades. If the social destruction perspective ever applied to Buffalo Creek in terms of neighbors and neighboring (and it probably did apply to a considerable extent for several years after the flood), it does not seem to apply very well any longer.

References to Disasters
Table 5.4 of appendix B provides data about the percentages of respondents who referred to the flood of 1972, or to other disasters, without being prompted to do so.[8] Then again, 20 percent of the respondents referred to the flood one to three times, but without manifesting very much disturbance of it. A small fraction of the respondents, 2 percent, referred to the flood of 1972 at least four times and seemed to be very conscious of it. In thinking about these data, we should keep in mind that these respondents were not asked about the flood through any of the items on the questionnaire and that every effort was made to minimize attention to the flood unless the respondents insisted on talking about it.

In an upcoming section of this chapter, we examine the kinds of respondents who referred to the flood on their questionnaires. For now, let us just keep in mind the facts that 78 percent of the respondents *never* referred to the flood, 20 percent of them did so once or several times, and only two of them did so repeatedly and still seemed to be bothered by their memories of the flood.

Estimates of Social Integration and Social Well-Being

Table 5.5 of appendix B presents data on the estimated levels of social integration and social well-being of the respondents based upon procedures that are explained in detail in appendix A and in brief at the bottom of the table. I estimated that 20 percent of the respondents were *very highly* integrated into Buffalo Creek as a social community. This means that these respondents scored very high on at least six of the seven indicators of social integration. Another 45 percent of the respondents were estimated to be *highly* integrated into Buffalo Creek. Combining these estimates, 65 percent—nearly two-thirds—of Buffalo Creek's respondents were estimated to have high or very high levels of social integration into Buffalo Creek. Conversely, only two of the ninety-five of the respondents were estimated to be socially isolated or alienated from Buffalo Creek. One of these people, whom we will refer to with the fictitious name of "Vera Grimm," was residing along Buffalo Creek at the time of the flood. The other person, whom we will name "Jimmy Joe Rooker," graduated from high school only a few years ago and is having trouble finding employment and contentment while living at home with his mother. Not surprisingly, both of these respondents also were estimated to be the only respondents to have very low social well-being. Only one other respondent scored this low along with them. Also not surprisingly, estimates of social well-being are similar to, but not identical with, estimates of social integration.[9] Slightly lower percentages of respondents are estimated to have "very high" and "high" levels of social well-being than social integration. However, slightly higher percentages of respondents score "moderate or mixed" and "low" on social well-being than on social integration, respectively. More importantly, however, as shown in table 5.6 of appendix B, the vast majority, 87 percent, of Buffalo Creek's respondents were estimated to be at least moderately well-integrated into Buffalo Creek *and* to have at least a moderate amount of social well-being. Surely, these findings support the social re-creation perspective much more strongly than the other perspective. *It is highly likely that the substantial levels of social integration and social well-being of these respondents are the result of re-creation of community life along Buffalo Creek since the flood of 1972.* If the flood destroyed social integration and social well-being along Buffalo Creek for these respondents, it did not do so completely or permanently except, perhaps, for the two decidedly unfortunate respondents: Vera Grimm and Jimmy Joe Rooker.

Vera Grimm: A Lonely Widow Cannot Forget the Flood

Vera Grimm surely is one of the most alienated respondents along Buffalo Creek. She seems almost "haunted" by the flood. She manifests many of the damages that Kai Erikson and some other authors attributed to Buffalo Creek's survivors of the flood. She is a sad, sickly, often bitter widow in her late seventies who lives alone in an old wood-frame house surrounded by a waist-high, steel-mesh fence. She says that its purpose is to "keep the dogs out." Vera has lived along Buffalo Creek for more than forty-five years, and in her current dwelling for more than thirty of those years.

At least five times during the interview (more than any other interviewee), Vera mentions "the flood," as she calls it, and conveys that her life has been miserable ever since then. She also claims that she has little relationship with any of her neighbors, or with anyone else, except for one son and one daughter. She has little good to say about anyone or anything.

Vera says that, while five of her seven close relatives live in Buffalo Creek, she has no close friends anywhere. "Most of my friends was killed in the flood." Asked what she likes best about living in Buffalo Creek, Vera says that "I liked it before the flood. I don't like it at all now. There's nothing to do now. Nothing here is worth much." She adds that this was the best place she ever lived up until the flood. "It messed everybody's life up." Before the flood, she says that she had happy years and events in her life: "When I got married and we loved one another. We had God. We had a happy home." Asked about what she misses most about the old community, Vera recalls, "The way everybody enjoyed life. Laughing. Talking. There's nothing for people since the flood. Now, since the flood, they don't mingle or nothing."

Regarding her neighbors, Vera claims that, "Other than my son—none." She does not feel that she has any. Yet, in responding to other questions, she reveals that she does have other neighbors, but that she does not feel that they are very neighborly towards her. She would recognize by sight "maybe ten" of her neighbors if she saw them outside of Buffalo Creek. She says that "[s]ometimes I sit on my porch and say 'hi,' but they just act like they don't know you." Although she knows the names of about nine of her neighbors, she says that she never gets a chance to talk with any of them. "They don't come near me." She adds that the neighbors "don't care if you lose a dog or a cat." She has been in two of her neighbor's homes, but never visits or socializes with any of them except for her daughter, who takes her to church. Vera notes that "my neighbor tries to borrow, but I don't fool with her." She concludes by observing that neighbors could be important, but are not. "They'd be important if they'd be neighbors." All she wants from them is that "they show you some respect."

In sum, Vera Grimm is perhaps the most bitter, negative, and alienated respondent from Buffalo Creek. She makes more frequent mention of the flood than does anyone else. She has nothing positive to say about anyone, anyplace, or anything since the flood. And yet, it is also true that Vera could have manifested even more bitterness, residual damage of the flood, and alienation. She has a daughter and a son, as well as a few close relatives who live along Buffalo Creek. She recognizes quite a few neighbors (but is bitter about how they react or fail to react towards her). She goes to church. And, although she more or less claims that the flood ruined social life for her and for Buffalo Creek, she still is able and willing to communicate her feelings to other people. Certainly, this is what she did with us. Therefore, it does not seem appropriate to portray her as being *totally* alienated. And still, there is no doubt that Vera Grimm is highly damaged and highly alienated.[10]

Jimmy Joe Rooker: Maybe a Few Friends
Jimmy Joe Rooker is an unemployed, frail-looking, single male in his twenties who lives with his mother in her trailer in one of the hamlets

midway up Buffalo Creek. Other than indicating that he has ten close relatives and two close friends who live along Buffalo Creek and that he was happier in high school, his responses are intemperate and often sarcastic, except that he wrote that he likes the "scenery" and the "peace" of Buffalo Creek. Jimmy dislikes the coal trucks, dust and trash, and most other features of Buffalo Creek's environment. "Nowhere" is his response to the best place he has ever lived. "Regular Nintendo" is his response to what he misses most from years ago along Buffalo Creek.

As to neighboring, Jimmy indicated that he has lived in his current dwelling ten years. He also indicated that he has six neighbors, recognizes all of them, but knows the name of only one of them. He has been in the house of only one neighbor. He never says "hello" or greets any of them (or so he claims). He never exchanges anything with any of them. He never discusses problems with them. He visits only one of them, and that is only "rarely." Jimmy wrote that neighbors are "not important" to him and that the most important quality is that neighbors "leave me alone."

Given these responses, it seems likely that, if Jimmy was being truthful,[11] he is highly alienated from almost every aspect of Buffalo Creek, except perhaps for a friend or two, and that his social well-being is very low. He seems embarrassed and bitter about being unemployed. He could be suffering from some other problems related to his health and personality that might aggravate his alienation. Sadly, he is the least comfortable and most negative young adult among our respondents.

Buffalo Creek as a Social Community
To summarize up to this point, Buffalo Creek's respondents generally are older people who have lived along Buffalo Creek for much of their lives and in their current dwellings for at least ten years, in many cases for at least thirty years. They have quite a few neighbors. They say that neighbors are very important to them. They are very familiar with their neighbors in basic ways such as saying "hello" and knowing their names, but they do not socialize very often with many of their neighbors. They regard trustworthiness, reliability, honesty, and friendliness very highly

in neighbors. Many of the respondents have high to moderate levels of social well-being and social integration into Buffalo Creek as a social community. Only a small percentage of them made reference to the flood of 1972, and only a few of them were highly conscious of the flood. It was the only disaster mentioned by any of them. Given all of these findings, it seems fair for us to believe that *Buffalo Creek is at least a moderately neighborly and socially integrated place to live*, according to the observations and the testimonies of the people we have interviewed in considerable detail, taken as a whole.

Now it is time to consider whether there are significant differences within this collection of respondents that relate to their familiarity with the flood. Are some of them—perhaps the ones who were most involved in the flood—less socially integrated than the others? Are they decidedly deficient in terms of neighborly relations and social well-being? Or, could it be that the cultural legacy of the flood has somehow "homogenized" all of these respondents?

THE FLOOD'S VICTIMS, WITNESSES, AND OTHERS

Now let us consider four categories of the respondents from Buffalo Creek according to how much direct experience they had with the flood, if any. Some of these respondents are classified as "victims." These people indicated that they experienced the flood in person and that their homes or other property were damaged or destroyed by it. They and members of their household may or may not have been physically injured in the flood. The other categories are: "witnesses" (respondents who indicated that they personally observed the flood and its immediate aftereffects without indicating that they or their property were damaged by the flood); "possible witnesses" (respondents who apparently were residing along Buffalo Creek the day of the flood but did not indicate that they observed the flood or that they or their property was damaged by the flood); and "nonwitnesses" (respondents who were not born by the time of the flood or who were residing outside of Buffalo Creek at the time).

Table 5.7 in appendix B presents basic demographic data on each of these four categories of respondents. These data indicate that ten of the ninety-five respondents (11 percent) were obvious victims of the flood, fifteen other respondents (16 percent) were witnesses to the flood, thirty-seven respondents (39 percent) were possible witnesses, and thirty-three (35 percent) were nonwitnesses. This being the case, the percentages for victims and witnesses are more sensitive to variations of only one or a few respondents in these categories. With this precaution in mind, we will report on the major patterns in the data that can help us determine whether some of the flood's victims and witnesses are different from other respondents in terms of neighboring, social integration, and social well-being. On the one hand, if they are not very different, then the social re-creation perspective will gain more support than the social-destruction perspective. On the other hand, if they are very different, then the social destruction perspective gains additional support.

Average Age of the Respondents: Not surprisingly, we found that the victims (average age sixty-five) and witnesses (average age sixty-three) are considerably older than the other respondents. This difference is partially the consequence of how we defined "nonwitnesses" (i.e., the "nonwitness" category includes some respondents who were born after the flood). And yet, it can be argued that differences in the ages of different categories of respondents also call into question some aspects of the social destruction perspective. If the flood was "totally" destructive, as claimed by some of the authors whose work was highlighted in chapter 2, then all of the witnesses would have been victims and none of the victims would have survived. It is also likely that no one else would have been willing to locate or relocate along Buffalo Creek, just as no one apparently was willing to relocate to Pompeii after the volcano erupted there in AD 79 (as discussed in chapter 2). This might have happened if reports of the tragic deaths created overwhelming fear and loathing throughout the land. People might fear that another disaster would occur at Buffalo Creek. They might fear that the Buffalo Creek Valley is forever polluted, tainted, or cursed. Also consider that, if the flood had been more destructive, then its few surviving victims and witnesses would have died of physical and emotional ailments since 1972. If any of them survived until I started my research there, they would have been unable or unwilling to communicate with me and to participate in any research project. Furthermore, the simple fact that ten victims have survived to the average age of sixty-five and that fifteen witnesses have survived to the average age of sixty-three weakens the proposition that the flood and its aftereffects were utterly destructive. This general line of reasoning also is reinforced by our finding that the highest percentage of lifelong residents among the respondents are flood victims (80 percent) and witnesses (53 percent). Would such large percentages of victims and witnesses be willing to remain as lifelong residents of Buffalo Creek if the flood was so overwhelmingly and permanently destructive to them?

Years Living in Current Dwelling: We found that most of the victims (80 percent), all of the witnesses (100 percent), and most of the possible witnesses (70 percent) have lived in the current dwellings along Buffalo Creek long enough (at least ten years) to be settled in, to know their neighbors, to interact with them, and to be socially integrated into Buffalo Creek.[12] By contrast, we also found that 55 percent of the nonwitnesses have resided in their current dwelling for *less* than ten years. This being the case, we might expect to find that nonwitnesses are somewhat less involved in neighboring and in community life than are the respondents in the other categories.

Close Relatives and Close Friends: Patterns are fairly complex regarding close relatives and close friends. Forty percent of the victims and 53 percent of the witnesses reported that they have ten or more close relatives and ten or more close friends who reside along Buffalo Creek. They are somewhat more socially connected in this regard than are the possible witnesses and the nonwitnesses. This pattern is consistent with the re-creation perspective in that the victims and witnesses have many more close relatives and close friends who reside along Buffalo Creek than do the respondents in the other categories. This fact implies that many of their close relatives and close friends did not perish in the flood or move away permanently from Buffalo Creek because of the flood. Then again, it is also true that a considerable percentage of the victims

(40 percent) reported that they had three or fewer close relatives and three or fewer close friends living along Buffalo Creek. This fact might mean that some of the victims (i.e., 40 percent) lost considerable numbers of close relatives and close friends in the flood. It also could indicate that victims lost close relatives and friends in the more than thirty years since the flood—but for reasons unrelated to the flood. It might be the case that the close relatives and friends that victims have lost were older people who died of age-related causes. Then too, this fact could indicate that 40 percent of the victim respondents have been unable to reestablish many close relations with relatives and friends because of the flood. These are speculations, of course, that might be answered in future research. For now, it seems prudent just to say that witnesses of the flood, and perhaps the flood's victims as well, are not disadvantaged in terms of having only a few close relatives and friends who live along Buffalo Creek.

In summary, the data in table 5.7 of appendix B provide considerable support for the social re-creation perspective, particularly when we keep in mind the fact that the respondents who are the flood's victims and witnesses are considerably older than their counterparts. Old age and declining health might be expected to have reduced the likelihood of their having many close relatives and close friends—of their being lifelong residents of Buffalo Creek—and of their being able to remain in their current dwellings for more than ten years. Rather remarkably, this has not been the case.

Attitudes About Living Along Buffalo Creek

Table 5.8 in appendix B displays the percentages of Buffalo Creek's respondents in each of the categories who hold various attitudes about living along Buffalo Creek. Generally speaking, the data in this table indicate that victims and witnesses are not very different from possible witnesses and nonwitnesses in their attitudes. In fact, the victims and witnesses often are *more positive* about living along Buffalo Creek than are the respondents in the other categories. These general patterns support the social re-creation perspective more than they oppose it.

Specifically, we found that only small percentages of respondents in each category feel closest to places outside of Buffalo Creek. In fact, 90 percent of the *victims* felt closest to their current village along Buffalo Creek, to some other village there, or to Buffalo Creek as a whole. This is not what we would expect if the flood permanently alienated its survivors from Buffalo Creek. The vast majority of respondents indicated that they feel closest to Buffalo Creek regardless of their classification. This finding constitutes very strong evidence that Buffalo Creek now is highly cherished by these respondents. This would not be the case if Buffalo Creek had been overwhelmingly and permanently damaged by the flood or if they felt that Buffalo Creek was unduly dangerous, cursed, haunted, or condemned.

We also found that substantial percentages of victims and witnesses identified many qualities that they like best about living along Buffalo Creek. These qualities often include social features of Buffalo Creek such as friends and other people who live along Buffalo Creek, neighbors, other qualities of the community such as "togetherness" and the presence of family members. Sizeable percentages of victims and witnesses also reported that they like the quietness, peacefulness, and safety of Buffalo Creek. These qualities probably would not be mentioned if the respondents were obsessed with their memories of the flood or if they feared that the flood could happen again.

As to qualities liked least, we found that a considerable percentage of victims (30 percent) reported that there was nothing objectionable about living along Buffalo Creek or that they liked "everything" about Buffalo Creek. Would this be the case if these respondents were still badly damaged by their experiences in the flood of 1972? In addition to this, none of the victims, and very few of the witnesses, reported that they disliked their neighbors or any other quality of the community. These percentages also are low for the respondents who are possible witnesses and for nonwitnesses. Not to be overlooked is the rather surprising fact that the most frequently cited qualities that were liked least about Buffalo Creek by victims and by the other respondents was being "far from" shopping, recreation, and other services. This response can hardly be attributed directly to the flood of 1972. And there is no reason to believe that this kind of inconvenience significantly reduced respondents' appreciation of Buffalo Creek. Many of the respondents, including the victims and witnesses, often emphatically vented their displeasure about other features of Buffalo Creek such as littering, noise from passing coal trucks, coal trains, speeders, and both stray and wild animals. These features cannot readily be associated with the flood of 1972 or with its immediate aftereffects. Actually, they might suggest the opposite image—that there is plenty of motion and commotion in the Buffalo Creek Valley these days.

As to qualities missed most from how Buffalo Creek was years ago, we found evidence that that victims are not radically different from other respondents, except perhaps for "other qualities missed most." More than two-thirds of the victims and witnesses indicated that they missed some of their family members and friends who have passed away over the years, not necessarily in the flood or because of it, but rather because of age related illnesses. Said another way, since the victims and witnesses are considerably older than the other respondents, they have a lot more to miss about the past because the past is much longer and more inclusive for them. In fact, it is the *non*witnesses who are more distinctive than the respondents in the other categories—usually because they are so young, relatively speaking (their average age is twenty-nine). Quite a few of the nonwitnesses were somewhat perplexed when they were asked about the past. They claimed that they were still too young to remember a past that was very different from Buffalo Creek's current condition. This attitude among the nonwitnesses also is reflected by the fact that few of them mentioned "other qualities" that they missed from Buffalo Creek's past. Most of the nonwitnesses who responded this way said that they missed friends who had left Buffalo Creek in order to attend college or to try to find better jobs outside the area. For these reasons, it seems fair to say that it is the nonwitnesses more than the victims and witnesses who are relatively unusual among Buffalo Creek's respondents regarding what they miss most about Buffalo Creek in the past. Since their past is relatively limited, it is understandable that they miss less about the past than do the other respondents, most of whom are much older and "experienced" in this regard.

Neighbors and Neighboring Along Buffalo Creek

Are the respondents who were the flood's victims and witnesses less neighborly than other respondents? Apparently not, according to the data presented in table 5.9 in appendix B.

Number of Neighbors: We found that a larger percentage of witnesses (60 percent) have ten or more neighbors than do the respondents in the other categories. Only 7 percent of the witnesses reported having fewer than five neighbors. The reports from victims, however, are more bifurcated. While 50 percent of the victims reported that they have ten or more neighbors, 30 percent of the victims reported that they had fewer than five neighbors. This percentage is twice as high as the percentage (15 percent) for the Buffalo Creek respondents taken collectively. This difference probably is a minor one. It could reflect little more than the fact that three of the victims are very old and that they have been more or less housebound for a number of years.

Basic Familiarity and Relations With Neighbors: At least 65 percent of the respondents in all categories, including victims (70 percent) and witnesses (87 percent) reported that they have *all* of the types of basic familiarity with *all* of their neighbors. We also found that at least 90 percent of the respondents in all categories reported basic familiarity with all or with most or many of their neighbors. Only 2 percent of the ninety-five respondents claimed that they did not have basic familiarity with any of their neighbors. One of these respondents is a nonwitness. The other one is a victim. Since only two of the ninety-five respondents reported that they have no basic familiarity with their neighbors, it seems reasonable for us to conclude that basic familiarity with neighbors along Buffalo Creek is typical and extensive. Only a tiny fraction of Buffalo Creek's respondents are un-neighborly in this regard.

Socializing With Neighbors: We found that victims and witnesses score above the norm of 11 percent in reporting that they socialize with all or most of their neighbors. Victims also score above the norm in socializing often or occasionally with more than a few of their neighbors. However, witnesses are somewhat deficient in this regard, for reasons that cannot be readily explained, even after the information that they provided on their questionnaires was reexamined. Witnesses are not overrepresented among the respondents who rarely or never socialize with any of their neighbors. Therefore, it seems that the underrepresentation of witnesses in some of the response categories is not unduly significant, especially in light of all of the other data in table 5.9 that show witnesses to be at least as neighborly as the other respondents in almost every other aspect.

Most Important Quality of Neighbors: Most respondents mentioned more than one quality in neighbors that is important to them, even though the questionnaire only asked them to identify one quality.[13] Victims are close to the norm for Buffalo Creek's other respondents, except for two rather slight differences. Thirty percent of the victims, in contrast to 11 percent of Buffalo Creek respondents as a whole, reported that having neighbors who are friends, intimates, or confidants is important to them. Yet only 10 percent of the victims, in contrast to 48 percent of the nonwitnesses, reported that being friendly (or friendliness) was important to them in their neighbors. One possible explanation for these somewhat surprising findings is that the nonwitnesses are much younger than are the ninety-five respondents as a whole. Apparently, younger respondents place a higher value on friendliness than on any other quality. This appears to be less true of the older people, including victims and witnesses. Older people value "help when needed" and having neighbors who are friends, confidants, and intimates.

Going further into these matters, we found that very few respondents in any of the categories identified the absence of negative qualities like nosiness and gossipers as being most important to them. The respondents focused on positive qualities. This attribute also seems to support the social re-creation perspective more than the destruction perspective. The facts that Buffalo Creek's respondents mentioned so many different positive qualities in neighbors, and that the respondents (except for 47 percent of the witnesses) were not overly concerned about help in crises, suggest that psychological damages from the flood have diminished to a considerable extent. At the same time, however, the fact that 47 percent of the witnesses mentioned "help in time of crisis" as an important quality in neighbors might indicate that there is some residual and very persistent psychological effect of the flood.

Importance of Neighbors: Some of the strongest data in support of the social re-creation perspective involve responses to questions about the importance of neighbors. Eighty percent of the victims and 73 percent of the witnesses claimed that neighbors are "very" or "really" important to them. Lower percentages of possible witnesses and nonwitnesses responded this way. We might ask ourselves if this could be the case if the victims and witnesses had permanently lost all sense of trust in their neighbors because of the flood of 1972. Surely, these data are more consistent with those elements of the re-creation perspective that contend that reactions to some disasters eventually re-create or even strengthen aspects of social community, such as importance of good neighbors.

Overall, then, we can conclude that the respondents who were victims of the flood, or witnesses to it, are just as neighborly as those respondents who were not victims and witnesses, if not more so.

Respondents' References to Disasters

How salient was the flood of 1972 and other disasters on the respondents' completed questionnaires? Notably, the questionnaire does not mention or inquire about the flood, disasters, or the year 1972. Nor does it prompt respondents to mention tragedies in their lives or in the history of Buffalo Creek. And yet, a small percentage of respondents made comments about the flood on their questionnaires and during their interviews. For example, in response to the question about what they missed most about Buffalo Creek in the past, one respondent said, "Getting to see my Mom and Dad everyday. They were killed in the flood." Another respondent wrote that she has lived in her current dwelling "since just after the flood." How common were comments like these among the four categories of respondents?

Table 5.10 in appendix B displays data that inform us about this matter. It reveals fairly dramatic differences among the categories of respondents as to references to the flood of 1972 (no disasters other than the flood of 1972 were mentioned by any of the respondents). Only respondents who were victims referred to the flood at least four times on their questionnaires. Twenty percent of the victims did this. Another 60 percent of the victims referred to the flood one to three times, as did 73 percent of the witnesses, and only 3 percent of the possible witnesses. None of the nonwitnesses referred to the flood on their questionnaires. Taken as a collectivity, a very large majority (78 percent) of Buffalo Creek's ninety-five respondents did not refer to the flood or to any other disaster. Only 2 percent of the respondents referred to the flood at least four times. Thus it seems valid to conclude that Buffalo Creek's respondents were *not* ostensibly conscious of, oriented towards, or obsessed by the flood when they completed their questionnaires.

In contrast, it is obvious that large majorities of the victims and witnesses (80 percent and 73 percent, respectively) were conscious of the flood when they responded to the items on the questionnaire. This fact does support the social destruction perspective more than the social re-creation perspective—at least regarding the victims and the witnesses. Most of the victims and witnesses mentioned the flood at least once even though they were not asked about the flood. Only one other respondent from Buffalo Creek did the same. This contrast constitutes rather powerful evidence that the flood of 1972 is not forgotten by those residents of Buffalo Creek who experienced it most directly.

Social Integration and Social Well-Being
How well are the respondents integrated into Buffalo Creek as a social community? How many of them have social well-being? We estimated the levels of social integration and social well-being of the respondents in the four categories based on all of the information that they provided on their questionnaires and in their interviews (as explained in appendix A and in the notes at the bottom of table 5.11 of appendix B).

We found that solid majorities of the respondents in all four categories, including victims and witnesses, are either very high or high in their level of social integration. Specifically, 70 percent of the victims, 73 percent of the witnesses, 57 percent of the possible witnesses, and 69 percent of the nonwitnesses are very highly or highly integrated into Buffalo Creek. These findings alone support the social re-creation perspective rather strongly. For, if the flood was such an overwhelming disaster for Buffalo Creek as an entire social community—as claimed by so many mass media articles and experts who published famous books about it—then it is unlikely that more than two-thirds of the respondents who are victims and witnesses of the flood would be so highly integrated into Buffalo Creek more than thirty years later. More emphatically, it is unlikely that Buffalo Creek would even exist as a viable social community today.

And yet, it is also true that a slightly smaller percentage of the victims than nonvictims were found to be very highly socially integrated. Then again, it also is true that just one of the ten victims (Vera Grimm) was found to be alienated from Buffalo Creek as a community. Only one other respondent (Jimmy Joe Rooker) from Buffalo Creek was found to be so alienated. That person is a *non*witness to the flood; he was born more than ten years after it.

I believe that these percentages are so low regarding alienation from Buffalo Creek as a social community that they can be considered very minor. Perhaps they are even *abnormally* low in comparison with other residential communities in the United States. Is it not likely that at least 2 percent—if not 10 percent—of the residents of almost every village, town, township, city, and suburb in the United States are isolated or even alienated from the other residents? Consider that the United States has more than 1,300,000 homeless people, 2,7000,000 incarcerated people, and about 4,000,000 people who are institutionalized for addictions and other ailments at any given time. If we assume that only one-half of these 8,000,000 people are socially isolated or alienated from the rest of U.S. society, then these 4,000,000 alienated people would constitute more than 1 percent of the U.S. population of about 300,000,000 people.[14] Also consider that there are probably at least several million people in the United States, if not tens of millions of them, who are not homeless, incarcerated, or institutionalized, but who are nonetheless alienated from their communities. Seen in this light, that 2 percent of Buffalo Creek's respondents might be socially isolated or alienated does not seem to be a very high percentage, as lamentable as that percentage might be in terms of human misery to those who are in situations such as these. Going just a little further on this point, let us think back to chapter 2 and the devastating portrayals of Buffalo Creek that were rendered by Nugent, Stern, Lifton and Olson, and Erikson. While they did not explicitly estimate the amounts of social isolation and alienation among the flood's survivors, their portrayals of the survivors certainly lead us to believe that social isolation and alienation were widespread, rampant, or even "total" after the flood.

My findings regarding social well-being generally reinforce my findings regarding social integration, although social well-being unfortunately lags behind social integration to some extent, probably because quite a few of the respondents are relatively old and in declining health.[15] The positive side of the story is that we found *more than one-half* of all of the respondents to have high or very high social well-being. This includes the victims and witnesses. Surely, there is no need to elaborate on the now frequent suggestion that we have been making so many times in this chapter: here is yet another finding that leads us to believe that many people of Buffalo Creek are not permanently "destroyed" by the flood of 1972. On the negative side, we also found that that about 30 percent of the respondents who were flood victims had low or very low levels of social well-being, in contrast to 14 percent of the witnesses, 8 percent of the possible witnesses, and 6 percent of the nonwitnesses. This being the case, the social destruction perspective cannot be dismissed out of hand. On the one hand, these lower levels of social well-being in about one-third of the victims could be the lingering consequence of the flood. On the other hand, they could be the consequence of the advanced ages and age-related ailments of some of the flood's surviving victims.[16]

Looking back momentarily, it is true that we have interpreted the data presented so far in this chapter as indicating that the respondents of

Buffalo Creek do not seem to be very damaged, deprived, or deficient in their neighborly relations, social well-being, and social integration into Buffalo Creek as a social community—at least not in some intuitive and absolute sense. This interpretation does *not* in any way deny the material presented in chapters 1–4 to the effect that many of Buffalo Creek's residents suffered horrible damages on February 26, 1972, and that Buffalo Creek was greatly damaged as a social community. This interpretation simply infers that more than ninety of Buffalo Creek's current and recent residents have rather strong social relations more than thirty years after the flood, and that this would not be the situation if the flood's negative effects were still overwhelmingly destructive and pervasive.

Now it is time to consider whether, comparatively speaking, Buffalo Creek's respondents are very different from respondents in two other places that did not suffer the flood or disasters of comparable magnitude.

BUFFALO CREEK, ELK CREEK, AND ST. JOHN: HOW DIFFERENT ARE THEY?

Elk Creek, West Virginia: A Quiet Haven Despite Losses

> Love thy neighbor as thyself. The Bible says it plain and clear. And that's how important neighbors are to me.
>
> —Roger Cline, a longtime resident of Elk Creek

References like this to The Bible are not uncommon among older folks along Elk Creek or Buffalo Creek, West Virginia. And this is just one of many other important similarities between the two places, as well as differences that could be crucial to the patterns of social life in both places.

Elk Creek is the local name for a small, unincorporated hamlet of about forty residences and 130 people. Most of the dwellings are located along a half-mile stretch of a shallow brook, barely twenty feet across in most places, just before it undercuts two-lane, rural Route 14 and merges with the muddy waters of the much wider Guyandotte River. The hamlet is about eight miles upstream from the juncture with the town of Man, where the creek of Buffalo Creek empties into the Guyandotte. Whereas Buffalo Creek consists of sixteen former coal camps that are spread along seventeen miles of Buffalo Creek, Elk Creek refers mainly to one former coal camp that occupies both sides of the creek of Elk Creek. Buffalo Creek had at least five active coal mines in 1972, but only one active mine in 2000 when I first visited it. Elk Creek had three active mines in 1972, but only one active mine when I first visited in 2001.[17] A recently closed coal tipple, a railroad yard, and an assortment of run-down brick utility buildings occupy twenty acres along a railroad track one mile up Elk Creek. Other than that, Elk Creek consists of houses, trailers, garages, sheds, a two-bay auto repair shop near the bottom of the hollow, and a small, white, wood-frame Baptist church two miles up the hollow. Driving up through Elk Creek conveys the image that this place truly is a quiet little "hamlet in the hollow."

Elk Creek was selected for comparison with Buffalo Creek because of its intriguing similarities to and differences from Buffalo Creek. The similarities include Elk Creek's propinquity to Buffalo Creek (ten miles) and its location along a creek that is smaller than but similar to the creek of Buffalo Creek (both are prone to flooding several times a year due to heavy rainstorms). Furthermore, both Elk Creek and Buffalo Creek are located in steep hollows that run perpendicular to the mighty, muddy (some locals say "mighty muddy"), and flood-prone Guyandotte River. Both places are located in Logan County and consist of unincorporated former coal camps that were built and operated for decades by many of the same coal companies. Many of the residents of both places are the descendants of coal miners. As such, many of the residents of both places might be expected to have very similar views about and experiences with mining, neighboring, and the contours of social life in places like these.

Differences between Elk Creek and Buffalo Creek obviously include the disaster at Buffalo Creek in 1972. To the best of my knowledge, Elk Creek never had either a "natural" or a "man-made" disaster similar to the flood at Buffalo Creek in its physical and social destructiveness. The closing down of the coal mine and the coal tipple along Elk Creek might constitute an economic disaster to some social scientists. Whether this is the case for Elk Creek's own residents will become more apparent shortly.[18] Another obvious difference (besides the difference in the animal mascots and namesakes of each place!) is size and plurality. Buffalo Creek includes about 3,100 residents living within and between sixteen former coal camps along seventeen miles of the creek of Buffalo Creek, for the most part. Elk Creek generally refers to about 130 residents who reside in forty dwellings in one former coal camp along about two miles of the creek of Elk Creek. Buffalo Creek has more than a dozen businesses and services, including pizza shops, two post office branches, a public school, at least fifteen churches, and several units of subsidized housing. By contrast, Elk Creek had none of these at the time of my last visit, except for the small Baptist church (which some residents of Elk Creek claimed was not a part of Elk Creek). Also in contrast to Elk Creek, Buffalo Creek is adjacent to the town of Man (population 950). Residents of Buffalo Creek can use several gravel and dirt roads to drive up over the mountains to other parts of West Virginia in addition to the two-lane, paved Highway 16 that runs the length of the valley. For all practical purposes, the residents of Elk Creek have access to only one road, Route 14, that leads into and out of their community.

Whether these differences between Elk Creek and Buffalo Creek have allowed Elk Creek to be much more neighborly and socially integrated than Buffalo Creek is one of the questions behind the material that follows.

As done in chapter 4 with residents of Buffalo Creek, let us first "meet" a few residents of Elk Creek through the interviews that we had with them: Wesley Westfall, Cookie Lincoln, and Danny and Julie Lawler.

Wesley Westfall: Reluctantly Retired Coal Miner

Wesley Westfall is a pleasant, somewhat reticent fellow in his fifties whose body is shifting from muscular to soft and portly. He admits having difficulty adjusting to two losses in the past few years that have left him hesitant and uncertain about the future: a divorce and an involuntary retirement when the last coal mine on Elk Creek closed. It had been his one and only job since he started working there after finishing high school. He bought this wood-frame home, perched precariously on a steep side of the Elk Creek hollow, to be close to his friends and to be able to walk to his work at the mine. Now he lives here with his son, an unsmiling, oversized boy-man who is wearing camouflage hunting clothes while he paces nervously through the back rooms of the single-story house. Wesley makes no effort to introduce us.

After twenty minutes of talking about coal mining, I ask Wesley the questions on the survey sheet. He thinks carefully before answering. He says that he feels closer to Elk Creek than to any other place. He has lived here since he was five years old. Ten of his twenty-two closest relatives live here, as do five of his twenty closest friends. Asked what he likes best about Elk Creek, Wesley ponders for a while and responds softly, "I guess I just like it. That's all. It's a quiet place." Asked what he misses about the "old community," he slowly says, "My workin' at the coal mine, most of all. And I miss the closeness of his friends there at the mine and up and down the hollow." He repeatedly laments how things have changed since the mine closed. He observes that the "The State don't take care of the road that goes up the hollow to the mine like it used to. I guess it's just out of their way now. And we don't get the same quality water and other services like we used to."

Wesley avows that he does more neighboring along Elk Creek than do most of the other residents, including his family and friends. It is obvious that he wishes that more of them reciprocated. He says that he has four-teen or fifteen neighbors, that he readily recognizes all of them, knows their names, greets all of them every time he sees them, and talks with some of them two or three times each week. He has been in the homes of ten or twelve of them and he exchanges tools with some of them "maybe every three or four months." In contrast, few of his neighbors have ever asked Wesley for advice. They do not visit very often, and they rarely go places together. Once a year, they might have a barbecue together. Wesley mentions that there is a reunion every summer in Elk Creek. He attended it and enjoyed it for years, but now he laments, "I don't go to them much anymore." He says that most residents of Elk Creek "keep to themselves now, mainly, so they aren't as important as friends as they used to be." The important quality now of a good neighbor is "someone who is helpful when you need it."

Looking back, it seems as though Wesley Westfall is a thoroughly decent fellow who is struggling to adjust to his recent losses and to find his way through the remainder of his life. He would like more neighboring, probably to help occupy his days and to reassure him that life is still worth living.

Cookie Lincoln: "Moved Back Home" to Elk Creek

Why would someone who was having a happy, active married life with kids and grandchildren out in a "big city out West" move back to Elk Creek? Silver-haired, robust, and confident Cookie Lincoln has a ready reply to that question:

> It was pretty exciting out there, I'll tell you that. Plenty to do. Great place to raise a family. No pollution. Good schools. Steady economy, and all of that, you know! All our kids and grandkids were born out there. They grew up out there. But then, when it came time to retire, me and my husband decided to come back home to Elk Creek. I mean, Elk Creek is our home. We feel closest to Elk Creek. Out West is good for the kids. We can go out there and visit pretty often. Sometimes they come here for a visit, too.

Cookie says that she had been a sales and service coordinator out West, but now she is "just a grandma and a homemaker." She and her husband, Ed, bought this new double-wide trailer when they moved back and had it installed on this well-shaded lot. Like a true West Virginia mountaineer, Cookie says "these mountains are what I like best about Elk Creek. The roads and water I like the least." Seventeen of her many close relatives and about the same number of her close friends live here, but many live elsewhere, including a lot of friends out West. Cookie admits that what she misses most from the Elk Creek of her youth is "the closeness of the family. Getting together in the evenings. Sitting on the porch visiting." She counts about nine people as her close neighbors. She recognizes, says "hello" to, and names all nine of them. She talks several times a week with some of them, has friendly talks with one of them fairly regularly, but has not been asked for advice by any of them ("at least not yet!"). She borrows magazines and food staples from one or two of them about once a week, has been in the homes of three of her neighbors, visits some of them about once or twice a week, and goes places with one or two of them once or twice a month.

It is no surprise to hear Cookie exclaim that neighbors are "very important when they are dependable, friendly, and helpful." At no point in the interview did Cookie indicate that she unduly missed being out West anymore, even though her children and grandchildren are there. She and her husband insist that they are comfortable in their decision to move back to Elk Creek.

> This is what we were looking for in our retirement years. Living here doesn't cost much. It's quiet, friendly, and real comfortable. We have plenty of relatives and friends around Logan County when we want to socialize. They aren't that far away. And we have our privacy right here when we want it, too. I think we are here to stay.

Julie and Danny Lawler: Young Marrieds Happy in Elk Creek

Julie and Danny Lawler are attractive young marrieds, in their twenties, with a new baby, a new trailer, and a very positive disposition towards everything, including living in Elk Creek. They insist on answering all of the survey questions as a couple. They say that they moved to Elk Creek four years ago from another little place in Logan County and bought this new trailer just for this lot. Danny works at a retail store about twenty miles away. Julie says that she is an "in-home, day care provider. I just love being with the little kids. They are *so* sweet." The Lawlers indicate that four of their thirty-five closest relatives live in Elk Creek, as do ten of their closest fifty friends. They still feel closest to their previous community, although they clearly are happy and well integrated into Elk Creek. They say "everyone is friendly here." Neither of them can think of anything that they "like least" about Elk Creek. They do not have a ready response to the question about anything that they might miss from the "old community."

As to their current neighbors, Julie and Danny estimate that they have "at least fifteen—maybe twenty neighbors here in Elk Creek." They say that they neighbor with at least two or three of those neighbors in almost all of the ways listed on the questionnaire. They recognize all of their neighbors wherever they happen to see them, even outside of Elk Creek. They know their names, talk with some of them "everyday," and have friendly talks with "most of them every so often." Two of their neighbors have "kinda asked us for some advice about problems they have." The Lawlers exchange recipes and tools with some of their neighbors "about once every week," visit with some of them "about every other day," entertain one another two to five times a year, and go places with some neighbors "maybe once a week."

Given these responses, it is not surprising to hear the Lawlers say that neighbors are very important to them. "We all try to be good neighbors that can count on each other." The Lawlers do not have any complaints, and they do not mention any problems in the past from their former home or their current one here in Elk Creek. Thus it seems that there is ample evidence that the Lawlers are neighborly, well integrated, and pleased with their social well-being in Elk Creek. There also is ample evidence that for them and for Cookie Lincoln, if not for Wesley Westfall, social life along Elk Creek is satisfying enough, given their life stages and expectations.

*   *   *

And now, we will turn to a place more than 2,000 miles away from Elk Creek and Buffalo Creek, West Virginia. In late summer, it is surrounded by rolling fields of golden wheat rather than by rugged mountains of green forests above deep seams of black coal. It is said to have been blessed with economic prosperity, social stability, and community spirit since it was founded more than one hundred years ago.

St. John: "Just Walk in and Make Yourself at Home"

> Just walk in and make yourself at home. The door is always open. The key is on the mantle inside.

So said Dorothy Lang, one of the four employees of St. John Phone Company. She had just phoned me in Seattle, 300 miles away, to tell me that the phone company's one-room "Super 1 Motel" (it only has *one* motel room—and no office) would be open and waiting for my wife and me when we arrived in a few days. Dorothy's invitation to "just walk in and make ourselves at home" would prove to be a fitting epigraph for most of our many experiences in and around St. John ever since then. We have found St. John to be an unusually cohesive and friendly community. This is one of our many findings that coincide with what John C. Allen and Don A. Dillman reported more than a decade ago in their intriguing sociological study of St. John, *Against All Odds: Rural Community in the Information Age.*[19]

> Can a meaningful sense of community exist within rural towns and villages of the United States...? The answer is a resounding yes for at least one rural community in the Pacific Northwest... Most of all _____ (a pseudonym) has a community spirit, an identity defended publicly and privately, and with anger or tears when necessary. The residents, most of whom are descendants or relatives of the original settlers, gauge both their actions and reactions according to what other community members expect of them.
> _____ is a tightly knit community of people whose daily actions, both economic and social, take into account a shared identity.[20]

St. John is an incorporated town that occupies about one square mile of bottomland in the smoothly contoured, rolling hills of the Palouse wheat-growing area of southeastern Washington State. The town has about 520 residents in 300 dwellings, as well as twenty stores and shops, three churches, two public schools (primary and high school), and an impressive number of recreational facilities that include a public swimming pool, several parks, and a six-hole golf course that is operated by the town's recreation department. Another 250 people who identify themselves with St. John, and pay school, fire, and other taxes to St. John, reside along the rural roads within ten or twelve miles of the town. Dozens of these people reside in farmhouses and own and operate wheat farms of more than 1,000 acres.

If neighbors and neighborly relations[21] can be found anywhere in the United States, they should be found in residential communities that are relatively small, stable, democratic, circumscribed, homogenous, and economically productive—places like St. John. This is exactly the reason why St. John has been included in this study. It is just rural enough to isolate its residents from having face-to-face relations with people from other towns, but it is compact enough to allow many of its members to have easy, face-to-face relations with one another at least several times a week. Admittedly, this is somewhat less true of St. John's outliers. And yet, many of these outliers reside along hard-surface roads that connect them more readily to "in-town" St. John (as it is referred to) than to the other villages and towns in Whitman County. Fortuitously, St. John is situated along a well-maintained, two-lane, improved roadway, Route 23, that has a fifty mph speed limit that is difficult to exceed safely. It links St. John with a major east-west interstate (I-90), twenty-seven miles to the northwest, that connects Spokane and Seattle, the two largest cities in Washington State. There is also a north-south interstate, I-70, fifteen miles to the east of St. John, that links Spokane to Pullman, the location of the second-largest state university, Washington State University, and to Colfax, the seat of Whitman County. St. John is at least a twenty-five–minute drive from a larger commercial area and about a ninety-minute drive from a large city, Spokane. It is less isolated than neighboring towns, villages, and hamlets. Its members can shop and socialize more conveniently in St. John than in the few other towns and villages within easy driving distance, if and when they want to do these things.

In part because of its fortuitous location, St. John has had remarkable prosperity, stability, and continuity since it was founded in 1904 as a trade center for wheat production (and named after one of its incorporators, Edward St. John). Growing wheat, barley, peas, lentils, and hay on family farms continues to be the primary productive activity, supplemented by services that cater to the needs of farmers: cooperative grain mills and storage facilities, state agencies that regulate land use, and businesses that sell fertilizers, herbicides, fuel, lubricants, and farm machinery. As might be expected, the social life of many of St. John's native-born residents resonates with the yearly cycle of repairing and fueling farm machinery, plowing and fertilizing the land, planting seeds, harvesting the crops, and trucking them to the massive grain silos along the railroad tracks in the middle of St. John. In addition to this kind of core economic activity, St. John's citizens smartly added other features to the town that helped it survive the years when harvests and market prices sagged and when wheat farming consolidated into large, capital-intensive farms in the 1960s and 1970s. They established a cooperative bank, a utility company, a six-hole golf course, housing for senior citizens, a large public swimming pool, and a year-round recreation program to maintain commerce and residential housing in the in-town area. All of these features can help St. John's citizens engage in plenty of positive social relations with one another on a daily basis. They also can take comfort and pride in the fact that St. John has flourished—in contrast to most of the other little towns and villages in the Palouse that have withered away since the end of WWII.

In recent years, a number of other features—inexpensive land, low cost of living, infrequent street crime, and the public golf course—have drawn dozens of recently retired couples and singles to St. John. Some of these newcomers are only part-time residents who have built rather ostentatious new homes around the golf course. They and their fancy homes are not necessarily appreciated by some of the longtime residents. It is also true that some of the older, deteriorated housing has been acquired by absentee landlords who rent it out to lower-income people who cannot find affordable housing in Spokane and other cities in the region. On the one hand, these newcomers are regarded with suspicion by some other residents who claim, sometimes with justification, that the newcomers have drug problems and deviant life styles. On the other hand, some of the newcomers complain that there is a surprising amount of bigotry, nosiness, prejudice, and status consciousness lurking below the surface of small-town communality in St. John. And so, it is very possible that perceived differences between the "natives" and the "newcomers" could have considerable bearing on the social lives and the sense of social well-being of considerable numbers of St. John's people.

Now then, rather than speculate further about social relations in St. John, let us meet a few of St. John's people who agreed to tell us about their experiences with neighbors and other residents of St. John.

John Landsman: A Quiet, Communal Man of the Land

John Landsman is an unassuming and laconic fellow in his forties. His slight build, eyeglasses, and sparse beard going gray seem incongruous with the fact that he owns and operates a well-kept and profitable wheat farm of more than 1,500 acres on the outskirts of St. John, where he lives with his wife, Ella, of twenty some years. His grown children have full-time jobs, take college courses during the winter, and help John, Ella, and two hired hands harvest the wheat crop in August by driving trucks to and from the towering grain silos that prevail over "downtown" St. John. John was born in St. John and has gladly farmed his entire working life. "I've enjoyed all of my years here in St. John, growing up, going to the schools, dating my wife, building our new house a few years ago and, of course, farming. I guess most of all I enjoyed the years my children were born."

On the questionnaire, John wrote simple responses without elaboration. What he likes best about living in St. John are: "location, community, and life." What he likes least are: "location, gossip, and nosiness." John did indeed write "location" for both his likes and dislikes: He likes the fact that the location gives him privacy, and he dislikes being so far away from salt water. "The togetherness" is what he wrote in response to the questionnaire about what he misses most about social life in the "old community."

John also wrote that eight of his fifteen close relatives live in St. John, as do "all but two" of his close friends. In response to the questions about neighbors and neighboring, John wrote that he has thirteen neighbors whom he knows by name, recognizes anywhere, and greets daily. He also wrote that he talks with all of his neighbors "all the time," including "friendly talks." He socializes with his neighbors fairly extensively: discussing problems with three or four of them and exchanging tools and household goods "all of the time" with them. John has been in the homes of all of his neighbors. He discloses with some regret that he and his neighbors only get to entertain one another "two or three times a year," that there is "not enough visiting" with his neighbors, and that he and his neighbors do not go places together as often as he would like. John also wrote that neighbors are "important a lot" to him and that he appreciates "their friendship" more than any other quality.

In evaluating John Landsman's comments, it should be noted that John is remarkably sincere and "down to earth," both literally and figuratively (after all, his surname means "farmer" in German). I have no doubt that his comments allow us to infer that John is highly integrated into St. John as a social community, that social life in St. John is very satisfactory to him, that he is a good neighbor and appreciates good neighbors, and that he has a strong but not exaggerated sense of social well-being. Beyond this, it is also apparent that John Landsman is the kind of citizen of St. John that Allen and Dillman portrayed so often in their astute book about St. John.

Emily Kellogg: Native Daughter of the Land

Emily Kellogg is a large, healthy, happy, and confident young woman in her twenties. She is college educated and well employed in agricultural research. During our first interview in a popular cafe in St. John, other customers often stop by our table to greet her warmly and to meet me. She is comfortable with all of them.

Eventually, we turn to the topics of my project and to the questionnaire. Emily says that she was born on the farm where her parents still live and where she lives whenever she returns for weekends and during harvest season to help them with the harvest. She considers sixteen people in the four houses closest to her parents' farm to be her neighbors. She recognizes all of these people no matter where she sees them, and she always says hello to all of them when she has the opportunity. She knows all of their last names, but perhaps only 80 percent of their first names. She explains that her parents taught her to show respect by referring to older people as "Mr." or "Mrs." Emily talks with her neighbors "all the time," and she has friendly talks with many of them about once a week. Most of her neighbors have asked Emily for advice at one time or the other on topics that they believe are related to her college education. She has been in the homes of all of her neighbors, starting when she was a school child "selling school stuff." Borrowing and exchanging things is common among the neighbors, she says. At least twice a year all of them have a dinner together—usually a "Hawaiian pig roast" and a "chocolate waffle feed" at Christmas—traditions that started many years ago. The neighbors also get together three or four times a year for graduations and weddings.

Given these responses, it is hardly surprising to hear Emily say that neighbors are "very important" to her "for the support, to keep an eye on things, to borrow from, and to take care of the animals when you aren't there." Emily adds that "[r]eliability is the first thing we need in neighbors. Friendship comes after that."

As to whether she misses anything about the way St. John was years ago, Emily affirms her grandmother's belief that "Neighborliness is less than before. Some people just aren't as reliable as they were years ago." Pressed for an example, Emily says that years ago, all of the neighboring farmers would immediately rush to the aid of any other neighboring farmer whose fields caught fire accidentally during harvest. However, recently, one farmer did not show up to help at a fire. This miscreant was "told flat out that he had better help out the next time. Years ago, neighbors wouldn't have to be reminded like that."

Emily definitely sees herself and her family being integral members of St. John even though they live miles outside of town and closer to another village with a few stores and a school. Years ago, Emily's parents decided to identify and associate with St. John because they felt that the services and schools were better in St. John. Emily readily names what she likes best about St. John: "community support, strong work ethic, the independence of the farming community, and it's so easy for children to know the adults everywhere in town." Emily explains that the children are not limited to conversing within their peer group when they are growing up.

Emily also notes that she has twelve to fifteen close relatives who live in or near St. John, and about thirty relatives who live elsewhere. She has two or three close friends here and ten to twelve living elsewhere, including quite a few of them in other towns in the Palouse. While she identifies readily with St. John as her home and the place that she feels closest to, she feels that the best place she ever lived was in a country on a distant continent, where she spent a year after college. "It was a lot more exciting over there—that's for sure!" She was happiest over there and during her high school years in St. John. "You got to know everyone so well. There were all sorts of activities at school and here in St. John and Whitman County. I loved participating in the stock shows and fairs. It was good growing up here."

Looking back, I was able to communicate with Emily Kellogg six or seven times over a two-year period. There is no doubt that she is very neighborly and very well integrated into St. John even though she no longer resides there on a full-time basis. She has a very strong sense of social well-being that is anchored in St. John and extends to friends that she makes wherever she goes.

Joleen Newport: Some Unique Insights by a Positive Newcomer

Joleen Newport is a large, robust woman in her fifties—remarried, and a proud grandmother. She readily fits into the friendship circle of ladies at an afternoon coffee klatch at a favorite cafe in town, despite her smoking (which she does outside) and her relatively short tenure in St. John.

Joleen wrote detailed, clear, and revealing responses on her questionnaire. Her response to the question about what she likes best about living in St. John provides an original and tolerant view of the town's cliques: "I like how versitile they are in the clicks [*sic*]. If you don't fit in one there's always another one you can join. People here all like to have fun and create fun with each other. Everyone enjoys each other's company and takes care of one another."

Joleen did not mention any dislikes about living in St. John. She indicated that St. John is the best place she has ever lived, although she misses the city and state where she spent most of her life. She wrote that twenty-five of her twenty-six close relatives live outside St. John, but that twenty-eight of her fifty-five close friends live here. This estimate seems rather remarkable insofar as she has only resided in St. John for a few years. Yet it is obvious that Joleen has a positive attitude about almost everything in her life, including: "When my sons were born. When I re-married my present husband we were working together to make a good family. When my grandchildren were born."

As to neighboring, Joleen has accomplished a lot in the few years that she has resided in her current dwelling. She estimates that she has about fifty neighbors in the twenty-eight dwellings that are closest to hers. She says hello or good morning to "everyone in town," knows the names of all the neighbors "who live on my street, but one," talks every day to many of her neighbors, has friendly talks with all fifty of them once in a while, has talked with twenty of them about their problems, exchanges things with "everyone," and has been inside the homes of "10 to 15" of them. As to visiting with her neighbors, Joleen wrote, "everyday in there [sic] yards or at the tavern or cafe at 2 p.m." She goes places together with her neighbors "every other month or so, sometimes every month." Not surprisingly, Joleen indicated that neighbors are "very important" to her because "[w]e all care what happens to each other. We all watch out for each other too. We even help raise each other's kids and grandkids." My sense is that Joleen is very sincere and accurate with this statement, at least insofar as it pertains to her circle of coffee-klatch friends. Possibly, she overgeneralizes by extending her assessment to St. John's population as a whole. She seems to blur the distinctions among "neighbors," the people who reside on her street, the ladies in her coffee klatch, the habitués of the favorite tavern in town, and folks she sees or meets casually on the streets around St. John. She might be something of a magnanimous Pollyanna in this regard. Possibly, she is still experiencing the euphoria of easy acceptance that she has found since moving to St. John a few years ago. Be that as it may, Joleen Newport certainly presents herself as being extremely neighborly, well integrated into St. John, and high on social well-being.

*   *   *

Return trips to St. John allowed us to interview some residents who are on the social margins of the community, in some ways. These include some single males of various ages, single mothers with kids, and young couples who are trying to find their ways economically and socially. Van Hegel and Heidi Hopewell are cases in point.

Van and Vanna Hegel: "It's More a 'Hi' and 'Goodbye' Kind of Thing"
We are sitting on the back porch of the home of a retired, divorced, handyman whom I will refer to as "Van Hegel." He lives alone now in this neat, often renovated wood-frame bungalow of 1920s vintage. This back porch protects us from the broiling sun and some of the ninety-eight degree heat that radiates off of the ten grain silos that tower over the center of town. Van is not one to talk about such things, or much else, unless asked. Often he stalls before saying something as simple as, "Well, I don't know much about that." He is slight, slender, approaching seventy, and wearing faded blue jeans, a plaid cotton shirt, and Vietnam-era scuffed black boots. His grown daughter, Vanna, has joined us at a picnic table on the porch. She is in the middle of a two-week summer visit from her home in the Midwest. A voluble and confident woman in her forties, she sits at the picnic table with an open fishing tackle box that is filled with a bright gallery of her cosmetics, nonchalantly applying makeup to her face during much of our interview. Vanna lived in St. John while finishing high school in the 1980s. She readily helps her father respond to our questions, sometimes answering for herself as well as for him.

After some smalltalk, Van mentions that he grew up in another part of eastern Washington and then "I bounced around some until I found myself here in St. John. That was years ago. There was work here and I didn't see much reason to leave, except maybe to go salt water fishing over in the (Puget) Sound whenever I could manage it." Asked to name three things that he likes best and least about living in St. John, Van eventually says, "Well, that's a hard one." Then Vanna chimes in for him: "It's really friendly, you know everyone, and its quiet, Right?" Then Vanna leaves the table to make a phone call in the living room. Van glances over at me and haltingly offers his own answers in his own way.

> I guess you can say my work environment was okay here. I've had some decent jobs since I've been here. Somebody always needs something repaired in their homes. Maybe another thing that's okay here is church. It's close by; just a few blocks away. I can walk there and most other places here in town. The Rialto (tavern) is close by. I can play cards there and spend time when I feel like it.

Van then lapses into stories about fishing. In time I ask Van if it would be fair to say that he likes the fishing around St. John. "Yes, I guess that's fair to say. There are some big rainbows (trout) in Rock Lake. Sometimes the kids here in town even catch some right here in the creek" (pointing to the almost dried-up ditch that bisects the town). Van seems a little downcast when I jokingly suggest that he might be trying to take advantage of his out-of-town interviewer. "Well, it might be hard to believe, but it's happened after big rains in the Spring."

Van is even less certain about what he likes least about St. John. "I don't know. I can't say much about that." Just then, Vanna returns to the table and helps Van decide that "It's kind of far from some things" (mainly from fishing over in Puget Sound). Vanna then mentions that "St. John has some cliques, you know. You either click with the cliques or you are out of luck." Van smiles a little, and agrees, "Well that's true. I guess I'm on the outside mostly." Vanna qualifies that by saying "Well yes—except down at the Rialto (tavern)." To this Van responds, "Yes, I guess that's so. Then again, most everyone is in at the Rialto so long as they are paying their own way. Some seem to forget, from time to time."

As we talk, Vanna helps Van determine that only one or two of his fifteen close relatives live in St. John and that he does not really feel too close to any of them. Van tries to explain that this is not because of overt conflicts so much as it is because he is not a person with high expectations about other people or about life in general. As to close friends, Van says, "I guess I got none outside of St. John. To be honest, even my friends here in St. John are only community friends, mainly the ones I talk with down at the Rialto, playing cards or just spending time." Vanna takes exception to this and mentions the name of a local fellow who seems to be friendly with Van: "Isn't he your friend?" "Well, I guess not really. I just help him out when he needs it. Fix his plumbing. Stuff like that. That's all."

Asked about the community he feels closest to, and what he misses most about social life in the "old community," Van characteristically answers, "I suppose this one (St. John). I've been here the longest. It hasn't changed much since I've been here. So I can't say as I miss much from years ago." I ask him about the often lamented outward migration of young people from little towns like St. John. Van responds, "I can't say as I have seen that. At church, when the preacher calls out for Sunday School, it seems like half the church empties out when the kids leave. So there's enough kids around, I guess."

As to neighbors and neighboring, Vanna and Van decide that he has six or seven neighbors in the three or four dwellings closest to him. The ambiguity occurs because one old woman who lived adjacent to him in a trailer has been living in an elderly care facility elsewhere in Whitman County for a few months. For many years, Van did odd jobs on her property for her, so he was more familiar with her than with his other neighbors. The other neighbors are two married couples who have lived adjacent to Van for years, and a young single mother, her young child, and a live-in male companion.[22] Of these six or seven neighbors, Van indicates that he recognizes all of them whenever he sees them and that he greets them whenever "it seems right." He talks with some of them "once or twice a month—but only the men." Without any affect, Van adds, "I don't bother with the women." He says he knows the names of three of the men, but only the name of one of the women, even though one of the unnamed women has been his neighbor for more than ten years and Van knows her husband rather well.

As a handyman, Van has been in the dwellings of all of his neighbors in order to make minor repairs.

> I guess they sometimes ask me to fix something in their homes for them. Lots of people in town do that. We don't visit each other

except when we are outside in our yards. Then we just talk a little. It's more a "hi" and "good-bye" kind of thing. Sometimes we might see each other at church or at the Rialto and play cards. We don't plan on it. It's like that with other people in town—at least with the men. It's not whether they live near me or not. It's that we just see each other around town.

This disposition towards neighbors carries over into Van's answer about the importance of neighbors. "I don't know how to answer that one. I guess I don't have to have neighbors. I don't spend time with them much because I'll see them in town or at the Rialto. I guess all six of them are good enough as neighbors. They don't cause me any problems or have wild parties or things like that."

Van's (and Vanna's) responses are included in this chapter because they represent some of the people of St. John who are neither advocates for nor critics of social life in St. John. Van seems to be living in St. John because it is where he happens to be. Life is tolerable for him in St. John, but certainly not exciting or rewarding. He does not see moving away from St. John "unless maybe the cost of housing got a lot lower over on the coast"—something that he does not expect to happen.

As to Vanna, she seems happy to be able to return to St. John each year to visit and "catch-up with old friends and on new gossip." She has no regrets about the years she lived in St. John while finishing high school. She does not indicate any desire to live here again.

As a postscript of sorts, consider this: A few minutes after leaving Van and Vanna on his porch, I encountered him on the corner of Main Street on his way to the Rialto Tavern. It was 3:30 p.m. on a weekday afternoon. We watched a freight train with more than sixty cars loaded with wheat slowly pass through St. John on its way to a shipping terminal on the Columbia River. Van nodded when I greeted him. I mentioned the passing train. He showed no more interest in it than in anything else we had discussed. Then he walked slowly across Main Street and disappeared into the Rialto. The train full of wheat rolled out of St. John into a landscape waving in golden wheat as far as the horizon, and beyond.

Heidi Hopewell: Getting by on the Margins of St. John Society

A small but growing number of St. John's in-town residents are people of modest means, on fixed incomes, or on one or more government assistance programs. They have moved to St. John, or back to St. John, primarily for the inexpensive housing that can be rented on a short-term basis. Some of these people are older women and a few men who have been left adrift by divorce, separation, or the death of their companions. Some of them can no longer drive or afford cars. Some others want freedom from or nearness to their relatives who live elsewhere in the Palouse. Others are people in their late teens and twenties, single moms, cohabiting couples, and a few young marrieds who ran into trouble with illnesses, job losses, drugs, violence, and other hazards in Spokane, Seattle, and other cities.

One of these people is a young mother in her twenties whom I will call Heidi Hopewell. She is a petite, polite, young woman who carefully cradles her infant in her arms while she gets to know us. During our hour-long conversation, her husband, a gangly, pleasant fellow dressed as a cowboy, comes into the cafe, says "hello" to Heidi and to the table of ladies who are sitting there drinking coffee, and leaves without introductions. Heidi tells us that she and her husband had difficulties with living conditions in a nearby city. They moved to St. John a few years ago for the low-cost housing and to be near some of his relatives. They have moved several times already within St. John whenever larger units become available that they can afford. Heidi indicates that they are struggling financially but that they certainly like St. John better than their previous situations. "We are trying to give our baby everything we didn't have when we were growing up. St. John seems like a good place to try to do that. But it hasn't been easy here, either. Jobs don't pay as much as in the city. We are dreaming that maybe someday we can afford to buy our own home here."

Asked what she likes best about St. John, Heidi says: "The schools are good here and this is a good place to raise kids. There are no gangs, violence, or drug problems here. The rents are real low, maybe $250 for a trailer and maybe $400 for a two bedroom house. There are some real nice people here, too."

Heidi is hesitant about mentioning any negative features of St. John. Eventually, she says, rather quietly:

> Some of the people here were nice at first. They brought us food and things for our place. But then they put you in categories that aren't very nice, just because we don't have money or a name that's important around here. It also seems like some people start rumors about you even if the haven't met you and they don't know you. And then there's the town's siren that goes off at noontime— it sounds like a war siren. It's so loud it scares the baby. The dust storms here are pretty bad, like the one we had yesterday. The dust blows right around the doors and windows into the house. And it gets really hot here, too. Just like now. What is it outside: 107 or 108? The place we are living in doesn't have air-conditioning. It's just as hot inside as outside. It's hard on the baby.

Despite these drawbacks, Heidi quickly answers that St. John is the best place that she has even lived and that she already feels closer to St. John than to any other community. She mentions that she wishes people would spend more time visiting one another outdoors and at their homes instead of watching so much TV, playing video games, and text messaging on their cell phones.

> It's kind of stupid, you know. People my own age spend so much time alone with these little electronic things. They are so small and hard to use anyway. Why can't people take the time to talk with each other more and make phone calls, write letters like they used to do? They don't spend time anymore talking with their families and with the people around them. This is what I miss most about how things were years ago.

Heidi adds that she often takes her baby in a stroller for walks around town during the day. She tries to meet new people and make friends as she goes along. Besides her husband and baby, only a few close relatives live in St. John. Eight to ten other close relatives live elsewhere in the nearby counties. Heidi feels that she already has ten fairly close friends here in St. John. "Only one of them is really close, I guess. We do a lot of things together with our babies." Another ten close friends reside in the city where Heidi lived until a few years ago.

Heidi discloses she really never had good neighbors until she moved to St. John. Now she feels that she has about twenty, even though she and her husband have only lived in their current residence for less than one year. She estimates that she says "hello" to ten or fifteen of these twenty neighbors. She knows the names of all of them and she has daily talks with some of them when she encounters them on her walkabouts around town. "I'm out walking my baby and riding my bike all the time, so I meet anyone who will talk with us." With a slight hint of annoyance, Heidi remarks that "[e]verybody here knows your name and business even before we have met them. They even know my baby's name. I'm not sure that I like that."

Heidi has friendly talks with five or six of her neighbors fairly frequently, and she estimates that five of them have told her about their personal problems. She exchanges or borrows things, "mainly magazines and stuff," with about five of her neighbors, "mainly with my best friend, Britney." Heidi says that she does not really visit them inside their homes so much as outside along the streets and in their yards. She only entertains and goes places with one of her neighbors. "We take our babies on walks together to the park or we drive over to the mall in Colfax when we have a car."

Heidi reports a strong appreciation for good neighbors. "I never had them before over in the other places I lived. So I think they are important. They can help you with health problems and with housework and repairs and childcare if you need help. They can check on your windows and doors when you are gone." Heidi adds that the most important quality of good neighbors is "respect. If you tell them something, then it's really important that they respect you and not go and tell the whole town about it. It's nice if they are friendly, too; but the respect is more important."

Summing up, Heidi Hopewell seems to be trying hard to be a good neighbor and to find a decent place for her husband and child in St. John's status system, but her youth, limited income, health problems, and short tenure in St. John are challenging her sense of social well-being. Let us hope that St. John will help Heidi and her young family thrive, as did so many of its other inhabitants over the last one hundred years.

*   *   *

And now, keeping in mind the preceding accounts of our interviews with people of Buffalo Creek, Elk Creek, and St. John, we will compare and contrast a larger number of respondents from these three places regarding the quantity and quality of their social relations.

COMPARING BUFFALO CREEK, ELK CREEK, AND ST. JOHN

How different are the respondents of Buffalo Creek, Elk Creek, and St. John in the quality and quantity of their social relationships and their attitudes towards social life in their communities? Are the respondents from Buffalo Creek deficient in ways that reveal the continuing legacy of the flood of 1972?

Tables 5.12 through 5.16 in appendix B present comparative data from the respondents from these three places on basically the same topics that we have been considering throughout chapter 4 and the preceding parts of this chapter. As might be expected, we found that Buffalo Creek and Elk Creek are very similar in their demographic characteristics. By contrast, the data for St. John reveal that its respondents are somewhat different from their counterparts in Buffalo Creek and Elk Creek in terms of the percentage who are female (76 percent), average age (fifty-six), the percentage who are lifelong residents (35 percent), and respondents with at least ten close relative and ten close friends who reside there (19 percent). This is in keeping with the historical profile of St. John earlier in this chapter. St. John's respondents have fewer close relatives and close friends living in their town, in contrast to their counterparts in Buffalo Creek and Elk Creek. St. John's respondents are more female and elderly. It is likely that these characteristics are the result of St. John having become both a retirement community and a refuge for people who are trying to escape the higher costs and social problems of Spokane, Pullman, and other cities in the region. Widows of deceased farmers move into town for their final years. Recently retired couples move to St. John for the public golf course and swimming pool and for the low cost of house lots, new homes, taxes, and just about everything else. Cheap rental apartments and old cottages attract low-income couples who have had economic, health, and social problems in the cities. For these reasons alone, we might expect that, even without a disaster like the flood of 1972 in St. John's history, its residents and these respondents might have fewer opportunities to be neighborly and socially integrated than do the respondents of Buffalo Creek and Elk Creek. And yet, the demographic similarities among the respondents of Buffalo Creek, Elk Creek, and St. John probably outweigh the differences. The respondents of all three places are rather old and female. They have lived in these places and in their current dwellings long enough to have neighborly relations, to be socially integrated into their communities, and to have a considerable amount of social well-being. Strong majorities of the respondents in all three places have lived in their current dwellings for at least ten years. Less than one-third of the respondents have lived in their current dwellings for less than ten years. Surely, these percentages indicate to us that there is considerable residential stability among the respondents in all three communities. These are not people who are so displeased with their residences and their communities that they leave them. Would this be the case if Buffalo Creek was utterly and permanently transformed by the flood of 1972?

Many of the respondents at all three places—but especially at Buffalo Creek—report that they have ten or more close relatives and ten or more close friends who reside in their hometown, or more than three close relatives and three close friends who reside in their hometown. Less than one-third of the respondents at each of the places report having three or fewer close relatives and three or fewer close friends in these places. These data thereby support the inference that the respondents in these three places, including Buffalo Creek, have far more close friends and close relatives than do many people in other places in the United States. Consider, for example, a study by sociologists Miller McPherson and Lynn Smith-Lovin. They examined data from the National Opinion Research

Center at the University of Chicago that involved a large national sample of Americans in the year 2000.[23] The respondents in their study claimed to have an average of only two "close friends" anywhere in the world—not just in their hometown! By contrast, we found that the average number of "close friends" reported by Buffalo Creek's respondents was 9.4. The comparable numbers of close friends reported by respondents from Elk Creek was 8.7, and for St. John it was 6.6. While our study does not use exactly the same questions and research procedures as does the other study, it is nonetheless very likely that respondents from Buffalo Creek, Elk Creek, and St. John are above the U.S. norm regarding the quantity of social relations with close friends. And thus, it seems reasonable for us to conclude that Buffalo Creek's respondents have far more close friends than do residents of many other places in the United States. Again, this conclusion is hardly what we would expect regarding a place that suffered so much damage in 1972 as Buffalo Creek.

Attitudes About Living in These Places
The data in table 5.13 of appendix B generally indicate that respondents from Buffalo Creek are *not* unusual, let alone negative, in their attitudes about living there. For example, 94 percent of the respondents from Buffalo Creek report that they feel closest to their village or hamlet along Buffalo Creek, or to Buffalo Creek as a whole. Not only is this percentage nearly optimal, but it is considerably higher than for Elk Creek (67 percent) and for St. John (76 percent).

On one hand, Buffalo Creek's respondents also are not very distinctive, let alone negative, as to what they like best and least about living where they live. On the other hand, St. John's respondents score relatively high on the quality of liking the friends or people of their community. St. John's respondents are very positive and distinctive in this way, and yet they are not so distinctive regarding the other qualities that they like least about their community. And so, it seems apropos to believe that the respondents from Buffalo Creek, Elk Creek, and St. John are quite similar as to what qualities they like *best* about their respective communities.

This same point also is true of the qualities that the respondents like *least* about their communities. The most common "complaint"—let us call it for convenience—for all of the respondents is that their communities are "far from" shopping and other services. Surely, this complaint is not very surprising, given that all three communities are rural communities (some city dwellers and cynics might even say "very" or "utterly" rural communities). Even so, however, less than 40 percent of the respondents in these three places proffer this complaint. Of course, the more relevant finding for us is that only very small percentages of respondents in the three places complain about neighbors or about some other quality that is lacking in the community such as cohesiveness, cooperativeness, or spirit. Interestingly, 19 percent of the respondents of St. John complained that their community was lacking in qualities such as these. The missing quality that they mentioned most often was "privacy" (as we heard in the testimony of several residents of St. John in a preceding section of this chapter). Often St. John respondents laughed with a touch of embarrassment when they mentioned this lack of privacy. They related it to the small-town atmosphere and to the tendency of St. John's people to be a little "nosey" and "gossipy." Several times, respondents laughed and expressed mild annoyance to me: "Seems like I'm often the last person to know *my own* business around here!"

For the most part, the differences are slight among respondents in the three communities regarding qualities that they missed the most in these places from years ago. Very small percentages of St. John's respondents indicated that they miss much of anything from St. John's past. These low percentages for St. John probably result from the fact that many of St. John's respondents are not lifelong residents of St. John. Quite a few of them (fourteen of the forty-two respondents, in fact) are widows who moved into St. John after they and their late husbands sold or bequeathed their family farms and retired. Nonetheless, the percentages of St. John's respondents who indicated that they missed qualities of their "neighbors" or their "community" from years past (2 percent and 12 percent, respectively) are somewhat lower than the comparable percentages for Elk Creek (5 percent and 24 percent) and for Buffalo Creek (7 percent and

20 percent). Unfortunately, we cannot say whether these differences in percentages, however small, can be attributed to the continuing effects of the flood of 1972 on Buffalo Creek's respondents, to the fact that many of St. John's respondents are less aware of social conditions years ago in St. John, or to some other factor. The fact that 31 percent of St. John's respondents indicated that they missed nothing from the past in St. John, or they indicated that they "can't say," probably reflects another fact— namely, that quite a few of the respondents (about 25 percent) had moved into the "downtown" area of St. John within the past few years.[24]

In sum, with but a few exceptions that are probably minor or negligible, we found that Buffalo Creek's respondents are not very different from Elk Creek's and St. John's respondents in their attitudes about their "hometown," so to speak. If the flood of 1972 was as destructive as portrayed by many of the authors who wrote about it years ago, that destructiveness is not very apparent in contemporary respondents from Buffalo Creek. Once again, the social re-creation perspective seems more applicable than the social destruction perspective concerning Buffalo Creek as a contemporary social community.

Neighbors and Neighboring
We found similar patterns when we compared these three places in terms of neighbors and neighboring, although there are a few exceptions of note. Data in table 5.14 of appendix B reveal that Buffalo Creek's respondents reported slightly fewer neighbors, on the average, than the respondents of Elk Creek and St. John. And yet, the percentages of respondents with ten or more neighbors are identical across the three communities. It is St. John's respondents—not Buffalo Creek's—who have fewer than five neighbors on the average. Once again, this lower number for St. John probably reflects the fact that a larger percentage of St. John's respondents have only lived in St. John for a few years since they retired. It has become a very popular place to retire, in part because local business leaders have had the foresight and the skill to advertise St. John as a great place to retire.

As to basic familiarity and socializing with neighbors, Buffalo Creek's respondents are just as neighborly as the other respondents, occasionally even more so. Buffalo Creek's respondents have the highest percentages of respondents who claim familiarity with all of their neighbors, of socializing with all of their neighbors at least occasionally, and of socializing occasionally with more than a few of their neighbors. These facts also are in keeping with the social re-creation perspective. Somewhat surprisingly, relatively more respondents from St. John (17 percent) than from Buffalo Creek (6 percent) and Elk Creek (0 percent) reported that they rarely or never socialize with their neighbors in any of the ways under consideration (as indicated in table 5.14). Based on these patterns, it seems judicious to contend that Buffalo Creek's respondents are just as active and positive as the other respondents when it comes to familiarity and socializing with their neighbors, if not more so.

This assertion also applies to all of the respondents in all three places regarding the most important quality of neighbors, and to the importance of neighbors to them. Specifically, respondents reveal similar levels of concern about having neighbors to help them in "crisis situations," to protect their property in their absence, to be friendly, and other positive qualities. In addition to this, Buffalo Creek's respondents are not unusual in claiming that their neighbors are "very important" or "real important" to them. Then again, and speaking comparatively, Buffalo Creek's respondents are somewhat more likely to appreciate neighbors who are trustworthy, reliable, and honest. They are a little less likely to appreciate neighbors who will be their friends, intimates, and confidants. They also are not very concerned about negative qualities in their neighbors such as nosiness and gossiping.

Therefore, as with so many of the other response categories that have been considered so far in this chapter, it seems reasonable to believe that the damages of the flood and its secondary effects no longer distinguish Buffalo Creek's respondents from their counterparts at Elk Creek or St. John as far as neighboring and neighborly relations are concerned.

References to Disasters

Was the Buffalo Creek flood of 1972 mentioned by any of the respondents from Elk Creek? Did respondents from Elk Creek and St. John mention *any* disasters at all? Did they use the word "disaster" or any synonyms, such as "catastrophe" or "tragedy?" The data presented in table 5.15 of appendix B endorse negative answers to all of these questions. None of the respondents of Elk Creek or St. John ever mentioned the Buffalo Creek flood or any other floods or disasters. They never used the word "disaster" or synonyms for it.

Of course, these findings are in contrast to Buffalo Creek's respondents, to some extent. As explained in a preceding section of this chapter, 22 percent of Buffalo Creek's respondents made reference to the flood (but to no other disasters). Two percent of them did so at least four times. A few of them were very conscious of the flood during our interviews with them, even though we tried our best to avoid the topic of the flood. And yet, 78 percent of Buffalo Creek's respondents did *not* refer to the flood or to any other disasters. Readers are encouraged to draw their own conclusions from these data. My belief is that Buffalo Creek's respondents are somewhat different from the others in this regard—but *not* decisively so. Over 75 percent of them are just like their counterparts in Elk Creek and St. John, none of whom made reference to any disasters.

Now, regarding the respondents of Elk Creek and St. John, allow me to mention that I found the data in table 5.15 to be somewhat surprising in at least two ways. One relates to Elk Creek. The other relates to St. John.

I expected that at least a few of Elk Creek's respondents would have used words like "disaster" and that they would have referred to some of the many floods of the Guyadotte River as disasters, if not specifically to the flood of Buffalo Creek in 1972. I say this because Buffalo Creek is only ten miles away from Elk Creek and both of them are more or less "perched along" the much larger Guyandotte River—which floods often, destructively, and sometimes lethally. Except for riders of "all-terrain vehicles" (ATVs), most of Elk Creek's residents cannot leave Elk Creek by motor vehicle without driving within thirty meters of the Guyandotte River. They see it directly in front of them every time they leave and return to Elk Creek. In order to drive to Logan, the county seat, or to Charleston, the state capital, and the only "big city" in the lexicon of most of the local people, Elk Creek's respondents are obliged to drive at least twenty-five miles along the muddy Guyandotte River. In doing so, they must traverse the creek of Buffalo Creek at Man, about eight miles downriver. Surely, we could expect that all of these factors would have produced a high level of consciousness of floods and of disasters among Elk Creek's respondents. And yet, they did not manifest this during the interviews that we had with them. This outcome surprised me all the more for two other reasons. As implied by its name, Elk Creek has its own creek. That creek bisects Elk Creek in such a way that most residents see the creek whenever they look out their front windows and whenever they drive to and from their homes. Although the creek of Elk Creek is only about one half as wide as the creek of Buffalo Creek, and it usually runs shallow, clear, and quiet, a day or two of heavy rain can turn this creek into a fast flush of raging, muddy water that alarms me, if not the local folks. In addition to this possible "disaster factor," active coal mining operations along Elk Creek ceased during the years that I was conducting interviews there. As indicated in the interviews with Elk Creek respondents earlier in this chapter, several of the respondents mentioned that they had lost their jobs in the mines. I would not have been surprised to hear them refer to these changes as being disasters, catastrophes, or crises. However, this was not the case. Elk Creek's respondents did not refer to events as disasters. They did not manifest what might be called a "disaster consciousness," let alone an obsession about disasters.

I also expected that at least a few of the old-timers at St. John would have used the word "disaster" or synonyms for it. I also expected that some of them would have made reference to some of the many destructive forces of nature for which eastern Washington State is famous: cyclones, flash floods, lightning-ignited fires flaming across thousands of acres of parched wheat fields in late summer, and, most of all, by sudden, blinding dust storms, the likes of which are permanently etched in my memory. And yet, none of the respondents of St. John referred to these often destructive and sometimes lethal meteorological events as "disasters." Six of the forty-two respondents did mention that dust storms were among the features that they liked least about residing in St. John. Probably, this happened because dust storms were dramatic and frequent in the month of August when we were in St. John conducting our interviews.[25]

Social Integration and Social Well-Being

Are Buffalo Creek's respondents decidedly disadvantaged in their levels of social integration and social well-being when compared with their counterparts along Elk Creek and St. John? There are two answers to this question, based on the data in table 5.16 of appendix B. Each of the answers requires some qualifications. Buffalo Creek's respondents are not disadvantaged when compared with their counterparts along Elk Creek, except in the cases of three respondents from Buffalo Creek. Admittedly, the respondents of both Buffalo Creek and Elk Creek are somewhat behind the respondents of St. John when it comes to scoring *very high* on social integration and social well-being—but not in other ways.

By way of explanation of these answers, we found that slightly larger percentages of Buffalo Creek's respondents score higher than Elk Creek's respondents on social integration and social well-being. However, offsetting this advantage to Buffalo Creek's respondents, to some extent, is the fact that very small percentages of Buffalo Creek's respondents score very low on social integration and social well-being, while none of Elk Creek's respondents score this low on either factor. In other words, except for two or three of Buffalo Creek's respondents who are very isolated or alienated, and who are very low on social well-being, Buffalo Creek's respondents are doing as well as Elk Creek's respondents in these aspects of their social relations—if not slightly better.

Furthermore, the respondents of Buffalo Creek and Elk Creek generally are similar to the respondents of St. John—with but two exceptions. Larger percentages of St. John's respondents score "very high" on social integration (33 percent) and social well-being (29 percent) than do Buffalo Creek's respondents (20 percent and 13 percent, respectively) and

Elk Creek's respondents (19 percent and 10 percent, respectively). In thinking further about these differences, let me suggest that this rather small advantage of St. John's respondents is offset by the fact that slightly smaller percentages of St. John's other respondents score "high" on social integration and on social well-being. In other words, St. John's respondents do better in scoring *very high* on these two factors, but respondents from Buffalo Creek and Elk Creek do better in scoring *high* on these same factors. We also found that the percentages of respondents who score "moderate" or "mixed" on social integration and on social well-being are very similar in all three localities.

Taken as a whole, then, our findings lead us to believe that St. John's respondents might be somewhat more socially integrated and have more social well-being than Elk Creek's and Buffalo Creek's respondents, but the respondents of Buffalo Creek are not obviously deficient in these regards, especially when they are compared with their counterparts at Elk Creek.

HAS COMMUNITY BEEN RE-CREATED ALONG BUFFALO CREEK?

Looking back over the dozens of findings that have been presented in this chapter, it is rather obvious that the people of Buffalo Creek, Elk Creek, and St. John provide us with plenty of evidence that neighboring, social integration, and social well-being are substantial in all three of these places. Buffalo Creek does *not* lag behind Elk Creek and St. John on any of these factors to an appreciable extent. Often it actually matches these other places or exceeds them in the quality and the quantity of social relations that we have examined. How is it possible that Buffalo Creek could be doing this well only thirty-five years or so after the disaster of 1972? Perhaps one of the two perspectives that we have been applying since chapter 2 can help us answer this question.

The social destruction perspective would lead us to expect that most respondents from Buffalo Creek would manifest the extraordinary destruction of social life and social well-being that is said to have been caused by the flood and by its secondary effects. It would also lead us to expect that a place like St. John, which has not suffered a disaster as cat-aclysmic as the Buffalo Creek flood of 1972, would be decidedly higher than Buffalo Creek on social integration, neighboring, social well-being, and perhaps every aspect of social life. Clearly, this has not been the case, based on the data presented in this chapter. Perhaps the flood did not damage social life along Buffalo Creek as thoroughly as reported by some authors. Perhaps social life has somehow been re-created substan-tially since then. And, quite possibly, perhaps both of these eventualities are true.

How about the social re-creation perspective? Do the data in table 5.16 and the other tables in appendix B convincingly support it?

Perhaps Buffalo Creek had much higher levels of neighboring, social integration, and social well-being before the flood than the levels that are indicated in table 5.16 for recent years. Perhaps 80 or 90 percent of its people would have scored very high on all of these factors if they had been interviewed in January 1972. Perhaps the flood "dropped" the very high scores on social well-being, let us say, on all but about 13 percent of Buffalo Creek's residents. If so, then it did not drop them very far—given that 13 percent of the respondents score "very high," 39 percent score high, 38 percent score moderate or mixed, and only 10 percent score low or very low on social well-being.

Therefore, it seems likely that the most valid answer to the question about the applicability of the social re-creation perspective to Buffalo Creek is a guarded "yes," based on the following logic. Consider that, as described by the authors whose works were reviewed in chapters 1 and 2, Buffalo Creek's residents before the flood of 1972 would have scored much higher on neighboring, social integration, and social well-being than did the respondents of Buffalo Creek whose scores are pre-sented throughout this chapter. Many experts described pre-flood Buffalo Creek as being a vibrant, productive, highly integrated social community where neighboring was extensive and most people felt very good about their social lives. Also consider that, as described by the authors whose works were reviewed in chapters 1 and 2, the flood was so devastating in the days, weeks, months, and years after the flood that many, if not all, of Buffalo Creek's survivors would have scored much lower on neighboring, social integration, and social well-being than the respondents of Buffalo Creek whose scores are presented throughout this chapter. As many of those authors described it, Buffalo Creek was utterly devastated, if not totally destroyed, as a social community. The flood washed out and then washed away "everything in its path," literally and figuratively. Mental health and social well-being plummeted. Survivors no longer cared about themselves or about one another.

Now, if the two preceding suppositions are valid, then the data that have been analyzed throughout this chapter reveal that social conditions along Buffalo Creek have improved substantially, but not totally, for Buffalo Creek's respondents since the flood. Sixty-five percent of Buffalo Creek's respondents are very highly or highly integrated into Buffalo Creek. Conceivably, the percentage could be higher—as high as 100 percent, perhaps. And yet, how many places in the United States can claim that more than 65 percent of their residents are highly integrated into their community as a whole? And how many places in the United States can claim that at least 52 percent of their residents have high social well-being?

Admittedly, these questions are rhetorical. My answer is "very few." I have searched the literature on contemporary hamlets, villages, towns, and cities in the United States. Many of the empirical studies—but certainly not all of them—portray many of these places as having lost a lot of the qualities that characterized them before the 1950s, including highly satisfying levels of neighboring, cohesion, social integration, and social well-being.[26] In fact, St. John is one of the more noteworthy exceptions to this rather depressing sociological template. This observation is underscored by the fact that the title of the book about St. John is *Against All Odds: Rural Community in the Information Age*. This is exactly the reason why I have included St. John in this report.

And so, it seems appropriate to conclude that, in all likelihood, an impressive amount of neighboring, social integration, and social well-being has been re-created along Buffalo Creek since the flood of 1972. Let me add that, if this was not the case, then, if nothing else, more than one of the ninety-five respondents from Buffalo Creek would have mentioned to me that he or she was sorry to be residing there still, after all of these years. More than one of the respondents would have complained that Buffalo Creek never has recovered anything. And more than one of the respondents would have attested that the flood took away "everything in its path" and that nothing has ever returned—despite the fact that she did return and spend the rest of her life along Buffalo Creek.

Therefore, it is reasonable for us to conclude that a great deal of community, of neighboring, and of social well-being has been re-created along Buffalo Creek since 1972. The creek still runs through Buffalo Creek's hamlets and villages. So does a lot of social life that is well worth knowing about—and appreciating.

ENDNOTES

1. Chapter 4 presents detailed information from and about twenty-two former, recent, and current residents along Buffalo Creek whom we interviewed since 2000. Twenty of these twenty-two interviewees were still living along Buffalo Creek when we interviewed them. The other two interviewees resided along Buffalo Creek at the time of the flood but never resided there again after their homes were destroyed in the flood. Both of them still live within ten miles of Buffalo Creek, however, and they say that they occasionally visit some of their relatives along Buffalo Creek.

2. To extrapolate from our descriptions of these two perspectives in chapter 2, consider that if the *social destruction perspective* is correct when applied to Buffalo Creek, then the flood of 1972 was overwhelmingly destructive to Buffalo Creek's people and to Buffalo Creek as a social community—just as it was portrayed in many of the mass media and by many of the authors. It was so destructive that all of the ninety-five respondents, or certainly the vast majority of them, will manifest low levels of neighboring, social integration, and social well-being. This will be especially true of the flood's victims. This also will be true, although possibly less strongly so, of witnesses who were not victims, and even the people who were born after the flood and people who moved to Buffalo Creek after the flood—for all of these people frequently are "contaminated," so to speak, by the negative cultural legacy of the flood that is transmitted to them, often unwittingly, from so many sources: other survivors, idle gossip, rumors, folktales, folk songs, and stories that they hear at church, school, parties, and on street corners, television, radio, and the Internet. By contrast, the residents of Elk Creek, West Virginia, and St. John, Washington, should manifest much higher levels of positive social relations because they have not experienced disasters so overwhelming as the flood of 1972. Then again, respondents from Elk Creek might be more similar to Buffalo Creek's respondents than St. John's respondents because Elk Creek is only ten miles from Buffalo Creek, both are situated along the Guyandotte River in Logan County, and the negative cultural legacy of the flood of 1972 at Buffalo Creek is likely to "spill over" to Elk Creek to some extent.

    On the other hand, if the social re-creation perspective is more correct than the social destruction perspective, the flood, and second-order damages that resulted from it, may or may not have been as destructive as portrayed by some of the mass media and experts who researched it. In either case, the damages are not nearly so pernicious and enduring as alleged by the social destruction perspective. This might be the case if the flood created common adversities and needs for most of the residents of Buffalo Creek who survived it and did not move away permanently from Buffalo Creek. Many of these survivors came to understand and appreciate these commonalities, as did many of the leaders of agencies, voluntary associations, and interest groups inside and outside Buffalo Creek. Many cooperative responses occurred that eventually led to the "re-creation" of appreciable amounts of neighboring, social integration, and social well-being along Buffalo Creek. Examples of these responses include the Buffalo Creek Citizens' Committee that hired the law firm of Arnold & Porter (as mentioned in chapters 1 and 2). And so, it is that the social re-creation perspective leads us to expect that Buffalo Creek's ninety-five respondents will manifest rather high levels of positive social relations. It is also likely that the flood's victims and witnesses have benefited from this re-creation of community, although possibly somewhat less so than nonwitnesses. As a result of this benefit, victims and witnesses are not radically different in social relations when compared with nonwitnesses, let alone wholly disadvantaged. Going even further with the re-creation perspective, Buffalo Creek's ninety-five respondents will not be very different or wholly disadvantaged when compared with respondents from nearby Elk Creek. They might even be similar in social relations to respondents from a location so far away in place, terrain, and economy as St. John, Washington, despite the many damages that they suffered more than three decades ago in the flood of 1972.

3. Copies of the "Community and Neighboring Questionnaire," the "Authors' Assertions about Buffalo Creek" form, and other instruments that were used in the research reported here are available from the author by written request.

4. As explained in chapter 4 and in appendix A, our selection process uses elements of what some sociologists refer to as "purposive" sampling and what some anthropologists refer to as "judgment" or "judgmental" sampling, rather than random sampling. On these types of sampling designs and their uses, refer to Delbert C. Miller, *Handbook of Research Design and Social Measurements*, 5th ed. (Newbury Park, CA: Sage, 1991), 60–64; Bernard S. Phillips, *Social Research Strategy and Tactics*. 2nd ed. (New York: The Macmillan Company, 1971), 94–96; and John J. Honigmann, "Sampling in Ethnographic Field Work," chap. 15 in *A Handbook of Method in Cultural Anthropology*, ed. Raoul Naroll and Ronald Cohen (New York: Columbia University Press, 1973), 266–279. One of the reasons for this is that

longtime residents of Buffalo Creek and Elk Creek are reluctant to allow researchers into their homes for face-to-face conversations and interviews unless they are introduced to them or they are referred to them by other residents whom they trust. This is a common phenomenon in relatively small, rural, and remote communities. As a result of the selection process we used, we can say a lot about social context and the people we interviewed, but we cannot generalize definitively to the entire populations of Buffalo Creek, Elk Creek, and St. John. In order to gain depth and richness of understanding, we sacrifice some generalizability. However, it is worth knowing that nonprobability sampling and probability sampling have been shown to produce similar results when used in relatively small, homogenous communities and when used within several relatively homogenous strata, cohorts, groups, and aggregates (see Honigmann, "Sampling in Ethnographic Field Work," 278–279). Buffalo Creek, Elk Creek, and (perhaps to a lesser extent) St. John are relatively small, homogenous communities with rather homogenous strata, groups, and cohorts.

5. Basic demographic data are not available for Buffalo Creek or for any of its sixteen former coal camps because they are unincorporated places, and the camps are part of at least two different census tracts. Census data for Logan County, which includes Buffalo Creek, indicate that the median age of the population in 2000 was thirty-nine years and that females constituted about 55 percent of the population. See "Logan County, West Virginia," *Wikipedia, the Free Encyclopedia*, 2007, http://en.wikipedia.org/wiki/Logan_County,_ WestVirginia (accessed April 25, 2007). Part of the population of the Buffalo Creek Valley belongs to the "Amherstdale-Robinette CDP." The U.S. Census for 2000 indicates the median age in this census tract is 39.1 years and that females constitute about 52 percent of the population (U.S. Census Bureau, *County and City Data Book 2000: A Statistical Abstract Supplement (County and City Data Book)*, 13th ed. (Washington, DC: Dept. of Commerce, Bureau of the Census, 2001), see "West Virginia: 2000, Summary of Population and Housing Characteristics," table 1). While our sets of respondents at Buffalo Creek and Elk Creek are older and more female than the population of Logan County as a whole, it is important to keep in mind that we selected respondents for purposes other than to be able to generalize definitively to the entire populations of Buffalo Creek and Elk Creek.

6. By the way, you might notice that the percentages in each of the sets of rows 3a–f, 4a–f, and 5a–e of table 5.2 cumulate to more than 100 percent. This is because they indicate the percentages of the ninety-five respondents whose responses fit into each of the categories. Respondents were not limited to

one category of response. This also is true of response patterns in many of the other tables in appendix B.

7. Respondents who reported going places with their neighbors often added that they went together to church services with one or two of their neighbors, sometimes as often as three or four times a week. This is a common practice along Buffalo Creek, where there are at least fifteen small churches (the number of churches seems to fluctuate every year) that hold services at least twice a week, often on Wednesday and Saturday evenings, as well as on Sundays.

8. None of the ninety-five respondents made reference to any "disaster" other than the flood of 1972. The most important finding in the table is that 78 percent of the respondents did not refer to the flood or to any other disaster at any time (row 2c).

9. As explained in the glossary and elsewhere, social well-being is a more inclusive concept than social integration. It takes into account all of the responses and comments that each respondent provided on the questionnaire and during the conversations and interviews that we had with them over a period of six years, 2000–2006. Social well-being scores in the table reflect how each of the respondents felt about their social lives along Buffalo Creek when we communicated with them. Social integration scores in the table reflect the quantity and quality of social relationships that each of the respondents reported having with other people, groups, and organizations in and around Buffalo Creek: family members, neighbors, friends, churches, schools, voluntary associations, and businesses. These two variables can be somewhat independent from each other, as when a person such as Woody Mercer or Tina Miner (as described in chapter 4) has a very low sense of social well-being, despite being fairly well integrated into Buffalo Creek. It is also possible for a person to have a high sense of social well-being even though he or she is not extensively integrated into the community. Examples of this kind of person are Mabel Church, Leroy Diggs, and Arnie Canfield, as described in chapter 4. This situation sometimes appears with middle-aged and elderly people who are physically healthy, independent, and not particularly gregarious. Perhaps they are considered by many people to be "loners." And yet, they are contented, even highly satisfied, with their social situation even though they are not highly integrated into the community as a whole. This does not mean that they are totally alone—without any family or friends—although they might be. What it means is that they do not have many social relations and bonds throughout the community. They are not highly socially integrated into Buffalo Creek. This does not necessarily bother them greatly. It does not necessarily

encroach on their sense of self-worth, happiness, and satisfaction with life. In fact, some of these people claim that they take pride in having few social relationships. For example, one respondent told me, "I'm mostly alone, that's true. But that don't mean I'm lonely. Just alone." Another one told me, "I get along real good with just me, myself, and I."

By the way, readers who are keenly interested in the relationship between social integration and social well-being might want to refer to table 5.6 in appendix B for a statistical estimate of this relationship.

10. While it might sound insensitive on my part, I have the sense that Vera might have misunderstood the purpose of the questionnaire even though none of the questions mention the flood and the questions are not designed to elicit statements about the flood. Yet, in her very old age, depressed state, and failing health, Vera might have assumed that there was a "hidden agenda" that related to the flood. She might have reverted to the kinds of statements that she had made or heard in her conversations with some other residents of Buffalo Creek many years ago. Admittedly, these are speculations on my part which, unfortunately, I have not been able to probe because Vera is not willing to be interviewed further. Having written this, however, I also have no doubt that memories of the flood continue to haunt Vera, and that the flood damaged her life profoundly and permanently.

11. Several of Jimmy Joe Rooker's peers and neighbors portrayed him as he portrayed himself—rather isolated and alienated, but also rather candid and truthful.

12. Beyond this, the considerable differences in the percentages across row 5a of table 5.7 probably reflect the fact that only 20 percent of the victims (cell A5a) have resided in their current dwelling for at least thirty years because many victims had to relocate after the flood in 1972. This was less true of the witnesses, 60 percent of whom (cell B5a) have been able to reside in their current dwelling for at least thirty years because the flood did not force them to relocate. By the same token, none of the nonwitnesses (0 percent—cell D5a) have resided in their current dwelling for at least thirty years because this category consists of people who are younger than thirty years of age; people who established their own residences along Buffalo Creek as they matured, got jobs, got married, and settled down; and people who moved to Buffalo Creek from other parts of West Virginia and the United States.

13. This is the reason that the percentages in each column (A through E) of rows 5a–g in table 5.9 cumulate to more than 100 percent.

14. On these population estimates, see *The World Almanac and Book of Facts* (New York: World Almanac Books, 2006), 204, 473, 475 passim.

15. Rows 3a–e of table 5.11 display the estimates of the social well-being of the respondents in all of the categories. In interpreting these data, we should keep in mind the facts that victims and witnesses are considerably older than the other respondents (average ages are sixty-five, sixty-three, fifty-eight, and twenty-nine , respectively, as shown in table 5.7), and that, for many or most people, social well-being surely is influenced heavily (but not completely) by physical well-being. Since this is the case, we should expect that victims and witnesses would score somewhat lower on social well-being even if they had not been victims of and witnesses to the flood. Many of them are old, and they are in declining health, based on the interviews that I conducted with dozens of them in their homes.

The data in rows 3a–e are consistent with this proposition. Notice that the nonwitnesses (column D) are estimated to have scores considerably higher on social well-being than the respondents in the other categories. Specifically, 24 percent of the nonwitnesses (cell D3a), but none of the victims (0 percent—cell A3a), are estimated to have very high levels of social well-being. The percentages of victims and witnesses who are estimated to be very high (row 3a) or high (row 3b) on well-being are lower than the percentages for the other categories of respondents.

16. Unfortunately, when I reexamined the data on these victims with low social well-being, I found that the results were mixed. One victim who had been badly damaged in the flood was elderly and in poor health after a lifetime of ailments and disappointments. Another victim who had been badly damaged in the flood was middle aged and had experienced relatively good health through the years. Yet another middle-aged victim, who had not been badly damaged in the flood despite having been in the floodwaters, was in poor health and was relatively bitter "about life," even though this person had quite a few relatives and acquaintances who lived along Buffalo Creek in fairly close proximity.

17. The coal mine closed during the next two years.

18. None of the residents of Elk Creek with whom I conferred mentioned any disasters in their lives or in the history of Elk Creek.

19. John Allen and Donald Dillman, *Against All Odds: Rural Community in the Information Age* (Boulder, CO: Westview Press, 1994).

20. Allen and Dillman, *Against All Odds*, xv–xvi. Readers might note that Allen and Dillman's book was published in 1994 and that much of the original field research was done by Allen in the 1980s. I found that some significant changes have occurred since then, especially in St. John's demographic base. As best as I can tell, most residents are no longer descendants

of the original settlers, and they are not blood relatives of the farm families in Whitman County. However, this is not necessarily a major change in terms of the topics of interest to us in this book—neighboring, social integration, and social well-being—but it could be.

21. The glossary defines the terms "neighboring" and "neighborly" as they are used in this book.

22. Interestingly enough, Vanna seemed to know these neighbors better than did Van. Also, at least one of the people Van identified as a neighbor did not consider Van to be a neighbor. This person did not even recognize Van by sight or by name.

23. Miller McPherson and Lynn Smith-Lovin, "Social Isolation in America: Changes in Core Discussion Networks Over Two Decades," *American Sociological Review* 71 (June 2006): 353–375. The findings in this article are mentioned only to provide a very general context for evaluating the significance of the number of "close friends" who were claimed by respondents in my study. Definitions and measurements of "close friends" are not identical in the two studies. Nonetheless, Buffalo Creek's respondents reported relatively large numbers of close friends when compared with other places and with the U.S. norm, as reported in the McPherson and Smith-Lovin study.

24. By the way, only two of the respondents in any of the three communities complained that their neighbors or fellow citizens spend too much time with electronic diversions and entertainments such as radio, TV, videos, home computers, the Internet, and cell phones. In contrast to respondents from Buffalo Creek and Elk Creek, few respondents from St. John mentioned local churches and local church activities as features of St. John that they like best, like least, or miss most from the past. St. John had at least three churches operating when I last visited it. Buffalo Creek had at least fifteen churches. Elk Creek had one church.

25. In fact, two of our interviews were occurring when howling dust storms suddenly swept into St. John, reducing visibility to about ten feet, at best. Even then, only one of the two interviewees mentioned "dust storms" as something to dislike about residing in St. John, but not as a "disaster," despite the amount of erosion that is caused by dust storms and the long and arduous task of cleaning up after them.

26. This is a major theme in many influential books over the years, including Arthur J. Vidich and Joseph Bensman, *Small Town in Mass Society: Class, Power, and Religion in a Rural Community* (Princeton, NJ: Princeton University Press, 1958); Maurice R. Stein, *The Eclipse of Community:*

An Interpretation of American Studies (Princeton, NJ: Princeton University Press, 1960); Thomas Bender, *Community and Social Change in America* (New Brunswick, NJ: Rutgers University Press, 1978); Roland Warren, *The Community in America* (Chicago: Rand McNally, 1978); Richard F. Hamilton and James D. Wright, *The State of the Masses* (New York: Aldine, 1986); Patricia D. Beaver, *Rural Community in the Appalachian South* (Prospect Heights, IL: Waveland Press, Inc., 1992); Janet M. Fitchen, *Endangered Spaces, Enduring Places: Change, Identity, and Survival in Rural America* (Boulder, CO: Westview Press, 1991); Kenneth P. Wilkinson, *The Community in Rural America* (Westport CT: Greenwood Press, 1991); Robert Wuthnow, *Loose Connections: Joining Together in America's Fragmented Communities* (Cambridge, MA: Harvard University Press, 1998); and Robert D. Putnam, *Bowling Alone: The Collapse and Revival of American Community* (New York: Touchstone/Simon & Schuster, 2000).

PART III

Now,
THE FUTURE,
AND THE PAST

CHAPTER 6

REPRISING AND REAPPRAISING OUR ACCOUNTS, METHODS, AND MEMORIES

I really don't remember much about that flood or for many days
after it. It's all kind of a blur now. I guess maybe I don't really
want to remember any of it.

—Flood survivor who was a teenager at the time

Oh, I remember the day it happened and the day after that just like
they were a few days ago. I can't forget them even if I tried.

—Flood survivor who spent days after the flood
helping less fortunate survivors

I remember it wasn't exactly a paradise up there before that flood. There was plenty of problems that people kind of forget about. The houses was packed together along the railroad tracks. Coal trains was loud, dirty, and dangerous. Coal smoke and soot was everywhere you went. People from the different camps didn't always get along. There was heavy drinking and fights on the weekends. That flood caused a lot of misery, no doubt, and for years. But you can say it kind of washed away some of the old problems up there, too. Maybe it even washed away some people's memories of them.

—Willy Homans,
a retired, local businessman

Let us now summarize what has been reported in the chapters up to this point. Then we will reappraise our findings in light of what other authors have written about Buffalo Creek and with regard to the limitations of human memory and of research methods in the behavioral sciences. There are many agreements among our accounts. There are also some differences among our accounts that are worth contemplating. By and large, however, our research work at Buffalo Creek, Elk Creek, and St. John builds upon and extends the good work of our predecessors. Taking all of our accounts as a whole, our works can have special relevance for understanding disasters and their long-term impacts on small communities in rural areas. These are the major topics in this chapter and the next one. Let us first return to an account of an encounter with one of the most colorful and iconoclastic survivors of the disaster at Buffalo Creek.

"GUNNER" McGRUFF

Recall that the preface introduced us to a fellow, Gunner McGruff, who barely escaped with his family from the flash flood. They relocated to the HUD trailer camps for many months after the flood. When I met him in 2000 at Three Forks, where the dams burst in 1972, he showed no special concern or reverence for the place. He was salvaging for scrap metal at an abandoned tipple less than one mile from the dam sites. He said that when he walked over the mountains from Lorado only a few days after the flood, he found Three Forks to be severely damaged—but not totally destroyed and lifeless. Several dwellings were still standing there, and members of one family, the Baileys, were still living there. As I got to know Gunner and met his family in his home, I came to understand why he attested that, looking back, the flood was mainly just another nuisance to him—another "pain in the ass"—just like so many other events and situations in his long and fitful life. There was little if any evidence of a long-lasting residual effect of the flood on Gunner McGruff. He expressed no sentimentality, fondness, or sense of loss about anything before or after the flood. Neighboring, community, and social well-being were not topics that interested him.

CHAPTER ONE:
BUFFALO CREEK BEFORE, DURING, AND SOON AFTER THE FLOOD

Chapter 1 described some of most relevant conditions and events in the Buffalo Creek Valley before, during, and in the first few months after the flash flood. In doing so, it revealed that some of the commonly held beliefs about these topics are mistaken. For example, the valley was not an unusually depressed area, economically and socially, whose residents were totally unaware of the dangers around them and whose employers, the coal companies, were completely unconcerned about the dangers. High production and profitability of the mines along Buffalo Creek in the 1960s enabled many of the families to buy their homes, modernize them, acquire many modern appliances and conveniences, and enjoy working-class lifestyles. Ownership of many of the mines shifted from small, local companies to regional companies and then to a powerful conglomerate with headquarters in New York City: The Pittston Company. Increased mechanization and centralization of the mines, combined with environmental regulations against the dumping of mine wastes directly into water courses, led to the proliferation of massive piles of mine waste and to deep gob ponds filled with wastewater and debris from the mines. Prompted by citizens' complaints about flash floods that occurred when gob ponds collapsed along Buffalo Creek, federal and state agencies conducted occasional inspections of dams, gob ponds, and related mining operations along Buffalo Creek and raised questions about the structural integrity of the dams at Three Forks. Because of these occurrences, some residents in the valley had been predicting for years that the dams at Three Forks would fail and the valley would suffer a devastating flash flood.

Sensing the danger the night before the flood, hundreds of Buffalo Creek's residents—off-duty miners in particular—were actively engaged in observing the creek and in communicating by phone with their friends and neighbors up and down the valley about the status of the dams. Dozens of residents in the upper valley evacuated to safer ground, some of them in response to warnings they received from coal company employees who were checking on the status of the dams every few hours. Some of the managers and employees of Buffalo Mining Company had been inspecting the dams periodically during the two days of heavy rains that preceded the flood. One manager ordered a work crew to install another diversion pipe in the dam that failed, only hours before it failed.

When the dams burst at about 8:00 a.m. on Saturday, February 26, 1972, many of the adult residents of Buffalo Creek already were awake. Some of them were notified of the bursting of the dams through telephone calls from friends and neighbors minutes before the floodwaters arrived. Many of them escaped death in the floodwaters as a result of these neighborly warnings.

Nonetheless, hundreds, possibly even thousands of the 4,950 residents of Buffalo Creek did not escape the floodwaters. Perhaps 4,000 of them were left homeless, at least temporarily. Hundreds were injured, many of them severely. Of the 125 people who died in the flood, 91 (73 percent) were residents of Lorado and Lundale, the two largest coal camps at the far end of the valley. Damages to public and private property exceeded $50 million. And so, there is not doubt whatsoever that this flash flood was highly unusual in its intensity, suddenness, shock effect, and destructiveness to the coal camps and inhabitants, particularly those in the upper half of the valley.

However, there is some disagreement among different sources as to how much the flood's survivors were able to help themselves and one another in the hours and days immediately after the flood. Some authors portray the survivors in general as having been so shocked, stunned, confused, and damaged that they were unable to function at all, let alone function effectively. And yet, anecdotal evidence and testimony from some survivors indicates that more than a few survivors were very willing and able to help their family members, neighbors, and even strangers as soon as the floodwaters raced by, sometimes even as they raced by.

Less controversial is the evidence that external recovery and relief agencies including the state police, National Guard, Civil Defense, firemen, and ambulance crews arrived at the town of Man, at the lower end of the valley, within hours after the floodwaters swept into the Guyadotte River. Unfortunately, they were unable to travel very far up the valley because huge piles of debris obstructed the roads and bridges. Most survivors had to fend for themselves and for one another that first night, some of them for many nights after that.

The next day, Sunday, February 27, large numbers of managers, employees, and voluntary workers from external relief agencies converged on the town of Man, ready to help survivors who were being evacuated by helicopters or were slowly finding their way down the valley in need of food, shelter, and medical assistance. Hundreds of survivors were clothed, housed, and fed at Man High School for weeks on end. In response to a request from Governor Arch Moore, the White House announced that $20 million would be made available to the state in disaster relief funds. The Army Corps of Engineers, the National Guard, and managers of some of the mines provided equipment and personnel to clear debris from the roads and bridges in the valley and to erect water supply points and sanitary facilities.

Relief and clearance efforts accelerated during the next few months. The U.S. Department of Housing and Urban Development established thirteen trailer camps with 700 trailers for more than 2,500 of the survivors, some of whom were from flooded coal camps in other parts of Logan County. Major controversies erupted that gained attention in the national news media and aggravated many of the survivors. Local media quoted coal company officials as saying that the flash flood was a "natural" disaster—"an Act of God"—rather than the result of human errors or negligence. Governor Moore and some coal company officials charged that coverage of the flash flood and recovery efforts by local news media were biased against them. Flood survivors complained that government and coal company officials were ignoring their plight by giving first priority to opening the rail lines so that coal shipments could resume, rather than opening the roads so that survivors could return to their former communities and start rebuilding their homes.

Months later, a Citizens' Committee to Investigate the Buffalo Creek Disaster charged that an Ad Hoc Committee appointed by Governor Moore to investigate the disaster was a "whitewash packed with people who have a personal interest in the findings." Complaints erupted about the living conditions and operations of the HUD trailer camps and about the disruptive and deviant behaviors of some of the flood's survivors who resided there. Investigations into the flood by federal and state agencies produced testimony that was highly critical of coal company operations, of federal and state laws that regulate coal company operations, and of enforcement of those laws. An announcement by the state of West Virginia—that it planned to build modern water and sewage systems and a new, straight highway up through the valley—became controversial as flood survivors realized that this would delay their moving back to their former homesites in the valley or that the state intended to confiscate their house lots in order to build the new infrastructure. They would never be able to return "home" again.

Seen in this light, it seems fair to say that, several months after the flood, the prospects for rebuilding Buffalo Creek and for the recovery of its survivors were mixed, at best. On the positive side, perhaps 1,000 of the Valley's 4,950 preflood residents had not been dislocated from their homes. The vast majority of the valley's people (4,825) had not been killed immediately in the flood. Many of them remained in Logan County. More than 2,000 of them were living in thirteen HUD trailer camps in the area. Many of them were inclined to move back into the valley as soon as they could. Quite a few of the families that had been dislocated had received, or would receive, up to $10,000 in compensation from the state or $8,000 from the Mine Workers Assurance Fund. Extensive efforts had been made to help survivors by county, state, and federal agencies and by national emergency relief organizations.

The mines were operating again and most of the survivors who were miners were working again. The governor and state agencies gave many indications that the infrastructure of Buffalo Creek would be rebuilt and modernized. Investigations of the disaster by federal and state agencies were ongoing, or they had produced testimony that was critical of mining practices that contributed to the disaster. Agencies promised to make necessary reforms in their regulations and practices so that similar disasters would not occur anywhere in the United States. The "disaster at Buffalo Creek" had become a major story of the year in the national news media. It had not been dismissed or discounted as just another coal mining accident in the long and pathetic history of coal mining accidents.

On the negative side, 125 people had died, hundreds had been injured severely, and about 80 percent of the valley's residents were dislocated from their homes. Many families were disrupted. Many of the survivors were suffering from repeated disappointments and a variety of stresses from the flood and from some of the reactions to it by external agencies and coal company officials. Damages to private and public property were astounding—far more than the $20 million that the White House had allocated for disaster relief. Most dwellings and commercial buildings had been demolished by the flood or by postflood clearance efforts along the creek at eight of the sixteen coal camps: Three Forks, Pardee, Lorado, Craneco, Lundale, Stowe, Crites, and Latrobe. Compensation to survivors' families for losses of real estate and personal property did not come close to covering replacement costs. The HUD trailer camps were increasingly congested, uncomfortable, constraining, and disturbing to many of the survivors who lived there. Survivors also were aggravated by controversies about culpability for the flood and plans for rebuilding the infrastructure of the valley in ways that would prolong uncertainty about whether survivors could ever move back to the sites of their former homes. Lawsuits were mounting by survivors against the coal companies and some government agencies. And these are just a few of the reasons why many of the survivors were uncertain as to whether they—and Buffalo Creek—had a future.

·

CHAPTER TWO: EXPERTS' ACCOUNTS OF DISASTERS
AND THE DISASTER AT BUFFALO CREEK

Accounts by Nugent, Stern, Lifton, and Erikson

As described in chapter 2, there are many similarities in the accounts of
the flash flood and its immediate aftereffects in the accounts of Thomas
Nugent, a journalist, Gerald Stern, an attorney, Robert Lifton, a psychiatrist, and Kai Erikson, a sociologist. Three of these authors were part of
the Arnold & Porter lawsuit on behalf of some of the flood's survivors
against The Pittston Company and Buffalo Mining Company. Although
none of the four authors had been to Buffalo Creek before the flood,
they portrayed preflood Buffalo Creek as a highly homogenous community comprising sixteen highly integrated coal camps. To them, it was
a thriving, industrious, rather isolated community with plenty of stores,
shops, and services for its residents. It had remarkable cohesion, social
well-being, and neighborly relations. Families and neighbors helped one
another without having to be asked. Everyone pulled together.

According to these authors, the flash flood swept away all of these
qualities, and much more. Most of the residents were asleep. They had
been completely unaware of the danger at the dams and gob ponds at the
upper end of the valley, even after two days of unusually heavy rains.
This was not the case with the executives and managers of the coal
companies, however. No. They had known for years that the dams were
unsafe and they had done nothing to reduce the danger. Agencies of state
and federal government had been negligent about enforcing regulations
that might have mitigated the disaster, and they had created regulations
that had contributed to the disaster.

And so, the residents of Buffalo Creek were caught totally unawares
and helpless when the dams burst and the flash flood raced down through
Buffalo Creek Valley. According to images in the accounts of these authors,
the physical destruction to the coal camps was overwhelming and without
precedent. Almost everyone was caught in the raging, ice-cold, black
floodwater, or they escaped by the thinnest of margins. They suffered so
much psychological shock that they were unable to care for themselves,

their families, their neighbors, or their friends. They had to wait for days until help arrived from external agencies of government and relief organizations. Almost everyone suffered psychological impairments such as anxiety, sleeplessness, despair, depression, hallucinations, and a wide range of phobias and compulsions. Psychiatrist Robert Lifton claimed that they were suffering from "the survivor syndrome" that he witnessed in the survivors of the atom bomb attack on Hiroshima, Japan. These impairments were aggravated, magnified, and prolonged for weeks, months, and even for years, by many inadequate, misguided, and mismanaged efforts of government agencies and by failure of the coal companies to demonstrate compassion for the survivors and to compensate them adequately for their losses. Some survivors were shocked again when they realized that they would not be able to return to their homes or to the sites of their former homes because the state was confiscating their property in order to restructure the floodplain in the valley, and to build new roads, bridges, and utility systems. And, according to sociologist Kai Erikson, survivors were shocked yet again when they realized, sometimes many months later, that the kind of quintessentially social community they had cherished and shared with one another before the flood could not be recovered. It was gone forever.

None of these authors portrayed significant rebuilding of Buffalo Creek or significant recovery of psychological and social well-being by survivors by the time they published their accounts one to four years after the flood. And yet, many of the survivors had received thousands of dollars in compensation. Hundreds of families had remained in the valley, and hundreds more had moved back by then to rebuild their homes or to build new ones.

Taken as a whole, the accounts of these four authors portray Buffalo Creek and its people as having been so severely damaged by the flood, and by responses to it by outside agencies, that virtually no recovery had occurred four years after the flood. They saw little reason to expect recovery in the years ahead. Even the distribution of millions of dollars to hundreds of plaintiffs in the Arnold & Porter lawsuit against the coal companies was considered to be inconsequential when contrasted to the totality and permanence of the destruction that had been done.

Accounts by Green, Gleser, and Associates

Perhaps more than just a little at odds with these four other authors are the books and research articles by psychologists Bonnie L. Green, Goldine C. Gleser, and their various associates. They focused on whether the flood produced significant psychological impairments in samples of the survivors who were litigants in the Arnold & Porter lawsuit and whether the impairments diminished between 1974 and 1989. Among dozens of other highly specific findings, one of Green and Gleser's most salient findings was that about two-thirds of the 600 plaintiffs—but not all of them—manifested some psychological impairments two years after the flood. In the absence of baseline data on Buffalo Creek's inhabitants before the flood, and given the fact that this level of impairment is much higher than estimates of impairment in the general population of the United States, Green and Gleser more or less assumed that this high level of impairment in their sample was attributable to trauma suffered in the flood by members of their sample. From a series of detailed and complex follow-up studies between 1974 and 1989, Green and Gleser then reported that they found considerable evidence of significant *decreases* in levels of psychological impairment among other samples of flood survivors who had been litigants in the Arnold & Porter lawsuit.

Writing years later, Green and her associates reached the rather remarkable conclusion that "the specific impact of the disaster was *no longer detectable* in these subjects" (emphasis added). As such, the Green and Gleser's findings are considerably *less* congruent with the social destruction perspective than are the portrayals by Nugent, Stern, Lifton, and Erikson. One could even go so far as to say that Green and Gleser's conclusion that "the specific impact of the disaster was no longer detectable in these subjects" is very much in keeping with the social re-creation perspective. The disaster of 1972 was not producing impairments in one-third of their subjects in 1974, and it was not producing abnormally high levels of impairment in samples of survivors by 1989. Less than one-third of them manifested psychological impairment. Could it be that many of them had recovered, reachieved, or re-created psychological well-being? If not, then perhaps the flood did not impair them too severely to begin with.

CHAPTER THREE:
REBUILDING THE INFRASTRUCTURE SINCE 1972

Currently, the Buffalo Creek Valley has about 3,100 residents, twenty-five services and businesses, two coal mines, one school, and fifteen churches. These are unevenly dispersed in a series of unincorporated villages and hamlets that once were its sixteen coal camps. This is in contrast to the situation in the valley before the flash flood in 1972, when it had an estimated 4,950 residents, more than one hundred businesses and services, five working mines, four schools, two hospitals, thirty churches, and more than forty industrial buildings related to the coal mines and the railroads. The resident population has not only shrunk by more than one-third, but it also has larger percentages of retired men, elderly women, and short-term renters of the dwellings in the valley, rather than owner-occupiers. As in so many places in rural America, Buffalo Creek has heavy outward migration of young people searching for jobs. Concurrently, it is experiencing limited inward migration of people in search of cheap housing and a change from the bustle, expenses, and social problems of daily life in metropolitan places.

Therefore, speaking solely in terms of the numbers of industries, services, buildings, and inhabitants, the Buffalo Creek Valley is less than two-thirds of what it was before the flood. Then again, it is now at least three times greater in its residential population and its services than it was in the days and weeks immediately after the flood.

However, much of its infrastructure is much more modern than it was before the flood. Some aspects of its infrastructure not only were rebuilt, but they were also modernized impressively by 1980, as called for in an ambitious plan created by the state of West Virginia and the Federal Regional Council, the Buffalo Valley Redevelopment Plan. These aspects

include a modern, two-lane, concrete highway (#16) from Crown to
Pardee, modern telephone and electric systems, and well-designed water
and sewage systems for the hamlets and villages that have replaced the
former coal camps in the valley. Many tracts of land in the floodplain
along the floor of the valley were altered in order to reduce the likelihood
of future flooding of housing and commercial buildings that survived the
flood and those that would be built in the future. Most, but certainly not
all of the new housing that has been built or moved into the valley since
the flood is located on these more-or-less flood-resistant tracts of land
in the upper half of the valley. Then again, some major improvements
in the infrastructure occurred in the 1990s after West Virginia and Logan
County formed new agencies that have included Buffalo Creek within
consolidated service districts so as to finance major improvements in
primary and secondary education, emergency rescue, and fire-response
services.

Some other aspects of infrastructure development have not been so
fully realized, despite the recommendations of the plan. Three "new
communities" of high-density housing have not been built. Only a small
fraction of the subsidized, low-income housing that was called for has
been built. A mass-transit system has not materialized. A comprehensive,
new community center has not been built in the center of the valley, nor
does the valley have its own police force or adequate law enforcement.
Only a small number of businesses, consumer services, and recreational
facilities have been restored to the valley, and only one primary school
remains there. Few health care services remain.

And so it is that many residents have mixed reactions to Buffalo
Creek's infrastructure. On one hand, they appreciate the highway,
the utilities, and the improved sense of safety that they feel regarding floods. On the other hand, they wish that there were many more
stores, physicians, dentists, clinics, job opportunities, and government
services close to them in the valley. They are hoping that their prospects for the future will benefit from the opening of new coal mines,
the reopening of the rail line up through the valley to Pardee, the
creation of a McCoy-Hatfield Feud Historic Route for tourists, rallies

for enthusiasts of "four-wheelin'," and some other recent efforts at economic redevelopment in Logan County.

CHAPTER FOUR: BEING WITH PEOPLE OF BUFFALO CREEK

Chapter 4 introduced us to twenty-two former and current residents of Buffalo Creek, many of whom witnessed the flood in 1972. Each of these twenty-two people revealed to us important insights about social life and social well-being recently and, in many cases, the changes that have occurred since the flood. Taken collectively, these respondents generally attested that the quality of social life was very satisfying before the flood. Damages inflicted by the flood were quite variable. Some of the respondents who witnessed the flood suffered severe damages. Some suffered moderate damages. Others suffered no direct damages at all, save for the loss of electricity and phone service for a number of days. The respondents also varied greatly as to whether they suffered physical or psychological impairments because of the flood. Only one of them reported being severely impaired in the flood. Six of the seventeen respondents who experienced the flood did not claim any direct impairments because of it. None of the respondents revealed that the flood caused increased deviant behaviors such as substance abuse or interpersonal violence by the respondents or by members of their households.

Of the seven respondents who had relocated to HUD trailer camps, four of them either appreciated the camps or they had few complaints about them. One of them recalled that her family was delighted by the gas range, the indoor plumbing, and other modern conveniences that were utterly new to them in the trailer they occupied. Another respondent vowed that she wanted to keep living at her HUD camp rather than move back to her former coal camp along Buffalo Creek. The three other respondents disliked the camps almost to the point of loathing them, perhaps even beyond that. Seven of the respondents reported that they received monetary compensation from the state of West Virginia for losses they suffered in the flood. Six of these people also received compensation from the Arnold & Porter law firm as a result of the settlement of the lawsuit against The Pittston Company. None of these six plaintiffs in the lawsuit indicated that their involvement in the lawsuit increased their stress levels or aggravated any psychological impairments that they might have had because of the flood. All seven respondents who received monetary compensation appreciated it, but they did not believe that the money dramatically changed the recovery process for them. Then again, a few of the respondents were skeptical about the veracity of the damage claims by some of the plaintiffs. They felt that compensation was not always allocated fairly. Some respondents also believed that some of the survivors who were in their late teens and twenties misused the money they received as compensation to avoid working and to engage in disruptive, deviant, and criminal lifestyles for ten or fifteen years after that.

Only three of the seventeen respondents who witnessed the flood received prolonged remedial health care for the impairments they suffered. One of these people, Sam Chance, was so severely injured that he was hospitalized for his physical injuries, and he missed months of work in the mines. And yet, despite these impairments that were directly attributable to what he experienced in the floodwaters, Sam subsequently was able to marry, raise two successful children, and work productively in the mines for more than twenty years after the flood.

The seventeen respondents who were able to react to major assertions by experts about the flood and about Buffalo Creek as a community did so in three different ways. Four of them generally agreed with the experts. Seven others partially agreed with the experts. It is also true that six of the respondents took strong exception to key assertions by the experts, including the claim that Buffalo Creek had been destroyed as a community and that survivors could no longer care about or for themselves, their families, or their neighbors.

Major events since the flood have been more positive than negative in the lives of fourteen of the twenty-two respondents and for nine of the sixteen respondents who witnessed the flood. Even the late Tina Miner, who was one of the most unfortunate respondents through much of her life, indicated that she had some positive experiences in the decades after the flood. She felt that the standard of living had improved for most people in the valley. She also explained how social conditions along Buffalo Creek before the flood were not always as idyllic as some authors depicted them to be—particularly for young wives when their husbands were working in the mines or were out carousing.

Chapter 4 also revealed to us that most of the respondents reported that they were quite active as neighbors and that they placed high value on neighboring and good neighbors. Fifteen of the twenty-two people were estimated to be rather well integrated into Buffalo Creek as a social community. These people participated in more than a few aspects of community life, and they had positive social relations with other people in addition to their family members and neighbors. Furthermore, even though a few of the elderly respondents were in such poor health that they were housebound, or nearly so, none of the respondents complained of being socially isolated, shunned, or discriminated against by other inhabitants of Buffalo Creek. Survivors of the flood did not indicate that they were treated any differently than anyone else, nor did they indicate that they had more or less prestige because they had survived the flood. They did not make disparaging remarks about people who had not experienced the flood or any other disaster.

These twenty-two respondents were estimated to be more varied and lower on social well-being than on any of the other factors. While eleven of them had high or very high social well-being, the others were not so fortunate, although few of them were suffering significantly in this regard. Some respondents, such as Lonnie McCain, have friends and family members whose company they enjoy, but their jobs or other obligations leave little time for socializing with them. Other respondents have limited amounts of social well-being, not so much because of what happened to them in the flood or its aftereffects, but because they have lost some of their hearing, eyesight, or physical mobility, and their life-long friends have died. These people can no longer drive to visit the few elderly friends who remain alive.

All of the respondents estimated that Buffalo Creek was doing at least moderately well as a social community. Ten of them estimated that it was doing even better than that. Those who had moderate views of Buffalo Creek's well-being did not attribute its shortcomings to the flood, but rather to other factors such as insufficient police protection in the valley and too few jobs, shopping outlets, and health care facilities in or near the valley.

Taken as a whole, these findings in chapter 4 lead us to conclude that most of the twenty-two respondents have been experiencing reasonably satisfying social lives in recent years. In part, this probably is because their expectations are moderate and realistic. They realize that they are no longer living in highly cohesive and industrious coal camps so much as in relatively rural and dispersed villages and hamlets. While the flood immediately changed many of the patterns of social life in some of the coal camps, many of those changes would have occurred anyway during the next three decades because of economic, social, and cultural trends in the United States as a whole. In some ways, it might be said that the flash flood "cleared the way" for both the infrastructure and the social structure to be modernized—albeit involuntarily, violently, and tragically. In any case, there is considerable evidence that most of the twenty-two respondents who were introduced to us in chapter 4 were doing reasonably well, socially—as was Buffalo Creek—more than three decades after the flood. Not one of the respondents indicated that she or he would leave, even if it was easy to do so. Not one of them indicated that he or she regretted his or her life along Buffalo Creek. Not one of them indicated that Buffalo Creek has failed to re-create at least a modicum of community well-being since the disaster of 1972.

CHAPTER FIVE: COMPARING PEOPLE OF BUFFALO CREEK, ELK CREEK, AND ST. JOHN

Chapter 5 reported on neighborly relations, social integration, social well-being, and other factors among ninety-five of Buffalo Creek's current and recent residents and among four categories of these residents: victims, witnesses, possible witnesses, and nonwitnesses of the flood. It also described two places that were spared from disasters—Elk Creek, West

Virginia, and St. John, Washington. It profiled a number of their residents. Then it systematically compared and contrasted residents from all three communities in such ways as to help us determine if Buffalo Creek is (still) socially damaged, relatively speaking.

Considering ninety-five of Buffalo Creek's residents collectively, chapter 5 showed us that the respondents are older people who have lived along Buffalo Creek for much of their lives and in their current dwellings for at least ten years. Many of them have lived in their current dwellings for at least thirty years. This is hardly what we would expect of a place that was reported to be irreparably destroyed. The respondents reported that they have quite a few neighbors and that their neighbors are very important to them. They are familiar with their neighbors in basic ways including saying "hello" and knowing their names. And yet, the respondents do not socialize very often with many of their neighbors other than in passing. They regard trustworthiness, reliability, honesty, and friendliness very highly in their neighbors. Based on our observations during interviews and on responses to our questions, we estimated that the respondents are rather highly integrated into Buffalo Creek as a community and that their level of social well-being is at least moderate to high. Only two respondents scored low on social well-being, and only one of these had been a victim in the flood. Only a small percentage of the respondents referred to the flood and only a few of them were very conscious of it. Taken as a whole, these findings led us to conclude that Buffalo Creek is a rather neighborly and socially integrated place to live, according to the testimonies of the people we interviewed and observed. Thus, the social re-creation perspective is a more appropriate way to view Buffalo Creek at this time.

*   *   *

Many of the comparisons between and among different categories of Buffalo Creek's respondents revealed that victims of and witnesses to the flood of 1972 were just as neighborly and well integrated into Buffalo Creek as were other respondents—if not more so. This also is in keeping with the social re-creation perspective. In fact, victims and witnesses were somewhat more socially connected to close relatives and close friends who reside along Buffalo Creek than were their counterparts who were nonwitnesses or were possible witnesses to the flood. They also were somewhat more positive about living along Buffalo Creek than were their counterparts. The vast majority of respondents in all four categories feel closest to their current hamlet or village along Buffalo Creek or to Buffalo Creek as a whole, rather than to some place outside of Buffalo Creek. Respondents in all four categories also indicated that they liked many of the social qualities of life along Buffalo Creek, although the older ones realized that social life had become less encompassing over the years. There were relatively few things that they disliked about living along Buffalo Creek. Being far from shopping outlets and similar conveniences was the most frequent complaint.

Solid majorities of respondents in all four categories, including victims, were estimated to be high or very high in their level of social integration into Buffalo Creek as a whole. Only two respondents were poorly integrated, one of whom had been a flood victim and was now very old and sickly. The other person, in his twenties and bitter about his life situation in general, had little awareness of the flood.

As to neighbors and neighborliness, chapter 5 showed us that all four categories of respondents have quite a few neighbors (more than eight neighbors on average) and that basic familiarity with neighbors along Buffalo Creek is typical and extensive in all four categories. Respondents focused more on positive qualities of neighbors—such as "help when needed" and friendliness—than on negative qualities such as nosiness and gossiping. Larger percentages of victims and witnesses than their counterparts reported that neighbors are "very" or "really" important to them. *All of these findings support the social re-creation perspective more than the social destruction perspective* by revealing that victims of and witnesses to the flood were not less socially integrated or less neighborly than other kinds of residents, and that people in all four categories were quite neighborly and socially integrated.

Nevertheless, there were a few ways in which the flood's victims and witnesses might still be disadvantaged by their experience in the flood or its aftereffects. Without being asked about the flood, large percentages of victims and witnesses mentioned it at least once during their interviews, whereas none of the nonwitnesses did so. Furthermore, two of the victims mentioned the flood at least four times and were very conscious of it—perhaps even to the point of obsession. One of these persons, whom we profiled with the pseudonym of "Vera Grimm," claimed that it had ruined her life. Surely *her* account is in keeping with the social destruction perspective. And yet, Vera is the one exception out of the ninety-five respondents. Nonetheless, it is also obvious that the flood of 1972 is *not* forgotten by those residents of Buffalo Creek who experienced the flood most directly.

Estimates of social well-being provide some support for both perspectives. More than two-thirds of all respondents were estimated to have high, moderate, or mixed levels of social well-being, regardless of their category. And yet, none of the flood's victims scored "very high" on social well-being, as did only one of the witnesses. Thirteen percent of the sample as a whole and larger (but still small) percentages of victims and witnesses scored "very low" on social well-being. These relatively slight differences in social well-being might be the result of lingering effects of trauma that some of the respondents suffered in or immediately after the flood. However, they also could be the result of aging. The victims and witnesses were appreciably older and less well, physically, than were their counterparts.

Be that as it may, chapter 5 revealed that most of the Buffalo Creek's respondents—including those who were victims in the flood and witnesses to its destructiveness—recently did *not* evince much evidence of damage, deprivation, or deficiency in their neighborly relations, social well-being, and social integration. On the contrary, they seemed to be doing rather well socially—much better than we might have expected, given the devastation some of them suffered and witnessed because of the flood and the cultural legacy that remains from it.

*   *   *

Chapter 5 also reported considerable evidence of social re-creation along Buffalo Creek when it was compared to Elk Creek, West Virginia, and

St. John, Washington. Elk Creek was described as one small, unincorporated hamlet of about 130 residents that had been a coal camp until its coal mines, tipple, and rail line closed in 2003. It has become a quiet refuge for many of its residents. A variety of its residents were profiled: a reluctant, retired coal miner; a married couple who eagerly moved back to Elk Creek from a midwestern city when they retired; and a young married couple who moved to Elk Creek from another small hamlet in Logan County for the friendliness and quiet security of the place.

St. John was described as a small town in the wheat-growing Palouse country of southeastern Washington State. It is well regarded for its economic vitality, cooperative business practices, good schools, recreational facilities, and community spirit. Once again, a variety of its residents were profiled: a quiet, community-oriented wheat farmer; a native daughter of the land; a recently remarried grandmother who moved to St. John a few years ago and enjoys the coffee klatches and variety of cliques; a laconic handyman who does not ask much of his neighbors, of St. John, or of his life; and a young married mom on the margins of St. John society who is trying her best to make a better life for her baby after disappointments in a big city.

Despite some obvious differences among Buffalo Creek, Elk Creek, and St. John—including population sizes and experiences with disasters—the respondents in all three localities have lived in their current dwellings long enough to have neighborly relations, to be socially integrated, and to have a considerable amount of social well-being. Many of them reported that they had ten or more close relatives or ten or more close friends who resided in these localities, or close by.

Chapter 5 also revealed that the respondents in all three localities are quite similar in having mainly positive attitudes about their localities. They liked the quietness, simplicity, security, sense of belonging, and the natural environments that surround them. There were relatively few complaints about the lack of neighbors, friends, cooperation, and community spirit—although complaints were more frequent at Buffalo Creek and Elk Creek than at St. John. The most common complaint in all three localities was that they are "far from" shopping and other services—a complaint that is hardly surprising, given that all three localities are rural in almost every respect, including distances from the nearest cities and from metropolitan areas.

As far as neighbors and neighboring is concerned, respondents in all three localities had similar numbers of neighbors, and the numbers are rather high (more than eight neighbors, on average). Furthermore, Buffalo Creek's respondents are just as neighborly as their counterparts, if not more so, when it comes to conversing with their neighbors on a daily basis, borrowing and loaning tools, recipes, and other amenities, and going to social functions with them. This is hardly what we would expect if the flood of 1972 permanently damaged social relations along Buffalo Creek and if the social destruction perspective applies to it without major qualifications.

Regarding social integration and social well-being, Buffalo Creek's respondents were similar to Elk Creek's respondents, but the percentages of St. John's respondents who score very high on social integration (33 percent) and social well-being (29 percent) were somewhat higher than for their counterparts in Buffalo Creek and Elk Creek. This fact leads us to believe that St. Johns' respondents might be somewhat more socially integrated and have more social well-being than their counterparts. At the same time, it appears that Buffalo Creek's respondents are *not* obviously deficient on these factors in that most of them were at least moderately well integrated. They also had at least moderate levels of social well-being.

These, then, are the reasons why chapter 5 generally concluded that neighboring, social integration, and social well-being are substantial in all three localities. This being the case, the findings are more congruent with the social re-creation perspective than with the social destruction perspective. Compared to their counterparts in Elk Creek and St. John, the vast majority of Buffalo Creek's respondents are *not* obviously deficient and damaged in their social relations. Given credible and rather unanimous testimony by so many authors that this was not the case in the wake of the disastrous flash flood of 1972, it is reasonable to conclude that considerable amounts of community and social well-being have been re-created along Buffalo Creek since 1972. For this we should be thankful. This is welcome news indeed.

More *Re-Created* Than Rebuilt, Recovered, or Resilient?

The bulk of the evidence presented in chapters 1–5 leads me to suggest that it is more appropriate to say that community and well-being have been re-created along Buffalo Creek rather than to claim that the community has recovered, been rebuilt, or been resilient. As indicated in the glossary at the end of this book, "re-creation" involves creating relatively new elements of community and well-being to replace those elements that were damaged and destroyed by a particular event—in this case, the flash flood in 1972. Re-creation does not deny that some of the former elements remain from the past. However, it emphasizes that many of the elements have changed appreciably, for better, worse, or a combination of both. The term re-creation also allows that the changes have been both intentional and unintentional.

"Rebuilding" is only partially applicable to the Buffalo Creek experience. As shown in chapter 3, more than one-third of the former elements of Buffalo Creek have not been rebuilt, such as about 600 of the estimated 1,800 dwellings that were occupied at the time of the flood. The mines, mine company offices, hotels, hospitals, and theaters are just some of the kinds of facilities that have not been rebuilt—or replaced, for that matter. Going further, most of the roads, bridges, and utilities have not been rebuilt so much as they have been radically modernized and relocated to other parts of the valley. None of the former coal camps exist as coal camps anymore. The settlements that remain exist as residential hamlets and villages, rather than as coal camps. People only *reside* in them—not work in them, shop in them, go to school in them, and play in them, for the most part. Several of them no longer exist even as hamlets or villages, per se. And several of the hamlets and villages that currently exist were built on new tracts of land, sometimes on an opposite side of the creek from their namesakes. These, then, are some of the reasons why it is not as accurate to say that Buffalo Creek has been "rebuilt" as to say that it has been "re-created."

It also is difficult to use with confidence the term "recovery" in portraying what has happened to Buffalo Creek and its people. Recovery conveys the notion that key elements of the community have been regained or restored to their previous state. Unfortunately, it is very uncertain as to whether much of anything has been restored to its previous state along Buffalo Creek. While it is true that some of the respondents whom we profiled in chapter 4 said that they believed that Buffalo Creek has recovered to a considerable extent, these respondents were in the minority. More of the respondents, and quite a few outside observers who are quoted throughout this book, indicated that Buffalo Creek never can recover fully. Consider, for example, just two of the elements of community that have been highlighted throughout this book—neighbors and neighboring. While quite a few respondents were at least moderately satisfied with their neighbors and with their neighboring activities, there is no doubt that the nature of neighbors and neighboring has changed appreciably since the 1970s, as has been the case in many places throughout America. Many of our interviewees from Buffalo Creek—especially interviewees less than sixty years of age—indicated that they were satisfied having just a few neighbors who were friendly enough to wave and say hello from time to time. They were not interested in more involved forms of neighboring such as dining and partying together, exchanging household goods, and going places together. For the most part, most neighbors have become simply "nearbys"—the people who just happen to reside nearby.

As far as "resilience" is concerned, we would like to be able to report that Buffalo Creek was "resilient" after the flood—that it rebounded quickly to its original shape, form, and functions. Sadly, this has not been the case. As shown in chapter 3, much of its original shape and many of its original functions are gone forever. As mentioned previously, none of the coal camps remain as coal camps. Some of them are deserted, or nearly so. Others have been moved to different tracts of land. The hamlets and villages that remain are much smaller and less multifaceted than they were before the flood. For most residents, they provide few functions other than residences, small gardens for vegetables and flowers, churches, and views of the surrounding hills. And yet, this is enough to satisfy many of the residents, especially the older ones. For them, Buffalo Creek is not what it once was—but it is "home." For them, this is enough.

MAJOR AGREEMENTS AMONG OUR ACCOUNTS

My account generally agrees with the accounts of Nugent, Stern, Lifton, Erikson, and Green and Gleser regarding the nature of social life along Buffalo Creek before the flood. We agree that some of the sixteen coal camps of Buffalo Creek—such as Kistler, Amherstdale, Lundale, and Lorado—were rather productive, thriving, internally cohesive, multifunctional communities. Many of the inhabitants in the camps experienced extensive and satisfying social relations with family members, relatives, friends, and neighbors. Many of the inhabitants had considerable psychological and social well-being, even if their social worlds were defined by and perhaps limited to the Buffalo Creek Valley, if not to their own coal camps. We agree that the flash flood was sudden, shocking, quick, and very destructive to private and public property and to the physical and psychological well-being of many of the inhabitants who lived along Buffalo Creek, particularly those who lived in the camps above Amherstdale. We also agree that the flood caused at least $50 million of damage and left the coal camps without electricity and phone service for many days. One hundred twenty-five of Buffalo Creek's 4,950 inhabitants died immediately in the flood. As many as 4,000 of the survivors were unable to live in their dwellings for at least a few nights. More than 2,000 of them eventually relocated to trailer camps that the HUD established for them and for survivors of other floods in Logan County.

We concur that many of the survivors were shocked, saddened, and depressed by what they experienced after the floodwaters passed by: seeing dead bodies and severely injured adults and children, attending impromptu funerals, being relocated several times to temporary shelters, losing neighbors and having to adjust to new neighbors, hearing unsettling rumors, and learning about political fights and controversies over the future of the Buffalo Creek Valley. We also agree that it is likely that most of the adult citizens of Buffalo Creek—even those who were not in the valley at the time of the flood—lost some very significant social relationships because the flood killed or impaired some of their acquaintances and forced others to leave the valley forever. Understandably, many of the survivors were devastated emotionally when they came to believe or to realize that they would not be able to return to their former homesites and to the kind of community life that they had known and cherished. Sadly, I must admit that I also agree with authors who speculated that some survivors were so severely devastated psychologically that they would never fully recover the levels of psychological and social well-being that they had before the flood. And so, it is obvious that all of us also agree that the flash flood at Buffalo Creek constituted a disaster—and an unusually concentrated, disruptive, and tragic one, at that.

These are just a few of the many things that we all agree upon.

Speaking for myself, Green and Gleser's findings also are very credible. They found that about two-thirds of the 600 plaintiffs in the Arnold & Porter lawsuit manifested one or more types of psychological impairments about two years after the flood. Beyond that, they found that the impairments declined appreciably among many plaintiffs over the next seventeen years—by 1989. We should also note, however, that in the absence of preflood data on the frequency of psychological impairments among Buffalo Creek's residents, Green and Gleser did not claim—and could not claim—that the psychological impairments they detected could be attributed only to the flood.[1]

SOME DIFFERENCES AMONG OUR ACCOUNTS

Even with the many points of agreement, there are some significant differences among our accounts that will just be summarized here. These differences relate to the period before 1989 because the accounts of the other authors do not go beyond that date.

Was Buffalo Creek a Single, Uniquely Homogenous, Cohesive, Peaceful, and Neighborly Community Before the Flood?

As shown in chapter 2, most of the other authors portrayed preflood Buffalo Creek as being a uniquely homogenous, cohesive, peaceful, and neighborly community comprising a highly integrated set of coal camps whose 5,000 or so people knew one another and were glad of it. While I generally agree that the camps in the Buffalo Creek Valley probably had more of these qualities than did many other places in Appalachia that were poorer and more urban, the research presented in chapters 3–5 indicates that some of the larger coal camps—such as Kistler, Amherstdale, Accoville, Lundale, and Lorado—were more self-contained, exclusionary, and competitive than some of the other camps. Distrust, animosity, and territorial disputes existed between and among some of the coal camps. These divisive features probably were most pronounced among teenagers and young adults in the larger coal camps. They also carried over into some of the HUD trailer camps after the flood. Displaced residents from some coal camps did not want to reside near displaced residents from some other coal camps.

Prior to the Flood, Were Buffalo Creek's Residents Generally Unaware of the Dangers Posed by the Gob Ponds? Were They Caught Unaware—Asleep in Their Beds—When the Flood Swept Through Their Coal Camps?

In contrast to all of the authors except Green and Gleser, I believe that it is highly inaccurate to answer affirmatively to these questions, without major qualifications. Based on the evidence presented in chapters 1 and 4, it is more correct to say that significant numbers of Buffalo Creek's residents—perhaps 30 percent or more of the adults—were well aware of the dangers posed by the gob ponds that collapsed at Three Forks. They knew that gob ponds frequently collapsed after two days of heavy rain. They knew that one of these ponds had collapsed a few years earlier. Many residents, including some employees of Buffalo Mining Company, were reacting to the dangers in the hours before the flash flood. Some of them visited dam #3 throughout the night. Others kept watch over the creek near their homes in the upper valley. Most of the residents of Three Forks had evacuated that camp for the night. Miners were returning to their homes from the "hoot owl shift" at the mines. Many of the other residents in the upper valley were not sleeping in their beds when the flood occurred at 8:00 a.m. on a Saturday morning. They had been warned of the danger and they were warning their relatives and neighbors of the danger. Many of them helped other people—including their neighbors and strangers—escape the flood and try to adjust to the flood's devastation.

Did the Flood Immediately Destroy the Social Cohesion, Communality, Neighborly Relations, and Social Well-Being of the Survivors?

Sadly, it probably is true that hundreds of the most severely injured people among the more than 4,800 survivors lost their social cohesion, communality, neighborly relations, and social well-being. There is no doubt that many of the plaintiffs in the Arnold & Porter lawsuit against the coal companies behaved in ways that convinced some of the authors that this had happened to them. Nonetheless—except for Green, Gleser and their associates—the authors neglected contradictory cases among their own interviewees, all or most of whom were plaintiffs. Then these authors overgeneralized from the most damaged plaintiffs to the thousands of other survivors as a whole. In contrast to accounts such as these, I found considerable evidence—occasionally within the authors' own accounts—that many survivors helped their families, friends, neighbors, and strangers during the flood, immediately after it, and ever since then. Molly Good, Wanda Mercer, Buck Miner, Goldie and Buddy Cummins, and Lureen and Jake Albro are just a few of the cases in point. At the very least, it is likely that social cohesion, communality, and neighborly relations remained strong in the side hollows of the valley and among the 1,000 residents who were not forced to leave their homes because of the flood or responses to the flood.

**Were All of the Survivors Psychologically Impaired Because
of the Flood or Because of Responses to the Flood's Damages
by Other People, Agencies, and Organizations?**

While there is no doubt that hundreds or even a few thousand of the survivors suffered psychological impairments because of the flood or responses to it, it also is likely that hundreds of survivors did not suffer psychological impairments. As indicated in chapter 2, there are major, underacknowledged differences among some of the experts as to the extent of psychological impairments that are attributable to the flood. Lifton and Erikson repeatedly asserted that all or nearly all of the survivors—not just the survivors who became litigants in the Arnold & Porter lawsuit—suffered significant psychological impairments as a result of the flood or of reactions to it by government agencies. By contrast, Green and Gleser contended that about two-thirds of the plaintiffs manifested psychological impairments. Even more by contrast, the psychiatrist hired by Pittston Company to defend it in the Arnold & Porter lawsuit found evidence of psychological impairment in less than 45 percent of the plaintiffs.

Before commenting one last time on these discrepancies among the experts, let me once again acknowledge that I am not a psychologist or psychiatrist by training. It also is true that my field research along Buffalo Creek was not designed to resolve this discrepancy among the experts. However, based on the evidence that I have presented throughout this book—particularly the testimonies of survivors of the flood in chapter 4—I believe that Lifton and Erikson overstated by a considerable margin the extent of psychological impairments in the 600 plaintiffs. They were even more mistaken when they generalized this level of impairment to the more than 4,000 survivors who were not plaintiffs. In all likelihood, Green and Gleser's estimate that about two-thirds of the plaintiffs were impaired is more accurate than Lifton's and Erikson's estimates, as well as the lower estimate that was averred by the psychiatrist for Pittston Coal Company.[2]

Was the Flash Flood Unprecedented and Unique in U.S. History?
The flood certainly was unusual in a number of ways. And yet, unfortunately and contrary to some of the authors, flash floods similar to this one have been rather frequent in mining and mill towns of the United States since the late nineteenth century when earth-moving machinery enabled organizations to build large reservoirs and impoundments.[3] For example, flash floods similar to the one at Buffalo Creek have been occurring in the Conemaugh River Valley of western Pennsylvania since 1864. The most notorious one of these occurred there on May 31, 1889. One of the largest earthen dams in the United States at that time collapsed during a severe storm that dumped eight inches of rain in a twenty-four–hour period. Water from a 470-acre impoundment surged down fourteen miles of the South Fork and Little Conemaugh River Valleys through more than a dozen mill towns and coal camps before it smashed into Johnstown. A total of 2,209 people drowned. More than 10,000 were left homeless. Damages to private and public property were estimated to exceed $5 million—in 1889 dollars. A controversy erupted as to whether the disaster was a consequence of an act of nature or an act of man. Investigations by an association of engineers and several newspapers determined that the flash flood was due to the negligence of the South Fork Fishing and Hunting Club, which owned the impoundment and the dam. Apparently, the directors of the club (which included Andrew Carnegie and other magnates in the coal and steel industries) had ordered the wastewater overflow gates to be closed in order to retain as much water as possible in the impoundment.[4]

Then again, in July 1977—almost one hundred years later, and five years after the disaster at Buffalo Creek—heavy rains caused earthen dams to collapse at several places in the Little Conemaugh Valley upstream from Johnstown. At least fifty-five people drowned. "In the seven-county disaster area along the Conemaugh Valley $200 million in damages and 50,000 homeless people testify to the monstrous proportions of the Flood of '77."[5] As was the case at Buffalo Creek, these flash floods in the Conemaugh River Valley occurred when impoundments collapsed. The floodwaters caught most of the victims in their homes.

Most of those victims were relatives of miners and mill hands rather than the workers themselves. This sounds similar to the disaster at Buffalo Creek, does it not? Or worse.

Was the Flash Flood Entirely "Unnatural"—
The Work of Human Beings Alone, and Not of Nature?

Contrary to the interpretations of some of the authors, the flash flood was only partially the work of human beings—and of many different human beings and organizations, at that. Humans did not create the ridges, the valley, the side hollows, and the other primary terrain features in the area. Humans did not cause the two days of heavy rain, the near-freezing temperatures, or the other major meteorological conditions of that time. The collapse of dam #3 would have been more exclusively the work of human beings if human beings had caused the two days of heavy rains in some way, perhaps by "seeding" the clouds with chemicals, or by using explosives to blow up the dam as a prank, sabotage, or act of terrorism. Even then, however, the flash flood that resulted from this kind of human interference might have been somewhat different in its physical characteristics than was the flash flood as it occurred on February 26, 1972. And yet, obviously, it is also true that the flood was primarily an event that resulted from the decisions and work of many different human beings and organizations over a number of years. As indicated in chapter 1, two of the three dams and most of the gob ponds were built, altered, and expanded at various times between 1947 and 1968 by work crews of small, local coal companies. Eventually, these properties were sold to Buffalo Mining Company before they were acquired by Pittston Company in 1970. Companies had been dumping mine waste and debris into these gob ponds for years. It also should be noted that human beings built the roads, bridges, and coal camps that were hit by the flood and, in the process, altered it and often became part of its mass and hydraulic structure as it surged down through seventeen miles of the valley. And so, it can be said that the flash flood at Buffalo Creek was primarily—but not entirely—the consequence of human decisions and actions.

Were Buffalo Mining Company and Pittston Company Totally Irresponsible and Negligent Regarding the Flash Flood?

In contrast to the other authors and to generally accepted public opinion on this question, I do not believe that these companies or any other entities were *totally* irresponsible and negligent regarding the flood. Surely, the facts presented in the preceding chapters indicate that Buffalo Mining Company and Pittston Company were more irresponsible and negligent than any other organization, agency, or person. However, the flash flood was not entirely the consequence of what they did. They did not cause the two days of heavy rains. They did not build most of the dams or the gob ponds, although they had purchased them from other companies and they were thereby legally responsible for maintaining them and for operating them safely. They did not build most of the roads, bridges, houses, and other buildings that were swept up in the flash flood, became part of its mass, and contributed to the deaths, injuries, and further damages to property downstream. A few days before the flood, senior executives had flown above the dams and had discussed their safety. On the night before the flood and early that morning, BMC superintendent Jack Kent and several employees periodically checked on the conditions at the gob ponds. One of the employees, Dennis Gibson, personally warned many residents of Three Forks about the dangers, and he encouraged them to evacuate for the night to the school building at Lorado. Many of them did so, but several residents disregarded the warning. Several hours before the flood, BMC's general manager Steve Dasovich ordered Jack Kent to have a twenty-four–inch drainpipe installed at dam #3 in order to divert rising water and release pressure in the dam. Dasovich then phoned his boss, BMC president I. C. Spotte, and informed him of the situation. Spotte approved the installation of the drainpipe. While these actions obviously did not preclude the dams from collapsing, they certainly establish that BMC and Pittston were *not totally* negligent and irresponsible regarding conditions at the dams and gob ponds. Some employees of these companies certainly miscalculated—significantly—and with tragic consequences. But this hardly constitutes "*total*" negligence, let alone willful negligence—other than in a court of law, perhaps.

Was "Everything" "Irreparably" Destroyed?

Chapters 3–5 indicate that, fortunately and in contrast to the claims of some of the authors, everything was not destroyed, let alone destroyed irreparably. Had this occurred, there would be no Buffalo Creek today. Had Buffalo Creek not survived, this book would have been not only unnecessary, but also impossible.

Was the Buffalo Creek Disaster a "Total" Disaster?

Contrary to author-psychiatrist Robert Jay Lifton, the disaster at Buffalo Creek was not a "total" disaster. It certainly was an unusual disaster in its intensity. Perhaps it came close to being a total disaster at Three Forks, Pardee, and parts of Lorado and Lundale. However, the disasters at Pompeii, AD 79, and Hiroshima, 1945, were far more" total" than was the one at Buffalo Creek.

WHY THE DIFFERENCES AMONG OUR ACCOUNTS?

There are at least four reasons why differences can exist between my findings and the accounts of the other authors, without any of us necessarily being in error: (1) differences in time frames and in time spent in the field, (2) differences in research methods and data collected through them, (3) differences in concepts, definitions, context, and syntax, and (4) fallibilities in the nature of human memory and in how people recollect and recount their memories to others.

Differences in Time Frames and Time Spent in the Field

None of us visited the Buffalo Creek Valley before the flood. Nor did we observe the flood. None of us started making direct observations in the valley until at least a few days (Nugent), a few weeks (Stern), a few months (Lifton), or more than a year after the flood (Erikson, Green and Gleser, and myself). Therefore, none of us have direct knowledge of what happened to Buffalo Creek and its people before, during, or immediately after the flood. All of us have had to rely upon documents, articles, and other people to provide us with crucial information. However, while I had no direct observations of Buffalo Creek until 2000, I have the advantage of being able to draw upon the accounts of all of these authors and on the accounts that have appeared in newspapers, journals, films, videos, and many other accounts since then. I have had the opportunity to weigh the discrepancies and the consistencies within each of their accounts and among them. I have also benefited from critiques that seventeen of the survivors provided me about major conclusions in the accounts of some of the authors. In addition to these advantages, I have spent more than seven years visiting Buffalo Creek in order to do my work. This is a much longer time frame than for the other authors—except, perhaps, for Green and Gleser. And, of course, my research considers changes that have occurred in the valley during the more than thirty-five years since the flood.

Differences in Research Methods,
Informants, and in Data Collected
Consider for the moment that it is impossible, ex post facto, to conduct a "perfect" research study of the psychological and social impacts of the flash flood and on the recovery process to date. At the very least, a perfect study would require a well-financed team of researchers skilled in a wide range of research methods to start collecting data along Buffalo Creek several weeks or months before the flood. Researchers would be obliged to use well-established techniques and measures in behavioral and social science to collect huge amounts of baseline data on dozens of individual-level and community-level variables at several of the coal camps, preferably at all sixteen of them. Advocates of ethnographic research and participant observation would want some of the researchers to reside with and work alongside Buffalo Creek's residents for many months before the flood, and to continue to do so during the flood and for many months after it. Ideally, for research purposes, some of the researchers would need to be caught up in the floodwaters along with other survivors so that they could witness directly how people reacted to their predicament and to others around them. Were the residents who were "good neighbors" before the flood more likely to

remain good neighbors during the flood and long after it was over? If so, were they more likely to help other "good neighbors" than to help "bad neighbors" or strangers? Were residents who were good neighbors more likely to escape psychological impairments and to retain their sense of social well-being after the flood?[6] These are just a few of the kinds of provocative questions about the disaster at Buffalo Creek that cannot be answered definitively by anyone, ex post facto. But we can at least try our best to derive empirically informed—if tentative—answers to these kinds of questions. We can remain open-minded about the possibility that each and every research method, when used skillfully, can help increase our knowledge and reduce our ignorance, to some extent, even if we can never attain perfect and complete understanding of what has transpired.

Obviously, none of us has come close to meeting the prerequisites of a perfect research project. This is no surprise, of course. To the best of my knowledge, a "perfect" research project never has been conducted on a human community—anywhere—let alone on a human community that has experienced a disaster as devastating as the one at Buffalo Creek.

Also consider that all of us who have studied Buffalo Creek have used somewhat different research methods. Nugent, a journalist, apparently used standard journalistic procedures when he talked with dozens of people along Buffalo Creek and reported on public meetings of government agencies in the months after the flood. His book focuses on how the flood occurred, who was to blame for it, and on recollections of the flood by some survivors and relief workers. As consultants to Arnold & Porter in the lawsuit against the Pittston Company, Stern, Green and Gleser, Lifton, and Erikson were hired to prepare testimony about psychological and social damages among the plaintiffs that would be relevant in the litigation process. They reported that they used research methods that they were qualified to use based on their academic credentials. Although they do not say so in their published accounts, they probably were under considerable time pressure and under additional pressure from the other consultants to produce testimony that would be consistent across the group of consultants. They were not hired to produce research papers for academic journals, although it would not be surprising to learn that, as career researchers who are expected to publish on a regular basis, this was in the back of their minds. In any case—except for Green and Gleser—these consultants seem to have assumed that the plaintiffs they reported on were key informants into what all of the other survivors were thinking, feeling, and experiencing. Apparently, the authors did not collect data systematically from the 1,000 or more survivors who were not dislocated from their homes and were not plaintiffs in the lawsuit. These consultants also seem to have assumed that the physical features of the valley as they observed them were the direct consequence of the flash flood alone rather than of the clearing, excavating, and salvage operations of the Army Corps of Engineers, the departments of public works, the coal companies, and even the survivors themselves. In other words, these authors occasionally might have mistaken physical reactions to the flood's damages for the direct damages done by the floodwaters. Still, I believe that the accounts of all of these authors are valid as descriptions of what their interviewees revealed to them about their experiences before, during, and after the flood.

Now, as far as my own research methods are concerned, consider that they are much more diverse than the methods that were used by the other authors (as indicated in appendix A and in the many of the endnotes throughout this book). This is not to claim that my methods are superior to theirs. Simply, it is meant to emphasize that my methods were chosen and employed in such ways as to build upon their work and to provide us with new insights—not definitive tests of hypotheses—about a wider range of topics than they addressed. Other authors focused on describing the flood and its short-term psychological and social impacts, whereas I reexamined these topics and then related them to the efforts that have been made in the past thirty-five years to rebuild, recover, and re-create communities since the disaster. I also wanted to be able to convey to many different kinds of readers—not just researchers in some specialized branches of sociology—what daily life is like for a variety of residents in these communities. In addition to this, as a human being and a humanist, as well as a social scientist, I wanted to be able to form lasting relationships with the people who participated in my research—with the people I "studied," so to speak—rather than just use them for data, and *as* data. These are the reasons why I combined research procedures and presentation styles from journalism, biography, history, ethnography, psychology, and four types of sociology: qualitative, humanistic, quantitative, and comparative.

I made field trips to Buffalo Creek, Elk Creek, and St. John many times for more than six years. I walked in and around these places, made observations of how the inhabitants interacted with one another, and got to know a variety of the residents so that I could estimate differences and similarities in the social relations of purposively selected, informed residents of these places. As shown in chapters 4 and 5, I conducted in-depth, structured interviews in the homes of many of these people and in public places in their communities. I have continued to communicate over the years with informed people in these communities so as to stay abreast of ongoing changes. I also have interviewed dozens of government officials and community leaders to get their views on how the communities have changed and on the prospects for the future. As a result of this combination of research procedures, I believe that we now have much deeper insights into the Buffalo Creek disaster and its aftermath. We also know a lot about social conditions in these places and about the social lives of some of their residents. I hope that now we can appreciate what has been accomplished at Buffalo Creek, rather than just be stunned and dismayed by what was destroyed there so many years ago.

Differences in Concepts, Definitions, Context, and Syntax
In some social circles, it is fashionable to dismiss disagreements between and among authors on the grounds that the disagreements are due to differences in syntax or to some other aspect of language. Yet it would be erroneous to attribute the differences among our accounts to supposed differences in language unless, perchance, some of the authors did not really mean "everything" when they repeatedly used that term in claiming that the

flood "destroyed everything," and they did not really mean "total" when they claimed repeatedly that the disaster was a "total disaster." Chapter 2 goes to great lengths in providing a context for understanding the accounts of the other authors. The authors are quoted often and in detail throughout this book in order to minimize the likelihood that I would misrepresent them. Furthermore, Kai Erikson and Bonnie L. Green graciously read and commented on material that I sent to them from chapter 2 that describes their published work about Buffalo Creek.[7] The glossary clearly identifies the relatively few instances where my definitions of key concepts differ from those of the other authors. Even in these instances, I believe that the differences are so minor that the substantive differences among our accounts about Buffalo Creek should not be attributed to differences in concepts, definitions, context, and syntax.

Limitations in Memory and Recollection

Memories and recollections have not been the focus of this book. In contrast to other books about Buffalo Creek, this book does not heavily rely upon the recollections of the flood and the days after the flood by some of the plaintiffs in the Arnold & Porter lawsuit against the coal companies—a woefully biased "sample" of the population of flood survivors. No. By contrast, this book uses official documents, newspaper articles, reports of academic studies, and direct observations that I made "in the field." Most of the people I interviewed were not asked to recall their very distant memories of the flood or of traumatic events in their lives, although some of them did so anyway, as reported in chapters 3, 4, and 5. And yet, it is also true that many of the people I interviewed recalled memories of social life years ago in order to explain to me "how things have changed." For this reason, we should consider how the limitations and distortions of human memory and recollection might relate to the differences among our accounts.

Despite decades of extensive research on human memory,[8] some experts on the topic concede that they have only limited understanding of how we remember and recount to others the events that we witnessed, or believed we witnessed, many years ago. There is considerable debate among scientists as to whether people can remember traumatic events more clearly than normal events. It is generally acknowledged that some people prefer to forget traumatic events in their lives, that their memories are repressed or distorted in various ways, and that they sometimes simply cannot or can no longer recall a traumatic event. In fact, I found that this was true of some of the people I interviewed along Buffalo Creek, as indicated in the first two epigraphs at the head of this chapter. And yet, there also is evidence that traumatic events often are remembered and recounted to others more accurately than are ordinary experiences. There also is evidence that, once memories are remembered, efforts to recount them and convey them to other human beings are influenced heavily by the recounter's current state of mind, the social context in which the recounting occurs, and several other factors. Among these other factors are the recounter's conscious and unconscious sense of the listener's empathy and ability to understand what the recounter wishes to convey.

With these limitations in mind, I believe that substantive differences among our accounts may be *partly* attributable to several differences that involved the memories and recollections of our interviewees. First, as stated previously, the other authors relied more heavily than I did on recollections of interviewees, plaintiffs in particular. Second, except for journalist Tom Nugent, the other authors were employees of, or consultants to, the law firm of Arnold & Porter. As such, they were much more interested in eliciting from their interviewees recollections of traumatic events and experiences than in knowing about how well their interviewees were recovering from these events and experiences and whether they were involved in the rebuilding of communities along Buffalo Creek. Third, as best as we can tell from the accounts of the other authors, often the social context in which the recounting of traumatic memories occurred was uncomfortable to the interviewees (in flood-damaged homes and neighborhoods and in the HUD trailer camps), and the interviewees were suffering from significant psychological impairments. As such, we might expect that the interviewees' "state of mind" would produce significant distortions in their memories and recollections. Nevertheless, and to their credit, I believe that the other authors probably were very compassionate and skilled. Because of this, they were able to convey to their interviewees the sense that they were empathetic listeners who could understand and appreciate the interviewees' recollections of traumatic experiences.

As to the interviewees who participated in my study, a small percentage of them recounted to me their memories of the flood or of other disturbing experiences that they had during the course of their lives (as reported in chapters 3–5) even though I did not ask them to do so. In general, I believe that they did so honestly and accurately. My sense is that flood survivors did not exaggerate the disruptions, difficulties, and disappointments that they experienced. If anything, they probably understated them, possibly because I did not dwell on these topics. When I crosschecked factual aspects of recollections from different respondents, I got the sense that accuracy in the recounting of past events was especially high with respondents who were in their fifties and sixties, were religious, nonaddicted, and had not suffered too many severe illnesses or family problems in the recent past. These respondents tended to be very measured and discerning in conveying their recollections to me. Family members who witnessed the recounted events often corroborated one another's recollections (as shown in the cases of Goldie and Buddy Cummins and Lureen and Jake Albro in chapter 4). Recounters also were judicious in statements of attribution about major events that had occurred during and since the flood. This is to say that very few recounters attributed blame or credit to any one person, event, or agency. They had moderate to subdued levels of affectation during the time I spent with them. Very few of them expressed high levels of anger, bitterness, elation, or euphoria. Recalling memories and recounting them to me was done voluntarily and did not seem to disturb the people who did so. In sum, the occasional recollections of the people I interviewed were relevant, even tempered, and credible.

*   *   *

Most importantly, let us recall that the primary purpose of this book has been to describe, analyze, and explain what has happened to Buffalo

Creek's communities and people in the more than thirty-five years since the flash flood. It has not been meant to focus upon what other authors said about the disaster only a few years after it occurred. Nor has it been intended as an exercise in what some people might dismiss as "academic nitpicking." So, let us now move on to consider the possible futures of Buffalo Creek and other small, rural communities. Then we will explain how the "Buffalo Creek experience" to date can help other communities prepare for disasters, reduce the likelihood of disasters, and, if the need arises, respond to them smartly. Surely, all of us can agree that the "disaster" part of the Buffalo Creek experience should not be suffered again.

ENDNOTES

1. If, for instance, 10 percent of the plaintiffs incurred psychological impairments before the flood that they continued to experience through the time that they were examined by members of the Green and Gleser team, then their psychological impairments cannot be attributed directly or indirectly to the flood. Even then, however, by subtracting this 10 percent of the plaintiffs from the two-thirds of the plaintiffs who were detected to have psychological impairments, we can infer that more than one-half of the plaintiffs who were examined by the Green and Gleser team were suffering psychological impairments that can be attributed to the flood or to responses to the flood. This estimate—roughly 55 percent—is much higher than most estimates of the frequency of psychological impairments in the general population of the United States, as estimated in Ronald C. Kessler et al., "Lifetime and 12-Month Prevalence of DSM-III-R Psychiatric Disorders in the United States: Results from the National Comorbidity Survey," *Archives of General Psychiatry* 51 (January 1994): 8–19.

2. In the spirit of full disclosure—but with considerable reluctance because I am not certified as a clinical psychologist or a psychiatrist—I offer the following estimates of the psychological well-being of the sixteen survivors who were residing along Buffalo Creek at the time of the flood and whose profiles are presented in chapter 4. As to the past, my sense is that eight of the sixteen survivors suffered psychological impairments such as sleeplessness, anxiety reactions, panic attacks, hydrophobia, and depression for at least several years after the flood and because of the flood or reactions to it by government agencies. This estimate of 50 percent splits the difference between the Green and Gleser estimate (about 66 percent) and the psychiatrist for the coal companies (less than 45 percent). However, in contrast to their estimates, my estimate of 50 percent refers to only those respondents whose psychological impairments are attributable to the flood or reactions to the flood. It excludes persons who might have had impairments before the flood.

More recently, since I began my field work along Buffalo Creek in the year 2000, my sense is that only three of these eight survivors continue to suffer one or more psychological impairments because of the flood or because of reactions to it. None of these three persons is so impaired as to be totally impaired or to require institutionalization. All three of them are able to care for their basic needs, to drive vehicles, and to carry on short but coherent conversations with me on a daily basis. And yet, all three of them are emotionally subdued and rather depressed. They have never expressed to me obvious enthusiasm about anything, although they were glad that they had respected jobs in mining after the flood.

However, I am a sociologist with more than thirty years of experience doing sociological research. As such, I feel more qualified to estimate the social well-being of these people. As indicated in chapter 4, I found none of them to be totally deprived, alienated, or disadvantaged in their social relationships—even those who were suffering terminal illnesses and were aware of their plight. I believe that most of the twenty-two people whom I profiled in chapter 4 had at least a moderate amount of social well-being. A number of them were doing much better than that. No less noteworthy is the fact that none the three people whom I estimated to still be suffering *psychological* impairments attributable to the flood had less than a moderate amount of social well-being. All three of them had intact marriages, resided with their spouses, and indicated that they had positive relationships with more than a few friends and relatives. Two of them have adult children and grandchildren. Both of them indicated that they have positive relations with their children and grandchildren. I have been in public places with two of these three people. Both of them interacted in normal ways with other members of the community whom they recognized. The other person was very hospitable to me during my visits to the family home and during the several phone conversations we had after those visits.

3. David McCullough's superb writing on the Johnstown (Pennsylvania) flood in 1889 also explains how flash floods of mining and mill towns became more common in the United States as corporations and municipalities built large impoundments and reservoirs. In fact, Johnstown has suffered highly destructive flash floods since 1864—not just since 1889. See his book, *The Johnston Flood* (New York: Simon & Schuster Paperbacks, 1968).

4. McCullough, *The Johnston Flood*, 230–238 passim.

5. J. Ververs Cruse and Elizabeth Taggart, eds., *The Johnstown Flood—1977* (Johnstown, PA: Jujulah Corporation, 1977), 14.

6. As indicated in chapters 4 and 5, my own data from Buffalo Creek generally indicate that the answers are affirmative to all of these questions. Survivors who were good neighbors before the flood tended to remain good neighbors after the flood, and they generally fared better than did lesser neighbors.

7. Furthermore, for more than five years, I communicated with Kai Erikson by phone, letter, e-mail, and in person in order to increase the likelihood that

I had accurately described his work. Of course, any errors or oversights are mine alone in my descriptions of his work and the work of other authors.

8. Scientific research on human memory is summarized and interpreted in Paul Antze and Michael Lambeck, eds., *Tense Past: Cultural Essays in Trauma and Meaning* (New York: Routledge, 1996); and in Daniel L. Schacter's *Searching for Memory: The Brain, the Mind, and the Past* (New York: Basic Books, 1996) and *The Seven Sins of Memory* (Boston: Houghton-Mifflin, 2001).

CHAPTER 7

FUTURE PROSPECTS AND RECOMMENDATIONS FOR BUFFALO CREEK AND FOR SMALL COMMUNITIES IN RURAL AMERICA

I believe that, socially speaking, the people of Buffalo Creek still have a sense of community. I don't know that they ever really lost that. That mountain ethic is still there. Most of the people try to be self-reliant and take care of their own families and kin. That hasn't changed. What they need now are more jobs and modern health care facilities close enough to keep them there with a decent quality of life.

—Raamie Barker, well-known local news reporter

I predict it will go steady around here for another ten to twenty years. They say there is another twenty years of easy coal up there in the mountains. Some of that's high BTU coal that's bringing in upwards of $100 a ton right now. That ought to keep us going pretty good for years to come.

—Willy Homans, respected, retired businessman

I guess you can say it's a kinda boom time again around here. There's that big, new strip mine up on Kelly Mountain. Trucks carrying heavy equipment are coming up and down the Valley at all hours now. In March (2006) the first train in thirteen years come up through Lorado after the tracks was cleared and repaired. People lined-up along the tracks and cheered. It means jobs again, or it's supposed to. Now there's a new load-out at Pardee. And new homes are going up, too. Already there are maybe ten of them down in Accoville hollow. Some of then are fancy ones, too.

—Molly Good, flood survivor and Buffalo Creek resident

People won't stop living here at Buffalo Creek. Everybody has cars and trucks now. The roads are getting better. Nowadays people don't mind driving more than an hour to get to jobs, go shopping, or do whatever they want. They like driving away, and they like coming back here where it's really home.

—Buddy Cummins, flood survivor and Buffalo Creek resident

$*$ $*$ $*$

What are the prospects for Buffalo Creek Valley and for its inhabitants? How can the "Buffalo Creek experience" help other small communities in rural America?

Of course, we hope that the prospects are bright and certain. So many of the people of the valley suffered far too much, and they have toiled long and hard to re-create social well-being for their families. Rather than use crystal balls, horoscopes, soothsayers, and swamis, we will employ several techniques that were made famous in the 1960s by the late "father of futuristics," Hermann Kahn, and his still influential Hudson

Institute.[1] Among other contributions to our modern lexicon, Kahn popularized the term "scenario" and used "alternative scenarios" to help government leaders and concerned citizens work towards "desirable futures" and reduce the chances of bumbling blindly into disastrous ones. Consider that the current international debate about "global warming" is flush with alternative scenarios that many concerned scientists (and at least one former vice president) have created about the possible consequences of excessive consumption of fossil fuels over the next ten, fifty, hundred, and thousand years.

In the pages ahead, we outline five alternate scenarios that might occur in and around the Buffalo Creek Valley over the next twenty years. These scenarios are based in part on what we have learned from the people of Buffalo Creek whom we profiled in chapters 4 and 5, from the dozens of government and business leaders in West Virginia whom we interviewed over the years, and from technical reports and other documents that were analyzed in chapter 3. By doing this, we can get a better sense of whether Buffalo Creek's "best days" could still be ahead of it and, if so, how this eventuality can become reality. We will also call attention to some dangers to be avoided so that its worst days will remain in the ever-more-distant past. Then we will explain why Buffalo Creek's experiences and prospects can be very relevant to many other small communities in rural America that are far from Buffalo Creek in geographical distance, if not from harm's way. Finally, we will offer a number of recommendations to residents of these small communities so that they are less likely to experience the worst of the Buffalo Creek experience.

FIVE SCENARIOS FOR THE BUFFALO CREEK VALLEY

Scenario I: Continuing the status quo—until the "easy" coal is depleted (and a promising extension)

Scenario II: Current efforts at economic diversification have moderate success

Scenario III: Major, new economic initiatives transform the valley

Scenario IV: Sudden decline in the coal economy and in support from external organizations

Scenario V: Another disaster

Some Competitive Advantages of the Buffalo Creek Valley

In reading through the scenarios that follow, it can be useful to keep in mind several of the competitive advantages that the Buffalo Creek Valley has over other locations in Appalachia for attracting new industries, new funding from government agencies, and new residents to reside there, pay taxes, and be active citizens. These advantages were explained in chapter 3.

1. Relatively new and recently upgraded water and sewage systems, modern bridges, and a wide, well-banked, modern, two-lane highway (Route 16) through fifteen of the seventeen miles of the main valley.

2. At least thirty acres of inexpensive, vacant land in several of the former coal camps that could be used for small industrial sites and for at least one hundred new homes, apartments, condominiums, or similar facilities. After the flood, this land was cleared of debris, was raised at least fifteen feet above the floodplain, and was planned for industrial or residential use that has not yet materialized.

3. Other popularly supported proposals in the 1973 Buffalo Valley Redevelopment Plan that have not yet been fulfilled, including extension of Highway 16 nine miles from Three Forks to Route 99 and the city of Beckley, and designs for three new residential communities on elevated land in the valley.

4. Public sympathy, goodwill, and a cultural legacy in some political circles that Buffalo Creek still deserves special consideration for economic development because of the disaster of 1972.

5. Recent and ongoing investments in economic diversification around the Buffalo Creek Valley including tourist attractions, small wells for natural gas, a huge, new "mountain topping" coal

mine above Pardee, and the reopening of the rail line from Fanco to Three Forks.

Some Competitive Disadvantages

Unfortunately, the Buffalo Creek Valley also has some competitive disadvantages that could offset its competitive advantages, as indicated in previous chapters of this book.

1. For all practical purposes, the Buffalo Creek Valley is a "dead end"—a cul de sac—in terms of ground transportation (see map of Buffalo Creek in front of book). The paved portion of Highway 16 ends before it reaches the tiny hamlet of Curtis, a few miles upstream from Three Forks.[2] Access to the upper valley also is restricted by an old, two-mile section of Highway 16 from Man through Kistler to Crown that was not modernized after the flood. It is so narrow and close to the creek bed that safe speed is less than 15 mph. Ground transportation to the valley and to the town of Man from Logan, Charleston, and urban areas to the north and west is severely restricted by a treacherous and utterly obsolete ten-mile section of Route 10 between Logan and Man.

2. A strong case can be made that the Buffalo Creek Valley never will have enough political clout unless it incorporates as a town, or some other entity, or unless at least one of its sixteen hamlets and villages does so. Longtime residents of the valley still seem to be divided as to whether incorporation should have passed when it was voted on in the 1980s.

3. There is only limited acreage on the valley floor above the fifty-year floodplain for new housing and for commercial and industrial uses (even though the acreage that is available provides some competitive advantages, as indicated in the preceding section).

4. Stores, shops, health care services, entertainment, and public transportation are scarce or nonexistent, particularly in the upper ten miles of the valley.

5. As part of Logan County, Buffalo Creek shares a number of the county's economic, social, and historical disadvantages, not the least of which is a reputation for "hillbilly" backwardness.[3]

This list might be expanded to include other features of the valley such as its limited access to strong educational facilities and the lack of political activism in its inhabitants, except for the fact that these features do not clearly distinguish Buffalo Creek from so many other small communities in rural Appalachia or in quite a few other parts of rural America.[4] As such, they probably are not competitive disadvantages for Buffalo Creek.

Scenario I: The Status Quo Continues Until the "Easy" Coal Seams Are Depleted (and a Promising Extension)

As indicated in one of the opening epigraphs, a popular assumption among local people is that there is enough high BTU coal (that is used for generating steam to electricity) in the readily accessible seams in the hills about the Buffalo Creek Valley to keep the mines operating for another ten to twenty years. If the mines continue to operate as assumed, then a small but significant number of the valley's residents will continue to be employed locally in the mines and in related service industries. Housing values will remain stable, most residents will be able to pay their taxes and afford living costs, and Logan County government will continue to maintain the infrastructure in and around the valley in reasonably good condition. If these things happen, the status quo should remain about the same as it is in terms of standard of living, quality of life, social integration, neighboring, and social well-being for most residents.

A Promising Extension

One variant on this scenario could extend the status quo for perhaps an additional twenty to thirty years—possibly to midcentury. This variant could occur if an increasingly popular energy-extraction technology is applied to reach much deeper coal seams around the valley or to reopen and tap into coal deposits that were abandoned as they deteriorated years ago. This technology is referred to with various names including "deep-seam coal gasification," "coal-bed methane development," "hydraulic fracturing," and "fracking."[5] In essence, it uses coal gas *wells* rather than coal *mines* to extract inanimate energy from the ground. It is expanding rapidly in some of the old coal fields in western Pennsylvania and some other parts of the United States, including the San Juan Basin in south-west Colorado and the Powder River Basin in Wyoming and Montana. It also is being used on a small scale at about eight locations in Logan County, West Virginia, not far from the Buffalo Creek Valley. This technology does not require much land per well (only about three to five acres of surface land, on average) and it is not very labor intensive, once the wells are in place and they are pumping on a consistent basis. While the technology requires the operation of dozens of wells above many miles of coal seams in order to be effective, and it has significant impacts on groundwater aquifers, it does not require much capital investment per well (about \$40,000–50,000) and it can generate "more than \$500,000 of revenue over the life of the well."[6] Wells can operate in place for twenty years or more with a moderate amount of maintenance. Therefore, if this technology can be used extensively to tap previously inaccessible coal seams near the Buffalo Creek Valley, it probably would sustain rather than transform the status quo of the people and their communities. It could maintain or enhance the tax revenues for the valley, but it probably would not produce many more jobs—directly or indirectly—or boost the standard of living for most of the inhabitants. Then again, more outsiders might be attracted to retire in the valley as methane gas wells replace coal mining operations because the wells occupy little surface space, they are less noisy and dusty than the mines, and they probably would be perceived to be much safer and more benign, environmentally, than are conventional coal mining operations.

Since I am not a geologist, a mining engineer, or an energy economist, I cannot attest to the economic feasibility of twenty more years

of coal mining or to the prospects for coal gasification in and around
the Buffalo Creek Valley. However, in May 2007, I found that a variety
of energy extraction methods were being expanded throughout Logan
County. There was considerable optimism among miners, drillers, managers, and heavy-equipment operators that the energy extraction business will remain robust for years to come, even if the markets for mined
coal fluctuate considerably from time to time. Thus it seems quite likely
that inanimate-energy production will help sustain community life along
Buffalo Creek at least for the next few decades.

SCENARIO II: CURRENT EFFORTS AT ECONOMIC DIVERSIFICATION BECOME MODERATELY SUCCESSFUL

> Route 10 needs to be modernized into a four lane highway from
> Logan City passing by the town of Man and going over across the
> belly of West Virginia to I-64 and I-77. Doing that would allow
> people to drive quickly to and from the Buffalo Creek Valley from
> hundreds of miles around.
>
> —A Logan County official

As indicated in chapter 3, several initiatives at economic development
have started in Logan County since 2000 that could have substantial long-
term benefits for the Buffalo Creek Valley. These include the rerouting
and modernizing of Route 10 from Logan City to and beyond the town of
Man, opening and promoting the Hatfield-McCoy Feud Historic Route,
and using tournaments and other incentives to promote an expanding
network of mountain trails for riders of "all-terrain vehicles" (ATVs).
If these efforts are successful over the next five years, they could produce moderate increases in local employment and in the number of high
school graduates who do not permanently leave the valley. Some young
adults and retirees might even move into the valley to establish their
homes on lots that have been made flood resistant but have remained
vacant for so long. In order for these three initiatives to be fully realized,
federal subsidies for the initiatives probably will need to continue for at
least another five years. However, if this happens, the benefits could be

quite substantial, particularly for start-up businesses in and around the valley.

The most important of these initiatives is the completion of the rerouting and modernizing of Route 10 from Logan City past the town of Man and the mouth of the Buffalo Creek Valley to the town of Gilbert, about twenty miles up the Guyandotte River. Doing this will connect the Buffalo Creek Valley more readily with Route 52, the southernmost highway that traverses the state. The current Route 10 from Logan to Man is one of the narrowest, most convoluted, and treacherous two-lane roads that I have traveled in West Virginia—and that is saying something! It is not to be experienced by the faint of heart—especially not at night, in rainy weather, or when loaded, sixty-ton coal trucks are fast approaching you. In local parlance, the recommended survival strategy in cases like these is to "double up on your prayin' and prepare to meet your maker as a pancake."

The good news is that a major section of this Route 10 renewal project was completed in 2005, reportedly at a cost of more than $10 million. It features an impressive, four-lane bridge of reinforced concrete that arches high above the town of Man near the junction of Buffalo Creek and the Guyandotte River. Of course, this bridge also allows traffic to bypass Man completely, and at more than 50 mph. A modernized Route 10 will make it much easier for Buffalo Creek's residents to drive to the services and jobs that they cannot find in the valley so that they do not feel compelled to move closer to those distant jobs.[7]

Overall, then, there is plenty of reason to believe that this scenario has a good chance of being realized so long as the West Virginia delegation in the United States Congress maintains enough seniority and influence to keep federal dollars flowing into Logan County.

SCENARIO III: MAJOR NEW PROJECTS AND INDUSTRIES REVITALIZE OR TRANSFORM THE VALLEY

There are a number of proposals for major new industries in and around the valley that have been mentioned to me by various people who have known Buffalo Creek since before the flood.[8]

- Economic development is the key to the future of Buffalo Creek and to Logan County area. Many of the young people would stay there, and many people would return to live there, if there were enough jobs, services, and opportunities down there. A number of proposals have been floating around for years. We've studied them and now we need to give them a try. We have a lot of "topless mountains" around here, as some folks call them. They are abandoned strip mines up on top of the mountains. The mountain tops were blasted away and leveled-off by heavy machinery so as to expose the coal. There's nothing up there anymore but wasteland. Those sites can be converted into recreational areas and resorts for tourists, maybe with gambling casinos and golf courses. You could even put an air-port up there to fly people in from all over the country.
- Arch Energy gave Logan County the deserted top strip mine at Becco with the proviso that it would be used for economic devel-opment. The State was going to build a new prison up there a few years back. Nothing has come of that so far—but it could happen in the next few years.
- The network of trails for the four-wheelers needs to be extended and marketed more heavily though the entire eastern U.S. We can even get riders from Germany, Japan, and China to come in here for yearly rallies if we do it right. Some of them have already been here and they love it.
- We need to re-open the hospital in south Man that closed years ago or we need to build a new critical access hospital or a care center that can provide what is called "urgent care."
- The state of West Virginia needs a new or remodeled mental health care facility with at least eighty-five beds down here in Southern WV. Building it in Man would help spur economic development by rehiring the former employees who lost their jobs when the hospital closed years ago.
- Years ago there was talk of creating a big trash recycling facility in one of the side hollows in the Valley. We could haul-in solid trash from Charleston and Huntington to fill in a lot of the old

gob ponds that we drained after the flood. Now they are just big, empty pits like something crashed into them from outer space. I say we should fill 'em up and cover 'em up.

- There's a lot of clean, cold, germ-free water up there in the old coal mines that are closed-up. That water can be used for fish farms where they raise catfish, trout, salmon, something called char, and other fish like that to sell year-round all over Appalachia. There's good jobs and money in that kind of business.

As indicated in these quotations, a number of prospects have been proposed in recent years that conceivably could revitalize and perhaps even transform the local economy as well as increase the political power of the communities in the valley. Converting the abandoned strip mines on the "topless mountains" around the valley into resorts and industrial sites is the prospect that excites politicians, business leaders, and the local populace the most.[9] If a major facility was built on one or more of the topless mountains above the valley (without housing being built up there for the employees), many of the employees could be expected to look for family housing down in the valley even though flood-resistant, vacant land is limited. Then again, a new facility also could prompt valley residents to try again to incorporate some or all of the sixteen hamlets and villages. Incorporation and completion of Route 16 over East Mountain to Route 99 and Beckley then could serve as catalysts to draw other industries into the valley or to bring them close by.[10] My sense is that major revitalization or transformation of the valley will not occur without one or two rather bold and dynamic catalysts such as these. Even then, the prospects probably are limited for a major transformation of Buffalo Creek during the next few decades.

SCENARIO IV: SUDDEN DECLINE IN THE COAL ECONOMY OR IN EXTERNAL FUNDING BY GOVERNMENT AGENCIES

The most obvious threat to the communities of Buffalo Creek is a sudden and enduring collapse in the markets for the kind of steam coal that is still fairly accessible around the valley. This could occur rather quickly if the next few administrations in Washington DC reverse the pro-coal policies of their predecessors and if Congress, the Environmental Protection Agency, and other federal agencies make concerted efforts to reduce the burning of coal for producing electricity. Growing international concerns about global warming and toxic emissions into the earth's atmosphere could prompt these changes within the next decade. Much of the coal from Logan County is transported to nearby power plants and chemical plants at Huntington, West Virginia, and Ashland, Kentucky. Enduring restrictions on the burning of Appalachian coal might close down these plants and produce significant unemployment—then depopulation—throughout the area, including the Buffalo Creek Valley.

A less obvious threat to the Buffalo Creek Valley has existed ever since the 1960s, when President Kennedy launched his War on Poverty program only a few years after he toured Buffalo Creek with the national press corps in tow. This is the threat of drastic reductions or terminations of federal programs that have been shoring up the local economy with funds for social welfare, infrastructure modernization, job training, education, and health care. Drastic changes like these could occur in the near future for any number of reasons. New foreign wars, a deep and lasting recession in the national economy, or a series of "mega" disasters like Hurricane Katrina on the Gulf Coast in 2005 could prompt governments to divert funding from areas like Logan County and Appalachia in order to meet more pressing exigencies elsewhere. A newly elected administration in DC could be politically indifferent or hostile towards the West Virginia delegation. The West Virginia delegation of very senior and influential senators (Byrd and Rockefeller) might be succeeded by members without enough influence to protect the interests of places like Buffalo Creek.

Given threats like these—no matter how unlikely they might seem to be at this time—residents of places like Buffalo Creek would be wise to pursue scenarios like II and III rather than run the risk of scenario IV striking them suddenly and unawares. This is even truer of the final scenario to be mentioned here, and with considerable trepidation—another disaster.

SCENARIO V: ANOTHER DISASTER

Rejecting Jeremiah, Cassandra, and other doomsdayers, let me post the best news up front: it is highly unlikely that another flash flood of the magnitude of the one in 1972 could occur again in the Buffalo Creek Valley. Probably, this could only occur if—for some reason that is not readily apparent—huge, new gob ponds were built, filled with massive volumes of liquid waste, and then suddenly destroyed by earthquakes or sabotage. Even then, such a flash flood would do much less damage to the valley than the one in 1972 because most of the buildings and residents are located on flood-resistant tracts of land that were reclaimed after the last flood. In addition to that, cell phones are so common in the valley that news of a collapsed gob pond or reservoir would spread so quickly that—I hope—most of the residents would be able to get out of harm's way.

And yet, we should at least consider the question that outsiders have asked me so often over the years—could it happen again? This subject has been mentioned to me from time to time by small numbers of the people whom I interviewed in the course of my research along Buffalo Creek. None of them ever spoke as Cassandras or Jeremiahs with predictions of apocalypse. In general, the older residents—particularly women who directly experienced the flood—expressed some concern that another flash flood could happen again, if smaller in scale. They did not contend that this is inevitable. They just do not have much faith in nature or in the workings of big organizations, from governments to coal companies. By contrast, people in business and government jobs, retired miners, and service workers generally felt that another flash flood as devastating as the one in 1972 could not occur again because, as several of them told me, "All the gob ponds have been drained. There's nothing in them anymore."

Curious about beliefs like these, I have done some exploring in the hills above the Buffalo Creek Valley. I have walked far up Middle Fork past the three dams that failed in 1972. I have walked up to and around a number of other former gob ponds above Buffalo Creek and Elk Creek. I have also spent an hour flying over the valley at 3,500 feet as a passenger in a helicopter in order to get an aerial view of former and current mining operations. Retired miners have driven me along Lorado Ridge in their ATVs in order to show me abandoned mines and old gob ponds. Of course, I am not a geologist, a civil engineer, or a physical scientist of any other sort. And I certainly do not want to be an alarmist. However, from what I have seen, heard, and read, I believe that the Buffalo Creek Valley is by no means invulnerable to flash floods, mud slides, rockslides, explosions, and fires from methane gasses in working mines and in mines that were abandoned long ago. It also is vulnerable to toxic wastes from former and current mining operations that contaminate mountain streams and the water table in the floor of the valley and, of course, the creek of Buffalo Creek itself. The geology and the hydrology of the area are not particularly stable because of human interference with deep-shaft mines, strip mines, explosives, and toxic wastes over the last hundred years. Former mines have been flooded and closed in rudimentary ways. There is evidence that some of them are "stewing" or "cooking" far underground, and that this can continue indefinitely.

Speaking from personal experience, I have found more than a few abandoned gob ponds that contain enough black liquid waste and suspended coal particles to fill several Olympic-sized swimming pools. I also have found that many of the old gob ponds that are "dry" still are blocked by earthen dams that conceivably could restrain thousands of tons of rainwater or other liquids until the dams become unstable and fail. I also saw one massive, active gob pond on the north side of Laurel Ridge above Rum Creek, less than ten miles from Buffalo Creek, that appeared to be filled with hundreds of tons of oily, black, mine wastewater.

Also unsettling to me is the fact that, as reported in chapter 4, flash floods still occur seasonally in some of the side hollows of the Buffalo Creek Valley. These flash floods frequently flood basements and wash away porches, vehicles, and small bridges. Occasionally, they even kill people—as happened during one of my visits to Buffalo Creek in May 2001.[11] It concerns me that incidents of nature and human interference such as these could occur on a massive scale or in rapid succession in the valley. Even if they did not destroy many lives or do much damage to private and public property, they could lead to a lot of pernicious rumors, to unfavorable publicity, and to exaggerated accounts of devastation. They could ignite old and new anxieties for Buffalo Creek's residents. The value of land and dwellings could plummet. County, state, and federal agencies might become reluctant to invest any further in the valley. Residents with sufficient means might decide that they have had enough troubles along Buffalo Creek and that it is time to move elsewhere. The valley might be more or less abandoned by external agencies and left to its own fates, all the more so if "mega disasters" like Hurricane Katrina's havoc to New Orleans and the Gulf Coast continue to occur and to absorb so much attention and revenue of the federal government. What few competitive advantages the Buffalo Creek Valley now has could disappear in a flash—and forever.

So, in sum, while a flash flood as disastrous as the one in 1972 is not likely to be repeated, the Buffalo Creek Valley still is vulnerable to lesser incidents of nature and human interference that, under the "perfectly" wrong circumstances, could lead to the rapid decline in the communities of Buffalo Creek. On a more positive note, however, this scenario of disaster (V) and the scenario of permanent decline in the coal economy (IV) can be rendered even less likely to occur if the people of Buffalo Creek can bring about scenarios II or III in the near future. The reason for this is that external agencies can be expected to eliminate or reduce the threats that constitute scenarios IV and V in the process of investing in the Buffalo Creek Valley.

PROSPECTS FOR ENJOYING LIFE IN THE VALLEY

Fortunately, the scenarios of sudden decline and of another major disaster are highly unlikely. Scenario II (current economic diversification) is underway and has been moderately successful so far. Without economic diversification, the status quo at Buffalo Creek is likely to continue for several more decades. Dramatic economic expansion probably is very unlikely unless Highway 16 is extended over the mountains to Beckley and the interstate highways. Even with the extension of Highway 16, however, it is unlikely that more than a few new industries will move into the valley.

So, given the widely varying likelihoods of these five different scenarios, longtime residents, as well as residents who have voluntarily moved to Buffalo Creek in recent years and have built homes, have good prospects for enjoying life in the valley for years to come. Retired and gainfully employed persons who enjoy life along Buffalo Creek certainly should stay. The odds are in their favor. Continuing improvements on Route 10 will make it easier for all residents with vehicles to get to Logan and to Route 119 to Charleston and to urban areas to the west and to the north. Buffalo Creek's worst years are over, as far as isolation from the cities to the north and west is concerned. Candidly put, however, highly motivated, upwardly mobile high school graduates who aspire to careers in professions that require advanced degrees in law, medicine, engineering, or the humanities probably have little prospect for these kinds of careers while living in or around this area. Of course, this also is true for these kinds of people who live in so many areas of rural America that are more than an hour's drive from at least one major metropolitan area.

With its quiet amenities, the Buffalo Creek Valley also should continue to attract as new residents early retirees who are still in good health and who want inexpensive housing in a rural setting surrounded by well-forested mountains that some people find to be comfortably protective. As one native-born "creeker" told me, "I don't feel right unless I'm in my mountains. They give me shelter." Living in the valley can be even more appealing for newcomers if they have adult children, grandchildren, and a few close relatives and friends who are happily residing in the valley or near it. The many small churches and friendly religious groups in and around the valley also can be attractive features. And, of course, the ridges above the valley can be paradise for anyone who loves riding ATVs/OMTs ("old men's toys").

RELEVANCE OF THE BUFFALO CREEK EXPERIENCE TO OTHER SMALL TOWNS IN RURAL AMERICA

It would be easy to dismiss the experience of Buffalo Creek as an aberration, an anachronism, dead history, or as a place whose story was over long ago. But it would be foolhardy to do so. At least three erroneous assumptions can feed this temptation to discount and ignore the relevance of the Buffalo Creek experience for so many other places in rural America:

1. That there is no other place like Buffalo Creek. It is utterly unique—exceptional.
2. That a flood like the one that struck Buffalo Creek is totally different from other incidents of nature and human intervention that cause disasters.
3. That federal, state, and local governments can now protect small communities from incidents like the flood at Buffalo Creek and from disastrous aftereffects and consequences.

All of these assumptions are dubious, at best. They are contradicted many times every year by incidents that produce disastrous consequences for many small communities in many areas of the United States and elsewhere in the world.[12]

The Buffalo Creek Experience Is Not Utterly Unique

I have driven on only a small fraction of the back roads in the coal counties of West Virginia, Tennessee, Kentucky, and Pennsylvania (where I lived for seventeen years). But I have found many places—"coal camp valleys," let us call them—that are very similar to the Buffalo Creek Valley in topography, hydrology, demography, economy, and community life. In fact, there are dozens of coal camp valleys like this just in the five counties (Boone, Logan, Mingo, Wyoming, and McDowell) along the "Coal

Heritage Trail" of southwestern West Virginia. These are steeply pitched, cul-de-sac valleys that are up to twenty miles long. One or more former coal camps are located in their very narrow floodplains along mountain streams that are prone to flash floods. To the extent that these places are different from their counterparts in the Buffalo Creek Valley, the differences often are to their disadvantage. Many of them are in much steeper valleys that are surrounded by older, less closely monitored gob ponds, reservoirs, and mines. Ironically enough, their roads, bridges, utilities, industrial buildings, and dwellings are older and more vulnerable than Buffalo Creek's to flash floods and other incidents of nature and/or human interference. This is because they have not had Buffalo Creek's experience with such major disasters as the one of 1972. In contrast to the Buffalo Creek Valley, their floodplains have not been elevated, contoured, and made more flood resistant. As a result, they are much more vulnerable targets for destructive incidents than is the Buffalo Creek Valley. Is it any wonder, then, that flash floods are so commonplace in these places?

In fact, the flash flood and the disaster at Buffalo Creek never were especially unique, from a historical standpoint. As indicated in chapters 1 and 6, there are many places in mountainous regions of the United States—such as Johnstown, Pennsylvania, and dozens of villages above and below it on the Conemaugh River—that have been suffering deadly flash floods for more than one hundred years. And there are even more villages in low-lying areas along mighty rivers such as the Ohio and Mississippi that continue to suffer devastating floods from time to time, just as they have since they were first inhabited more than one hundred years ago, despite the enormous investments made by governments and the Army Corps of Engineers to preclude them from occurring.[13]

Of course, we should not need to be reminded that floods occur not just when it rains too heavily, for too long, and when gob ponds collapse. Obviously, floods also occur when water reservoirs fail, when levees burst, and when hurricanes inundate communities. Seen in this way, it should be no surprise for us to learn that hundreds of hamlets, villages, and small towns in the United States suffer devastating floods each year. These include little places like Rocky Creek and Princeville,

North Carolina, Hannibal, Missouri, and the hundreds of little villages and towns along the Gulf Coast in Mississippi, Louisiana, Alabama, and Florida that are swamped whenever hurricanes come their way.

Many Other Places Are Vulnerable to Incidents and to Disasters Similar to the Buffalo Creek Experience

Buffalo Creek's experience is relevant not just to hamlets, villages, and small towns that are vulnerable to floods, tornadoes, and forest fires. Its relevance applies to the thousands of small places in America and elsewhere in the world that are in or near hazardous sites where "incidents of nature and human interference" can turn into disasters. Included here are places that are closely tied to nearby extractive industries such as oil and gas wells, copper, lead, uranium, sulfur, nitrate, and iron mines, and to "volatile" or toxic production and distribution facilities such as oil refineries, chemical plants, paper-pulp plants, and laboratories that produce and store materials for biological warfare. Examples include petroleum refineries at Grand Isle, Louisiana; the paper-pulp plants at Grassy Narrows, Ontario; the nuclear-waste storage facility at Yucca Mountain, Nevada; and the crude-oil–shipping facilities and operations at Valdez, Alaska. In all of these cases, local residents had been somewhat aware of some of the hazards around them, but they were unprepared for the kinds of devastating incidents that occurred and for the disastrous consequences that continued for years. They also relied too heavily upon large corporations and governments to protect them and to help them recover from the damages they suffered.[14]

Federal, State, and Local Governments Often Cannot Preclude Incidents and Disastrous Consequences Similar to the Buffalo Creek Experience

In this era of "mega disasters" such as Hurricanes Katrina and Rita, small rural communities in the United States that suffer disasters will be competing for government aid and resources against big cities, metropolitan areas, and multistate regions of the country. The megadisasters, and the threat of more of them, will monopolize the attention and the funding of government agencies, interest groups, and charitable organizations. Already there is a tendency for the Federal Emergency Management Agency and the Army Corps of Engineers to overlook localized disasters at small rural communities and to discourage survivors from rebuilding and resettling there.[15] For example, in 1999 the Tar River overflowed a levee that was supposed to protect Princeville, North Carolina, from flooding. It flooded so severely that almost every building and home was totally submerged, except for the steeple of one of its churches. Officers from the Army Corps of Engineers and from the Federal Emergency Management Agency who visited the disaster site tried to convince the survivors that Princeville should be cleared of debris and abandoned forever. Residents who insisted on moving back to Princeville after the floodwaters receded were assigned to trailers in a HUD trailer camp in a haphazard manner similar to what had occurred at the HUD trailer camps in and around Buffalo Creek in 1972.[16]

CONCLUDING RECOMMENDATIONS FOR SMALL, RURAL COMMUNITIES

Given the obvious relevance of the Buffalo Creek experience for so many small communities in harm's way in America, allow me to conclude this book with some recommendations based upon the Buffalo Creek experience. Some of these recommendations are preventive and proactive. Others are reactive. All of them supplement the many suggestions that have been made in conjunction with various major findings that are presented in the preceding chapters of this book. Let me also suggest that these recommendations might have reduced the likelihood of the flash flood and the disaster at Buffalo Creek in 1972. More importantly, let me affirm to you my belief that these recommendations can help prevent disasters in many small communities in rural America.

Some Preventive and Proactive Recommendations

1. If possible, at least once a year, personally visit the hazardous sites in the catchment, containment, and contaminant zones nearest to

your community, or observe them from a safe distance, when it is reasonably safe to do so. You can learn a lot about potential hazards just by walking, hiking, or driving around the periphery of sites that might be hazardous. Observe the sites from high ground or from the air when you fly over the area. Pay attention to wind direction, gullies, water courses, vegetation, dumps, storage facilities, and obstacles created by humans that can influence how the products are distributed and the wastes are dispersed under normal conditions and under extreme conditions. If you cannot do these things yourself, then try to encourage other trustworthy and mature members of your community to do so, such as ministers and teachers. Show your appreciation when they inform you of what they see and learn from their own personal reconnaissances.

2. Pay attention to plausible rumors and to credible reports of minor accidents and incidents at nearby sites that could indicate that there might be systemic safety problems at the sites or that conditions are deteriorating there. In responsible ways, encourage editors and reporters from the nearest news media to investigate credible reports of accidents and incidents at the sites and to publish articles about the sites based on their own visits to the sites.

3. Be sure to invite employees and managers of the sites to participate fully in public events in your community, such as picnics, parades, and functions at the schools and churches. Help them to feel comfortable when they do so. Talk to them at opportune times about their work at the sites, but refrain from interrogating them or making them feel defensive. Reassure them that you and other members of your community are interested in them, their work, and the sites because all of you share the same environments and communities. Also try to encourage members of the labor force at the sites to buy property and reside within your community so that they are direct stakeholders in its well-being.

4. Acknowledge, appreciate, and commend members of your commu-
    nity who exercise an active interest in the sites. At the same time,
    do not tolerate pranksters, jokesters, sensationalists, and antago-
    nists who spread outrageous rumors about the sites or interfere
    with the operations at the sites in hazardous ways. Recall from
    chapter 1 that some residents of Buffalo Creek had discounted
    the likelihood of the dams collapsing at Three Forks on February
    26, 1972, because for many years, pranksters had been driving up
    and down the valley on rainy nights, blaring on the horns of their
    vehicles, and yelling out false alarms about the collapse of the
    dams: "The dams just broke! Head for the hills!" Therefore, do
    not tolerate pranks and intentionally false alarms. Persuade the
    pranksters to desist—or have them chastised or prosecuted, if
    need be.
5. Protective political actions: Residents of small, rural communi-
    ties that are not incorporated and are without their own elected
    leaders, police, fire, rescue, and other services can take a number
    of actions that will reduce the likelihood of dangerous incidents
    at hazardous sites and will keep such incidents from becoming
    full-blown disasters.

Identify and engage elected and appointed officials and bureaucrats in
your county and state government agencies who are willing to help your
community reduce hazards at the nearby sites and who will be ready to
respond to dangerous incidents that might occur at the sites. For example, encourage elected members of county and state government to provide incentives (such a tax credits) to hazardous-site operators who will
share their emergency fire-and-rescue equipment with your community
whenever it is needed.

Form an association or a group of volunteers (a "watch-guard" rather
than a "watchdog") that will actively monitor the hazardous sites in
responsible ways, anticipate how incidents at the sites could become
disasters for the community, and serve as a liaison between residents
of your community and the managers of the hazardous sites. A volun-

tary association such as this can invite suggestions regarding its purposes and plans from all the other residents of the community, from managers at the hazardous sites, and from officials in county and state government. The association also can invite experts to help it anticipate and understand the kinds of incidents that might occur at the hazardous sites and the kinds of disasters that might result from these incidents. Association members can be encouraged to become familiar with "the Buffalo Creek experience" and with other reports on how other small communities have experienced disasters. The association might decide to form teams such as an "Incident Preparation Team" (IPT) and an "Incident Remediation Team" (IRT). As implied by their names, these teams would focus, respectively, on preparation for and remediation after disastrous incidents.[17]

The association as a whole can decide upon primary and alternative locations in the community where members can assemble and operate if incidents occur at the hazardous sites. Central crossroads and the porches and parking spaces at churches, schools, and private homes might be good choices for such "coordinating centers" (not to be confused with the "command centers" of official agencies). Establish reliable procedures so that association members can readily communicate with one another, around the clock, and so that all other members of the community can get in touch with association members through a variety of media (face to face, cell phones, CB radios, an association Web site on the Internet, etc.) whenever the need arises. The association also might identify the safest locations for emergency shelters, food and water supply points, sanitary facilities, aid stations, morgues, and temporary trailer camps in the event that major disasters occur. Then the association will be ready to inform the managers of the hazardous sites and officials in county and state government, the Red Cross, and other rescue and relief agencies of what it has accomplished and how the association and its IRT can (and should) be used if emergencies occur.

And, of course, you might consider the benefits of incorporating your community either by itself or in conjunction with other small communities that are near the same hazardous sites. If this is not feasible, then consider the possibility of using existing laws or having new laws created that will allow your community to increase its political influence by joining into a coalition or a "quasicorporation" with other small communities in the area, preferably without extraordinary increases in taxes or in financial liability. Consider that the flash flood at Buffalo Creek probably would not have occurred if one or more of the sixteen coal camps had been incorporated and had a responsible town council at least several years before the flood. And consider that a responsible town council could have helped the Buffalo Creek Valley rebuild and recover more quickly and more fully than it has, to date.

Some Reactive Recommendations

Here are some reactive measures to employ if and when incidents occur at hazardous sites that spill over onto or into your community and threaten to become disastrous. While reading through these, keep in mind that Kai Erikson and the authors of other worthwhile books about Buffalo Creek credibly established that some of the well-intended but misguided reactions of some government agencies to the flash flood were just as disastrous to the well-being of the survivors as was the flash flood itself.

Activate your community's IRT "Incident Remediation Team" (or form such a team if it has not already been formed) as soon as an incident occurs at a hazardous site that might jeopardize the well-being of your community. Of course, it is very important to do this in responsible ways so as not to interfere with the operations of police, fire, and emergency rescue crews from the county and state; but do not be surprised if assistance from external organizations takes longer to arrive and is less organized than you might expect. It can be helpful if members of the IRT assemble at one of the predesignated points in the community and divide into three or more subunits with the ability to maintain frequent communication with one another, through cell phones or other handheld electronic devices. Members of one subunit might deploy to the two or three primary avenues into the community in order to meet relief personnel from external agencies when they arrive and to help guide traffic, if this is appropriate. Members of another subunit might circulate throughout the community to assess any damages, render immediate aid to people in need, and assure other residents that their interests are being served. Other subunits might concentrate on working with county and state officials when they arrive in the area, and on coordinating communications with members of the news media and relief agencies such as the Red Cross. Several members of the IRT should remain at the designated assembly point in order to coordinate the operations of the subunits and keep a detailed written record of the major events that occur as external agencies respond to the incident and its threat to the community.

Once trustworthy personnel from external agencies have arrived in your community, members of the IRT can monitor their work in unobtrusive ways, provide assistance when needed, and help coordinate the use of other volunteers from inside and outside the community. Of course, it is important to understand that IRT members do not have any official authority or legal standing unless, perchance, they are deputized or hired on the spot as temporary workers. And yet, it is also true that, as citizens of the state and as residents of the community in danger, they have many rights and more than a few obligations to protect themselves, their property, their homes, their families, their neighbors, and the community at large.

Other lessons to be learned from the Buffalo Creek experience that can help your community respond to hazardous incidents and to disasters include the following.

Be willing to help and to receive help not only from your family members and friends, but also from your neighbors and from all members of your community. Do not expect outside agencies to be able to do for you and your community as much as you can do for one another, especially in the minutes and hours immediately following an incident.

Anticipate that the "confusion factor" and the "convergence factor" will occur in the days immediately after an incident. Your small community will probably be overloaded with more outsiders than it could ever accommodate without mass confusion. These will include employees from many different outside agencies and organizations, volunteers from nearby communities and relief organizations, concerned relatives of members of your community, members of news media from all over the United States, and, of course, the inevitable parade of gawkers and hawkers. Based on what we have learned from careful studies of hundreds of other disasters, very few outsiders will be inclined towards mischief, larceny, looting, or mayhem—but there might be a few of these. So, be prepared to help your neighbors maintain surveillance and security over your neighborhoods in discreet and lawful ways.

As shown in the Buffalo Creek experience, realize that sustaining social support networks and building new ones (part of what is sometimes referred to as "social capital") can help in the recovery of psychological and social well-being and the re-creation of the kinds of social relations that made your locale into a real community that is worth re-creating. However, social capital alone probably will *not* be sufficient to accomplish these things, in part because disasters often do the most damage to those places and people with relatively little social capital to begin with.

Be prepared for the possibility that government agencies—such as the highway department and the public works departments of the county, the Army Corps of Engineers, and the Federal Emergency Management Agency—will be inclined to engage in excessive clearing of damaged parts of your community rather than save, salvage, and rebuild them.

Expect that rebuilding the infrastructure of your community will take many months, if not years, and that there will be many frustrations along the way as government agencies stall, bog down in bureaucratic squabbles and budgetary shortfalls, and occasionally reverse their plans and procedures. Also expect that some of the infrastructure will *not* be rebuilt, at least not by government agencies.

Be prepared for what seems to be a limitless number of lawsuits by and against members of your community, businesses, county, state, and federal government agencies, the operators of hazardous sites, and by all sorts of external interest groups whose interests might have little to do with the interests of your small community. Be aware that lawsuits and the "litigation process" sometimes complicate the rebuilding and recovery process in some small, rural communities that have suffered major disasters (although this does not seem to have been the case at Buffalo Creek—in contrast to what is reported to have happened at the Love Canal in New York and at Valdez, Alaska). Realize that community members have the right to sue individually for damages sustained because of hazardous incidents and disasters. However, realize that collective actions can be very successful, less controversial, and less divisive, even though they tend to take longer to resolve. They also can contribute to re-creating positive social relations throughout small communities.

* * *

Last, but certainly not least, be prepared for the interest that writers, researchers, clinicians, and scholars will express in you and your community if a major disaster materializes there. Chances are that they will be sincerely interested in what happened, and why. They will be shocked and saddened by the destruction that they observe in and around your community. They will want to convey to others the depth of your suffering and your losses. If you are able to do so, help them understand fully what has transpired and what it means to you and to others. However, unless everything has been lost, help them to understand that, despite all of the devastation and the personal tragedies, some things have not been lost—things that perhaps you and many others hold most dear. Help them to understand that while the quintessential qualities of human communities can be very fragile and fleeting, they also can be concealed by the devastation of disasters—unless we know how and where to find them. Help them to understand that—thankfully and despite the odds against them—humans and the communities that they create often are able to re-create themselves *if* they are allowed enough time, resources, and respect.

Fortunately for humankind, few disasters have been as "total" in their destructiveness as was the volcanic eruption of Mount Vesuvius to the Roman city of Pompeii in AD 79 (as analyzed in chapter 2). And as we now know, Buffalo Creek certainly is not one of them. It continues to provide at least moderate amounts of community and social well-being for many of its people. Surely, all of us can be thankful for this.

ENDNOTES

1. Herman Kahn and Anthony J. Wiener, *The Year 2000: A Framework for Speculation on the Next Thirty-Three Years* (New York: The Macmillan Company, 1967). For one of many examples of the use of scenarios and "alternative futures" for improving social life in small, rural communities, see chapter 17 of Janet M. Fitchen, *Endangered Spaces, and Enduring Places: Change, Identity, and Survival in Rural America* (Boulder, CO: Westview Press, 1991).

2. A tortuous gravel road somehow manages to cross over the mountains eastward from Three Forks to Route 99, but only the most courageous or desperate souls are inclined to chance this hair-raising experience.

3. Basic demographic and economic data are available for Logan County and for the Amherstdale-Robinette census tract, but not for Buffalo Creek as a whole or for any one of its sixteen former coal camps. Despite the abundance of coal and gas reserves, Logan County and the local census tract are relatively poor, low in educational attainment, and high on infant mortality, compared to state and national averages. For example, the poverty level in Logan County is 23 percent, in contrast to 16.8 percent for West Virginia, and 13.3 percent for the United States. Median household income is $22.7K for Logan County, in contrast to $27.4K for West Virginia and $37.5K for the United States. See U.S. Census Bureau, *County and City Data Book 2000: A Statistical Abstract Supplement (County and City Data Book)*, 13th ed. (Washington, DC: Dept. of Commerce, Bureau of the Census, 2001), tables A1–12, B1–12, and "West Virginia: 2000, Summary of Population and Housing Characteristics," tables 3, 15, and 23.

   Unfortunately, several other facts about Logan County tend to sully its reputation, in addition to the legendary feud between the Hatfield and McCoy clans (some of whose members lived in Logan County) and much of what has been written by other authors about the "Buffalo Creek disaster." In the early 1800s, settlers of European descent nearly exterminated the Mingo tribe that inhabited the area. In 1921, an effort to unionize coal miners in Logan County turned into the notorious and bloody "Battle of Blair Mountain," less than twelve miles from Buffalo Creek. Adding to this image of deprivation is the fact that Logan County has more than a few unincorporated communities with names that cartoonists, comedians, and critics use to conjure up "hillbilly" stereotypes: "Black Bottom," "Crooked Creek," "Frogtown," "Rum Junction," and (believe it or not) a "Sodom" and an actual "Dog Patch." Some business owners in Logan County even appear to enjoy the stereotype with the names of their businesses: "Hillbilly Barber Shop" (on the main street of the town of Man) and "Hillbilly Pawn Shop" (in Logan).

In fact, the hillbilly stereotype is reinforced in some ways at the senior high school in south Man that serves the students of the Buffalo Creek Valley. Colorful banners and billboards around the high school and its ball fields proudly display a cartoon "hillbilly" as the school mascot and proclaim the nickname of the school, "MAN HIGH SCHOOL. HOME OF THE HILLBILLIES."

Quite a few local people—working-class males in particular—often identify themselves as hillbillies, perhaps as a badge of honor, sometimes with a dash of self-deprecating humor. "Hillbilly—and proud of it," "Hillbilly Heaven," "Moonshiner," "Moonshine Madness," "Redneck," and "Rednecks Rule" are popular proclamations on the bumper stickers and window decals on their trucks and every other sort of vehicle. This is *self*-stereotyping—not prejudicial labeling by external bigots and elites.

Given these realities, at times it seems that the people who are most offended by the hillbilly stereotype—almost to the point of loathing it—are not the common folk of Appalachia so much as some of the scholars in "Appalachian studies" who go to great lengths to deny the existence of hillbillies. For examples, see various chapters in Dwight B. Billings et al., eds., *Confronting Appalachian Stereotypes: Back Talk from an American Region* (Lexington: The University Press of Kentucky, 1999).

4. On the scarcity of political activism in many parts (but certainly not all parts) of rural America, see Philip J. Obermiller and Michael E. Maloney, eds., *Appalachia: Social Context Past and Present* (Dubuque, IA: Kendall-Hunt Publishing Company, 2006); Janet M. Fitchen, *Endangered Spaces, and Enduring Places: Change, Identity, and Survival in Rural America* (Boulder, CO: Westview Press, 1991); and various articles in David L. Brown and Louis E. Swanson, eds., *Challenges for Rural America in the Twenty-First Century* (University Park, PA: The Pennsylvania State University Press, 2003), such as chapter 15, "Community Agency and Local Development," by A. E. Luloff and Jeffrey C. Bridger, 203–214.

5. Briefly stated, with this technology, well-drilling machinery is mounted on the beds of trailer trucks that are driven to small parcels of land (three to five acres) above deep coal seams. Steel pipes are drilled down hundreds or thousands of feet beneath the earth's surface into coal seams that cannot be reached economically by more conventional mining techniques. Then, in

a complex series of operations, water is forced down through pipes under extreme hydraulic pressure that fractures the coal seams into releasing methane gas ("coal gas") from the coal. The gas is extracted by pipes to the surface, where it is collected in storage tanks or piped overland to central collection points or to industrial sites that use the gas for manufacturing processes, to produce chemicals such as nitrogen for fertilizer, or to generate electricity. For more information on this technology, see Western Organization of Resource Councils, "Coalbed Methane Development: Boon or Bane for Rural Residents?" Washington DC, http://scholar.google.com/scholar?q=coal+gasification+hydraulic+fracture (accessed March 2003).

6. Ibid. This information about coal-bed–methane-development technology is based on a number of additional sources, including my conversations with various coal mine employees in Logan County, West Virginia, May 2007; as well as my conversations with Calvin Elder Pollins, a landowner who has three coal-bed–methane-gas wells operating on his farm at the time of this writing.

7. Unfortunately, in 2006 Governor Mankin suspended further improvements on Route 10 until the state's budget crisis is resolved.

8. These quotations are from Logan County government and business leaders, ministers, and supervisors in the Buffalo Valley Service District.

9. The topless parts of the "topless mountains" are not very accessible by ground transportation, and they are rather shocking sights to experience in person (even for an adult)! I have driven my tired but true minivan up the daunting, serpentine, rocky trail from Becco to the top of Lorado Ridge where, as rumor had it, the state of West Virginia was about to build a medium-security prison. The four-mile trip took me almost one hour to climb the inclines and to zigzag back and forth across steep ravines and washed-out gullies. Once I arrived at the "top," I found that the mountain really was "topless." It was a barren, boulder-strewn wasteland. It appeared that the tract of land was large enough—more than 500 acres—that it could accommodate an airfield for all but the largest jet aircraft. Otherwise, the cost of building a modern, two-lane highway from Route 16 on the valley floor would be extremely expensive, if not prohibitive. On the nature of "mountaintop removal," see Shirley Stewart Burns, *Bringing Down the Mountains: The Impact of Mountaintop Removal on Southern West Virginia Communities* (Morgantown, WV: West Virginia University Press, 2007).

10. As explained in chapter 3, both of these catalysts were proposed and almost came into being in the years immediately after the flood. One of these was promised in the Buffalo Valley Redevelopment Plan that was

issued by Governor Moore and the Federal Regional Commission in 1973. This was the proposed extension of Highway 16 from the eastern end of Buffalo Creek at Three Forks over the mountains to join up with Route 99. It would provide quick access from the valley to the city of Beckley and the two interstate highways (I-77 and I-64) that link south-central West Virginia to Virginia, North Carolina, Kentucky, and Ohio. The other catalyst would be the incorporation of one, several, or all of the hamlets and villages in the Buffalo Creek Valley into a town or some other form of municipality. Recall that a referendum to incorporate all of the former coal camps into one municipality was defeated around 1980. There still is considerable support among local people (some of whom were profiled in chapter 4) for incorporating some of the former coal camps, provided that local taxes would not increase too dramatically.

11. As reported in chapter 3, two adults and a child perished in May 2001 when they were caught trying to drive across a ford of Buffalo Creek at Robinette during a flash flood. When I interviewed some local residents about this incident the next day, I was alarmed to hear that they were *not* alarmed by it. One of them appeared to speak for the others when he told me that "[y]ou got to be smart enough to know when you can't get across that creek."

12. Summaries and descriptions of some of the many disasters that happen to small communities in the United States each year can be found in the annual reports of the Federal Emergency Management Agency and in Ted Steinberg's *Acts of God: The Unnatural History of Natural Disasters in America* (Oxford and New York: Oxford University Press, 2000). Also see documents of the Federal Emergency Management Agency (FEMA), including "2007 Federal Disaster Declarations," http://www.fema.gov/news/disasters.fema?year=2007 (accessed August 11, 2008).

13. Many of these flash floods, floods, and other disastrous incidents are described and documented in Ted Steinberg's *Acts of God: The Unnatural History of Natural Disaster in America*.

14. Often these are the kinds of communities that rely heavily—even exclusively—upon one industry, plant, or facility that is hazardous or that can become hazardous over the years. It is not unusual for the site to be operated by a subcontractor for an absentee subsidiary of a huge multinational corporation in ways that complicate matters of accountability, transparency, and liability. Many of these sites are in remote areas of the nation, far from metropolitan areas and government centers, and thus are likely to be ignored. Often the facilities use processes and produce products that

are perceived by the public to be unpleasant, "dirty," unstable, somewhat embarrassing, and controversial. These are places where hazards might brew, percolate, leech, or cumulate slowly for years before they become incidents that suddenly seem to explode into the mass media and the public conscience. Examples include the "Love Canal" toxic-waste controversy in upstate New York in the 1980s; the release of highly toxic fumes at the chemical plant near Bhopal, India, in the 1980s; and, of course, the nuclear power plant accidents at Three Mile Island, Pennsylvania, and Chernobyl, USSR, in the 1980s. Looking to the immediate future, we might call attention to the current proliferation of ethanol from corn-production refineries near so many small towns and villages in the Midwest thanks to government subsidies, tax breaks, and other incentives. Can these sites endanger the small communities closest to them? If so, the recommendations that conclude this chapter can help to reduce the hazards and the likelihood that disasters will materialize from incidents of nature or of human interference.

15. This increasing tendency of federal agencies to overlook disasters to small rural communities and to discourage survivors from rebuilding is developed in Steinberg's *Acts of God*. Several case studies of this tendency are presented in Jake Halpern, *Braving Home: Dispatches from the Underwater Town, the Lava-Side Inn, and Other Extreme Locale*s (Boston: Houghton Mifflin Company, 2003).

16. Information about the flooding and the disaster at Princeville, North Carolina, in 1999 is based on personal interviews that I conducted there in May 2001, on *Braving Home* by Halpern, and on an article in the *Raleigh News and Observer*, "Delia Perkins: The Waters Came Down," interview by historian David Cecelski, April 8, 2007, 6D. By the way, it is generally accepted that Princeville was the first town in the United States to be founded and chartered by former slaves, in 1865. It has been suggested that this fact, combined with the fact that Princeville had been recognized as a national historic site for this reason, made it more difficult for state and federal agencies to abandon Princeville.

17. Omitting the word "disaster" from the names of these two teams might be necessary in order to avoid alarming some members of your community and, even more so, from alienating the managers of the hazardous sites.

EPILOGUE

Each day when I drive through my little residential neighborhood in Chapmanville, West Virginia, I pass by the residence of my friend Grace Adkins, a survivor of the Buffalo Creek flood. Grace is an appropriate name for this gentle, Christian lady, because it is only by the grace of God she is able to live to tell of her harrowing—yet true—story of that terrible day in Logan County history. Blessed with longevity of years most of us could only hope for, Grace experienced that violent flash flood in a way that could have claimed her life and that of her husband. There are many stories like hers—stories of sheer terror—but only a few of them end as happily as hers.

Now, largely confined to her house to be cared for by others, Grace lives in an area not far from the Guyandotte River, into which those deadly waters flowed. It is on higher ground, but in the back of her mind, there is something that makes her uneasy every time it rains. As one who experienced many river floods, even I consciously feel a bit uneasy during heavy rains. A psychologist friend of mine tells me that it is not uncommon for us to experience this phobia—living, as we do, with the memory of floods and the disaster at Buffalo Creek.

Several years ago, Grace explained to me that she and her late husband were trying to drive out of the Buffalo Creek Valley on that Saturday morning of the flood, February 26, 1972. They had been warned that the dam at Saunders (Three Forks) might collapse. As they drove down along the creek in their pickup truck, they encountered many other residents who were trying to escape on the narrow, winding road that ran the length of the valley. Suddenly, she and her husband saw a huge gob of everything imaginable coming at them as they sat, stalled in their truck. She told me how the rolling mass essentially picked up their truck— much like a surfboard would rise on a wave. Somehow it deposited Grace and the truck on the porch of a house. Her husband was tossed out of the window of the truck. He disappeared in the raging floodwaters.

Other than a few minor injuries and the shock (which would come to anyone who had been through such an experience), Grace immediately felt that she had been saved, as she put it, by the hand of God. She set out, on foot, walking down through the valley in search of her husband. She did not know if he was dead or alive, but her faith kept her searching for him. Hours passed. She grew very tired. Then, looking up, she saw him walking up the valley looking for her! He was shaken and injured, but well enough to embrace her. Unfortunately, more than one hundred of Buffalo Creek's sons and daughters did not live to experience reunions such as this.

I was a public school teacher and a reporter in Logan County at the time of the flood. The summer before the flood, I had supervised a crew of about twenty Buffalo Creek teenagers who were paid to repair a fire-tower road close to the dam that failed at Three Forks. You can imagine how shocked I was when, as a reporter, I discovered that some of those teenagers died in the flood. I also covered funerals where small clusters of survivors moved from one hastily dug grave site to another. Many of them were bandaged, in casts, cut and bruised, on crutches, or in wheelchairs. In many instances, I knew the deceased persons or members of their families. Still, I felt like an intruder. But I was convinced then, as I am today, that the world needs to know what had happened to these people and why it happened. More importantly, we need to do our best to make certain it will not happen again. Here is a book that can help us achieve this goal.

Even then, I knew that, because of the nature of news reporting and the press, it would not be long until they would forget about Buffalo Creek and move on to the next disaster. All too often, only the survivors remember a disaster for very long. I did not want this to happen to the disaster at Buffalo Creek. So, I am especially gratified to see the publication of this book, *After the Disaster: Re-creating Community and Well-Being at Buffalo Creek since the Notorious Coal Mining Disaster in 1972*. I am even more gratified to read that it is not just about the disaster. It is even more concerned about what has been accomplished since then by many of the survivors of that flood and by the many agencies of state, county, and federal government that worked so hard to rebuild the valley. As an observer and a reporter of West Virginia politics for more than forty years, I can tell you that this book gives due credit to the hard work of government and political leaders then and now in the rebuilding of Buffalo Creek.

Let me also report that memorial ceremonies for the disaster victims still are held every year on February 26 along Buffalo Creek, elsewhere in Logan County, and at the statehouse in Charleston. However, it would be unfortunate if Buffalo Creek is remembered only for the many personal tragedies that occurred there in 1972. Rather than abandon the valley in horror, fear, and utter defeat, many of the survivors—but certainly not all of them—remained in or near the valley. Others moved back, over the years. Many of them did this because they hoped to reestablish the strong sense of community and well-being they had before the flood. As this book reveals, many of them have been relatively successful in this regard. Yet it also reveals that some of them have not been successful. The horror of the flash flood probably has not been erased—but perhaps it has been subdued and surrounded by more pleasant experiences since then.

For those who have been relatively successful, many of them could not have been successful without substantial financing from outside agencies and through the cooperation of dozens of state, county, and federal offices, along with help from unions, private companies, and voluntary organizations. T. P. Schwartz-Barcott helps us understand how this was accomplished, often in the words of current residents of Buffalo Creek who experienced it for themselves. Knowing how this happened—and how it is still happening along Buffalo Creek—can help citizens in other communities that are vulnerable to disasters. They can be more prepared for disasters. And they can be more realistic in their expectations and efforts, if and when disasters occur.

I am certain that Grace Adkins and many current residents of the Buffalo Creek Valley will be heartened to know that their experiences, as portrayed in this book, might help other people far beyond Buffalo Creek appreciate what has been accomplished, as well as what has been lost—for this is a book by an author who does not oversimplify what was, is, and forever will be a very complex, tragic, yet rather remarkably inspiring story of thousands of human endeavors. There is no doubt that the flash flood was a tragedy—a terrible tragedy that must never be forgotten. In reality, much has been accomplished since then. It has become a testament to the perseverance and resilience of many of its survivors and to those people in governments and other organizations who have continued to care about them.

And so, this is a story well worth telling. Here is a book that does it. Read it. Study it. Think about it. Learn from it, but, by all means, do not think of Buffalo Creek only as a disaster. Too many of its residents have spent much of their lives overcoming that unfortunate label. For them, Buffalo Creek is alive. It is their home. It is where they belong, where their roots are, where their hearts always will reside...still...forever.

Raamie Barker, Chief of Staff to West Virginia
Senate President/Lt. Governor Earl Ray Tomblin, and
Assistant to former Governor Arch A. Moore, Jr.

Research Methods

General Overview

A number of research methods favored by ethnographers, historians, journalists, psychologists, and sociologists were used in this study in order to avoid relying on any one method that is favored by a particular group of specialists in one discipline. The purpose of this research is to deepen our understanding of disaster-related community life and recovery at Buffalo Creek and other small communities in the United States—*not* to conduct definitive tests of established research hypotheses or to repudiate the findings and arguments of other researchers.

Most of the research to collect primary data for this book occurred between March 2000 and June 2007. It included seven field trips to Buffalo Creek, six field trips to Elk Creek, and four field trips to St. John, Washington. During these visits, I resided in rented rooms and in an apartment along Buffalo Creek for periods of five to fourteen days so that I could get to know the local people and the rhythms of daily life in the neighborhoods. At St. John, I resided in apartments and houses for periods of four to eight days. It soon became apparent that standard sampling techniques, such as random sampling and "cold-calling" by telephone and with mailed questionnaires, do not work very well in communities such as these—at least not for the purposes of this research. For example, at Buffalo Creek and Elk Creek, many residents are unwilling to meet an "outsider"—let alone be interviewed at length—unless they are introduced by another resident with whom they are familiar. Residents do not have mailboxes at their homes. They get their mail at post office branches that may be in their postal district, near their workplace, elsewhere in Logan County, or in surrounding counties. Quite a few residents do not have home phones, or their phone numbers are unlisted. In addition to this, quite a few residents—especially residents in remote locations—discourage outsiders with warning signs ("No Trespassing," "Go Away," "Armed and Dangerous," "Protected by Smith & Wesson"), barbed wire, "junk-yard dogs," and other discouragements.

Given these constraints, it was necessary to start by identifying and establishing rapport with several key informants in each of these localities. These are people who had resided in these localities for decades, who knew many of the other residents, who were well regarded by many of the other residents, and who were willing to share their knowledge of the locality with me for extended periods of time. These key informants helped me identify and meet a variety of other residents who had a variety of experiences and views about their localities, and had resided in their current homes for at least two years so that they had enough time to become familiar with their neighbors.

After this was accomplished, a number of data collection techniques were devised that could be applied to all three locations. At Buffalo Creek, these included: (1) both structured and open-ended interviews with more than one hundred respondents in their homes or in public places in their communities, (2) administering the "Community and Neighboring Questionnaire," (3) getting reactions from seventeen respondents to the "Authors' Assertions about Buffalo Creek" Form, (4) interviews with dozens of community leaders regarding the history, current status, and future prospects of their communities, and (5) attending church services and public events including cookouts and softball games in the communities and spending countless hours driving and walking through the communities in order to meet residents, engage in casual conversations, and observe the quantity, quality, and variety of social relationships at various times throughout the week, including weekends. Follow-up phone calls and interviews were conducted over a period of seven years with dozens of the respondents and community leaders.

THE "COMMUNITY AND NEIGHBORING QUESTIONNAIRE"*

This questionnaire modifies a number of measures of respondents' self-reported attitudes about behaviors regarding family life, neighboring, and other aspects of community life as reported in Delbert C. Miller's *Handbook of Research Design and Social Measurement* (1991), including Paul Wallin's "Scale for Measuring Neighborliness" (1953).

The questionnaire was administered to more than one hundred adults, ages 18–78, who had been residing along Buffalo Creek from Kistler to Three Forks (Saunders) for at least five years. Special effort was made to meet and to interview residents of the upper valley, particularly the two former coal camps that were damaged so heavily—Lorado and Lundale—who resided there at the time of the flood in 1972. After completed questionnaires were received from fifty of these residents, a concerted effort was made to meet with and to interview at least forty-five residents, ages 18–40, who had not resided in the Buffalo Creek Valley at the time of the flood or who had no obvious direct recall of the flood because they had not been born yet or they were too young to remember it. Our primary purpose in using this selection process was to enable us to compare residents who had experienced the flood with residents who had not experienced the flood, in terms of their perceptions of neighboring and social well-being in their residential communities. This selection process has elements of "purposive sampling" and "judgment sampling" (also called "judgmental sampling" by some researchers) rather than random sampling (on these types of sampling designs, see Delbert C. Miller, 1991, 60–64; Bernard S. Phillips, 1971, 94–96; and John J. Honigmann, 1973, 266–279). Using this selection process allowed us to gain access to the homes of residents and to spend considerable amounts of time getting to know the residents in depth. As a result of this, we can report much more about the social context and the people we interviewed than we could report by using random sampling, but we cannot generalize definitively to the entire populations of Buffalo Creek, Elk Creek, and St. John—nor is this the purpose of our study.

This questionnaire also was administered to more than twenty-one adult residents of Elk Creek and to more than forty-two adult residents of St. John, Washington. An effort was made to include residents with various social characteristics, life experiences, and attitudes about their current situation in their communities. Very few of the people we approached to serve as possible respondents in Buffalo Creek, Elk Creek, and St. John refused to participate, probably because we were introduced to them or referred to them by other residents whom they trusted. None of the people who agreed to participate terminated our interviews while they were in progress. However, a small percent of the questionnaires were discounted because the respondents did not respond to enough of the items to allow us to include these respondents in the quantitative analysis that is presented in chapter 5.

No claim is made that this selection process produced a representative sample of all of the residents of these communities at a given point in time—nor was this our intention. Rather, our goal was to generate relevant information and insights about community life, neighboring, and well-being from a wide variety of residents who could and would inform us about these topics. For researchers interested in replicating our work, or in developing it further, it is worth knowing that more than 70 percent of our respondents voluntarily provided their names and contact information to us and asked that we inform them of the results of our research. Many of the respondents have indicated that they will be glad to participate in further research about their localities and that they are not concerned about being contacted again in this regard.

THE "AUTHORS' ASSERTIONS ABOUT BUFFALO CREEK" FORM*

Seventeen of the principal respondents who resided along Buffalo Creek were asked to react to a number of the most salient assertions made by authors of books about the flash flood at Buffalo Creek and its impacts, based on the respondents' experiences before the flood and since then. Respondents were also asked to explain their reactions to the assertions. Why did they agree or disagree with the authors?

MEASURING SOCIAL WELL-BEING AND SOCIAL INTEGRATION OF RESPONDENTS

Social well-being is a more expansive and subjective concept and measure than is social integration. It takes into account all of the responses, comments, and behaviors that each respondent provided on the questionnaire and during the conversations and interviews that we had with them over the period 2000–2007. Social well-being scores in the tables in appendix B reflect how each of the respondents felt about all aspects of their social relationships with other people, groups, and organizations along Buffalo Creek or the other communities when we communicated with them. Social integration scores in the table reflect the quantity and quality of social relationships that each of the respondents reported having with other people, groups, and organizations in and around Buffalo Creek or the other communities: family members, neighbors, friends, churches, schools, voluntary associations, and businesses. As explained in chapter 5, these two variables are not totally interdependent, although often they are interrelated. An estimation of the statistical nature of the relationship between these two variables is presented in table 5.6 of appendix B.

Level of social integration was estimated to be based on seven items in the "Community and Neighboring Questionnaire": (1) a respondent's estimate of the number of close friends and close relatives who reside along Buffalo Creek, (2) the respondent's identification of Buffalo Creek or one of the hamlets or villages in the Buffalo Creek Valley as "the community that I feel closest to," (3) the respondent's responses as to what he or she likes best and least about living along Buffalo Creek, (4) the respondent's responses as to what he or she misses most about Buffalo Creek in years past, (5) the respondent's estimate of the number of neighbors, (6) the respondent's responses on the four questions related to basic familiarity with his or her neighbors, and (7) the respondent's responses to the six questions related to how often the respondent socializes with his or her neighbors.

Very high = high on at least 6 of the 7 items
High = high on 5 of the 7 items
Moderate or mixed = high on 3 or 4 of the 7 items
Low = high on 2 of the 7 items
Isolated or alienated = high on only 1 or none of the 7 items

Level of social well-being was estimated based on all of the conversations and observations that we had with each respondent from 2000 to 2007 and on all of the respondent's responses to all of the items on the "Community and Neighboring Questionnaire," with particular emphasis on how satisfied the respondent was with his or her situation along Buffalo Creek or the other communities, the things that the respondent missed most from the past, and responses to the question about the "happiest years" in the respondent's life. For example, respondents who indicated that they had experienced many "happy years" in their life—including the current year and recent years—were estimated to have a very high level of social well-being so long as this also was true of their behaviors and their responses to the other items.

*Note. Copies of the questionnaire, the form, and other instruments that were used in the research reported here are available from the author by written request.

APPENDIX B

TABLES FOR CHAPTER 5

TABLE 5.1. Demographic characteristics of Buffalo Creek respondents.

	Buffalo Creek
1. Number of respondents (% of total respondents from Buffalo Creek)	95 (100%)
2. Average age (age range) of respondents	48 (18–78)
3. % who are female	63%
4. % who are lifelong residents	44%
5. Years living in current dwelling	
a. At least 30 years	22%
b. 29 to 10 years	45%
c. Less than 10 years	33%
6. Close relatives and close friends who reside in this village/community	
a. Ten or more of each	34%
b. Three or fewer of each	19%
c. Other configurations	47%

Note. Other configurations include respondents who report having nine to four close relations and nine to four close friends who reside along Buffalo Creek, respondents who report having more than ten of one category of close contacts but fewer than ten of the other category of close contacts, and respondents who report having three or fewer of one category of close contacts but more than three of the other category of close contacts.

TABLE **5.2.** Respondent attitudes about living in Buffalo Creek.

	Buffalo Creek
1. Number of respondents (% of total respondents from Buffalo Creek)	95 (100%)
2. % who feel closest to this place	
a. To this village in Buffalo Creek	71%
b. To some other village in Buffalo Creek or to Buffalo Creek as a whole	23%
c. To a place outside of Buffalo Creek	6%
3. Qualities liked *best* about Buffalo Creek	
a. "Friends" or "people"	23%
b. "Neighbors"	22%
c. "Community" or some quality of the "community" (e.g., "togetherness")	29%
d. "Family" is here or near here, it's my "home"	36%
e. "Quiet(ness)," "Peace(ful)," "Safe(ty)"	27%
f. Other qualities liked best*	60%
4. Qualities liked *least* about Buffalo Creek	
a. Few jobs, wages, or other aspects of the local economy	15%
b. "Neighbors" are objectionable or lacking in some way (e.g., nosy, unfriendly, rowdy)	8%

c. "Community" is lacking is some way (e.g., too crowded, no spirit or togetherness)	3%
d. Far from shopping, etc.	34%
e. Nothing is objectionable (i.e., likes everything here)	7%
f. Other qualities liked least**	53%
5. Qualities missed most about Buffalo Creek in the past	
a. Adequate jobs, wages, or other aspects of the local economy	14%
b. "Neighbors" (or "neighboring") were more valuable or valued years ago	7%
c. Was more "community," togetherness, and/or valued social activity years ago	20%
d. Miss nothing from the past, is the same, or can't say	16%
e. Other qualities missed most***	44%

* Other qualities liked best by at least three respondents include "the mountains," "4-wheeling" and "ATV-riding," "scenery," "convenience," "outdoors," "wildlife," "hunting," "close to work," and "churches."

** Other qualities liked least by at least three respondents include "trash," "litter," "dust," "4-wheelers," "(coal) trucks," "(coal) trains," "speeding," "mountain roads," "stray animals," "wild animals," "noise from the mines," "coal companies," "poor services," "drug problems," "loud parties," "the weather," and "nothing to do."

*** Other qualities missed most about Buffalo Creek in the past that were mentioned by at least three respondents include "friends who passed away," "friends who left the area," "kindness," "family/spouse was here," "more services/conveniences/things to do," "stores," and "dances."

TABLE **5.3.** Neighboring in Buffalo Creek.

	Buffalo Creek
1. Number of respondents (% of total respondents from Buffalo Creek)	95 (100%)
2. Number of neighbors	
a. Average number of neighbors per respondent*	10.8
b. % of respondents with ten or more neighbors	48%
c. % of respondents with nine to five neighbors	37%
d. % of respondents with fewer than five neighbors	15%
3. Basic familiarity and relations with these neighbors**	
a. % of respondents who report familiarity with all of these neighbors	78%
b. % of respondents who report familiarity with most or many of these neighbors	20%
c. % of respondents who report familiarity with few or none of these neighbors	2%
4. *Socializing* with these neighbors***	
a. Often, and with all or most of these neighbors	11%
b. Occasionally with more than a few of these neighbors	52%
c. Infrequently and only with one or a few of these neighbors	31%
d. Rarely or never with any of these neighbors	6%

5. Most important quality of neighbors

a. For help in crises and when needed	20%
b. To protect property when respondent is absent	5%
c. To be friends, intimates, or confidants	11%
d. Be trustworthy, reliable, or honest	35%
e. Be friendly/ friendliness	31%
f. Other positive qualities****	24%
g. Not be nosy, rowdy, gossipy, obnoxious, etc.	9%

6. % of respondents who report that neighbors are

a. "Very" or "really" important to them	64%
b. Less than "very" or "really" important to them	36%

* "Average number of neighbors per respondent" excludes the estimates provided by a few respondents that exceeded sixty neighbors. These respondents seemed to ignore the definition of "neighbor" that is provided on the questionnaire and that is used throughout this research.

** That is, recognize these neighbors anywhere, know their names, usually greet these neighbors when encountered and converse with some of them.

*** That is, conversing with, discussing problems with, visiting, exchanging items with, entertaining, and going places with these neighbors.

**** "Other positive qualities" that were mentioned by respondents include "respect," "loyal," "keep company," "compassion," and "nice."

TABLE 5.4. Respondent references to the flood in Buffalo Creek or to other disasters.

	Buffalo Creek
1. Number of respondents (% of total respondents from Buffalo Creek)	95 (100%)
2. % of respondents who referred to the flood of 1972 or to other disasters	
a. At least four times and were very conscious of the flood	2%
b. One to three times	20%
c. At no time	78%

TABLE 5.5. Estimates of respondents' level of social integration into Buffalo Creek as a social community, and estimates of respondents' level of social well-being.

	Buffalo Creek
1. Number of respondents (% of total respondents from Buffalo Creek)	95 (100%)
2. Estimated level of social integration* of the respondents into Buffalo Creek as a social community	
a. Very high	20%
b. High	45%
c. Moderate or mixed	27%
d. Low	5%
e. Isolated or alienated	2%

3. Estimated level of social well-being** of the respondents

a. Very high   13%

b. High   39%

c. Moderate or mixed   38%

d. Low   7%

e. Very low   3%

* Appendix A explains how "level of social integration" was estimated. In general, the estimate was based on seven factors: (1) a respondent's estimate of the number of close friends and close relatives who reside along Buffalo Creek, (2) the respondent's identification of Buffalo Creek or one of the villages in Buffalo Creek as "the community that I feel closest to," (3) the respondent's responses as to what he/she likes best and least about living along Buffalo Creek, (4) the respondent's responses as to what he/she misses most about Buffalo Creek in years past, (5) the respondent's estimate of the number of neighbors, (6) the respondent's responses on the four items related to basic familiarity with her/his neighbors, and (7) the respondent's responses to the six items related to how often the respondent socializes with her/his neighbors.

Very high = high on at least 6 of the 7

High = high on 5 of the 7

Moderate or mixed = high on 3 or 4 of the 7

Low = high on 2 of the 7

Isolated or alienated = high on only 1 or none of the 7

** Appendix A explains how "level of social well-being" was measured. It takes into account all of the respondent's responses to all items on the questionnaire, with particular emphasis on how satisfied the respondent was with his or her situation along Buffalo Creek, the things that the respondent missed most from the past, and responses to the question about the "happiest years" in the respondent's life.

TABLE **5.6.** Correlation between social integration and social well-being.

Social Integration	A Very High or High	B Medium	C Low or Very Low	D Total
			Social Well-Being	
1. Very High or High	42	19	1	62
2. Medium	7	15	4	26
3. Low or Very Low	1	1	5	7
4. Total	50	35	10	95

Note. df = 4.
$\chi^2 = 42.519$.
$p \leq 0.0001$.
The distribution is significant.

Explanation. Table 5.6 displays how the ninety-five respondents were cross-categorized in terms of social integration and social well-being. It reveals that the correlation between these two factors is high and statistically significant—but not total or "perfect" (to use a term popular with some statisticians). Each of the cells presents the number of Buffalo Creek's ninety-five respondents who were estimated to have specific levels of social integration (rows 1–3) and specific levels of social well-being (columns A–C). For example, cell A1 indicates that forty-two respondents scored very high or high on social integration and very high or high on social well-being. Cell B2 indicates that fifteen of the respondents scored medium on both of these variables. Cell C3 indicates that five of the respondents scored low or very low on both of these variables. In order for social integration and social well-being to be totally correlated, the scores for all ninety-five respondents (not just for sixty-two of the respondents) would need to fall in these three cells (A1 + B2 + C3). However, the scores for thirty-three of the respondents do not fall into these three cells. Rather, the other thirty-three scores are found in cells A2, A3, B1, B3, C1, and C2. These are the scores of the thirty-three respondents who score higher on social integration than on social well-being, or vice versa. Thus, from the data in Table 5.6, we can infer that social integration and social well-being are not identical. We can also infer that it is highly unlikely that they are uncorrelated. Rather, they are correlated, but they are not perfectly correlated.

Not reflected in the table is the fact that neither social integration nor social well-being is correlated very highly with the number of times that respondents referred to the flood or to other disasters. Other calculations revealed that chi-square coefficients were *not* significant at the .05 level for either variable in cross-tabulations with the number of references made to disasters by the respondents. In other words, those respondents who frequently referred to the flood were not always the ones who were estimated to be low on social integration and social well-being.

By the way, it should be noted that the chi-square statistic is presented with this table only in order to provide us with some general sense of the nature of the correlation between social integration and social well-being as variables and the probability that this correlation could happen solely by chance. Many of the conditions for appropriate use of this statistic—including random sampling—are not compatible with the design of this research, for reasons that are explained in appendix A.

Finally, it also is worth noting in Table 5.6 that a considerable number of the respondents ($N = 42$, cell A1) score very high or high on social integration as well as on social well-being. Furthermore, most of the respondents ($N = 83$, cells A1 + A2 + B1 + B2) score "medium" or higher on both variables. The remainder of the respondents ($N = 12$, cells A3 + B3 + C1 + C2 + C3) score low or very low on both variables. Thus, it can be said that the vast majority, 87 percent, of Buffalo Creek's ninety-five respondents were estimated to be at least moderately well-integrated into Buffalo Creek and to have at least a moderate amount of social well-being. Surely, these findings support the social re-creation perspective much more strongly than the other perspective. It is highly likely that the substantial levels of social integration and social well-being of these respondents are the result of re-creation of community life along Buffalo Creek since the flood of 1972.

TABLE **5.7**. Demographic characteristics of Buffalo Creek respondents—by category.

	A Victims	B Witnesses	C Possible Witnesses	D Nonwitnesses	E Total
1. Number of respondents	10	15	37	33	95
(% of total respondents from Buffalo Creek)	(11%)	(16%)	(39%)	(35%)	(100%)
2. Average age	65	63	58	29	48
(age range) of respondents	(42–78)	(41–76)	(36–77)	(18–71)	(18–78)
3. % who are female	80%	60%	67%	55%	63%
4. % who are lifelong residents	80%	53%	46%	27%	44%
5. Years living in current dwelling					
a. At least 30 years	20%	60%	27%	0%	22%
b. 29 to 10 years	60%	40%	43%	45%	45%
c. Less than 10 years	20%	0%	30%	55%	33%
6. Close relatives and close friends who reside in this village/ community*					
a. Ten or more of each	40%	53%	24%	33%	34%
b. Three or fewer of each	40%	20%	22%	10%	19%
c. Other configurations	20%	27%	54%	57%	47%

* Other configurations include respondents who report having nine to four close relations and nine to four close friends who reside along Buffalo Creek, respondents who report having more than ten of one category of close contacts but fewer than ten of the other category of close contacts, and respondents who report having three or fewer of one category of close contacts but more than three of the other category of close contacts.

TABLE **5.8.** Respondent attitudes about living in Buffalo Creek—by category.

	A Victims	B Witnesses	C Possible Witnesses	D Nonwitnesses	E Total
1. Number of respondents (% of total respondents from Buffalo Creek)	10 (11%)	15 (16%)	37 (39%)	33 (35%)	95 (100%)
2. % who feel closest to this place					
a. To this village in Buffalo Creek	80%	73%	78%	58%	71%
b. To some other village in Buffalo Creek or to Buffalo Creek as a whole	10%	7%	19%	39%	23%
c. To a place outside of Buffalo Creek	10%	20%	3%	3%	6%
3. Qualities liked *best* about Buffalo Creek					
a. "Friends" or "people"	50%	53%	16%	9%	23%
b. "Neighbors"	30%	27%	19%	21%	22%
c. "Community" or some quality of the "community" (e.g., "togetherness")	30%	47%	21%	27%	29%
d. "Family" is here or near here, it's my "home"	30%	53%	39%	27%	36%
e. "Quiet(ness)," "Peace(ful)," "Safe(ty)"	40%	20%	19%	36%	27%
f. Other qualities liked best*	40%	53%	57%	72%	60%

(continued on next page)

TABLE 5.8. (continued)

	A Victims	B Witnesses	C Possible Witnesses	D Nonwitnesses	E Total
4. Qualities liked *least* about Buffalo Creek					
a. Few jobs, wages, or other aspects of the local economy	10%	27%	11%	15%	15%
b. "Neighbors" are objectionable or lacking in some way (e.g., nosy, unfriendly, rowdy)	0%	7%	13%	6%	8%
c. "Community" is lacking is some way (e.g., too crowded, no spirit or togetherness)	0%	7%	3%	3%	3%
d. Far from shopping, etc.	50%	40%	27%	33%	34%
e. Nothing is objectionable (i.e., likes everything here)	30%	7%	8%	0%	7%
f. Other qualities liked least**	40%	47%	49%	64%	53%

5. Qualities missed most about Buffalo Creek in the past

a. Adequate jobs, wages, or other aspects of the local economy	10%	33%	11%	9%	14%
b. "Neighbors" (or "neighboring") were more valuable or valued years ago	10%	13%	8%	3%	7%
c. Was more "community," togetherness, and/or valued social activity years ago	20%	33%	22%	12%	20%
d. Miss nothing from the past, is the same, or can't say	10%	0%	11%	30%	16%
e. Other qualities missed most***	70%	67%	43%	27%	44%

* Other qualities liked best by at least three respondents include "the mountains," "4-wheeling" and "ATV-riding," "scenery," "convenience," "outdoors," "wildlife," "hunting," "close to work," and "churches."

** Other qualities liked least by at least three respondents include "trash," "litter," "dust," "4-wheelers," "(coal) trucks," "(coal) trains," "speeding," "mountain roads," "stray animals," "wild animals," "noise from the mines," "coal companies," "poor services," "drug problems," "loud parties," "the weather," and "nothing to do."

*** Other qualities missed most about Buffalo Creek in the past that were mentioned by at least three respondents include "friends who passed away," "friends who left the area," "kindness," "family/spouse was here," "more services/conveniences/things to do," "stores," and "dances."

TABLE **5.9.** Neighboring in Buffalo Creek—by category.

	A Victims	B Witnesses	C Possible Witnesses	D Nonwitnesses	E Total
1. Number of respondents (% of total respondents from Buffalo Creek)	10 (11%)	15 (16%)	37 (39%)	33 (35%)	95 (100%)
2. Number of neighbors					
a. Average number of neighbors per respondent*	9.1	9.5	10.7	11.2	10.8
b. % of respondents with ten or more neighbors	50%	60%	60%	30%	48%
c. % of respondents with nine to five neighbors	20%	33%	24%	57%	37%
d. % of respondents with fewer than five neighbors	30%	7%	16%	13%	15%
3. *Basic familiarity and relations* with these neighbors**					
a. % of respondents who report familiarity with all of these neighbors	70%	87%	65%	91%	78%
b. % of respondents who report familiarity with most or many of these neighbors	20%	13%	35%	6%	20%

c. % of respondents who report familiarity with *few or none* of these neighbors***	10%	0%	0%	3%	2%
4. Socializing with these neighbors*					
a. Often, and with all or most of these neighbors	20%	20%	8%	6%	11%
b. Occasionally with more than a few of these neighbors	60%	33%	46%	67%	52%
c. Infrequently and only with one or a few of these neighbors	10%	40%	41%	21%	31%
d. *Rarely or never* with any of these neighbors	10%	7%	5%	6%	6%
5. Most important quality of neighbors					
a. For help in crises and when needed	20%	47%	19%	9%	20%
b. To protect property when respondent is absent	10%	7%	5%	3%	5%
c. To be friends, intimates, or confidants	30%	20%	11%	3%	11%
d. Be trustworthy, reliable, or honest	30%	27%	38%	36%	35%
e. Be friendly/ friendliness	10%	20%	24%	48%	31%

(continued on next page)

TABLE **5.9.** (continued)

	A Victims	B Witnesses	C Possible Witnesses	D Nonwitnesses	E Total
f. Other positive qualities****	20%	33%	24%	21%	24%
g. Not be nosy, rowdy, gossipy, obnoxious, etc.	10%	13%	11%	6%	9%
6. % of respondents who report that neighbors are					
a. "Very" or "really" important to them	80%	73%	65%	55%	64%
b. Less than "very" or "really" important to them	20%	27%	35%	45%	36%

* "Average number of neighbors per respondent" excludes the estimates provided by a few respondents in each category that exceeded sixty neighbors. These respondents seemed to ignore the definition of "neighbor" that is provided on the questionnaire and that is used throughout this research.

** That is, recognize these neighbors anywhere, know their names, usually greet these neighbors when encountered and converse with some of them.

*** That is, conversing with, discussing problems with, visiting, exchanging items with, entertaining, and going places with these neighbors.

**** "Other positive qualities" that were mentioned by respondents include "respect," "loyal," "keep company," "compassion," and "nice."

TABLE **5.10.** Respondent references to the flood or to other disasters—by category.

	A *Victims*	B *Witnesses*	C *Possible Witnesses*	D *Nonwitnesses*	E *Total*
1. Number of respondents (% of total respondents from Buffalo Creek)	10 (11%)	15 (16%)	37 (39%)	33 (35%)	95 (100%)
2. % of respondents who referred to the flood of 1972 or to other disasters					
a. At least four times and were very con- scious of the flood	20%	0%	0%	0%	2%
b. One to three times	60%	73%	3%	0%	20%
c. At no time	20%	27%	97%	100%	78%

TABLE **5.11.** Estimates of respondents' level of social integration into Buffalo Creek as a social community, and estimates of respondents' level of social well-being—by category.

	A Victims	B Witnesses	C Possible Witnesses	D Nonwitnesses	E Total
1. Number of respondents (% of total respondents from Buffalo Creek)	10 (11%)	15 (16%)	37 (39%)	33 (35%)	95 (100%)
2. Estimated level of social integration* of the respondents into Buffalo Creek as a social community					
a. Very high	10%	33%	16%	21%	20%
b. High	60%	40%	41%	48%	45%
c. Moderate or mixed	10%	20%	41%	22%	28%
d. Low	10%	7%	2%	6%	5%
e. Isolated or alienated	10%	0%	0%	3%	2%
3. Estimated level of social well-being** of the respondents					
a. Very high	0%	7%	8%	24%	13%

b. High	30%	33%	41%	42%	39%
c. Moderate or mixed	40%	46%	43%	28%	38%
d. Low	20%	7%	8%	3%	7%
e. Very low	10%	7%	0%	3%	3%

* Appendix A explains how "level of social integration" was estimated. In general, the estimate was based on seven factors: (1) a respondent's estimate of the number of close friends and close relatives who reside along Buffalo Creek, (2) the respondent's identification of Buffalo Creek or one of the villages in Buffalo Creek as "the community that I feel closest to," (3) the respondent's responses as to what he/she likes best and least about living along Buffalo Creek, (4) the respondent's responses as to what he/she misses most about Buffalo Creek in years past, (5) the respondent's estimate of the number of neighbors, (6) the respondent's responses on the four items related to basic familiarity with her/his neighbors, and (7) the respondent's responses to the six items related to how often the respondent socializes with her/his neighbors.

Very high = high on at least 6 of the 7
High = high on 5 of the 7
Moderate or mixed = high on 3 or 4 of the 7
Low = high on 2 of the 7
Isolated or alienated = high on only 1 or none of the 7

** Appendix A explains how "level of social well-being" was measured. It takes into account all of the respondent's responses to all items on the questionnaire with particular emphasis on how satisfied the respondent was with his or her situation along Buffalo Creek, the things that the respondent missed most from the past, and responses to the question about the "happiest years" in the respondent's life.

TABLE **5.12.** Demographic characteristics of Buffalo Creek, Elk Creek, and St. John respondents.

	A Buffalo Creek	B Elk Creek	C St. John
1. Number of respondents (% of total respondents)	95 (100%)	21 (100%)	42 (100%)
2. Average age (age range) of respondents	48 (18–78)	46 (23–75)	56 (20–96)
3. % who are female	63%	62%	76%
4. % who are lifelong residents	44%	38%	35%
5. Years living in current dwelling			
a. At least 30 years	22%	38%	33%
b. 29 to 10 years	45%	47%	35%
c. Less than 10 years	33%	19%	32%
6. Close relatives and close friends who reside in this village/community			
a. Ten or more of each	34%	38%	19%
b. Three or fewer of each	19%	10%	21%
c. Other configurations*	47%	52%	60%

* Other configurations include respondents who report having nine to four close relatives and nine to four close friends who reside here, respondents who report having more than ten of one category of close contacts but fewer than ten of the other category of close contacts, and respondents who report having three or fewer of one category of close contacts but more than three of the other category of close contacts.

TABLE **5.13.** Respondent attitudes about living in Buffalo Creek, Elk Creek, and St. John.

	A Buffalo Creek	B Elk Creek	C St. John
1. Number of respondents (% of total respondents)	95 (100%)	21 (100%)	42 (100%)
2. % who feel closest to this place			
a. To this place	94%	67%	76%
b. To some other place	6%	33%	24%
3. Qualities liked *best* about this place			
a. "Friends" or "people"	23%	33%	52%
b. "Neighbors"	22%	24%	17%
c. "Community" or some quality of the "community" (e.g., "togetherness")	29%	14%	31%
d. "Family" is here or near here, it's my "home"	36%	29%	17%
e. "Quiet(ness)," "Peace(ful)," "Safe(ty)"	27%	43%	33%
f. Other qualities liked best*	60%	67%	52%
4. Qualities liked *least* about this place			
a. Few jobs, wages, or other aspects of the local economy	15%	5%	14%
b. "Neighbors" are objectionable or lacking in some way (e.g., nosy, unfriendly, rowdy)	8%	5%	7%
c. "Community" is lacking is some way (e.g., too crowded, no spirit or togetherness)	3%	0%	19%

(continued on next page)

TABLE 5.13. (continued)

	A *Buffalo Creek*	B *Elk Creek*	C *St. John*
d. Far from shopping, etc.	34%	19%	38%
e. Nothing is objectionable (i.e., likes everything here)	7%	10%	0%
f. Other qualities liked least**	53%	43%	48%
5. Qualities missed most about this place in the past			
a. Adequate jobs, wages, or other aspects of the local economy	14%	10%	5%
b. "Neighbors" (or "neighboring") were more valuable or valued years ago	7%	5%	2%
c. Was more "community," togetherness, and/or valued social activity years ago	20%	24%	12%
d. Miss nothing from the past, is the same, or can't say	16%	14%	31%
e. Other qualities missed most***	44%	43%	21%

*Other qualities liked best by at least three respondents include "the weather," "farms," "stores," "the mountains," "4-wheeling" and "ATV-riding," "scenery," "convenience," "outdoors," "wildlife," "hunting," "close to work," and "churches."

**Other qualities liked least by at least three respondents include "the heat," "dust storms," "winter," "trash," "litter," "dust," "4-wheelers," "(coal) trucks," "(coal) trains," "speeding," "mountain roads," "stray animals," "wild animals," "noise from the mines," "coal companies," "poor services," "drug problems," "loud parties," "the weather," and "nothing to do."

***Other qualities missed most about this place in the past that were mentioned by at least three respondents include "friends who passed away," "friends who left the area," "kindness," "family/spouse was here," "more services/conveniences/things to do," "the farms," "stores," and "dances."

TABLE **5.14.** Neighboring in Buffalo Creek, Elk Creek, and St. John.

	A Buffalo Creek	B Elk Creek	C St. John
1. Number of respondents (% of total respondents)	95 (100%)	21 (100%)	42 (100%)
2. Number of neighbors			
a. Average number of neighbors per respondent	10.8	13.4	11.7*
b. % of respondents with ten or more neighbors	48%	48%	48%
c. % of respondents with nine to five neighbors	37%	33%	24%
d. % of respondents with fewer than five neighbors	15%	19%	28%
3. Basic familiarity and relations with these neighbors**			
a. % of respondents who claim familiarity with all of these neighbors	78%	76%	60%
b. % of respondents who claim familiarity with most or many of these neighbors	20%	24%	40%
c. % of respondents who claim familiarity with few or none of these neighbors	2%	0%	0%
4. Socializing with these neighbors***			
a. With all of these neighbors at least occasionally	11%	5%	2%
b. Occasionally with more than a few of these neighbors	52%	43%	36%
c. Infrequently and only with one or a few of these neighbors	31%	52%	45%

(continued on next page)

TABLE 5.14. (*continued*)

	A Buffalo Creek	B Elk Creek	C St. John
d. Rarely or never with any of these neighbors	6%	0%	17%
5. Most important quality of neighbors			
a. For help in crisis situations	20%	10%	19%
b. To protect property when respondent is absent	5%	10%	5%
c. To be friends, intimates, or confidants	11%	29%	26%
d. Be trustworthy, reliable, or honest	35%	29%	24%
e. Be friendly/friendliness	31%	38%	29%
f. Other positive qualities****	24%	24%	19%
g. Not be nosy, rowdy, gossipy, obnoxious, etc.	9%	19%	17%
6. % of respondents who claim that neighbors are			
a. "Very" or "really" important to them	64%	76%	60%
b. Less than "very" or "really" important to them	36%	24%	40%

* This 11.7 average number of neighbors excludes the estimates of three respondents who considered everyone in St. John to be "their neighbors" despite the definition specified for this concept on the questionnaire.

** That is, recognize these neighbors anywhere, know their names, and usually greet these neighbors when encountered and converse with some of them.

*** That is, conversing with, discussing problems with, visiting, exchanging items with, entertaining, and going places with these neighbors.

**** "Other positive qualities" that were mentioned by respondents include "respect," "loyal," "keep company," "compassion," and "nice."

TABLE **5.15.** Respondent references to the flood or to other disasters—Buffalo Creek, Elk Creek, and St. John.

	A *Buffalo Creek*	B *Elk Creek*	C *St. John*
1. Number of respondents (% of total respondents)	95 (100%)	21 (100%)	42 (100%)
2. % of respondents who referred to the flood of 1972 or to other disasters			
a. At least four times and were very conscious of the flood or disasters	2%	0%	0%
b. One to three times	20%	0%	0%
c. At no time	78%	100%	100%

TABLE **5.16.** Estimates of respondents' level of social integration into Buffalo Creek as a social community, and estimates of respondents' level of social well-being—Buffalo Creek, Elk Creek, and St. John.

	A *Buffalo Creek*	B *Elk Creek*	C *St. John*
1. Number of respondents (% of total respondents)	95 (100%)	21 (100%)	42 (100%)
2. Estimated level of social integration* of the respondents into the social communities			
a. Very high	20%	19%	33%
b. High	45%	43%	40%
c. Moderate or mixed	27%	29%	21%
d. Low	5%	10%	5%
e. Isolated or alienated	2%	0%	0%
3. Estimated level of social well-being** of the respondents			
a. Very high	13%	10%	29%
b. High	39%	38%	29%

c. Moderate or mixed	38%	43%	36%
d. Low	7%	10%	7%
e. Very low	3%	0%	0%

* Appendix A explains how "level of social integration" was estimated. In general, the estimate was based on seven factors: (1) a respondent's estimate of the number of close friends and close relatives who reside near him/her, (2) the respondent's identification of his/her community as "the community that I feel closest to," (3) the respondent's responses as to what he/she likes best and least about living here, (4) the respondent's responses as to what he/she misses most about living here in years past, (5) the respondent's estimate of the number of neighbors, (6) the respondent's responses on the four items related to basic familiarity with her/his neighbors, and (7) the respondent's responses to the six items related to how often the respondent socializes with her/his neighbors.

Very high = high on at least 6 of the 7
High = high on 5 of the 7
Moderate or mixed = high on 3 or 4 of the 7
Low = high on 2 of the 7
Isolated or alienated = high on only 1 or none of the 7

** Appendix A explains how "level of social well-being" was measured. It takes into account all of the respondent's responses to all items on the questionnaire with particular emphasis on how satisfied the respondent was with his or her situation in the social community, the things that the respondent missed most from the past, and responses to the question about the "happiest years" in the respondent's life.

GLOSSARY

Several definitions are provided for some of the following terms in order to demonstrate that these terms are used in this book in ways that are congruent with—but are more specific and relevant to this study than in *The Living Webster Encyclopedic Dictionary of the English Language*, in Erikson's book, *Everything in Its Path*, and in other major references (with page numbers indicated, where appropriate).

COMMUNALITY

Webster: Group solidarity. Communal character or state. Similar opinions and feeling in a group (204).

Erikson: A state of mind among a particular gathering of people (189). A constant readiness to look after one's neighbors (190, 194).

Here: A pervasive set of beliefs, feelings, and sentiments—within a group or collectivity—that all or most of the members belong together at a specific location such as a neighborhood, village, nursing home, or other place, and that they will try to help one another when their help is urgently needed, regardless of whether it is requested. (NB: Communality is one of several dimensions, aspects, and characteristics of a complete community. See the definition of *community* as follows).

COMMUNITY

Webster: A number of persons having common ties or interests and living in the same locality (204).

Erikson: The locus for activities that are normally regarded as the exclusive property of individuals (193).

Here: Geographical places such as hamlets, villages, and towns where most of the residents share a common identity, a strong sense of communality, a common culture, many social experiences, and considerable interdependency.

DISASTER

Webster: A calamitous event, especially one occurring suddenly and causing great loss of life, damage, or hardship, as a flood, airplane crash, or business failure (561).

International Encyclopedia of the Social Sciences (Charles E. Fritz): An event, concentrated in time and space, in which a society, or a relatively self-sufficient subdivision of a society, undergoes severe danger and incurs such losses to its members and physical appurtenances that the social structure is disrupted and the fulfillment of all or some of the essential functions of the society is prevented (202).

International Encyclopedia of the Social and Behavioral Sciences (Gary A. Kreps): Disasters are non-routine events in societies or their larger sub-systems (e.g., region and communities) that involve conjunctions of physical conditions with social definitions of human harm and social disruption (3718).

FLOOD

Webster: A great flowing or overflowing of water, esp. over land not usually submerged (736).

INFRASTRUCTURE

Webster: The fundamental facilities and systems serving a country, city, or area, such as transportation and communication systems, power plants, and schools (980).

LOCALITY

Here: Geographical places such as hamlets, villages, and towns which may or may not have the essential elements of [community,] including common identity, a strong sense of communality, a common culture, many social experiences in common, and considerable interdependency.

NEIGHBOR(S)

Webster: Near dweller. One who lives near another. One in close proximity. One's fellow man. One who is kind or helpful (637).

Erikson: Those with whom one shares bonds of intimacy and a feeling of mutual concern (187). A neighbor, then, is someone you can relate to without pretense, a familiar and reliable part of your everyday environment; a neighbor is someone you treat as if he or she were a member of your immediate family (188).

Here: The people (including renters—not necessarily owners) who reside in households close(est) to other households.

NEIGHBORHOOD

Webster: The region near or about some place or thing. A district or locality, often with reference to its character or inhabitants (as run down or fashionable) (637).

Here: An area or locality, particularly in terms of households, dwellings, and residences that are in close proximity to one another (normally within easy walking distance of one another).

NEIGHBORING

Webster: Being in the vicinity, adjoining, next to (637).

Here: Mutually voluntary, usually amicable, face-to-face social interactions between at least one resident in each of two or more households that are relatively close to one another (and are considered to be within the same neighborhood).

NEIGHBORLY

Here: An expressed, positive attitude by a member of a household towards face-to-face interactions with one or more members of other households in the neighborhood.

REBUILDING (OF A LOCALITY)

Here: The physical activities that are intended to build the infrastructure of places such as hamlets, villages, towns, cities, counties, states, and societies after the infrastructure has been severely damaged or destroyed by events such as disasters and wars.

RECOVERY (OF COMMUNITY)

Here: The regaining and restoring of the elements that constituted a community before it was damaged by events such as disasters and wars.

RECOVERY (OF WELL-BEING)

Here: The regaining and restoring of the elements that constituted an individual's sense of psychological and social well-being before the person was disturbed or damaged by some event, such as a disaster.

RE-CREATION (OF COMMUNITY AND WELL-BEING)

Here: The creating of relatively new forms of community and well-being in a locality in place of those that were damaged or destroyed by a particular event such as a disaster. Also, the creating of relatively new relationships, groups, and institutions in a locality in place of those that were damaged or destroyed by a particular event.

RESILIENCE (OF A COMMUNITY)

Here: The ability of a community to rebound quickly to its former shape, forms, and functions following a disruptive event such as a disaster.

SOCIAL INTEGRATION

Here: The extent to which the people, families, and other groups who reside in a locality participate fully and harmoniously in the social life of the locality. Also, the process through which people, families, and other groups within a community participate fully and harmoniously in the social relations of the community.

WELL-BEING

Webster: Welfare; the condition of happiness, prosperity, and good health (1128).

Diener: A subjective, positive, emotional state with general life satisfaction (16451).

WELL-BEING (AN INDIVIDUAL'S SENSE OF THE COMMUNITY'S WELL-BEING)

Here: A person's beliefs about and evaluation of the general standard of living, quality of life, and social problems of the community in which he or she resides.

WELL-BEING (AN INDIVIDUAL'S SENSE OF HIS OR HER SOCIAL WELL-BEING)

Here: A person's beliefs about and evaluation of the quantity and quality of social relationships that he or she with other people, including neighbors.

BIBLIOGRAPHY

Allen, John C., and Don A. Dillman. *Against All Odds: Rural Community in the Information Age*. Boulder, CO: Westview Press, 1994.

Angell, Robert Cooley. "Social Integration." In vol. 7 of *International Encyclopedia of the Social Sciences*, edited by David Sills, 380–386. New York: The Macmillan Company & The Free Press, 1968.

Antze, Paul, and Michael Lambeck, eds. *Tense Past: Cultural Essays in Trauma and Meaning*. New York: Routledge, 1996.

Babbie, Earl. *The Basics of Social Research*. Belmont, CA: Wadsworth Publishing Company, 1999.

Barton, Allen H. *Communities in Disaster: A Sociological Analysis of Collective Stress Situations*. New York: Doubleday, 1969.

Beaver, Patricia D. *Rural Community in the Appalachian South*. Prospect Heights, IL: Waveland Press, Inc., 1992.

Beck, Ulrich. *Risk Society: Towards a New Modernity*. London: Sage Publications, 1992.

Beckman, L. F. "Social Integration, Social Networks, and Health." In vol. 21 of *International Encyclopedia of the Social and Behavioral Sciences*, edited by Neil J. Smelser and Paul B. Baltes, 14327–14332. Amsterdam: Elsevier, 2001.

Bender, Thomas. *Community and Social Change in America*. New Brunswick, NJ: Rutgers University Press, 1978.

Bernard, H. Russell. *Research Methods in Anthropology: Qualitative and Quantitative Approaches*. New York: AltaMira Press., 1998.

Bernard, Jessie. "Community Disorganization." In vol. 3 of *International Encyclopedia of the Social Sciences*, edited by David Sills, 163–168. New York: The Macmillan Company & The Free Press, 1968.

Billings, Dwight, and Sally Maggard. Review of *Everything in Its Path*, by Kai T. Erikson. *Social Forces* 57, no. 2 (December 1978): 722–723.

Billings, Dwight B., G. Norman, and K. Ledford, eds. *Confronting Appalachian Stereotypes: Back Talk from an American Region*. Lexington: The University Press of Kentucky, 1999.

Blackhall, Susan. *Tsunami*. Surrey, U.K.: TAJ Books, 2005.

Bloland, Sue Erikson. *In the Shadow of Fame: A Memoir by the Daughter of Erik H. Erikson*. New York: Viking, 2005.

Bolin, Robert C. *Long-Term Family Recovery from Disasters*. Boulder, CO: University of Colorado Press, 1982.

Brinkley, Douglas. *The Great Deluge: Hurricane Katrina, New Orleans, and the Mississippi Gulf Coast*. New York: William Morrow/Harper-Collins Publishers, 2006.

Brown, David L., and Louis E. Swanson, eds. *Challenges for Rural America in the Twenty-First Century*. University Park, PA: The Pennsylvania State University Press, 2003.

The Buffalo Creek Flood and Disaster: Official Report from the Governor's Ad Hoc Commission of Inquiry. 1972. http://www.marshall.edu/library/speccoll/virtual_museum/buffalo_creek/html/GAHCI-Report.pdf (accessed August 11, 2008).

"Buffalo Creek Report." http://www.marshall.edu/speccoll/Virtual Museum/Buffalo Creek/HTML/depositions.html.

Buffalo Valley Redevelopment Plan. Prepared by the Office of the Governor [of West Virginia], Federal/State Relations in Conjunction with Federal Regional Council (III). Charleston, WV, July 1973.

Burns, Shirley Stewart. *Bringing Down the Mountains: The Impact of Mountaintop Removal on Southern West Virginia Communities*. Morgantown, WV: West Virginia University Press, 2007.

Caplow, Theodore, and Louis Hicks. *Systems of War and Peace*. 2nd ed. Lanham, MD: University Press of America, 2002.

Carmon, N. "Neighborhood." In vol. 15 of *International Encyclopedia of the Social and Behavioral Sciences*, edited by Neil J. Smelser and Paul B. Baltes, 10490–10496. Amsterdam: Elsevier, 2001.

Caudill, Harry M. "Buffalo Creek Aftermath." *Saturday Review*, August 26, 1972, 16–17.

————. *Night Comes to the Cumberlands*. Ashland, KY: Jesse Stuart Foundation, 2001. Originally published by Little, Brown and Company, 1963.

Church, J. "The Buffalo Creek Disaster: Extent and Range of Emotional and/or Behavioral Problems." *Omega* 5 (1974): 61–63.

Collins, Randall. *Four Sociological Traditions*. Oxford and New York: Oxford University Press, 1994.

Conway, M. A. "Memory, Autobiographical." In vol. 14 of *International Encyclopedia of the Social and Behavioral Sciences*, edited by Neil J. Smelser and Paul B. Baltes, 9563–9566. Amsterdam: Elsevier, 2001.

Crouser, Brad. *Arch: The Life of Governor Arch A. Moore, Jr.* Chapmanville, WV: Woodland Press, LLC, 2006.

Cruse, J. Ververs, and Elizabeth Taggart, eds. *The Johnstown Flood— 1977*. Johnstown, PA: Jujulah Corporation, 1977.

Dale, Ann, and Jenny Onyx. *A Dynamic Balance: Social Capital and Sustainable Community Development*. Vancouver: UBC Press, 2005.

Deitz, Dennis, and Carlene Mowery. *Buffalo Creek: Valley of Death*. South Charleston, WV: Mountain Memory Books, 1992.

Denzin, Norman, and Yvonne S. Lincoln, eds. *Handbook of Qualitative Research*. London: Sage Publications, 1994.

Derogatis, L. R., R. Lipman, K. Rickels, E. H. Uhlenhuth, and L. Covi. "The Hopkins Symptom Checklist (HSCL): A Self-Report Symptom Inventory." *Behavioral Science* 19 (1974): 1–15.

Diener, E. "Social Well-Being (Subjective), Psychology of." In vol. 21 of *International Encyclopedia of the Social and Behavioral*

Sciences, edited by Neil J. Smelser and Paul B. Baltes, 16451–16454. Amsterdam: Elsevier, 2001.

"Disaster at Buffalo Creek." Symposium presented at the meeting of the American Psychiatric Association, Anaheim, CA, 1975. Proceedings published in the *American Journal of Psychiatry* (March 1976): 133.

Drabek, Thomas E. *Human System Responses to Disaster: An Inventory of Sociological Findings*. New York: Springer-Verlag, 1986.

———. "Taxonomy and Disaster: Theoretical and Applied Issues." In *Social Structure and Disaster*, edited by Gary A. Kreps, 317–329. Newark, DE: University of Delaware Press, 1989.

Dunn, Janet, ed. "Looking Ahead," *HUD News*, November 1972, May 1973. Office of the Department of Housing and Urban Development, Man, WV.

Dynes, Russell R. Review of *Everything in Its Path*, by Kai T. Erikson. *Social Forces* 57, no. 2 (December 1978): 721–722.

Eller, Ronald D. *Miners, Millhands, and Mountaineers: Industrialization of the Appalachia South, 1880–1930*. Knoxville: University of Tennessee Press, 1982.

———. "Modernization, 1940–2000." In *High Mountains Rising: Appalachia in Time and Place*, edited by Richard A. Straw and H. Tyler Blethen, 197–219. Champaign, IL: University of Illinois Press, 2004.

Emerson, Robert M., Rachel I. Fritz, and Linda L. Shaw. *Writing Ethnographic Fieldnotes*. Chicago: University of Chicago Press, 1995.

Encyclopedia Britannica, vol. 18. Chicago and London: Encyclopedia Britannica, Inc. William Benton Publisher, 1975.

Erikson, Kai T. *Everything in Its Path: Destruction of Community in the Buffalo Creek Flood*. Hardcover ed. New York: Simon & Schuster, 1976).

———. *Everything in Its Path: Destruction of Community in the Buffalo Creek Flood*. Paperback ed. New York: Touchstone/Simon & Schuster, 1976.

————. *In the Wake of the Flood*. British edition of Erikson's *Everything in Its Path*. London: George Allen & Unwin, 1979.

————. "Loss of Communality at Buffalo Creek." Paper presented at the American Psychiatric Association meetings, Anaheim, CA, May 1975.

————. *A New Species of Trouble: The Human Experience of Modern Disasters*. New York: W. W. Norton & Company, 1994.

————. "Trauma at Buffalo Creek." *Society* (1976). Reprint *Society* 35, no. 2 (January/February 1998): 153–161.

Etzioni, Amitai. *The Spirit of Community: Reinvention of American Society*. New York: Touchstone/Simon & Schuster, 1994.

Ewen, Lynda Ann, and Julia A. Lewis. "Buffalo Creek Revisited. Deconstructing Kai Erikson's Stereotypes." *Appalachian Journal: A Regional Studies Review* 27, no. 1 (Fall, 1999) 22–45.

Falk, William W., Michael D. Schulman, and Ann R. Tickamyer, eds. *Communities of Work: Rural Restructuring in Local and Global Contexts*. Athens, OH: Ohio University Press, 2003.

Federal Emergency Management Agency (FEMA). "2007 Federal Disaster Declarations." http://www.fema.gov/news/disasters.fema?year=2007 (accessed August 11, 2008).

Fischer, Henry W. III. *Response to Disaster: Fact Versus Fiction and Its Perpetuation: The Sociology of Disaster*. 2nd ed. Lanham, MD: University Press of America, 1998.

Fitchen, Janet M. *Endangered Spaces, Enduring Places: Change, Identity, and Survival in Rural America*. Boulder, CO: Westview Press, 1991.

Freudenberg, William R. "Contamination, Corrosion, and the Social Order: An Overview." *Current Sociology* 45 (1997): 19–40.

————. "Risk and Recreancy: Weber, the Division of Labor, and the Rationality of Risk Perceptions." *Social Forces* 71 (1993): 909–932.

————. "The 'Risk Society' Reconsidered: Recreancy, the Division of Labor, and Risk to the Social Fabric." In *Risk in the Modern Age: Social*

Theory, Science and Environmental Decision-Making, edited by Maury J. Cohen, 107–120. New York: St. Martin's Press, 2000.

Friesma, H. P., J. Caporaso, G. Goldstein, R. Lineberry, and R. McCleary. *Aftermath: Communities after Natural Disasters*. Beverly Hills, CA: Sage, 1979.

Fritz, Charles E. "Disasters." In vol. 4 of *International Encyclopedia of the Social Sciences*, edited by David Sills, 202–207. New York: The Macmillan Company & The Free Press, 1968.

Gill, Duane, and J. Steven Picou. "The Day the Water Died: The *Exxon Valdez* Disaster and Indigenous Culture." In *Modern American Disasters*, edited by Steven Biel, 277–301. New York: New York University Press, 2001.

Gleser, Goldine C., Bonnie L. Green, and Carolyn Winget. *Prolonged Psychosocial Effects of Disaster: A Study of Buffalo Creek*. New York: Academic Press, 1981.

Green, Bonnie L., Goldine C. Gleser, Jacob D. Lindy, Mary C. Grace, and Anthony C. Leonard. "Age Related Reactions to the Buffalo Creek Dam Collapse: Second Decade Effects." In *Aging and Posttraumatic Stress Disorder*, edited by P. Ruskin and J. Talbott. Washington, DC: American Psychiatric Press, 1996.

Green, Bonnie L., Jacob D. Lindy, Mary C. Grace, Goldine C. Gleser, Anthony C. Leonard, M. Korol, and Carolyn Winget. "Buffalo Creek Survivors in the Second Decade: Stability of Stress Symptoms." *American Journal of Orthopsychiatry* 60 (1990): 43–54.

Green, Bonnie L., M. Korol, Mary C. Grace, M. G. Vary, Anthony C. Leonard, Goldine C. Gleser, and S. Smitson-Cohen. "Children and Disaster: Age, Gender, and Parental effects on PTSD Symptoms." *Journal of the American Academy of Child Adolescent Psychiatry* 30 (1991): 945–951.

Green, Bonnie L., Teresa L. Kramer, Mary C. Grace, Goldine C. Gleser, Anthony C. Leonard, Marshall G. Vary, and Jacob D. Lindy. "Traumatic Events over the Life Span: Survivors of the Buffalo Creek

Disaster." Chap. 13 in *Clinical Disorders and Stressful Life Events*, edited by Thomas W. Miller. Madison, CT: International Universities Press, Inc., 1997.

Green, Bonnie L., Jacob D. Lindy, Mary C. Grace, Goldine C. Gleser, Anthony C. Leonard, M. Korol, and Carolyn Winget. "Buffalo Creek Survivors in the Second Decade: Stability of Stress Symptoms." *American Journal of Orthopsychiatry* 60 (1990): 43–54.

Green, Bonnie L., M. G. Vary, T. L. Kramer, Goldine C. Gleser, and Anthony C. Leonard. "Children of Disaster in the Second Decade: A 17-Year Follow-Up of Buffalo Creek Survivors." *Journal of the American Academy of Child Adolescent Psychiatry* 33 (1994): 71–79.

Greer, Scott. "Neighborhood." In vol. 11 of *International Encyclopedia of the Social Sciences*, edited by David Sills, 120–125. New York: The Macmillan Company & The Free Press, 1968.

Gunter, Valerie, and Steve Kroll-Smith. *Volatile Places: A Sociology of Communities and Environmental Controversies*. Thousand Oaks, CA: Pine Forge Press, 2007.

Halpern, Jake. *Braving Home: Dispatches from the Underwater Town, the Lava-Side Inn, and Other Extreme Locales*. Boston: Houghton Mifflin Company, 2003.

Hamilton, Richard F., and James D. Wright. *The State of the Masses*. New York: Aldine, 1986.

Harshbarger, D. "Draft of Research and Intervention Project." 1972. Quoted in G. H. Sage. "The Universal Effects of Mass Disaster upon People." Manuscript.

―――. "An Ecological Perspective on Disastrous and Facilitative Disaster Intervention Based on the Buffalo Creek Disaster." Presented at a National Institute of Mental Health continuing-education seminar on emergency mental health services, Washington, DC, June 22–24, 1973.

Holahan, C. J., and R. H. Moos. "Community Environmental Psychology." In vol. 4 of *International Encyclopedia of the Social and Behavioral*

Sciences, edited by Neil J. Smelser and Paul B. Baltes, 2351. Amsterdam: Elsevier, 2001.

Honigmann, John J. "Sampling in Ethnographic Field Work." Chap. 15 in *A Handbook of Method in Cultural Anthropology*, edited by Raoul Naroll and Ronald Cohen. New York: Columbia University Press, 1973.

Hunter, Lori M. "Growth, Decline, Stability and Disruption: A Longitudinal Analysis of Social Well-Being in Four Western Rural Communities." *Rural Sociology* 66, no. 3 (September 30, 2001): 425–450.

Jacobs, B. "Community Sociology." In vol. 4 of *International Encyclopedia of the Social and Behavioral Sciences*, edited by Neil J. Smelser and Paul B. Baltes, 2383–2387. Amsterdam: Elsevier, 2001.

Kahn, Herman, and Anthony J. Wiener. *The Year 2000: A Framework for Speculation on the Next Thirty-Three Years*. New York: The Macmillan Company, 1967.

Kempf-Leonard, Kimberly, ed. Vols. 1–3. *Encyclopedia of Social Measurement*. Amsterdam: Elsevier Academic Press, 2005.

Kessler, Ronald C., Katherine A. McGonagle, Shanyang Zhao, Christopher B. Nelson, Michael Hughes, Suzann Eshleman, Hans-Ulrich Wittchen, Kenneth S. Kendler. "Lifetime and 12-Month Prevalence of DSM-III-R Psychiatric Disorders in the United States: Results from the National Comorbidity Survey." *Archives of General Psychiatry* 51 (January 1994): 8–19.

Kessler, Ronald C., A. Sonnega, E. Bromet, M. Hughes, and C. B. Nelson. "Posttraumatic Stress Disorder in the National Comorbidity Survey." *Archives of General Psychiatry* 52 (December 1995): 1048–1060.

Kliegl, R. "Memory, Aging, Cognitive Psychology of." In vol. 14 of *International Encyclopedia of the Social and Behavioral Sciences*, edited by Neil J. Smelser and Paul B. Baltes, 9556–9560. Amsterdam: Elsevier, 2001.

Kreps, Gary A. "Disasters, Sociology of." In vol. 6 of *International Encyclopedia of the Social and Behavioral Sciences*, edited by Neil J. Smelser and Paul B. Baltes, 3718–3721. Amsterdam: Elsevier, 2001.

————, ed. *Social Structure and Disaster*. Newark, DE: University of Delaware Press, 1989.

Kurtz, Richard A., and H. Paul Chalfant. *The Sociology of Medicine and Illness*. 2nd ed. Needham Heights, MA: Allyn & Bacon, 1991.

Lees-Haley, Paul R. "Litigation Response Syndrome." *American Journal of Forensic Psychology* 6 (1988): 3–12.

Lenski, Gerhard. *Ecological-Evolutionary Theory: Principles and Applications*. Boulder, CO: Paradigm Publishers, 2005.

Levy, Robert I., and Douglas W. Holland. "Person-Centered Interviewing and Observation." Chap. 10 in *Handbook of Methods in Cultural Anthropology*, edited by H. Russell Bernard. Walnut Creek, CA: AltaMira Press, 1998.

Lifton, Robert Jay. *Death in Life—Survivors of Hiroshima*. New York: Random House, 1967.

Lifton, Robert Jay, and Eric Olson. "The Human Meaning of Total Disaster. The Buffalo Creek Experience." *Psychiatry* 39 (1976): 1–18.

The Living Webster Encyclopedic Dictionary of the English Language. Chicago: The English Language Institute of America, 1975.

"Logan County, West Virginia." *Wikipedia, the Free Encyclopedia*, 2007. http://en.wikipedia.org/wiki/Logan_County,_West Virginia (accessed April 25, 2007).

Luey, Beth. *Handbook for Academic Authors*. 4th ed. New York: Cambridge University Press, 2002.

Luloff, A. E., and Jeffrey C. Bridger. "Community Agency and Local Development." Chap. 15 in *Challenges for Rural America in the Twenty-First Century (Rural Studies)*, edited by David L. Brown and Louis E. Swanson, 203–213. University Park, PA: The Pennsylvania State University Press, 2003.

Luloff, A. E., and R. S. Krannich, eds. *Persistence and Change in Rural Communities: A 50 Year Follow-Up to Six Classic Studies*. Oxfordshire, U.K.: CABI Publishing, 2002.

Mandell, Judy. *Book Editors Talk to Writers*. New York: John Wiley & Sons, 1995.

McCullough, David. *The Johnston Flood*. New York: Simon & Schuster Paperbacks, 1968.

McHugh, John, and William Black. "Death Toll Stands at 55; At Least 100 Missing." *The Tribune-Democrat* (Johnstown, PA), July 22, 1977, 1.

McPherson, Miller, and Lynn Smith-Lovin. "Social Isolation in America: Changes in Core Discussion Networks Over Two Decades." *American Sociological Review* 71 (June 2006): 353–375.

Miller, Delbert C. *Handbook of Research Design and Social Measurements*. 5th ed. Newbury Park, CA: Sage, 1991.

Nelson, Geoffrey, and Isaac Prilleltensky, eds. *Community Psychology: In Pursuit of Liberation and Well-Being*. New York: Palgrave Macmillan, 2005.

Newman, C. J. "Children of Disaster: Clinical Observations at Buffalo Creek." *American Journal of Psychiatry* 133 (1976): 306–312.

Nugent, Thomas. *Death at Buffalo Creek: The 1972 West Virginia Flood Disaster*. New York: Norton, 1973.

Obermiller, Philip J., and Michael E. Maloney, eds. *Appalachia: Social Context Past and Present*. Dubuque: Kendall-Hunt Publishing Company, 2006.

Petersen, R. A., Jr. "Community Organization and the Life Course." In vol. 4 of *International Encyclopedia of the Social and Behavioral Sciences*, edited by Neil J. Smelser and Paul B. Baltes, 2367–2371. Amsterdam: Elsevier, 2001.

Phillips, Bernard S. *Social Research Strategy and Tactics*. 2nd ed. New York: The Macmillan Company, 1971.

Pickering, Mimi. "The Buffalo Creek Flood: An Act of Man," and "Buffalo Creek Revisited." DVD by Appalshop Films. Whitesburg, KY, 2006.

Picou, J. Steven, Brent K. Marshall, and Duane A. Gill. "Disaster, Litigation, and the Corrosive Community." *Social Forces* 82 (June 2004): 1493–1522.

Polsby, Nelson. "Community Power." In vol. 3 of *International Encyclopedia of the Social Sciences*, edited by David Sills, 156–162. New York: The Macmillan Company & The Free Press, 1968.

Putnam, Robert D. *Bowling Alone: The Collapse and Revival of American Community*. New York: Touchstone/Simon & Schuster, 2000.

Quarantelli, Enrico L. *What Is a Disaster: Perspectives on the Question*. London: Routledge, 1998.

Quarantelli, Enrico L., and Russell R. Dynes. "Response to Social Crisis and Disaster." *Annual Review of Sociology* 3 (1977): 23–49.

Rabinowitz, D. "Community Studies: Anthropological." In vol. 4 of *International Encyclopedia of the Social and Behavioral Sciences*, edited by Neil J. Smelser and Paul B. Baltes, 2387–2389. Amsterdam: Elsevier, 2001.

Raleigh News and Observer. "Delia Perkins: The Waters Came Down." Interview by historian David Cecelski. April 8, 2007, 6D.

Ritzer, George. *Contemporary Sociological Theory*. New York: McGraw Hill, 1992.

———. *Encyclopedia of Social Theory*. Thousand Oaks, CA: Sage Publications, 2005.

Rodriquez, Havidan, Enrico L. Quarantelli, and Russell R. Dynes, eds. *Handbook of Disaster Research*. 1st ed. New York: Springer, 2007.

Sanders, Irwin T. "Community Development." In vol. 3 of *International Encyclopedia of the Social Sciences*, edited by David Sills, 169–173. New York: The Macmillan Company & The Free Press, 1968.

Schacter, Daniel L. *Searching for Memory: The Brain, the Mind, and the Past*. New York: Basic Books, 1996.

———. *The Seven Sins of Memory*. Boston: Houghton-Mifflin, 2001.

Schooler, T. Y. "Disasters, Coping with." In vol. 6 of *International Encyclopedia of the Social and Behavioral Sciences*, edited by Neil J. Smelser and Paul B. Baltes, 3713–3718. Amsterdam: Elsevier, 2001.

Schwartz-Barcott, T. P. "Recovering Community on the Anniversary of the Buffalo Creek Disaster." *Footnotes of the American Sociological Association* (April, 2002): 7–8.

Spence, Beth. "A Story of Broken Promises: Buffalo Creek." *The Mountain Call* (Kermit, WV) 1, no. 9 (July/August 1974): 8–13.

Spites, R. L., J. Endicott, A. M. Mesnikoff, and M. S. Cohen. *The Psychiatric Evaluation Form*. New York: Biometrics Research, 1968.

Stein, Maurice R. *The Eclipse of Community: An Interpretation of American Studies*. Princeton, NJ: Princeton University Press, 1960.

Steinberg, Ted. *Acts of God: The Unnatural History of Natural Disaster in America*. Oxford and New York: Oxford University Press, 2000.

Stern, Gerald M. *The Buffalo Creek Disaster: The Story of the Survivor's Unprecedented Lawsuit*. New York: Random House, 1976.

———. *The Buffalo Creek Disaster: How the Survivors of One of the Worst Disasters in Coal-Mining History Brought Suit Against the Coal Company—and Won*. New York: Vintage Books, 1976.

Straw, Richard A., and H. Tyler Blethen, eds. *High Mountains Rising: Appalachia in Time and Place*. Champaign, IL: University of Illinois Press, 2004.

Taylor, Steven J., and Robert Bogdan. *Introduction to Qualitative Research Methods: The Search for Meanings*. 2nd ed. New York: John Wiley & Sons, 1984.

Tierney, Kathleen J., and B. Baisden. "Crisis Intervention Programs for Disaster Victims: A Sourcebook and Manual for Smaller Communities." U.S. Department of Health, Educational and Welfare. Publication no. (ADM) 79–675, 1979.

Titchener, James L., and Frederic T. Kapp. "Family and Character Change at Buffalo Creek." *American Journal of Psychiatry* 133 (1976): 295–299.

———. "Family and Character Change in Buffalo Creek." Paper presented at the American Psychiatric Association meetings, Anaheim, CA, May 1975.

U.S. Census Bureau. *County and City Data Book 2000: A Statistical Abstract Supplement (County and City Data Book)*. 13th ed. Washington, DC: Dept. of Commerce, Bureau of the Census, 2001.

U.S. Congress. Senate. Committee on Labor and Public Welfare. *Buffalo Creek (W.Va.) Disaster, 1972*. 99th Congress, May 30–31, 1972. Washington, DC: U.S. Government Printing Office.

Vidich, Arthur J., and Joseph Bensman. *Small Town in Mass Society: Class, Power, and Religion in a Rural Community*. Princeton, NJ: Princeton University Press, 1958.

Wallin, Paul. "A Guttman Scale for Measuring Women's Neighborliness." *American Journal of Sociology* 59 (1953): 243–246.

Warren, Roland. *The Community in America*. Chicago: Rand McNally, 1978.

Webb, E. J., D. T. Campbell, R. D. Schwartz, and L. Sechrest. *Unobtrusive Measures: Nonreactive Measures in the Social Sciences*. Chicago: Rand McNally, 1966.

Weller, Jack E. *Yesterday's People: Life in Contemporary Appalachia*. 1965. Lexington, KY: The University of Kentucky Press, 1995.

Western Organization of Resource Councils. "Coalbed Methane Development: Boon or Bane for Rural Residents?" Washington, DC. http://scholar.google.com/scholar?q=coal+gasification+hydraulic+fracture (accessed March 2003).

Wilkinson, Kenneth P. *The Community in Rural America*. Westport, CT: Greenwood Press, 1991.

Woodruff-Pak, D. S., and S. K. Lemieux. "Memory, Aging, Neural Basis of." In vol. 14 of *International Encyclopedia of the Social and Behavioral Sciences*, edited by Neil J. Smelser and Paul B. Baltes, 9560–9562. Amsterdam: Elsevier, 2001.

The World Almanac and Book of Facts. New York: World Almanac Books, 2006.

Wright, James D. "Small Towns, Mass Society, and the 21st Century." *Society* (Transaction) 38, no. 1 (November/December 2000): 3–10.

Wright, James D., Peter H. Rossi, Sonia R. Wright, and Eleanor Weber-Burden. *After the Clean-Up: Long Range Effects of Natural Disasters.* Beverly Hills, CA: Sage, 1979.

Wuthnow, Robert. *Loose Connections: Joining Together in America's Fragmented Communities*. Cambridge, MA: Harvard University Press, 1998.

INDEX

About the Author

T. P. Schwartz-Barcott is a sociologist (PhD, University of North Carolina, Chapel Hill) who has taught sociology and conducted sociological research at Brown University, Providence College, the University of Connecticut, and the University of Delaware. His sociological research has appeared in *The Sociological Quarterly*, *Footnotes of the American Sociological Association*, *Teaching Sociology*, and other journals and anthologies. Currently, he is the director of Social Research Services, a research and consulting firm in Rhode Island.

He was raised in both Monessen and Latrobe, Pennsylvania, and is the grandson of immigrant coal miners and steel workers who worked in local mines and mills.

Printed in the United States
137651LV00003B/1/P